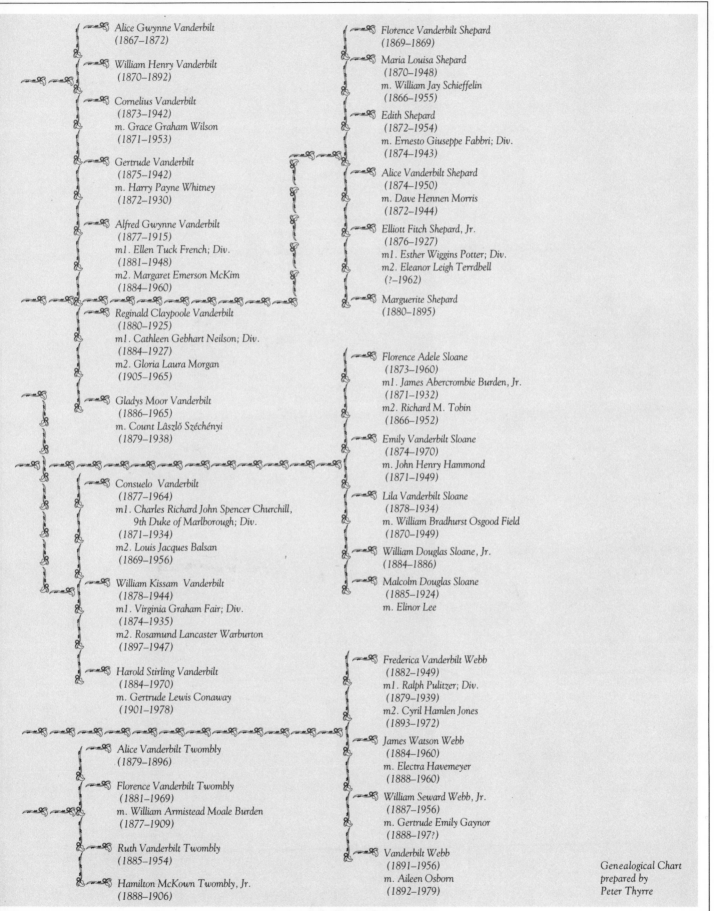

Alice Gwynne Vanderbilt
(1867–1872)

William Henry Vanderbilt
(1870–1892)

Cornelius Vanderbilt
(1873–1942)
m. Grace Graham Wilson
(1871–1953)

Gertrude Vanderbilt
(1875–1942)
m. Harry Payne Whitney
(1872–1930)

Alfred Gwynne Vanderbilt
(1877–1915)
m1. Ellen Tuck French; Div.
(1881–1948)
m2. Margaret Emerson McKim
(1884–1960)

Reginald Claypoole Vanderbilt
(1880–1925)
m1. Cathleen Gebhart Neilson; Div.
(1884–1927)
m2. Gloria Laura Morgan
(1905–1965)

Gladys Moor Vanderbilt
(1886–1965)
m. Count Lâszló Széchényi
(1879–1938)

Consuelo Vanderbilt
(1877–1964)
m1. Charles Richard John Spencer Churchill,
9th Duke of Marlborough; Div.
(1871–1934)
m2. Louis Jacques Balsan
(1869–1956)

William Kissam Vanderbilt
(1878–1944)
m1. Virginia Graham Fair; Div.
(1874–1935)
m2. Rosamund Lancaster Warburton
(1897–1947)

Harold Stirling Vanderbilt
(1884–1970)
m. Gertrude Lewis Conaway
(1901–1978)

Alice Vanderbilt Twombly
(1879–1896)

Florence Vanderbilt Twombly
(1881–1969)
m. William Armistead Moale Burden
(1877–1909)

Ruth Vanderbilt Twombly
(1885–1954)

Hamilton McKown Twombly, Jr.
(1888–1906)

Florence Vanderbilt Shepard
(1869–1869)

Maria Louisa Shepard
(1870–1948)
m. William Jay Schieffelin
(1866–1955)

Edith Shepard
(1872–1954)
m. Ernesto Giuseppe Fabbri; Div.
(1874–1943)

Alice Vanderbilt Shepard
(1874–1950)
m. Dave Hennen Morris
(1872–1944)

Elliott Fitch Shepard, Jr.
(1876–1927)
m1. Esther Wiggins Potter; Div.
m2. Eleanor Leigh Terrdbell
(?–1962)

Marguerite Shepard
(1880–1895)

Florence Adele Sloane
(1873–1960)
m1. James Abercrombie Burden, Jr.
(1871–1932)
m2. Richard M. Tobin
(1866–1952)

Emily Vanderbilt Sloane
(1874–1970)
m. John Henry Hammond
(1871–1949)

Lila Vanderbilt Sloane
(1878–1934)
m. William Bradhurst Osgood Field
(1870–1949)

William Douglas Sloane, Jr.
(1884–1886)

Malcolm Douglas Sloane
(1885–1924)
m. Elinor Lee

Frederica Vanderbilt Webb
(1882–1949)
m1. Ralph Pulitzer; Div.
(1879–1939)
m2. Cyril Hamlen Jones
(1893–1972)

James Watson Webb
(1884–1960)
m. Electra Havemeyer
(1888–1960)

William Seward Webb, Jr.
(1887–1956)
m. Gertrude Emily Gaynor
(1888–197?)

Vanderbilt Webb
(1891–1956)
m. Aileen Osborn
(1892–1979)

Genealogical Chart
prepared by
Peter Thyrre

THE VANDERBILTS AND THE GILDED AGE

John Foreman and
Robbe Pierce Stimson
Introduction by Louis Auchincloss

ST. MARTIN'S PRESS   NEW YORK

"We shape our buildings, and afterwards our buildings shape us."

—Winston Churchill

Chapter 1

THE VANDERBILTS AND THE GILDED AGE

The perfect image of a Vanderbilt;
Alfred Gwynne Vanderbilt (holding
the ribbons) with his wife, the former
Ellen Tuck French, coaching with
friends, circa 1905.

HIS book about the Vanderbilts and their houses is different in several respects from those written previously. It seeks to dispel extravagant and unrealistic images that have clung for too long to people such as the Vanderbilts. The private lives of the rich are too often portrayed as a sequence of bizarre indulgences motivated largely by whim. This is particularly the case with regard to their great houses, elaborate entertainments, and majestic life-styles.

The popular view of the rich as merely a frivolous and eccentric group of robber barons, alternately dangerous and foolish, and apt to do just about anything in the name of social climbing stems from the essential unfamiliarity most people have with great wealth. To own a yacht, give a ball, or commission the construction of a palace on Fifth Avenue are pleasures most will never savor. Hence, there is a vicarious thrill—piquant with a hint of envy—that we all get from reading about the Gilded Age and its lifestyle.

The trouble with this is the inevitable distortion it causes in our assessment of individual motive and accomplishment. Everybody knows that riches, in and of themselves, neither guarantee happiness nor automatically confer strength of character. We tend to forget, however, that eccentricity, like any other human trait, is also no more prevalent among the rich than among anybody else.

All this flies in the face of a sort of conventional wisdom in this country. This would have us believe that some of America's greatest architectural undertakings are to be explained purely in terms of Mrs. A.'s self-centered desire to build a larger house than her sister-in-law, or Mr. B.'s abject surrender—since he is assumed to have been as pretentious and uncultured as he was rich—to an egotistical architect.

The problem with defining great architecture in terms of social climbing is that it trivializes the buildings themselves. Presumably, it also makes them accessible to the public. However, it does so at the expense of obscuring the significance of some of America's greatest buildings. The importance of such architecture speaks to critical issues such as cultural continuity, traditions of fine design and domestic craftsmanship, and the role that tangible reminders of the past play in connecting us to our shared American history.

One important way in which the rich are indeed different from the rest of us is that they are conspicuous. This is true in spite of their best efforts to the contrary. At the beginning of the twentieth century, during what Louis Auchincloss has termed the "Vanderbilt Era," there was little effort made to hide one's riches. Many rich people saw themselves as flesh and blood fulfillments of the American dream. Such a belief is reflected in the words of John D. Rockefeller: "God gave me my money."

The reasoning that led men to build private palaces was usually quite sound. Such buildings were, of course, visible symbols of power and backdrops for lavish entertainments. However, they were also state-of-the-art machines uniquely representative of the late Victorian era's combination of mechanical innovation and cheap and abundant labor. Large and elaborate houses were furthermore an expression of high fashion. Their design often represented the cutting edge of national taste. Just as today's Paris haute couture is simultaneously patronized by the rich and recognized by the French nation as a part of its cultural heritage, so during the Vanderbilt Era were the great houses of the rising plutocracy consciously viewed, by builders and public alike, as attempts to beautify the American scene and enrich our own infant culture.

Not all the large houses were great, of course. If we can hold on to our sense of perspective, however, the great ones can be seen quite clearly as logical, functional, and beautiful adjuncts to the lives of the people who built them. By virtue of their beauty, they enhanced life in every community in which they stood.

Much of the life that was lived within those great houses was quite captivating. Certainly it was theatrical. The extravagant dinners and balls, the gleaming equipages and liveried servants, the aura of luxurious women and powerful men fascinate us still. We should not forget that the great house and the great party are both constants in human experience. And in that regard, the Vanderbilts and their set at the turn of the twentieth century were not very different from the Forbes and Rothschilds of our own times.

In this book, we not only want to demythologize the people who built these houses but also to upgrade the national appreciation of the houses themselves. Our scope of inquiry is limited to the grand old houses built between 1879 and the First World War. We hope that an increased appreciation of them will naturally stimulate appreciation of other worthy buildings from the past.

It was not very long ago that the demolition of a house by McKim, Mead & White was viewed almost as an act of patriotism. Despite the recent growth of the historic preservation movement, there is still considerable prejudice against the private palaces of that opulent era. Marble House, Biltmore, The Breakers, 660 Fifth Avenue, Florham, Woodlea, and so on are particularly representative of the time in which they were created. These are not bogus Parisian palaces, ersatz English country houses, or "exact copies" of anything. How disappointed Charles McKim would be to hear his great masterpieces such as the University Club in New York or the Vanderbilt house in Hyde Park, New York, complacently dismissed as "copies."

The Vanderbilt houses and the many other

great structures like them in the United States are eclectic but are also distinctly characteristic American works of art, expressions of the American Renaissance. One apostle of modernism, Le Corbusier, acknowledged this fact. He wrote in 1935, "In New York, then, I learned to appreciate the Italian Renaissance. It is so well

There were those who uncritically revered the engineers of American capitalism. The Monitor Oil Stove Company of Cleveland, Ohio, gave the rapacious Jay Gould precedence over William Henry Vanderbilt himself.

done that you could believe it to be genuine. It even has a strange new firmness which is not Italian, but American."

One sees here that Le Corbusier granted the uniqueness of the American Renaissance. It was "not Italian, but American." And what set it apart was the "new firmness." This is a subtle concept for those unaccustomed to looking carefully at old buildings. As we shall see in the chapters ahead, however, "firmness" and all it entails is germane to the issue.

American architects of the Vanderbilt Era naturally spoke with a Renaissance vocabulary. This was our imperial period, both politically and artistically. In recent years, we have tended to associate imperialism with exploitation. This, in turn, has clouded our view of the American Renaissance. During this period, which stretched roughly between the 1880s and the First World War, the torch of Western culture was consciously transferred from the Old World to the New. The age of European preeminence was

over; the America Era had dawned. Our artistic and commercial elite joined forces as self-designated successors to the enlightened princes of the Italian Renaissance. The zeitgeist of the times was understandably expansive.

Of course, it would be naïve to suggest that people who built houses such as those of the Vanderbilts were insensible to the effect that a mansion had on one's social standing. A person's house speaks volumes, and its messages are among the most acutely perceived by the rest of the world.

However, because of the broad streak of morality that is a fundamental part of the American character, the matter is complicated where the rich are concerned. The fact is, as Americans, we are prone to stern judgments. Ostentation has never been a popular trait in the United States. And if there is one thing consistently criticized as ostentatious, it is Vanderbiltian decor. The sin of ostentation, coupled with the supposed self-centered zaniness of the American millionaire, has caused the superb quality of late-nineteenth- and early-twentieth-century interior design and construction to be discounted. In fact, some of the best rooms in the world—in terms of proportion, design, and execution—were created in America, inside the very houses that for so long have been dismissed as ugly, unoriginal, and irrelevant to the American experience.

Commodore Cornelius Vanderbilt, whose palace-building descendants would conquer American society, was born and raised in this humble Staten Island farmhouse.

The family of William Henry Vanderbilt, painted by Seymour Guy in 1874. Nearly everyone responsible for the houses in this book is portrayed here, in the salon of a Vanderbilt mansion at Fifth Avenue and Fortieth Street. They are, left to right: William Henry Vanderbilt, seated; son Frederick William, with hand on his mother's chair; Mrs. Vanderbilt, née Maria Louisa Kissam; little George Washington, aged twelve; his sister Florence Adele, gazing off to her right; William Kissam, beside his sister Florence; fourteen-year-old Lila Osgood, seated, facing her little brother George; William Henry's eldest daughter Margaret; Margaret's husband, Col. Elliott F. Shepard; a servant; Emily Thorn, in white gloves; another servant; Alice Gwynne Vanderbilt (wife of Cornelius II); William Douglas Sloane, helping wife Emily with her gloves; and, standing at far right, Cornelius II.

It is only very recently that it has begun to be realized how fine the music room at The Breakers, or the library at Biltmore, or the dining room at Marble House really are. These three houses happen to be open to the public, and their interior decoration has been the subject of scholarly attention. There are many other comparable houses in America whose interior work is just as good, however.

Fine old mansions with white and gold ballrooms, extravagantly carved marble stair halls, paneled libraries, and—least loved of the beautiful orphans—vintage glass and marble bathrooms still exist all across the country. However, the owners of these old mansions too often are businesses or institutions, or even individuals, who shortsightedly view themselves as the last in the chain of ownership. Too frequently, these owners have little respect or understanding for the houses they own. Certainly, the notion of sacrificing immediate convenience in the name of preserving fine interior work from the past has yet to make real inroads on the American mindset. Once eviscerated, a great house is forever compromised.

Vanity plays a natural role in the human desire to create the best of anything. The Vanderbilts, and in particular that single amazing group of siblings responsible for the houses in this book, set out consciously to build the best. And, indeed, why not? Who else would do it? These people were not just promoting themselves; they also were attempting to give this country a category of buildings it had previously lacked. It is to their everlasting credit that, in order to accomplish this goal, they sought out the greatest talent available. Artists such as Richard Morris Hunt, Charles Follen McKim, Stanford White, Robert Swain Peabody, John La Farge, Louis Comfort Tiffany, Augustus Saint-Gaudens, Lucien Alavoine, Gilbert Cuel are a few such creative geniuses.

The houses these people created were purposely intended to fill a gap in American culture or, if you will, a blank in the American landscape. Whereas there had been palaces in Europe for millennia, there was at that time not a one in America. To men such as Richard Hunt or Cornelius Vanderbilt II, this was a situation that needed to be addressed.

The Vanderbilt family is so large and complex that one must take care not to confuse the third generation, who constitute the principal players in this book, with the others. Actually, the family had been in the United States for five generations before the birth of Cornelius Vanderbilt, known as the Commodore. Tradition designates him as the first generation only because of his success at business. It is also important to understand that whereas his grandchildren might have, therefore, been the third generation of rich Vanderbilts, they were only the first generation of social Vanderbilts.

As noted above, all the houses in this book save one were built by the members of a single group of siblings. There were eight of them— four boys and four girls. Their grandfather, the Commodore, had many other descendants. These other branches of the family all descended through female lines, however. The Commodore was a classic nineteenth-century male chauvinist and believer in the tradition of primogeniture. He passed along his great fortune, virtually intact, to his eldest son. In the wake of this, both he and historians after him consigned his daughters to the dustbin of history.

The third generation, the first of the social Vanderbilts and the builders of these houses, were the children of the Commodore's eldest son, William Henry Vanderbilt, and his wife, Maria Louisa Kissam. They were born in the following order:

> Cornelius II (1843–1899)
> Margaret Louisa (1845–1924)
> William Kissam (1849–1920)
> Emily Thorn (1852–1946)
> Florence Adele (1854–1952)
> Frederick William (1856–1938)
> Eliza (Lila) Osgood (1860–1936)
> George Washington (1862–1914)

These children comprised about as varied a group, in terms of personality, as one could possibly imagine. Cornelius II (Corneil) was a pillar of the community, a man so moral, so honest, so ethical, and so religious as to be the despair of mere mortals; Margaret (Maggie) was the long-suffering wife of a man her own father described as a "crank"; Willie K. was the prince of playboys, an all-around good fellow and a superb host; shy Emily Thorn loved her family and raised it like royalty; Florence (no nickname for her) was a frosty socialite with a bitter tongue and a notable lack of patience; Fred married a woman twelve years his senior and remained a cipher ever after; Lila remained faithful and gracious throughout her beloved husband's shameful "illness"; and George was the baby, cultured and incompetent, impulsive, and ultimately a victim of what one suspects was medical malpractice.

This group of brothers and sisters formed the nucleus of the family's social triumph. They had children, and the "cousins," as those children were called by later historians, had, in turn, many more children of their own. Many houses would be built by and for each succeeding generation. However, it was the first remarkable group of siblings, that third generation, that emerged from the chrysalis of mere wealth and became legend.

As a matter of fact, probably at no other time in U.S. history has a single group of brothers and sisters been to so unfettered a degree consistent builders of such good architecture. Not just a few but every single one of them built at least one great house—and Willie built four.

It is not the purpose of this book to trace in a detailed manner the evolution of the Vanderbilt fortune, but it is interesting to note a few facts about the Commodore, the man responsible for amassing the family wealth.

Cornelius Vanderbilt (1794–1877), the intimidating patriarch of the Vanderbilt family, was nicknamed "Commodore" on account of his large shipping interests. The Commodore was not an ordinary man. According to *Munsey's Magazine*, he "would have become rich on a desert island." Cornelius Vanderbilt was not only canny, sly, and immensely energetic, he was also big, fearless, muscular, naturally athletic, and enormously attractive to women.

New York society was in a tizzy because of his loud voice and uncouth manners. In retrospect, it seems as if he cultivated this persona to some extent. It is well known, for example, that he cussed with originality and passion, and delighted in ridiculing his children before strangers. *Blatherskite,* a word seldom heard in modern times, was a favorite insult reserved for his eldest son, William Henry. This is an ironic touch, considering that this much-maligned son would eventually become his father's principal heir.

Commodore Cornelius Vanderbilt "would have become rich on a desert island."

The Commodore was also a notorious pincher of shapely servant girls, a confirmed chewer of plug tobacco, and a fervent believer in the occult. Totally unschooled, he lifted himself from rustic obscurity on Staten Island to become the largest private employer in the United States.

This coarse and brilliant man was one of the great builders of America. He did not plunder other men's capital investments in the manner of his rivals, Jay Gould, Daniel Drew, or Jim Fisk. They were true robber barons; Vanderbilt was not. As a matter of fact, Vanderbilt never speculated in stocks at all. His riches came from the development of immense transportation systems.

First, he was in shipping. Then, at the age of seventy, he began to invest heavily in railroads. While his detractors characterized him as vicious and piratical, no one ever called him a liar. To the general public, he became something of a grand old man.

Commodore Vanderbilt died on January 4, 1877, at the age of eighty-two. The disposition of his fortune, which turned out to exceed the cash reserves of the United States government on that day, is an apt sketch of the man's character. The Commodore sired thirteen children in the course of his life, ten of whom survived him. Less than 2 percent of his more than $100 million fortune was divided among eight daughters and a no-good son named Cornelius Jeremiah. Virtually all the rest went to the underestimated William Henry.

The purpose of his will was not to bestow belated parental approval on a formerly unloved son. Rather, it was to keep intact the great fortune after the Commodore's death. His personal feelings about his children, including his principal heir, had very little to do with his will in its final form. Those children were either used or discarded to further the testator's goal: namely, the creation of a dynasty whose name would forever glorify its founder.

The Commodore liked his grandson Cornelius II (later of The Breakers and 1 West Fifty-seventh Street) much more than his own son. Several tokens of this esteem appear in the will, most notably a bequest of $5.5 million in bonds, as well as stewardship of the family portraits. Cornelius II, or Corneil as the family called him, thus was designated the eventual head of the family almost nine years before his own father's death.

Gay and charming Willie K., who was Corneil's younger brother, also inherited a tidy sum from his grandfather: $3 million. His two other brothers, Fred and George, received $2 million apiece. William Henry's daughters got nothing, but because they were women, nothing was expected.

Commodore Vanderbilt as the grand old man at home in New York.

Death watch on Washington Place; crowds outside #10 await news of the dying Commodore.

The expectations of William Henry's sisters, as well as his brother Jerry, were another thing. The Commodore's bequests to them were so comparatively insignificant that they banded together to contest the will. A sensational trial ensued in late 1878 and early 1879. Dutiful, honorable, religious, William Henry Vanderbilt, husband of a minister's daughter, a man who throughout his life had done only what his father told him, was forced to endure a scandal of horrific proportions.

His brother and sisters alleged in court that he had willfully manipulated their father for the express purpose of disinheriting them. Of course, it was the Commodore's desire that the fortune be preserved as intact as possible. William Henry was less an heir than a caretaker. The maintenance and cultivation of so great a sum of money—and one must remember that $100 million was an inconceivably large amount in 1877—was at least as much a burden as it was a boon.

William Henry was accused of procuring comely parlor maids to indulge his father's goatish proclivities. He was said to have colluded with fraudulent mystics so as to confuse the Commodore and influence the will. It was said he had struck a coldhearted bargain with the Commodore's second wife, a young woman with the delicious name of Frank Crawford, wherein she would abet his schemes for a price. "The haughty house of the Vanderbilt railroad king," gloated the Boston *Herald*, "is, for a parvenu race, possessed of quite a respectable collection of family skeletons." William Henry formerly had been quite close with his sisters and several of their husbands. At the time of the trial, he found himself pitted against precisely those who once had been at the bosom of his own family.

William Henry eventually made a deal with his siblings wherein each sister would receive half a million dollars in bonds over and above the lesser sums the Commodore had left them. Brother Jerry, true to traditions of Victorian chauvinism, got an entire million. William Henry Vanderbilt physically delivered the new bequest, driving from the house of one sister to that of the next in his carriage. This must surely be one of the more vivid images of America's past, that of the railroad king buying off his siblings with millions of dollars of negotiable bonds stashed in a carriage.

William Henry was rich, but he was no socialite. Nor did he pine for society any more than his father had. It is one thing for a man of means to expect recognition, and perhaps even a degree of deference, from the world at large. It is quite another, however, to expect to be a participant in that bright and amusing round of parties that characterize fashionable society. For, as many a rich and powerful person knows quite well, high society is not always all it appears to be. Nonattendance at its glittering functions is not always a bad thing.

During the 1870s, 1880s, and well into the 1890s, Mrs. Caroline Schermerhorn Astor, wife of William Backhouse Astor, reigned supreme in New York society. She and her majordomo, a former Savannah lawyer by the name of Ward McAllister, devoted their entire energies to defining and, more importantly, to regulating society. In those days, Mrs. Astor faced a tidal wave of arrivistes who poured into New York from all over the country in the hopes of breaking into society. Many were literally uncouth. One cannot blame Mrs. Astor too much for excluding certain of them, rich as they may have been.

Commodore Vanderbilt was this latter sort of a person. He could affect a temporary veneer of politeness if circumstances required, but he was much too rough around the edges in general conversation. And worse, he was given to dressing people down in coarse language. The old Staten Island ferryman simply wasn't refined enough for McAllister's and Caroline Astor's vision of what New York society ought to be. As long as he was alive, no Vanderbilt really could be considered part of New York's topmost elite.

By the same token, however, it would be absurd to think that an overwhelmingly powerful personality such as Commodore Vanderbilt really could have given a tinker's damn whether an epicene fop like McAllister or an overweening old biddy like Caroline Astor accepted him or not. He could have felt only contempt for such people. The assertion that he yearned for their company at fashionable dinner parties is simply farfetched. He had his cronies; he had his amorous liaisons; he had his young second wife (Frank Crawford was forty-five years his junior); he was already a member of the fashionable Union Club, at least until he resigned his membership. Vanderbilt was a Saratoga man, a gambler with an eye for fast horses, big stakes, and shapely ankles. He did not need Mrs. Astor's New York society to show him a good time.

Nor was his son William Henry any more of a candidate than his father for the glittering world of McAllister's Four Hundred. William Henry Vanderbilt was a bookkeeper at heart, a devoted husband, and a family man very much in the churchgoing Victorian mode. He could not have approved much of the antics of society types such as James Gordon Bennet, who is said to have delighted in driving his coach and four stark naked up Riverside Drive in the middle of the night, or the habit among upper-crust men (including his own son Willie) of keeping mistresses.

Neither William Henry Vanderbilt or his wife particularly regretted that they were not invited to Ward McAllister's *fêtes champêtres* in Newport or to Mrs. Astor's famous January ball. William Henry was far more interested in opera. When the socially prestigious Academy of Music refused to sell him a box, he and his sons, plus assorted other rich Academy rejects, organized the Metropolitan Opera Company. Hearing the music was more important to William Henry than being in the right theater, although, as things turned out, the Metropolitan eventually eclipsed the old Academy in social cachet.

The yacht *North Star*, over whose railing the young William Henry Vanderbilt tossed a cigar and turned down $10,000.

William Henry Vanderbilt was so overshadowed by his megalomaniacal father that his own personality is hardly known about today. He was a very careful man, as indeed one would have to be with such a father. Back in 1853, the Commodore had taken the whole clan to Europe aboard what was then the largest private yacht afloat. Called the *North Star*, she was 270 feet in length, with interiors that were *le dernier cri* in plush and rosewood. Besides the Commodore's family, their spouses, servants, and a private doctor, the party included one Reverend J. O. Choules, who remarked later that "the Commodore did the cussing and I did the praying."

The following tale speaks volumes about the man whose children built the Vanderbilt mansions. On deck one pleasant night, William Henry Vanderbilt, by this time a married man

of thirty-two, was discovered by his father smoking a cigar. Said the Commodore: "Tobacco is a dirty habit, Billy. I'll give you ten thousand dollars if you never touch it again." Without hesitation, son Billy reportedly popped his Havana overboard. "The money won't be necessary, Father," he replied. "I will do it to please you." So pleased, in fact, was the old man that he pulled out a cigar of his own, smiled broadly, and lit up.

Billy was, at this time, pursuing a modest career as a farmer on Staten Island. After his marriage to Maria Louisa Kissam, he had worked so hard in the Wall Street offices of his father's future enemy Daniel Drew that he suffered a nervous breakdown. Disgusted, the Commodore bought him a seventy-acre farm on Staten Island and packed him off out of sight.

William Henry had unsuspected talents, however. He worked diligently on that farm, and he prospered. Within a decade, he had increased the original 70 acres to 350. One day, he approached his father with an offer to buy manure from one of the Commodore's horse-car lines. It may be of interest to note that a wagonload of horse manure cost about two dollars in pre–Civil War New York. William Henry offered four dollars a load. Delighted, and disinclined to question the higher price, the Commodore accepted.

Subsequently, the old man visited his son at a dock where Staten Island–bound scows were being loaded with cartfuls of manure. "About how many loads can you fit on that scow?" asked the father. "Only one," replied the son. "The deal was four dollars a *scowload.*"

The Commodore was so amused by this affair that, instead of becoming angry, he started taking his son seriously. For instance, it was William Henry, and not his father, who originally saw the profit potential in railroads. The old man took his son's advice. As the Commodore moved aggressively into rails and laid the foundation for what eventually would become the vast New York Central system, a whole series of important directorships and vice presidencies came in rapid succession to the son. It has been suggested by historian James T. Maher that the beautiful houses of William Henry's children were all, in a way, built upon a scowload of manure.

In 1864, the Commodore not only made William Henry the vice president of the New York and Harlem Railroad, he also built him a fine

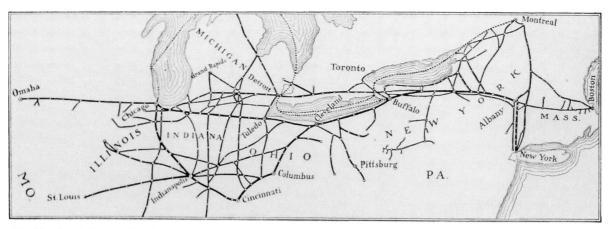

The Vanderbilt Railway Empire.

brownstone house on the southeast corner of Fifth Avenue and Fortieth Street. Thus ended the latter's Babylonian Captivity on Staten Island.

By the time he died, Commodore Vanderbilt successfully had molded his eldest son. The son obeyed the father's dying wish and devoted the remainder of his own life to protecting and nurturing the family fortune. He did it well, paying decent wages, adopting a consistently conciliatory manner in labor disputes, giving the American public its dollar's worth in transportation, and providing the nation with a first-rate and immensely valuable integrated system of railroad lines. However, perhaps he was just too rich for Americans to take him to heart.

In 1882, William Henry Vanderbilt made a careless remark that was reprinted, probably, in every newspaper in the country. In October of that year, he embarked on a junket in his private railroad car, accompanied by a congenial group of captains of industry, a few fellow railroad moguls, and his sons Fred and Willie. One afternoon, while the car was parked in a siding at Michigan City, Indiana, Vanderbilt agreed to be interviewed by a group of reporters. One of these was a free-lancer named Clarence Dresser, on assignment from the Chicago News. Many topics were touched upon. The atmosphere was manly, relaxed, and friendly.

An amusing footnote to this interview was William Henry's observation that antimonopolists were the cheapest legislators to buy. It was another remark, made in the easy atmosphere of the afternoon, that ultimately dominated the attention of the entire nation and haunted Mr. Vanderbilt for the rest of his life, however.

The conversation had got around to the Chicago Limited, the New York Central's crack passenger service between Manhattan and the Midwest. Many compliments were bandied about concerning this train, amidst which a relaxed Mr. Vanderbilt allowed as how Central wouldn't even bother with it but for the competition from the Pennsylvania Railroad. Dresser asked whether Central didn't feel that quality passenger service was a duty to the public. To this, William Henry Vanderbilt replied, no doubt with an easy laugh, that "the public be damned," it was the Pennsylvania who was responsible for the service.

Everyone present that day knew very well that Vanderbilt had no personal contempt for the American people. Whatever the faults of the New York Central in 1882, abuse of the public on passenger trains was not among them. However, Dresser went out and wrote the story with a sensational slant. Almost overnight, William Henry Vanderbilt became the man whose motto was "The Public Be Damned!"

He subsequently acquired a ruthless and aggressive image that had nothing whatsoever to do with his real personality. He was by turn shocked, wounded, and harried almost beyond endurance. This experience has been taken to heart by latter-day public figures.

Possibly the "Public Be Damned!" affair was what finally induced Vanderbilt to retire, which he did in May of 1883. His income at this time was 10 million tax-free dollars a year. Day-to-

day control of the vast Vanderbilt railroad interests was handed over to his two eldest sons,
polo-playing William Kissam Vanderbilt and his
Sunday-school–teaching brother, Cornelius Vanderbilt II. William Henry then attempted to re-
lax and enjoy himself.

His retirement was permeated by anxiety,
however, and played out to the accompaniment
of nationwide cartoons that showed him dancing
upon helpless writhing Americans while singing
"The Public Be Damned!" Aside from the indignity of being thus caricatured on a regular
basis, he had other worries, too. His youngest
son, George, didn't seem to be going anywhere
or doing much of anything; the responsibility of
the enormous family fortune remained a crushing
daily burden; his sons-in-law Seward Webb and,
especially, Elliott Shepard endlessly provoked
him; and, worst of all, he was beginning to experience ill health.

It didn't seem that anything serious was wrong,
at least not at first. Then suddenly, the hopeful
retiree had a stroke. This left him blind in one
eye. Almost immediately after, he was involved

The press of the era
singled out William
Henry Vanderbilt for
special vilification.

in a carriage accident. Although not badly hurt, he was severely shaken. So much so, in fact, that he soon after parted with his beloved trotter, Maud S. He sold her for forty thousand dollars, even though she was eleven years old. In 1884, feeling mortality close at hand, he hired Richard Morris Hunt to design the Staten Island mausoleum his father had made him promise to build.

On December 8, 1885, while lunching at his Fifth Avenue home with son-in-law Hamilton Twombly, Mr. Vanderbilt was interrupted by an unexpected caller. It was Robert W. Garret, President of the Baltimore and Ohio Railroad. B & O management was disgruntled over a disagreement with Central concerning connections to New York. Garret, not deigning to bother with the young Vanderbilt brothers, took his grievance directly to the top.

Little was said during the interview with Vanderbilt. Almost as soon as Garret arrived, Vanderbilt fell to the floor and died. His cause of death was another stroke.

The Commodore hadn't been dead quite nine years at this point. However, the fortune he left by now had grown from $100 million to over $200 million. William Henry Vanderbilt was the richest man in the world in 1885. Whether this was ultimately a testament to his financial acumen or simply a case of a vast sum of money acquiring a life of its own is moot.

Like her husband, Mrs. William Henry Vanderbilt had never cared much for the fashionable blandishments of New York society. The same could not be said of her eight children, though. In fact, by 1885, those children had already scaled society's walls, and many were included in McAllister's famous Four Hundred.

This third generation eventually came to define *society* in the popular mind. What enabled them to live as they did was their father's will. Unlike the Commodore's, this was a very subtle document.

The last will and testament of William Henry Vanderbilt also reveals how profoundly different the man was from his egotistical father. The founder of the family fortune was a bombastic berator of his children. William Henry was tactful and indulgent with his. The Commodore had strong views on the limited usefulness of women. William Henry treated his sons and daughters equally.

It is also true that by the time William Henry

William Henry Vanderbilt's famous trotter, Maud S., one of her harried owner's most treasured possessions.

died, the Vanderbilt fortune had become so huge that there really was more than enough for everyone. Even today, $200 million is a tidy fortune. Back in 1885, it had the value—and certainly the emotional impact—of far more.

William Henry once described this fortune as "too great a load for any brain or back to bear. . . . I have no son whom I am willing to afflict with the terrible burden." He solved this dilemma, and remained true to the Commodore's dying wishes, in the following manner. "I want my sons to divide it and share the worry which it will cost to keep it."

On first reading, this does not sound advantageous for the Vanderbilt daughters. It will be remembered, however, that William Henry Vanderbilt knew the lengths to which disappointed heirs will go. The core of his will was a

pair of $40 million trusts, each to be shared equally by all eight children. One trust was in bonds that could not be touched during the recipients' lifetimes. The interest was enormous, enough to support yachts, mansions, servants, and pretty much anything else the heirs might want. The trust itself would outlast them all and survive to enrich future generations of Vanderbilts, no matter what the present generation did with itself.

The other trust was in bonds, too, but these could be cashed at will. This arrangement provided each of Vanderbilt's eight children with a minimum inheritance of $10 million. This may seem modest compared to $200 million plus, but in the words of Central president Chauncey Depew, 10 million at the time was "beyond the grasp" of most people.

The rest of the money, after sundry other millions were dispensed, worked out to something on the order of $130 million. This he divided equally between his two eldest sons, Willie K. and Corneil. These men had been running the New York Central system for over two years, acting in a sort of joint consulship. By dividing the residual estate between them, and empowering them to act as trustees for everybody else's trusts, William Henry actually succeeded in distributing his fortune and keeping it together at the same time.

Alva Vanderbilt's famous ball of March 26, 1883 (described in Chapter 1) had eliminated any lingering doubt that the third generation of Vanderbilts had now entered society. In the wake of their father's death, however, all eight siblings embarked upon a new and even more lavish era. The remarkable part of the story is the consistency with which they all reacted. Every single one promptly went out and built an enormous and beautiful house. True, Willie and Corneil already had built fine houses, paid for with legacies from their grandfather. However, with coffers newly overflowing, even they went back and built some more.

These great houses, and others like them that were soon to rise all across the country, were the stages upon which a particularly luxurious chapter in the annals of American society was played out. It was an era when lavishness was commonplace, money flowed unashamedly, and life—for the fashionables, anyway—was literally an unrelenting round of dinners, balls, house parties, foreign travel, and jolly little excursions aboard somebody's coach, yacht, or private car.

"Your pace is charming, but can you keep it up?" Thus, according to his 1890 memoir *Society As I Have Found It*, was Ward McAllister once queried. Everyone did manage to keep it up. Of course, the men tended to die young, a function of a box of cigars a day, three-hour dinners, and a great deal of drinking. Despite this, the surface glamour of it all was quite breathtaking.

A typical top-drawer New York society family would spend the fall season in New York, dining out and/or going to the opera or attending a ball, as likely as not, almost every night. Their New York season might be interspersed with flying visits to a country place on the perimeter of the New York metropolitan area. Indeed, the same sorts of people still retreat to the same kinds of houses, in the same tristate area, to this very day. Of course, whether or not a society family ever spent much time out of town during the season was doubtful. Gertrude Vanderbilt's diary for one autumn in the early nineties, for example, notes that she has attended over ninety dinner parties.

After Mrs. Astor's January ball, society families with any sort of pretentions would as likely as not be bound for a spa. Here, they would try and get some sleep, and perhaps filter some of that foie gras out of their collective bloodstream. Grace Vanderbilt and Margaret Shepard were both partial to the Homestead in Hot Springs, Virginia.

Spring was the signal for different types of restorative trips, usually to Europe. It was in the spring that New York society people shopped in Paris for gowns, antique furniture, and so forth. Then came shoulder-season parties, perhaps at some great house in the country, or maybe on a yacht. After that, it was on to Newport in late June.

After the glories—or social thuds—of the Newport season, it was back to New York for the fall round of operas and dinners, culminating again in January with Mrs. Astor's annual ball, after which, the whole process repeated itself.

Their regular migrations, amidst baggage, servants, private railroad cars, and suites aboard ocean liners and in great hotels and houses, was as measured and grandiose, and even as inexorable in its way, as the passage of the seasons.

The world of high society occasioned consid-

erable mirth at the time. Mark Twain neatly
skewered the post–Civil War nouveau riche in
The Gilded Age. In 1904, the Rev. Charles Wilbur de Lyon Nichols published a small book titled
The Ultra-Exclusive Peerage of America. It is unclear to what extent the Rev. Nichols was pulling
America's leg, as opposed to setting forth genuinely helpful advice on how to break into society. One tends to believe the latter; certainly
he took himself seriously. His advice is certainly
practical, even today.

The first step was to acquire a town house in
Manhattan. The house shouldn't be too flashy,
and under no circumstances should it be on the
West Side. The idea was to avoid living in anything too-noticeable until such time as one could
be assured of filling it with fashionable guests.
Ideal location: close to, but not right on, Millionaires' Row on Fifth Avenue.

Next, the neophyte was instructed to employ
a press agent. This canny individual would keep
one's womenfolk away from the wrong sorts of
clubs and charities, and insure that one's sailings
and arrivals were posted in the right sorts of
papers. The point of this was to accustom the
right sorts of people to seeing one's name while
scanning the papers for the comings and goings
of their socialite friends, much as "nouvelle society" was to do in the 1980s.

"If your early training in drawing-room de-
portment has been defective or wholly lacking,"
says the Rev. Nichols, adding, "and as likely as
not it has—place yourself at once under such a
social mentor as Miss d'Angelo Bergh." Miss
Bergh was a "leader of the metropolitan musical
smart set." She or somebody like her could give
you "society intonation," teach you how to enter
and leave a drawing room, etc.

Fourth: Find a poor patrician woman who
knows everybody and loves to spend money. You
needed her to warn you off "detrimentals," whose
friendship might hamper you at a later date.

Fifth: Cultivate a visiting nobleman, but only
"if fully assured he is not an imposter." Feed him,
too; he probably needs it. Above all, be seen
with him.

Sixth: Don't worry unduly about "social
thuds" as the Rev. Nichols calls them. They are
inevitable; your day will come.

Seventh: "Be philanthropic, even though the
heart responds but feebly." This ranks interestingly low on the Nichols list, compared to its

The casino at Newport, Rhode Island, New York
society's summer mecca.

high priority for today's social climber.

Eighth: Be churchwise. "The Episcopalian
church and the Catholic church are the churches
of beautiful manners, and if your birth has placed
you under the social ban of being a dissenter,
cultivate Episcopal emotions and shuffle off the
mortal coil of Presbyterianism, on as short notice
as possible."

Ninth: Send your daughters to a convent (for
manners).

Tenth: Rent yachts, never houses. Reason: In
the event of a serious "social thud" you can sail
away on the yacht, but the empty rented house
will be a symbol of your social failure.

Eleventh: Keep cultivating the right people.
No matter how studied their disinterest may
seem, you will eventually be rewarded with an
invitation to a wedding, or at least to the church
ceremony. This will give you the opportunity to
purchase a costly and artistic gift. "Provided the
marriage is not altogether a cold blooded one of
convenience, a feeling towards yourself closely
simulating gratitude may well up in the hearts of
the bride and family." Plus which, the society
reporters, whom your press agent has advised
you to cultivate with tips and champagne, may
mention your gift in the papers. If they do,
others will assume that you were invited to the
reception.

Twelfth: Give musicales, receptions, clever
entertainments, etc., always with an important
guest. The people you hope to entertain likely
as not don't care particularly to see you.

Thirteenth: Learn to love horses.

So endeth the lesson. The book terminates
with a cautionary tale about a certain Mrs. Det-

rimental and her daughter from Denver. Mrs. D. doesn't follow the rules, fails, and commits suicide. In lieu of sympathy this final act of desperation evokes but clucks of disapproval from the Rev. N.

Frank Crowninshield's 1908 book *Manners for the Metropolis* is full of tongue-in-cheek observations on the life that was lived in New York society.

> "If a bachelor receives a dinner invitation from people who are not really 'in the swim' (people, let us say, like old friends, classmates, and business associates, who are, so to speak, 'on the green, but not dead to the hole') he should simply toss it into the fire. This plan will prevent any more invitations from so undesireable a quarter. Were he to answer these people politely, they would certainly annoy him again at a later date. Remember that 'the coward does it with a kiss, the brave man with a sword.' "

On dinner party conversation:

> "At a very large dinner, the lady beside you is almost certain to be one who entertains generously and, as such, should be treated with a certain degree of politeness. Try to suppress, however, all sentiments purely human in their nature, such as pity, kindness of heart, sympathy, enthusiasm, love of books, music and art. These ridiculous sentiments are in exceedingly bad taste and should be used but sparingly, if at all."

Crowninshield was for many years the editor of *Vanity Fair*, as well as a fellow resorter with the William Douglas Sloanes (she was Emily Vanderbilt, one of the eight siblings) in the Berkshires.

Crowninshield was not the only dinner-party wit. Mrs. Winthrop Chanler invented a scheme against dinner party bores. All of her friends paid a little premium, and then gave Mrs. Chanler a list of the men they most dreaded to be seated beside at dinner. If they got stuck with their nemesis, they could collect payment from Mrs. Chanler's fund, and this would at least enable them to buy a new hat.

All the money saved on taxes during this era was sometimes barely enough to cover the es-

sentials. An upper-class family in New York society was expected to maintain houses in Manhattan, Newport, and oftentimes at some mock country seat in Connecticut or New Jersey, as well. Wherever they were in residence, at the minimum they were expected to employ a chef, plain cook, kitchen maid, scullery girl, two laundresses, parlor maid, butler, second man, and at least two additional footmen for dining room work and occasional valeting. This didn't count a man's personal valet or his wife's personal maid.

Society people ate, drank, partied, and they certainly dressed. For a shooting weekend at Blenheim, Consuelo Marlborough—daughter of Willie K. and Alva Vanderbilt—had to change clothes all day long. She describes this in her 1952 book *The Glitter and the Gold*:

> Even breakfast . . . demanded an elegant costume of velvet or silk. Having seen the men off to their sport, the ladies spent the morning round the fire reading the papers and gossiping. We next changed into tweeds to join the guns for luncheon which was served in the High Lodge or in a tent. Afterward we usually accompanied the guns and watched a drive or two before returning home. An elaborate tea gown was donned for tea, after which we played cards or listened to a Viennese band or to the organ until time to dress for dinner when again we adorned ourselves in satin, or brocade, with a great display of jewels. All these changes necessitated a tremendous outlay since one was not supposed to wear the same gown twice. That meant sixteen dresses for four days.

"Taking a drive" on Bellevue Avenue, Newport, Rhode Island. The display of horseflesh and equipage was an afternoon ritual during the summer season.

Ward McAllister, who became America's first legitimate social oracle during his association with Caroline—*the* Mrs.—Astor, once opined that although a gentleman might walk places, his equipage must never be shabby. This could be a significant financial burden, considering that the prototypical New York household of the first order was expected to possess an entire fleet of carriages, plus horses, grooms, and stable buildings, both in Manhattan and at Newport.

At the minimum, according to the Reverend Nichols, one would need the following: an opera bus; a brake for fashionable four-in-hand driving; a victoria; a spider phaeton; a runabout; a station wagon for hauling luggage; a mail phaeton for the man of the house's recreational driving; a one-horse cabriolet; a two-wheel gig; a basket phaeton for the young women in the family; a one-horse bachelor brougham; a pair of two-horse bachelor broughams; and a hansom. Between six and ten horses were required to keep this flotilla on the move. And, lest one suspect Reverend Nichols of simply showing off his carriage knowledge, be advised that in the same year that his book was published, Neily Vanderbilt kept more carriages than this just in Newport—plus fifteen horses and thirty salaried Rhode Island grooms.

Nichols was actually describing Vanderbiltian standards in his book. This is understandable, because by 1904, the Vanderbilts epitomized America's image of high society. This was a neat bit of work on their part, seeing as how by then they were neither the richest nor the grandest family in the country. However, they did have a very particular style, characterized by a peculiarly American kind of expansiveness. This style evolved over generations. Its earliest blossoming was evidenced in the houses described in this book.

Americans traditionally have entertained a lively ambivalence toward our country's millionaires. People love to live in neighborhoods beautified by great estates and to point out palatial houses to relatives and visitors. They love equally to hear tales of the mighty brought low, however. This is unfortunate, since our great estates are oftentimes today in the hands of descendants who can barely afford to support them. To a certain extent, everyone is impoverished when people are chased from their stately homes be-

A family scene at Shelburne Farms. Lila Vanderbilt Webb seated at center with her husband, Dr. William Seward Webb.

cause of punitive taxes and shortsighted zoning.

Prior to the Vanderbilts' social ascendancy, no truly sophisticated private palaces, at least none of any scale, had been erected in the United States. Before Richard Morris Hunt's post-Civil War return from the École des Beaux-Arts in Paris, there weren't any professionally trained American architects. The kind of house the typical rich American considered a palace was dismissed by Edith Wharton as nothing more than an overblown "*maison bourgeoise.*"

The Vanderbilts were not alone in changing this state of affairs. By the late eighties, there were plenty of other rich, sophisticated architectural clients in America. However, no other single group, and certainly no other group of siblings, set out to change things with such panache and on such an enormous scale as did the Vanderbilts.

The themes and details of these first palatial houses were refined by subsequent generations in subsequent houses. These Vanderbilt houses, however, occupy a watershed position in American history, both social and architectural. Those that survive deserve sensitive preservation. Of the thirteen houses built by the third generation of Vanderbilts, ten still exist. They are, quite simply, cultural artifacts with enormous importance for the nation as a whole.

These houses, and many like them that still survive in our country, are integral parts of our heritage. To dismiss them as inconsequential aberrations of the social order is ultimately injurious to that heritage. Unless they are treasured, they will be lost. If that happens, all Americans will be the poorer.

The respective fates of these thirteen Vanderbilt houses illustrate almost everything that can, should, and should not be done to a fine old house. The three that once stood on Vanderbilt Row on Fifth Avenue have all perished. The other ten are still extant. The Breakers, Marble House, Hyde Park, and Biltmore are now museums, the largest and most elaborate, Biltmore, remains in Vanderbilt family hands. Florham and Idle Hour are colleges, and their conversions demonstrate only too well what should—and should not—be done in the field of adaptive reuse. Woodlea is a country club, which has survived the years in gratifyingly un-

The third-floor billiard room at 1 West Fifty-seventh Street.

A detail of the original 1 West Fifty-seventh Street built for Cornelius Vanderbilt II.

abused condition. Shelburne is a country inn. It exemplifies how well preservation can be implemented and how an old house can play a role in the modern world. Elm Court, still in family hands, has degenerated into a vandalized ruin, complete with peeling damask wall coverings and gaping windows open to the weather. Only Rough Point, a Newport cottage now owned by an enigmatic American billionairess—not a Vanderbilt herself—is still maintained in Vanderbiltian condition.

The story of these houses—and of the fascinating period of American history in which they played so great a role—is the subject of this book. One hopes that along with pleasure, *The Vanderbilts and the Gilded Age* will inspire an interest in historic preservation. It is certainly through preservation that tribute can be paid to the great American houses and what they have contributed to the American experience. In this way, they can be accorded the respect and deference they deserve.

—John Foreman
Millbrook, New York

Chapter 2

660 FIFTH AVENUE

660 Fifth Avenue

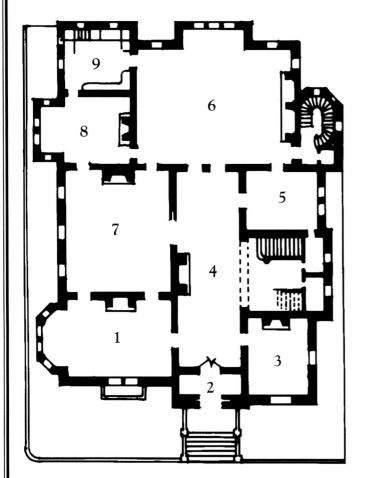
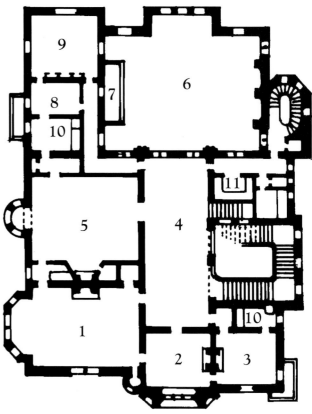

1st Floor
1. Grinling Gibbons Room
2. Vestibule
3. Library
4. Main Hall
5. Billiard Room
6. Dining Hall
7. Drawing Room
8. Breakfast Room
9. Serving Pantry

2nd Floor
1. Mrs. Vanderbilt's Bedroom
2. Mrs. Vanderbilt's Boudoir
3. Bedroom
4. Second Floor Hall
5. Bedroom
6. Upper Part of Dining Hall
7. Musicians' Gallery
8. Nurse
9. Child
10. Bathroom
11. Linens

660 Fifth Avenue (center), the heart of "Vanderbilt Row."

Location: New York City
Architect: Richard Morris Hunt (1827–1895)
Commissioned by: William Kissam Vanderbilt (1849–1920)
House completed: 1882

W. K. VANDERBILT'S urban château on the northeast corner of Fifty-second Street and Fifth Avenue was built for the ages but stood for only forty-four years. It was a much-loved landmark throughout its existence, an ornament to the city of New York, and an eloquent symbol of American wealth and culture.

Shortly after its completion at the end of 1882, this house achieved national prominence as a result of events that took place there on the night of March 26, 1883. This was the date of Willie and Alva Vanderbilt's official housewarming, a fancy dress ball of such surpassing elegance and style that social legend has credited it ever since with catapulting the formerly outré Vanderbilts to the very pinnacle of New York society.

The main stair at 660 Fifth Avenue, showing the magnificent carved Caen stone walls.

It was the genius of Willie and Alva to have their ball, like their house, remembered as the greatest of the century. Of course, there had been other great costume balls in New York before this, and others would follow. However, Alva sensed correctly that an unusual party held at her splendid new house would do much to certify her own and her husband's social standing. Her childhood friend Consuelo Yznaga, married to the Duke of Manchester and known as Lady Mandeville, agreed.

Lady M.'s powerful patronage did a great deal to attract the cream of New York society to Al-va's ball. Let no one suppose, however, that the Vanderbilts in 1883 were social nobodies. Willie and Alva by that date already had attended their first Patriarchs Ball. The Patriarchs, founded in the 1870s by social arbiters Ward McAllister and Mrs. Astor, was the oh-so-social annual gathering of New York's fashionable elite. The invitation list officially separated mere social hopefuls from those who had truly arrived.

Nobody disputed the wealth of the Vanderbilts, but their level of culture was something else. The manners of the coarse and bombastic Commodore, dead less than six years at the time of Alva's ball, were still fresh in New York's social memory. The architectural magnificence of 660 Fifth had undone the reserve of Ward McAllister, a man who prided himself on spotting up-and-comers. However, Patriarchs or no, as yet not a single one of the really good gentlemen's clubs had invited any Vanderbilt to join. New York's most select drawing rooms were not open to them or their wives. Nor had any of the family as yet been introduced to Mrs. Astor.

Caroline Schermerhorn Astor was the wife of William Backhouse Astor, "the landlord of New York." In the words of Reverend William de Lyon Nichols, she "rose to the leadership of American society by the acclamation of society itself." Historian James T. Maher more precisely termed her a "regulator." She was a woman who had lots of money, knew how to entertain with panache, and possessed a personal vision of what "good society" should be like and who should be in it. New York was awash in those years with "Avenoodles," people who'd suddenly struck it rich in mining camps out West (or something similar), and now lived in big houses on Fifth Avenue. The great desire of their ambitious wives was to break into New York society. It was Caroline Astor's self-appointed task not to let them all in.

The measure of her success was the fact that nobody in post–Civil War New York considered himself or herself really in the top drawer without her approval. Mrs. Astor had observed the rise of the Vanderbilts, and had been appalled by the personality of their progenitor the Commodore. Up until the date of Alva's ball, she had never cared to know any of them. To her, they simply did not exist.

The enormous amount of publicity surrounding Alva's ball changed all this. Mrs. Astor's daughter Carrie, like every well-connected young society woman in New York, was not about to miss what promised to be the best party of the year. According to legend, Carrie Astor and her friends had begun rehearsing a formal quadrille. (This was in the days before modern social dancing; for a quadrille, groups of guests would get together in advance and rehearse what was essentially an elaborate square dance). Miss Astor's quadrille was to be called the Star Quadrille. She and seven other society girls were to dress up as stars, in blue, yellow, purple, and white. Her mother was said to have

660 fifth Avenue, northwest corner of Fifth Avenue and Fifty-second Street, in 1926.

drilled the young ladies personally.

The legend continues that Mrs. Astor, at the eleventh hour, realized that she still hadn't received an invitation. Discreet inquiries were made. Alva admitted that, much as she regretted it, the Astors were not on the invitation list. After all, Mrs. Astor had never called. This remark was carried directly to the great lady of Thirty-fourth Street, who hastily boarded her carriage and dropped her card at 660 Fifth.

Appealing as the legend is, it is unlikely that Caroline Astor, the queen of propriety, would have undertaken elaborate preparations to attend a party to which she had not been invited. James Maher pointed out that the newspapers of the period, while reporting virtually every event and rumor connected with the ball, contain no mention whatsoever of her supposed exclusion. There probably is some truth to the tale; but instead of the dramatic last-minute gallop to Fifty-second Street, Mrs. Astor no doubt squared herself with Alva well before daughter Carrie started rehearsing the Star Quadrille.

The Vanderbilt ball, according to the papers, "disturbed the sleep and occupied the waking hours of social butterflies for over six weeks." Sixteen hundred invitations, sent out two months in advance, went to people as far afield as Philadelphia and Boston. When the night of

A contemporary newspaper artist's rendering of the Vanderbilt Ball of March 26, 1883.

March 26 arrived, cordons of police had to hold back curious mobs milling in the streets. Inside, the house presented a decidedly royal aspect. Klunder, society's florist of the hour, had been given carte blanche. Probably every rose and orchid on the Eastern Seaboard was in a gilded basket on Fifty-second Street that night. The third-floor gymnasium, transformed for the evening into a supper hall, was, according to the *Times*, "like a garden in a tropical forest." Even the potted palms were hung with orchids, and everywhere were great blossoming garlands of bougainvillea (or "vougen villa," as one reporter phonetically spelled it).

The guests began arriving at half past eleven. A dazzling procession of liveried coachmen and shining carriages lined up at the door. One costumed socialite after another stepped down onto a crimson rug that ran from the front door to the curb. The costumes were extraordinary. Alva wore Catherine the Great's pearls over a gown of white and yellow brocade that shaded from canary to deep orange. She said she was a Venetian princess. Willie was resplendent in yellow silk tights and a velvet cloak. He had copied the outfit from that worn by the Duc de Guise in a famous portrait owned by Willie's father. Brother Cornelius Vanderbilt II was dressed, appropriately given his character, as Louis XVI. His wife, Alice, wore a diamond-studded satin gown intended to symbolize "Electric Light."

Most of the other Vanderbilt brothers and sisters were there, too. Lila Webb came as a hornet; Emily Sloane as Bopeep; Margaret Shepard was a marquise in gold and olive brocade; Florence Twombly came as "Modern Beauty" in a blue outfit quilted with diamonds. Wall Street socialite Henry Clews, as well as the bogusly hyphenated Four Hundred member James Bradley-Martin, both came as Louis XV. Augustus Gurney wore *two* costumes, appearing alternately as a Moldavian chieftan and a Turkish pasha. Willie's drinking and yachting buddy F. O. (Freddy) Beach (the ladies called him "Beauty Beach" and shuddered with excitement over his raffish reputation) dressed up as a Spanish gypsy. William Henry and his good friend former President Ulysses S. Grant eschewed fancy dress, appearing instead in tails. Society photographer Mora captured everybody on film, and Alva kept an album of them all at Marble House in Newport for many years.

When the quadrilles were announced, a grand procession of princes and brigands, dairymaids and empresses, monks and knights all descended the stairs from the supper room to the main floor. It must have been quite a sight. Besides the Star Quadrille were Mrs. Howland's Hobby Horse Quadrille, Mrs. Perkins's Mother Goose Quadrille, Alva's sister Mrs. Jenny Yznaga's (married to Lady Mandeville's brother, Fernando) Opera Bouffe Quadrille, and Mrs. Strong's Dresden Quadrille. It all went on until dawn, when the last guests went home and an army of servants moved in and cleaned up the place.

According to Henry Clews, Alva's ball put the Vanderbilts "at the top of the heap in what is recognized as good society in New York." Certainly it proved the effective use to which a great house could be put. In the more political words of the New York *Sun*, the affair was "gorgeously accomplished with no interruption by dynamite." The New York *World*, with a Victorian fascination for dollar sums, estimated the total cost at a quarter of a million dollars, broken down as follows: costumes, $155,000; flowers, $11,000; carriage hire, $4,000; hairdressing, $4,000; champagne, catering costs, and music, $65,000; miscellaneous, $11,000. "Until Mrs. William K's advent," the *World* opined, "the Vanderbilt family was unheard of in New York Society, except occasionally when it was abused for watering railroad stock or damning the public." The ball changed all that.

It was another interesting sign of the Vanderbilt magic that they managed to get away with it. Alva's party made her a celebrity. Others who tried the same thing didn't fare so well. For example, in February of 1897, amidst a serious economic depression, the extravagant Mr. and Mrs. Bradley-Martin threw a fancy dress ball at the Waldorf-Astoria. Bradley-Martin allowed in print as how the total cost of the evening would probably approach $370,000. He then congratulated himself on pumping needed cash into the economy.

The ball "disturbed the sleep and occupied the waking hours of social butterflies for over six weeks."

The same public that had been titillated by the Vanderbilt ball was offended by the Bradley-Martin one. Teddy Roosevelt, New York's commissioner of police at the time, publicly declined his invitation. The rector of St. George's Church muttered darkly, "This affair will draw attention to the growing gulf which separates the rich and the poor and serve to increase the discontent of the latter needlessly." A perfect blizzard of bad press grew as the party approached, and engulfed

the hapless Bradley-Martins afterward. To their dismay, their town house was reassessed. Such was the continued tempo of angry articles that they eventually left New York for an extended stay in Paris, whence they effectively never returned.

In 1905, James Hazen Hyde gave a similarly ill-received ball at Sherry's. (At twenty-eight, Hyde had taken the reins of the immensely prosperous Equitable Life Assurance Society from his father, its founder). Young Hyde hired socialite architect Whitney Warren to transform Sherry's ballroom into a garden at Versailles, complete with banks of roses, garlands of orchids, and statuary imported for the evening from France.

The public response to this wanton expenditure led directly to the formation in 1905 of the Armstrong Insurance Committee of Investigation, which revealed so many iniquities in the life-insurance industry in general, and Equitable in particular, that in the midst of the proceedings, young Hyde executed a Bradley-Martin–style exit to the real Versailles in France. He, too, never returned. A joke of the period compared the strenuous life as personified by Teddy Roosevelt to the Equitable Life as exploited by James Hazen Hyde.

The Vanderbilts were more fortunate, or perhaps public opinion in the early eighties was just more innocent. Whatever the case, the upshot of their ball was social triumph. Willie now tackled the most exclusive clubs. In May of 1883, he invited the entire Coaching Club to Idle Hour, his estate on the South Shore of Long Island. The club accepted. And eleven months later, they even asked him to join. In rapid succession, he was admitted to the Union, Knickerbocker, Racquet and Tennis, Turf and Field, and New York Yacht clubs. In January of 1884, even Mrs. Astor succumbed and invited him and his wife to her annual ball.

All this must have been gratifying indeed for a man like Willie Vanderbilt. Finally, he was beginning to receive the sort of treatment he had every reason to expect. Willie was more than the scion of America's richest family. He was also a highly sociable creature and a veritable prince of good fellows. In his personal relations, he was tact and kindness personified. Genial, gracious, considerate, and generous to a fault, he was also an amusing raconteur with a huge fund of good stories.

William Kissam Vanderbilt, the builder of 660 Fifth Avenue. "Besides native charms [he] possessed a highly cultivated intelligence."

Besides native charm, Willie Vanderbilt possessed a highly cultivated intelligence. He had been educated in Switzerland, and as such was a rarity in his day. Few Americans of the time possessed the means, let alone the inclination, to send their sons abroad to school. Willie became a true sophisticate at an early age. He was fluent in French, and a connoisseur of European culture, art, and manners. The scandalmongering tabloids of the era loved to portray the Vanderbilts as coarse parvenus. However, the truth in the case of Willie's generation—and especially in the case of Willie himself—was precisely the opposite.

In Europe, Willie had been accorded that measure of deference that rich Americans traditionally receive overseas. He had witnessed firsthand the last effulgent splendors of the Second Em-

pire. He was an intimate of the nobility, studying with their sons and visiting in their houses. In Geneva and Paris, Willie Vanderbilt naturally traveled in the highest social circles. His wit and geniality, combined with his fluent French and huge wealth, made him a favorite at luxurious entertainments given by the most fashionable of the elite. What a shock it must have been to return to New York and find himself snubbed by the likes of Caroline Astor.

New York in the 1870s was vibrant and exciting. Culturally, however, it remained a provincial outpost compared to Paris or London. For a sensitive and naturally gregarious young man like Willie Vanderbilt, the dismissive treatment that greeted him upon his return home must have been terribly wounding. His subsequent ascendance to the heights of American society is usually explained away as merely incidental to the social successes of his wife. According to most historians, it was she alone who lusted for high society and all it entailed. Actually, her husband felt the sting of exclusion far more than she did; also, his hide was a good deal less tough than hers. There is no question that they both aspired to social success. Alva did not drag Willie along behind her, though; they were equal partners from the start.

Alva Vanderbilt called 660 Fifth Avenue her "little Château de Blois," and the house has sometimes been called a replica of that royal château. True, its architect, Richard Morris Hunt, was an ardent Francophile with a particular taste for the early French Renaissance. However, 660 was far from being a copy. It was a wholly original composition, inspired by the artistic legacy of the Renaissance but adapted to the needs of a powerful American family of the Industrial Age.

Although Willie paid the bills, he was not involved with the design of 660 Fifth. Hunt dealt almost exclusively with Alva, who plunged into the task of the design and made a lifelong friend of Richard Hunt in the process. It is incorrect to characterize 660 Fifth as nothing more than a tool of social aggrandizement. Alva Vanderbilt commissioned many fine mansions before she died. Houses were her art, and throughout her life she immersed herself in every detail of a considerable amount of construction. Her debut was 660 Fifth. Alva's personality was aggressive and domineering, but she was also a woman who

Mrs. William K. Vanderbilt, with son William K. Vanderbilt, Jr., daughter Consuelo, and baby Harold Stirling (Mike), in 1885.

aspired to the best in everything she undertook. She was as ambitious in the social arena as in the architectural one. And she was successful in both.

Actually, Alva's father-in-law, William Henry Vanderbilt, and her brother-in-law Cornelius Vanderbilt II, were both building palaces along Fifth Avenue at the same time she was. The family's building efforts on Fifth Avenue in the Fifties were a coordinated endeavor from the start. William Henry particularly encouraged his daughter-in-law to get involved in the construction of her new house. She did so joyfully. In those days, there were not many things a woman was allowed to do. The design and construction of 660 Fifth was a rare opportunity for Alva to express herself creatively. There is no question that she expected recognition as the chatelaine of so fine a town house. By the same token, she took special pains from the start to build a house that would be a municipal ornament. It was this desire, and not simply the dream of social conquest, that motivated her to build the best.

The house at 660 Fifth Avenue boasted a full one hundred feet on the avenue, which even in the 1880s was an extravagant lot size. Vanderbilt told Hunt that he wanted a house with plenty of light around it. To this, Hunt replied that Vanderbilt had better buy up the entire block-front. Willie didn't, and later regretted it. Actually, the rapacious growth of business in what we today call midtown very soon made Vanderbilt regret building south of Central Park at all.

The corner location gave 660 Fifth a high visibility on the avenue, especially when approached, as most often it was, from the business district downtown. The dominant element of the composition was a three-story attached tourelle that nestled against the entrance bay. This turret enclosed a private interior stair that connected Mrs. Vanderbilt's second-story corner bedroom with her husband's suite above. It gave the house a distinctive look, quite unlike anything that had been seen in New York up until that date. It is hard to adequately convey the visual shock value of this French-style limestone mansion in the brownstone-fronted world of New York in 1882. Edith Wharton described the city then as "cursed with its universal chocolate coating of the most hideous stone ever quarried." In that context, 660 Fifth was revolutionary indeed.

A few other private houses had broken the

pattern of the squared-off Italianate brownstones that dominated so many of the city's residential quarters. Notable among these were merchant prince A. T. Stewart's marble palace at Thirty-fourth and Fifth (1865) and Mary Mason Jones's famous Marble Row at Fifth and Fifty-seventh (1869). However, it was still 660 Fifth that was credited with shattering the tyranny of the brownstone front, probably because it inspired a host of imitators.

Then as now, there were architectural critics in New York who wrote about the cityscape and the individual buildings within it. These people had considerable influence on artistic opinion at the time and, by extension, on the careers of the architects they praised. Almost without exception, they loved 660 Fifth. Royal Cortissoz called it "a tour de force . . . an isolated triumph of lightness and vivacious beauty." Barr Ferree termed it "beautiful, stately and harmonious." Charles Moore related that he had "often walked up Fifth Avenue late at night with Charles McKim, who said he slept better for enjoying the sight of Hunt's W. K. Vanderbilt house; and having taken a look at it, he was ready to return home for another cigar before going to bed."

Richard Morris Hunt, the architect of 660 Fifth Avenue.

There were some ambivalent notes. The *American Architect and Building News* in 1881 complained that the skyline was "needlessly tormented." The author of the piece didn't care for the "colorlessness" of the limestone facade, either. Herbert Croly admired the house's "ease, grace, and urbanity," but added that he thought Hunt's decoration was "scholarly to the verge of pedantry." In this respect, 660 was ahead of its time. A decade later, the most fashionable of America's architects would be precisely those best able to employ architectural elements with historical accuracy.

Louis Sullivan, an acknowledged pioneer of the American skyscraper, struck a positively misanthropic note. "Must you wait until you see a gentleman in a silk hat come out of it before you laugh?" he asked cruelly. Sullivan asserted that no man could live in such a house, "morally, mentally, or spiritually. . . . [H]e and his house are a paradox, a contradiction, an absurdity." Voices such as this were in the minority, however.

The most elite residential quarter of New York, prior to the construction of 660 Fifth Avenue, was probably Fifth Avenue in the Forties. William Henry Vanderbilt lived at Fifth and Fortieth, in a house his father had built for him, and which he himself would later leave to his son Fred. Other of his children were billeted in a cluster of brownstones he had bought for them on East Forty-fourth Street.

By the late 1870s, the Fifties between St. Patrick's Cathedral and Central Park, were in the direct line of changing fashion. Prior to the arrival of the Vanderbilts, however, this stretch of the avenue had not yet developed a distinct character of its own. It was the construction of the Vanderbilt houses, and most particularly 660 Fifth Avenue, that confirmed at last that this part of town had arrived.

Many fascinating personalities were connected with the building of 660 Fifth. Perhaps none was as unusual as Mrs. Vanderbilt herself. Born Alva Erskine Smith, on January 17, 1853, at Mobile, Alabama, she was married to William K. Vanderbilt in 1875. Alva Smith's maternal ancestors were the Deshas (pronounced de-SHAY) of Kentucky. This was a noble old family with roots that legitimately included English aristocrats and prominent American pioneers.

Alva's father was a gracious sort, one of those members of polite society who are unsuited to making money yet always living in genteel surroundings. Murray Forbes Smith started as a lawyer, married the daughter of General Robert Desha of Kentucky, and wound up in Mobile, managing his father-in-law's cotton-shipping business. Alva's earliest memories were of building houses with books from her father's extensive library. Like many Southerners of breeding, the Smiths summered in the north, in Newport, Rhode Island.

On the eve of the Civil War, the Smiths decamped for New York. This was not done for political reasons. The move was caused by the new importance of railroads in the transport of cotton. Murray Smith moved to New York because New York was the acknowledged railroad capital of America. He purchased a house at 40 Fifth Avenue and a box at the fashionable Academy of Music, the latter being something the Vanderbilts never managed to do.

Alva's mother, Mrs. Phoebe Smith, was quickly welcomed into New York society. In 1860, she was on the receiving line at the Fifth Avenue Hotel to welcome the Prince of Wales on his famous visit to New York. The war, however, soon made life in New York an unpleasant matter for Southerners. Getting the cotton out of General Desha's plantations also proved impossible. After Lincoln's assassination, things became too uncomfortable for the Smiths and they decided to sell 40 Fifth. On her last Sunday in New York, outside the Church of the Ascension on lower Fifth Avenue, Alva got into a fight. A little boy in the Sunday school singled her out and began to taunt her about her French hat. She chased after him, pulled him down into the gutter, and beat him up. After this symbolic farewell to Manhattan, she accompanied her mother and sisters to Paris, where Mrs. Smith had visited frequently before the war. Mr. Smith, meanwhile, went to Liverpool to try and make a living.

Paris was inexpensive then and the Smiths were, after all, well connected. Emperor Napoleon III had rather a penchant for rich Americans with pretty daughters, and he showed the Smiths special favor. Alva attended a select girls school in Neuilly and, if nothing else, picked up a fluency in the language. She also took piano lessons, from an Italian teacher who made the mistake one day of taking her fingers a little too roughly and banging them onto the correct keys. She yanked her hand free, slapped him soundly across the face, and never took a lesson again.

Paris was brilliant in the late 1860s, and the last gorgeous years of the Second Empire had as great an influence on Alva's tastes and expectations as they had on those of her future husband. The struggle to make a living compelled Murray Smith to take his family back to New York, however. As it turned out, this was a good thing, since Paris fell to the Communards a short time afterward.

In New York, things went from bad to worse. Alva's mother died. Her father's investments soured. They moved to progressively less fashionable addresses. One day, Alva's father took her aside and said that if things didn't improve, "we shall have to keep a boarding house." At this point, enter William K. Vanderbilt.

Willie—or Willie K. as people sometimes called him—had a lot in common with Alva. They were both vivacious and attractive, each had firsthand experience with European society of the best sort, both were fluent in French and familiar with French culture, and neither one had a very solid footing in New York society. Each also had something the other needed. Alva's pedigree was impeccable, but she was impoverished; Willie was the son of the richest man in the world, but Mrs. Astor and her set refused to acknowledge them, and as a result, the family possessed zero social cachet in their own hometown.

Mrs. Astor's father-in-law, John Jacob Astor I, was almost a contemporary of Commodore Vanderbilt. Yet the Astors passed as "old money," while the Vanderbilts were accused of being "nouveau." Conventional wisdom has it that this was a silly prejudice without foundation in fact. However, the Astors really were better connected than their Vanderbilt competitors. John Jacob Astor's daughter Eliza had married a German count, and Astor himself had been presented to both Louis Philippe and Charles X. He was also a patron of Washington Irving, and his country house at Hell Gate in Northern Manhattan was the resort of all manner of amusing and important people from Daniel Webster to Samuel Ward. Astor also gave half a million dollars to found a public library, something no Vanderbilt as yet had done.

Willie Vanderbilt met Alva at a dance in New York and followed her to White Sulphur Springs, West Virginia. To her father's enormous relief, he proposed to her shortly thereafter. On April 20, 1875, at Calvary Episcopal Church in New York, he became the second Vanderbilt to wed a Mobile girl, the Commodore having been the first. Before Alva left for the church, her bedridden father took her hand in his and confessed with great emotion that her marriage had taken a crushing burden off his mind. Two weeks later, he died.

Alva immediately hit it off with her new father-in-law, whom she later described as her "boon companion." William Henry Vanderbilt was very taken by his son's new wife. He liked her style and her good looks, and he admired her intelligence and ebullience. She was the sort of person who literally crackled with energy, which she combined with the sort of genteel charm that rarely fails to win an older man's heart. When Murray Smith died, William Henry Vanderbilt begged Alva to consider him as her father henceforth.

The attraction between daughter-in-law and father-in-law was based not just on mutual admiration but on shared interests. William Henry Vanderbilt had come to a stage in life where he wanted to build something of beauty, something that would outlast him. The block-long palace he had constructed at 640 Fifth Avenue was as much an expression of his own creativity as 660 Fifth was a stage for the creative talents of Alva and architect Richard Morris Hunt. William Henry spent endless hours with her, sharing his plans and dreams for the great new house he planned to build for himself, as well as the additional houses—at 642 Fifth, 2 West Fifty-second Street, 680 and 684 Fifth—he planned for his married daughters.

It was in this context that William Henry Vanderbilt became Alva's close friend, and in which he encouraged her to involve herself in the design of 660. She basked in his fatherly love and encouragement. There is no doubt that he provided much of the early impetus for her subsequent interest in building houses.

Money woes, the bane of Alva's youth, were simply not part of the Vanderbilt equation. Willie started at the bottom of the family business but was rapidly promoted. In 1877, at the age of twenty-eight, he became second vice president

"Almost without exception [the critics] loved 660 Fifth."

A detail of 660 Fifth
Avenue.

of the New York Central. A good salary undoubtedly accompanied the new position. More importantly, at least from Alva's standpoint, he also inherited $3 million from his grandfather.

Although their marriage ultimately collapsed, Willie and Alva were a remarkably effective pair in the beginning. Together, they laid siege to New York society with a concentrated élan that proved irresistible. They carefully cultivated people; they assumed fashionable attitudes; they spent money to entertain in whatever amounts were necessary; they made full use of Alva's excellent social connections. It should be remembered, too, that this pair was also witty, cultured, widely traveled, sophisticated (though this actually could count against you in New York), and good-looking, all in addition to being rich.

By 1878, despite steady progress, they still were not where they wanted to be. That was the year that planning began for 660 Fifth Avenue. From the outset, these young Vanderbilts surely realized the value of an impressive house in the social sweepstakes. Richard Morris Hunt gave them a work of art instead of something vulgar and merely expensive.

Richard Morris Hunt, the "Father of American Architecture," was a well-established New York architect when the Vanderbilts first engaged him to design their Long Island country house, Idle Hour, in 1877. Ground was broken there in 1878, the same year planning began for the Fifth Avenue house. It was 660 Fifth Avenue, however, that made Hunt famous, nationally and internationally. His work on this house started a châteauesque revival that was felt across the entire country.

Hunt was born in 1827 in Vermont. His father Jonathan, a member of Congress and an intimate of Daniel Webster, died early, leaving the upbringing of seven children to a resourceful widow. She was an early sojourner in Paris, that formerly low-cost retreat to which many Americans repaired in times of financial reverse.

After schooling in Geneva, Hunt went to Paris to study architecture in the atelier of Hector-Martin Lefuel. This was a coup; Lefuel was the official architect of France's Second Empire; even better, the master approved of young Hunt, soon became his mentor, and urged him to enter the École des Beaux-Arts. This he did—after two tries at the entrance exam—in 1846.

Until this time, no other American had ever enrolled at the École's school of architecture. In the United States, architectural schools didn't even exist. Architecture on this side of the Atlantic was the province of talented amateurs and builders. There was no professional tradition, no recognized course of study, nothing save a lively national taste for the eclectic. Hunt was painfully aware of what he considered to be his country's lack of an architectural heritage. "Why should not our public hotels," he wrote to his mother at the end of late 1855, ". . . rival or even surpass the palaces of Europe?"

Hunt was lean and handsome in his Paris years, quite a physical contrast to the portly little old man he became. He drank tea by the potful, sported romantically drooping mustaches, spoke French like a native, even adopted the Continental manner of gesticulating with his hands.

He spent almost nine years in Paris, studying art and sculpture as well as architecture. He fell in love with Gallic culture; Frenchmen often took him for a native. In 1855, despite Lefuel's urgings that he stay and make his life in France, Hunt returned to the United States. From that point until his death in 1895, he was a literal whirlwind of professional activity.

After a short stint working for Thomas U. Walter on alterations to the U.S. Capitol, Hunt returned to New York and opened his own office. One of his early clients was the Hudson River School artist Thomas P. Rossiter. Rossiter's father-in-law, a miserly dentist by the name of Eleazar Parmly, had promised to pay for the design of a house to be built for the artist on West Thirty-eighth Street. However, when the bill came, he refused to pay. Hunt sued.

This was a landmark case for American architecture, and Hunt's pursuit of it had far-reaching implications for his profession. Although Hunt was not able to collect the entire fee, the judge did order Parmly to pay a portion of it. Thus is Hunt remembered as the first man to get an American court to uphold the concept of an architectural design fee calculated as a percentage of costs.

The tempo of Hunt's professional life steadily increased throughout the 1860s. During this time, he was associated with the so-called Stick Style of architecture. Stick Style houses were all the rage for a short while in the 1860s and 1870s. They were bulky, asymmetrical, all-wood American versions of the Tudor method of half-timbering with stucco infill. The idea was to suggest the structural nature of a building by means of an exterior skin composed of skeletal-looking beams. Actually, the beams (or "sticks," as they were called) that went up and down and crossways across the facade were all applied. They had an original look, however, and one that was uniquely American. Hunt's identification with the popular Stick Style underscored his position at the forefront of architectural trends in this country.

Hunt's New York atelier was in the Studio Building at 51 West Tenth Street, a brick-fronted concoction of his own design. The Studio was filled with famous and artistic individuals. Frederick Church, J. W. Casilear, and John LaFarge all rented space there. The building was not really overly attractive—it looks rather garagelike in old pictures—but in its day it was a center of artistic life in the metropolis.

Hunt took in students in the manner of the Beaux-Arts ateliers of Paris; that is, in lieu of classroom instruction, he provided them with the chance to work directly on whatever projects happened to be on hand at the time. This was how Lefuel had taught him. Charles Gambrill, George Browne Post, William R. Ware, Frank Furness, and many other architects who later rose to prominence were students of Richard Hunt on Tenth Street.

To a Beaux-Arts–trained architect, every building represented a challenge for which he needed to find the ideal solution. His *parti* was the specific arrangement of interior spaces whereby the problems posed by the building's intended use would best be solved. Up to this point, Beaux-Arts training is not much different from that of any other architectural school.

However, every Beaux-Arts *parti* was also informed with a special sort of ideal geometry based on balance. To this end, the architect employed a variety of axes, both major and minor, along which he arranged rooms in order of importance. Good Beaux-Arts buildings have a very calculated dramatic effect. Facades and entries were held to be crucial in establishing important initial reactions to the building's use and importance. Sizable halls and corridors, typical victims of twentieth-century economics, were another hallmark of Beaux-Arts design. They also helped create the stateliness one feels when moving around a Beaux-Arts building.

People today have a vague idea that Beaux-Arts means a specific architectural style. Actually, the École itself did not champion any particular style. The Art Deco Chrysler Building in New York City is as true to the principles of Beaux-Arts design as the Paris Opéra. Despite that, the Modern French style popular at the close of the nineteenth century, and later derided as "cartouche" architecture, has incorrectly come to be called Beaux-Arts, even though in itself it has no particular association with Beaux-Arts design principles.

In 1861, the very polished, talented, and socially acceptable young Richard Hunt married an extremely rich young woman. Catherine Clinton Howland Hunt came from a shipping and merchant family with a country seat on the Hudson (which Hunt designed) and extensive social connections. Hunt's widening circle of wealthy acquaintances kept the commissions rolling in.

He did numerous—mostly Stick Style—houses in Newport, and in 1869 he designed the famous Stuyvesant Apartment House on East Eighteenth Street for socialite Rutherfurd Stuyvesant. At the time, "French flats" were held in low repute; they were thought to be "too close for comfort," or for propriety. But the Stuyvesant, probably as a result of its owner's social cachet, filled up rapidly with middle-class types and even a few blue bloods. So it was that Hunt pioneered apartment living in today's apartment capital of the world: New York.

By the 1870s, the workaholic Hunt was in his glory. His practice was now swollen with commercial as well as residential contracts. He designed numerous skyscrapers, a notable one being the now-demolished 1873 Tribune Building on Park Row in Manhattan. His houses got progressively grander—and the variety of their locations attests to Hunt's growing reputation—as he designed for a wider and wealthier circle of clients. There was nothing he wasn't building in these years, from tenements, to churches, to libraries, to ever-more-elaborate private houses.

Much of Hunt's work up to this point, including the Stick Style house he did for Willie Vanderbilt at Oakdale, Long Island (finished in June of 1879), was a far cry from the pale Renaissance palaces with which he would later be so associated. Buildings such as the Tribune Building or the Studio Building look distinctly

Victorian and fussy to the modern eye. All that changed with 660 Fifth Avenue. In the words of architectural historian Joy Wheeler Dow, Hunt's years of "mediocrity" came to an abrupt end with that building. According to Dow, Hunt henceforth dispensed with his "staccato style" and embraced "adaptation."

Historically, adaptation has been derided. In unskilled hands, it is true that a pinch of this and a soupçon of that, drawn from too many or uncomplementary architectural traditions, easily can add up to an awful-looking botch. Such was hardly the case with Richard Hunt, however. His best buildings successfully adapted ancient Western principles of architectural proportion and decoration to modern American conditions.

Hunt was subsequently attacked as a copyist. There were those in the seventeenth century who belittled Hardouin-Mansart's work on Versailles. Ruskin belittled Inigo Jones and Sir Christopher Wren as uninspired, too. The buildings thus disparaged all represented little renaissances of their own. Likewise, Hunt's Vanderbilt houses, and 660 in particular, are legitimate examples of an American Renaissance. They are cases in point of the periodic resurgence of classic principles of Western beauty that never die. These principles were established in ancient times, and have reemerged at intervals ever since. They informed the Italian and the French Renaissance, and among other things inspired the Vanderbilt house at 660 Fifth Avenue.

It took a client such as Alva Vanderbilt to effect this sort of a sea change in the career of an already well-known professional, for 660 Fifth signaled an entirely new direction for Richard Morris Hunt. He took the spirited Victorian taste for elaboration, put it through a screen of cosmopolitanism and architectural knowledge, and produced the first in a series of authentically American palaces. Hunt's great houses were beautiful, functional, and instantly understandable. People marveled at them.

Hunt loved the early French Renaissance. This was a period that struck responsive chords in his inner being, and it was his association with Alva Vanderbilt that brought this love to concrete fruition. He especially loved the Château de Blois. A number of his big houses—particularly 660 Fifth, E. T. Gerry's house at Fifth and Sixty-first Street, and Biltmore for George Vanderbilt—are referred to as his "Blois Group."

They echo the palate, the massing, and the exquisite detail—if not the *parti*—of the original, although they do so with a distinct American accent. Like all of Hunt's subsequent palaces, 660 was a public demonstration of American savoir faire as much as it was a house for a rich client.

When built—and for more than a generation thereafter—660 Fifth Avenue was acknowledged as Hunt's most perfect creation. It also established the concept in America of the European architect-decorator. Hunt imported from Paris the notion that the designer of a great house should do the whole place, including the interior design, right down to the furniture. The common practice in this country at the time, even for the best houses, was to hire one individual to build the envelope and another to decorate it. The nonarchitectural approach of most interior decorators led architect Ogden Codman to condemn American interior design as a "branch of dressmaking."

The most handsome rooms are those whose good architecture is complemented—and not obscured—by carefully considered decoration and furnishings. The task of the architect-decorator is to keep this final goal in mind. He creates rooms with good proportions, then makes sure those good bones won't be carelessly obscured by someone else. This is not to say that the architect-decorator designs every single interior himself. However, he does oversee the total process, right down to the placement of the furniture.

What usually happened in Hunt's large houses was a collaboration between himself and one or more (usually French) *décorateurs*. Hunt would determine the purpose of the space, position it in the house, and indicate the size and location of doors and windows. Then the French decorator would design the boiserie, the floor, the ceiling treatment, the fireplaces, the hardware, and everything else required to produce a finished space. Hunt, of course, reviewed the progress of the design and made such suggestions for changes as he thought necessary.

Some interiors the architect would design himself. There was a sort of "floating crap game," as James Maher puts it, of skilled artisans working in New York at the time. Hunt could call upon any number of craftsmen to execute his designs in wood, bronze, and marble. The French designers typically had their work executed in Europe. Great rooms destined for American houses were routinely assembled in Europe, right down to the light fixtures on the walls and the hinges on the doors. They were then dismantled, packed in moisture-proof tin cases, shipped to New York complete with a French installation team, and reassembled on site complete with furniture.

Hunt's favorite decorating firm was a Parisian outfit called Jules Allard et Fils. He provided them with such a crush of work in the wake of 660 Fifth that in 1884 they opened a New York office of their own at 304 Fifth Avenue. Thanks to the association with Hunt, Allard became the best known of the Parisian firms working in the States at the end of the last century. There were others, however, now mostly forgotten. The rooms they produced were and are (many still exist) perfectly exquisite.

Mere elaborateness is not what sets these rooms apart. They exemplify superb craftsmanship, beautiful design detail, and an understanding of the beauties of good proportion. Edith Wharton called proportion the "good breeding of architecture." The subtle knowledge of how high to make a door, how elaborate the fireplace mantel, how heavy the cornice, the proportions of the wall paneling, how high the baseboards, and so on makes all the difference in a room's final effect. Many of our great American rooms are in special peril today because too many restorations either neglect to preserve enough of the interior fabric or render it unrecognizable through unsympathetic alteration.

The fact is that it was hard, even for a Beaux-Arts–trained American like Richard Hunt, to do French rooms with a truly authentic touch. Few Americans could; they hadn't grown up with the proportions. Francophile that he was, Hunt was quite aware of this, so he made Allard a virtual partner on many of his palace projects. Hunt still assumed total responsibility for the final product, however. He learned that from Lefuel, and taught it in his own atelier on Tenth Street. His students spread this gospel across the United States. They spread Hunt's love of French culture across the country, too, which eventually helped fuel a raging fashion in this country in the 1890s for French eighteenth-century design.

Alva Vanderbilt might have been Hunt's dream client. Dictating her (never-published) memoirs in 1917, she recalled her relationship with him as "one of the greatest companionships of my life." She claimed to have felt the sort of inspiration around him "that only comes from contact with greatness." They worked endless hours together in his office, sometimes daily, "pondering over drawings of the great buildings of Europe, fascinated with every detail and determined to reproduce in this modern city of the new world a structure that would recall the sure inspiration of the old-world builders."

"My house was the death of the brownstone front," she asserted. And it was part of some sort of Vanderbilt genius that, even though the house really was not the first to break with the brownstone tradition, somehow it still got the credit for doing so. "I wanted to put my whole soul into the construction of the house on Fifty-second Street," she wrote. What she and Hunt were trying to do was import culture—specifically that of Western Europe—to the descendants of those who had created it.

Always the perfect gentleman, Hunt never belittled or obscured the design contributions of his patroness. Both had strong opinions and demanding personalities, however, and they did not always agree. "Damn it, Mrs. Vanderbilt," Hunt once exclaimed, "who is building this house?" To which she replied, "Damn it, Mr. Hunt, who is going to live in it?" Plans for 660 Fifth were filed in December of 1879. Almost immediately afterward, by mutual agreement between herself and Hunt, Alva left for Europe to study interior decoration.

Construction work on 660 started at the end of 1879. The stone carving on this house was, in a word, sublime. The exterior was clad in "tooled" Indiana limestone. This means that each block of surface stone, instead of being left smooth, was worked over with a hand chisel. The result was a subtly textured surface surrounded by a smooth perimeter border. The facades were further enlivened by the opulent, if judicious, application of sensuously carved foliage, cherubs, dogs, and sundry additional architectural motifs derived from Renaissance French models.

There was marvelous stonework inside, as well. Both the central hall and the main stairway were paneled in Caen stone. This is a type of French limestone, imported from quarries near

The double-height dining hall at 660 Fifth, from whose second floor musicians' gallery the Vanderbilt children watched their parents' guests.

a city of the same name. When finished, it has a velvety surface texture not unlike etched glass. Caen stone is at once luxuriously smooth and suggestive of great substance.

In the vestibule off Fifth Avenue, the Caen stone walls were carved to look like hung fabric with fringed edges. The grand stairway to the second floor was a tour de force of trophies, fruit, masks, and cherubs holding aloft the letter V, all exquisitely executed in Caen stone. The effect was more than just grand and spacious. It was opulent, intricate, and beautifully proportioned. Looking at old pictures of these vanished interiors, one wonders how the wrecking crew in 1926 could have brought themselves to smash it all to pieces. Yet that is precisely what they did.

Some of the most beautiful craftsmanship at 660 was in the great double-height dining hall

that paralleled Fifth Avenue at the back of the house. The walls here were decorated with panels of "quartered" oak, quartering being a specific process of milling that results in advantageous display of hardwood grain. These panels were carved in low relief and filled with fanciful creatures and graceful movement. They were modeled in such a manner that background elements disappeared delicately into a flush surface at the perimeter of the composition. Each was left unstained and was finished with layers of hand-applied wax. The result was a mellow golden tone that went nicely with the dual stone fireplaces at the end of the room and with the elaborate tapestries that decorated the walls above. Architectural critic John Vredenburgh Van Pelt, writing in the twenties, noted that "The weakest point in the American Renaissance is perhaps the inadequate supply of high grade workmen. The Vanderbilt house is as notable for the beauty of the hand work on it as for the beauty of Hunt's design."

Many other parts of this house deserve credit, as well. The windows in the dining hall, for example, were made in France from "cathedral" glass, bits of medieval stained glass salvaged during repairs to cathedral windows. Historian James T. Maher described the style of the Louis XV drawing room as "Alva Vanderbilt French Revival." Napoleon III, patron of the opulent, was spiritual godfather to the look, a role he shared with Hector Lefuel and Charles Garnier (architect of the Paris Opéra). Alva's drawing room was anything but chaste, in the sense of the eighteenth-century French look that would come to dominate fashionable American inte-

riors by the 1890s. However, it was vigorous and glamorous, and it worked as well as it did due to the "nonchalant perfection" of people such as Jules Allard.

A number of rooms at 660 were redecorated over the years by different people, in different styles. This is typical of any large house. Even from the beginning, however, the interiors here represented the work of various decorators. The great dining hall, for example, with its beautiful quartered oak panels and the cathedral-glass windows, was the work of Herter Brothers, then the most prominent decorating firm in the United States. Hunt himself was responsible for the Moorish Room, an Islamic tour de force that housed the billiard table. The execution of this room was a marvel of detail and craftsmanship attributed to a furniture maker named Leon Mar-

"Alva Vanderbilt French Revival"; the Louis XV drawing room at 660 Fifth.

cotte. On the third floor, adjacent to Willie Senior's suite of rooms, was a big gymnasium. In 1898, this was turned into a supper room by Richard Howland Hunt, son of the original architect.

Willie and Alva's daughter, Consuelo, was six years old when the family moved from 5 East Forty-fourth Street to 660 Fifth. Already cowed by a tyrannical mother, little Consuelo found small comfort in her parents' vast new stone palace. It was huge and scary, rather like her mother. "How long and terrifying was that dark and endless upward sweep": This was how she described the staircase in her memoir *The Glitter and the Gold.* The double-height dining hall was another matter. She provides a charming vignette of herself and her little brother Willie Junior crouched on the musicians' gallery while peeking down at their parents' guests. The house was ablaze with light, filled with music and flowers and laughter. And unseen above the fashionable throng were two little children observing their parents' guests in the time-honored manner of children. Except these children were looking through a carved railing above gentlemen in evening dress and ladies "aglitter with jewels" all seated at high-backed tapestry-covered chairs, with footmen in knee breeches poised behind each.

Alva's suite on the second floor had a bathroom lined with plate-glass mirrors painted with blooming cherry trees. "Quite captivating" was how architectural historian John Vredenburgh Van Pelt described the effect just prior to the house's demolition. The tub in this room was carved from a single block of white marble. It, together with the mirrors, probably sits at the bottom of some New Jersey landfill today, an early victim of America's disregard for vintage plumbing.

The floor plan of 660 Fifth is a very good Beaux-Arts one because it particularly suited the life-style of the wealthy and important family for which the house was built. One passed from the vestibule into a sixty-foot-long hall, at the end of which were twin doors, hinting at something still grander in the distance. This wonderful hall, broad and richly decorated with carved stone and tapestries, was like a royal road to pleasure. It was a dramatic approach to the lavish entertainments that constituted one of the major requirements of the family, and it focused on the dining

A carved Caen stone panel on the main stair at 660 Fifth.

The Caen stone newel post on the main stair at 660 Fifth.

hall at the far end. When one reached that dining hall and passed through the twin doors, one's gaze was swept up to the ceiling, a full two stories above.

The main hall also provided access to a variety of other important rooms on the main floor. The drawing room was in a perfect spot for the ladies to retire after dinner, while the men could be assured of privacy in the billiard room. The Grinling Gibbons Room, named after the famous seventeenth-century sculptor and wood-carver whose heavily modeled foliate motifs inspired the room's decoration, could be thrown open during large entertainments, or used as an intimate reception room for daytime callers. The library was a retreat, located adjacent to the major traffic area yet offering seclusion if that was what was desired. All these rooms radiated off of the main hall and related to it in such a manner that they could be thrown open and used in combination with one another, on a gala evening, for example, or kept closed and private for various uses at other times.

The dominant characteristic of this plan is a respect for privacy, which is perhaps the ultimate luxury. The concept of privacy was a new one in the United States, where primitive conditions had traditionally encouraged a communal style of life. From the earliest of the New England cottages, focused around a central hearth, to the Queen Anne and Shingle Style houses of the late 1800s, with their wide-open living halls, American architecture had not been greatly concerned with the normal human desire to get away from the bustle. It was not until the era of the Beaux-Arts architects that American house design began to accommodate a more refined way of life based on European notions of the desirability of personal privacy.

For ten years after it was built, the Vanderbilts used 660 Fifth for the winter season in New York. Summers at first were spent at Idle Hour. By the mid-1880s, however, Newport began to attract trendsetting New Yorkers. Neither of the Vanderbilts cared much for Saratoga. And Alva, of course, knew Newport well from her childhood. They kept Idle Hour for the fall and spring, but began to rent in Newport for July and August. By 1888, they had decided to build. And in 1892, Marble House was opened.

The acrimonious demise of the Vanderbilts' marriage is described in Chapter 9. By 1894, they were separated. The divorce decree was signed in 1895; after that, 660 Fifth was used rarely. Alva was offered the house as part of the settlement, but she declined, feeling it was too expensive to maintain. Willie spent less time in New York; whenever he was in town, it was simpler to stay at the Metropolitan Club.

As late as the 1890s, many New Yorkers were convinced that Forty-second Street would remain the permanent dividing line between Manhattan's business districts to the south and its residential districts to the north. Speaking specifically of Vanderbilt Row, one architectural critic observed that "it does seem as though the stretches just below the Park can never be abandoned by those who have built themselves such comfortable, such enormously expensive, and

Willie Vanderbilt's yacht *Alva* sank in 1892; her replacement was *not* christened *Alva*.

The Vanderbilts' marriage finally came apart on the maiden voyage of this yacht, the *Valiant*, in 1894.

sometimes such very beautiful houses."

By 1901, however, the line already had been breached. Fifth Avenue below Central Park was becoming a world-class shopping street that would soon eclipse Bond Street and the rue de la Paix. Despite growing crowds and traffic, the Fifties still preserved an outward serenity. As late as 1904, Willie and his daughter-in-law bought two lots immediately north of 660 Fifth for the purpose of building another family house. In 1905, McKim, Mead & White designed a beautiful town house for the W. K. Vanderbilt, Jr.'s. This luxurious mansion, at 666 Fifth Avenue lasted scarcely twenty years.

VANDERBILTS SPEND MILLIONS FOR SELF-PROTECTION—IT IS AN EXPENSIVE LUXURY TO LIVE IN FIFTH AVENUE AND KEEP BUSINESS ENCROACHMENTS AT A DISTANCE. This headline appeared above a real estate article published in *The New York Times* on May 1, 1904. According to the *Times*, the family had already expended $4 million to keep their surroundings residential.

666 Fifth Avenue, designed by Stanford White for the Vanderbilts' son, William K. Vanderbilt, Jr., was built next door to Hunt's masterpiece in 1905.

"The Vanderbilts have decided to stay where they are and, if money can accomplish it, with the most desirable surroundings possible."

This undertaking was hindered by the fact that Willie, head of the family since the death of his brother Cornelius II in 1899, was so often in France. When the Catholic Orphan Asylum, which occupied the Fifth Avenue blockfront from Fifty-first to Fifty-second streets, came on the market in 1902, a serious opportunity was missed. The Union Club promptly bought the Fifty-first Street end of the Fifth Avenue blockfront and set about erecting a fine new clubhouse. The lots at the Fifty-second Street end, however, remained unsold.

The Vanderbilts at first did nothing. Then plans were filed for an eighteen-story hotel on the site. Blasting had already begun when Willie Vanderbilt belatedly acquired title—at a very inflated cost—and halted construction. His brother George then engaged Richard Hunt's son to design a pair of town houses to be erected on a portion of the site. These houses became known as the Marble Twins, and one of them, though much abused, is extant today at 647 Fifth Avenue.

The corner lot on Fifty-second Street turned into something of an albatross. Willie placed a restriction on the deed, which prohibited any use other than private residential. Then he set out to find a millionaire willing to build a suitable house. Everybody else saw what was happening south of Central Park, however, and nobody wanted to build. Finally, Morton Plant obliged and built the fine house that stands on the site today.

Shortly after this, the old Langham Hotel across Fifty-second Street came on the market. Mindful of the fiasco with the Asylum property, the Vanderbilts immediately purchased the Langham for $1,325,000, tore it down, and again restricted the site to single-family residential use. Now they had another albatross around their necks. This time, the property proved completely unsalable, at least as a site for a private residence.

Years passed and businesses and office buildings crept relentlessly northward. The price of land on Fifth Avenue was doubling every other year. Non-Vanderbilts on Vanderbilt Row began selling out one by one. By the eve of the First World War, Fifth Avenue from Thirty-fourth to Fifty-ninth streets had become the premiere shopping district of New York. Handsome new retailing palaces were everywhere: Gorham at Thirty-sixth; Tiffany and Lord & Taylor at Thirty-eighth; Arnold Constable on the site of William Henry's original house at Fortieth; W. and J. Sloane at Forty-sixth; Davis, Collamore at Forty-eighth; Duveen's at Fifty-sixth. In addition, a broad assortment of smaller shops aimed at the carriage trade had invaded former town houses on virtually every block. Vanderbilt Row was reduced to a scattered archipelago of private islands in a sea of boutiques.

When the war in Europe broke out in 1914, Willie Vanderbilt and his second wife, Anne, stayed in France to help the war effort there. They made periodic visits to the States, he to attend to railroad business and she to raise money for the war effort. The Langham site had been kept vacant for many years in the hope of eventually getting somebody to build. When war came, however, Willie must have decided that this was an impossible dream. The world as he had known it was passing, at least on Fifth Avenue in the Fifties. So he sold the Langham site. An eight-story loft building occupied by a dressmaking firm was promptly erected there facing Morton Plant's house across Fifty-second Street and 660 Fifth across the avenue.

Rather than endure the increased crowds and lunch-hour commotion, Morton Plant deserted his beautiful house in 1916 and joined the social migration uptown, in his case to Fifth Avenue and Eighty-sixth Street. According to contemporary accounts in *The New York Times*, Plant sold the house for a million dollars to William K. Vanderbilt, who then rented it to the jeweler Cartier. It was Plant, however, who some years later signed the sale contract to Cartier when the latter bought the house. Plant and Vanderbilt must have collaborated somehow on the transfer, however, as Vanderbilt alone had the ability to remove the residential deed restrictions he himself had placed upon it. Possibly the property was transferred back and forth between them, and simply not recorded.

The press of 1916 was scandalized by the arrival of a jewelry store in the heart of the Vanderbilt block. The *Times* lamented at length the "examples . . . within very recent years of the abandonment of fine Fifth Avenue private residences." Cartier made no overt changes to the exterior of the place. Willie is said to have made a packet on the rental deal. However, this act by the head of the Vanderbilt family was enormously symbolic. Although the side streets in the Fifties remained solidly single-family in 1916, no one in his right mind would have dreamed of building on the busy avenue itself.

Of course, there was no sudden overnight abandonment by those whose houses still fronted on Fifth. Willie's nephew Neily, for example, had only just completed half a million dollars' worth of Horace Trumbauer–designed alterations to the great brownstone cube William Henry had erected at 640 Fifth. Neily's wife, Grace, would stay there until 1945. As late as 1918, the W. B. Osgood Fields (she was Willie's niece, the daughter of his sister Emily Sloane) were still renting one of the Marble Twins at 645 Fifth. Willie's sister-in-law Alice, widow of Cornelius II, would continue to occupy her vast château at 1 West Fifty-seventh Street for another decade. All sorts of other socialites still clung to grand old mansions in the Forties and Fifties. These people, like the Vanderbilts, were all holdouts. And they all knew what was coming.

When the war ended, Willie and Anne Vanderbilt were living in France—although not always together. They remained American citizens but their Normandy château, the location of Willie's famous French racing stable, and a Paris town house at 10 rue Leroux were their real homes. By 1919, Willie was quite ill. He visited New York that winter and had to be carried aboard the ship that returned him to France. Then in April of 1920, he collapsed during the Grand Prix at Auteuil, having prophetically told friends that he would be there even "if it's the last race I see."

It was. He lingered three months, confined to his bed. His daughter, Consuelo, and his son Harold flew over from London on the eve of his death. On July 23, 1920, at the age of seventy, he succumbed to a heart attack, kidney trouble, and angina pectoris. According to Dr. Edmund L. Gros, Willie's fatal illness was the result of a lifetime of heavy smoking. Willie Vanderbilt once averaged a box of cigars a day.

Like his father, Willie, too, had once made some unfortunately unguarded observations to the press. These were reprinted time and again over the years, to the general detriment of his image. When he died, they were resurrected in every obituary in the land. His death, it should be noted, was front-page news around the world.

"Inherited wealth," he was quoted as saying, "is a big handicap to happiness. It has left me with nothing to hope for, with nothing definite to seek or strive for. . . . It is as certain death to ambition as cocaine is to morality." Finishing on the same lugubrious note, he added that a rich man "must labor, if he does labor, simply to add to an oversufficiency."

These words were excerpted from an interview given in the midst of his divorce. The man was understandably depressed at the time, and if he sounded self-pitying, it should be remembered that his normal personality was invariably jolly and gracious. Obituary writers had a field day bashing him as "The Melancholy Dane of Finance" and the like. However, this was an unfair characterization of the man, calculated more to sell papers than to accurately describe the deceased. According to his daughter, Consuelo, Willie invariably bore his troubles with dignity. He was never one to burden friends or family with sorry tales. Everybody who knew him knew that.

Willie's son, William K. Vanderbilt, Jr., would later build a yacht called *Alva* for himself.

The body was transported back to the States, and a small funeral was held at 660 Fifth. Interment was on Staten Island, in the Richard Morris Hunt–designed Vanderbilt Mausoleum.

After Willie died, there was no longer anyone named Vanderbilt on the list of America's top ten millionaires. The Commodore's original fortune by now had been divided into thirty-two parts. Frederick W. Vanderbilt alone, among all the men and women who bore the Vanderbilt name, still earned a million dollars a year.

Willie had rarely used Idle Hour during his

last years, but he never changed his official address. It was only fitting, really, for the first gentleman among the Vanderbilts to reside officially at a country seat. As a result, his estate provided the county of Suffolk with a $2 million windfall in the form of the largest inheritance tax ever collected in the county up until that date.

Of the approximately $53 million left after the tax was collected, Vanderbilt University received a quarter of a million; the local Episcopal church near Idle Hour got fifty thousand; the Metropolitan Museum received Vanderbilt's magnificent collection of art and furniture, including works by Gainsborough, Rembrandt, Reynolds, Holbein, Boucher, and Van de Velde. His widow got a life interest in the Paris town house and two French country estates that would eventually revert to Consuelo. Willie's grandsons, the Marquis of Blandford and Lord Ivor Churchill, sons of Consuelo and the ninth Duke of Marlborough, both received a million dollars apiece. Assorted other grandchildren received various additional trusts of a million or so apiece. All the rest was divided equally between sons Willie Junior and Mike.

If this sounds as though Willie's daughter, Consuelo, was shortchanged, it should be noted that her father made her an outright gift of $15 million immediately prior to his death. He created an $8 million trust for his wife at the same time. He also probably would have made similar arrangements for his other heirs had he had the time, since he was known to have been worried over the impact of the recently enacted inheritance tax. Such were the last concerns of the man who lamented the curse of inherited wealth.

Willie was barely in the ground when his sons put 660 Fifth Avenue on the market. In late 1920, there was some talk of preserving it as a museum, but nothing came of the idea. In the meantime, the best of the paintings and furniture were carted off to the Metropolitan. Then in October of 1921, the American Art Galleries removed and sold much of the paneling. For a while, it looked as if the house might be partly saved by converting it into an office building and preserving the exterior, but the deal fell through.

And so the old house sat, stripped of its furniture and much of its interior decoration, liable to taxes on an assessed valuation of $2,125,000 ($175,000 of which was allotted to the building),

and sealed shut. Meanwhile, in an act highly symbolic of the new directions in American taste and fashion, Anne Vanderbilt headed east. In 1921, she paid fifty thousand dollars for a nondescript house at One Sutton Place and hired society architect Mott B. Schmidt to transform it into an elegant small Georgian town house. Elsie de Wolfe did the interiors. Anne's good friends Elizabeth Marbury and Anne Morgan (J.P.'s sister) followed her lead, and Sutton Place was soon transformed from a borderline slum to a center of fashion. It remains so today; as does One Sutton Place, which is still a private house.

Finally in 1925, the heirs agreed to sell 660 Fifth to developers for a reported $3,750,000. Only a few voices of protest were raised at the time, among them that of Richard Howland Hunt, son of the original architect, and designer of Willie's second house at Idle Hour. Hunt and other members of the Municipal Art Society vigorously protested the unrestrained proliferation of skyscrapers in the midtown area. However, they were ahead of their time and no one paid much attention.

The American Architect, in a piece entitled "Scrapping an Architectural Masterpiece," observed that the city of New York was going to be the real loser, culturally, aesthetically, and historically; but a tone of abject resignation pervaded the piece. The author acknowledged that the land was worth more to industry, and concluded unhappily that this fact was sufficient reason for any sort of sacrifice. Compare this attitude to the sort of outraged public opinion that greeted and ultimately thwarted recent proposals to tear down New York's Villard houses and mutilate Grand Central Station.

The wreckers arrived in February of 1926. As has been the case with numerous of New York City's demolished landmarks—the old Astor Hotel and Pennsylvania Station among them—they didn't have an easy time of it. "The shades of the workmen of the past may thus have some measure of vengeance on the destroyers of the present," observed John Vredenburgh Van Pelt. A banal five-story office building, little more than a taxpayer really, rose on the site in 1927. Today, the entire Fifty-first to Fifty-second Street blockfront is occupied by a boxy office tower dating from the 1960s, known as 666 Fifth Avenue.

Chapter 3
1 WEST FIFTY-SEVENTH STREET

1 West Fifty-seventh Street

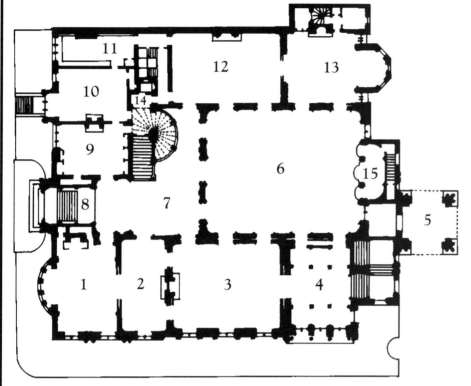

Fifth Avenue

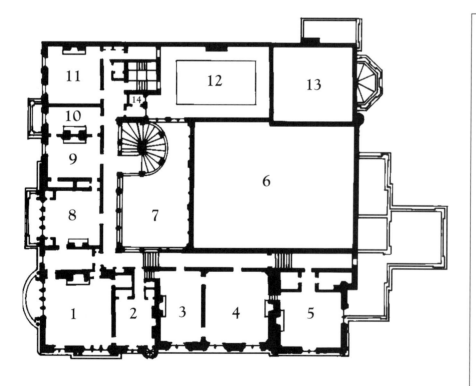

1st Floor
1. Library
2. Small Salon
3. Large Salon
4. Watercolor Room
5. Porte Cochere
6. Ballroom
7. Main Hall
8. Vestibule
9. Office
10. Breakfast Room
11. Serving Pantry
12. Dining Room
13. Moorish Room
14. Elevator
15. Musicians' Alcove

2nd Floor
1. Mrs. Vanderbilt's Bedroom
2. Mrs. Vanderbilt's Boudoir
3–4. Bedrooms
5. Boudoir
6. Upper Part of Ballroom
7. Upper Part of Main Floor Hall
8. Mr. Vanderbilt's Bedroom
9. Nurse
10. Baby
11. Sitting Room
12. Upper Part of Dining Room
13. Upper Part of Moorish Room
14. Elevator

Location: New York City

Architect: Original house: George Browne Post (1837–1913)

Addition: Post and Richard Morris Hunt (1827–1895)

Commissioned by: Cornelius Vanderbilt II (1843–1899)

House completed: Original house: 1882

Addition: 1894

*O*NE West Fifty-seventh Street was the stage set for perhaps the most publicized of all the Vanderbilt family scandals. Neither of the adversaries in this melodrama was a bad man. To the contrary, Cornelius Vanderbilt II (known as "Corneil" to his friends and intimates) was a saint. His handsome son Cornelius III (known as "Neily") was the personification of youthful honor. Yet honor pitted against sainthood resulted ultimately in some very unsaintly behavior.

Generations passed before the degree of damage that this falling out between father and son caused was evident. When the New York Central lost Neily, which it did because of his father's autocratic behavior, the Vanderbilt family lost the one member of its rising generation who was the most willing, and the most able, to continue the traditional family involvement with the source of their wealth. There might still be Vanderbilts in transportation—just as there are Fords and du Ponts and Rockefellers in the fields that made their families rich—had Corneil behaved differently to Neily back in 1896.

Our image of the Vanderbilts is due in great part to Cornelius Vanderbilt II. He neither extended his family's rail empire nor increased its legendary treasure to any notable degree; in fact, he was an unimaginative businessman and a mediocre investor. By virtue of the manner in which he lived, however, Cornelius Vanderbilt II engraved his name upon the national consciousness forever. The Vanderbilt name signifies unfettered opulence, New York-style, because of this man. His greatest legacy was not his many charities, although the list of these is impressive. Rather, it is his fantastic houses in Manhattan and Newport. Surely the most splendid of these was his town house at Fifty-seventh Street and Fifth Avenue. They reflected Corneil's unique sense of personal grandeur.

The Commodore contributed materially to this exalted self-image. Young Corneil was not only the eldest son of the Commodore's eldest son, he was also his grandfather's personal favorite. When the Commodore died in 1877, he left million-dollar legacies to each of William Henry's other sons. Corneil's share, however, was almost twice that of his brothers, a tidy $5.5 million to be precise.

The Commodore liked Corneil's industry, his modesty, and, above all, his obedience. It was a mark of the old man's favor that he personally supervised Corneil's schooling and early career moves. At the age of sixteen, the boy was put to work at the Shoe and Leather Bank. At twenty, he was transferred to Kissam Brothers, a private banking house controlled by his mother's family. In 1865, at the tender age of twenty-two, Corneil became assistant treasurer of the New York and Harlem Railroad. This was the beginning of an impressive climb to the top of the family business ladder, culminating in a sort of joint consulship with his brother William K.

Corneil's mature personality was gentle-mannered, considerate, and invariably courteous. However, according to his grandson Cornelius Vanderbilt IV (known as "Neil"), he possessed "a certain chilling look of command [that] belied his quiet courtesy. . . . Here was a man who expected to be obeyed, and instantly." If Corneil was irreproachably honest and moral, he was also utterly humorless. He would have nothing to do with horse racing, yachts, fads, personal hobbies, or licentious entertainments. He was instead forever being flattered for his supposed "simplicity,"

in spite of what grandson Neil called the "terrible splendor of his kingly dwelling places."

What Corneil lacked in imagination he made up for with good deeds. As a young man, his spare time was entirely devoted to church work. Later in life, he became a major philanthropist, whose charities included the Metropolitan Museum of Art, the New York Botanical Garden in the Bronx, a slew of hospitals (most notably St. Luke's), the College of Physicians and Surgeons, and the YMCA. His passion, however, was church work. This manifested itself in tireless support of the General Theological Seminary, the Cathedral Church of St. John the Divine, and the many efforts at missionary work supported by the Episcopal church, both in the slums of New York and abroad.

Cornelius Vanderbilt II was a major presence in New York, and a man whose name was known around the world. Almost every morning, he received requests for his entire annual income in the form of begging letters. According to Chauncey Depew, Corneil donated between a third and a half of his income to charity every year. There can be no doubt that he did a tremendous amount of good with his money—and not just for Episcopalians.

Corneil could be holier than thou, but he was also a gentleman. When Ward McAllister died, reviled and ridiculed by New York's elite in the wake of his embarrassing memoir *Society as I Have Found It*, Corneil was one of the few in New York society who behaved with respect. The very night before the burial, Mrs. Astor gave a dinner party, really a posthumous slap in the face to her former favorite, whom she had not deigned to notice since the publication of his book. Corneil was invited to that party but didn't attend out of respect for McAllister. The next day, he acted as one of the pallbearers, too, even though society shunned the affair en masse. The bottom line was that Corneil was a man with good manners.

Everybody treated Cornelius Vanderbilt with deference, which was probably the way he liked it. It was part of his personal genius to invest both this deference and the grandeur in which he lived with a moral message. Duty, or rather Corneil's acute sense thereof, had brought him to sublime heights. One had only to gaze upon 1 West Fifty-seventh Street or The Breakers to realize just how sublime. He was a living mon-

Cornelius Vanderbilt II.

ument, in his own eyes, to the rewards due the dutiful son. He possessed an enormous sense of self-importance, which is understandable given the experience of his own life.

In 1867, the year in which he was promoted to treasurer of the New York and Harlem, young Corneil married Alice Claypoole Gwynne. Alice-of-the-Breakers, as Harry Lehr would later tag her, was twenty-two at the time; Corneil was twenty-four. She was the daughter of a prominent Cincinnati lawyer named Abram E. Gwynne; the great-great-granddaughter of Captain Abraham Claypoole, an original member of the Society of the Cincinnati; and a direct descendant of Oliver Cromwell. Corneil had met her while they were both teaching Sunday school at St. Bartholomew's in New York.

The Gwynnes were distinguished, if not exactly social. The match was a good one for young Vanderbilt, whose family was still being dismissed by New York society as a collection of vulgar arrivistes. Alice was a dainty little woman, quite pretty, simple-mannered, and supposedly disinterested in society. Then again, her husband was supposedly not interested in club life, although at the time of his death he belonged to many clubs: the Metropolitan, Knickerbocker, Union, Union League, Century, Racquet and

Tennis, Lawyers, Players, St. Nicholas, St. Nicholas Society, Tuxedo, Riding, Westchester Polo, Grolier, New York Yacht (despite the fact he didn't own one), City, and even the Farmers (he did have a farm, just outside Newport).

For the first eleven years of their marriage, Corneil and Alice migrated restlessly from one fashionable quarter of the city to the next. Then in 1878, the year after the death of the Commodore, they purchased not one but two handsome contiguous brownstones on the west side of Fifth Avenue just above Fifty-seventh Street, plus a lot immediately to the west. These two houses, 742 and 744 Fifth Avenue, were the southernmost in a row of eight first-class brownstones that had been erected speculatively on the avenue a few years earlier. Corneil and Alice had no intention of living permanently in either one; they just wanted the land.

During the late 1870s, William Henry Vanderbilt and his two eldest sons, Corneil and Willie K, were engaged in a coordinated effort to create an urban family preserve along this part of Fifth Avenue. William Henry's great Triple Palace along the Fifty-first to Fifty-second Street blockfront, Willie K's 660 Fifth at Fifty-second Street, William Henry's houses for his daughters Mrs. Webb and Mrs. Twombly at Fifth and Fifty-fourth Street, plus Corneil's manse on the northwest corner of Fifth and Fifty-seventh Street were all built simultaneously. At one stroke, Fifth Avenue in the Fifties became New York's most

Alice Gwynne Vanderbilt in costume as "Electric Light" for Alva's famous ball of March 26, 1883.

sumptuous residential district, unsurpassed even by later development overlooking Central Park.

It comes as a surprise today that Corneil should have engaged George B. Post to design this major house. One would have expected it to have been Richard Hunt or Stanford White or any of the others who became known as the premier society architects of the time. The strength of Post's practice never lay in handsome town- or country-house designs. To the contrary, he was an engineer celebrated for the technical brilliance of his skyscrapers and commercial buildings.

Post, interestingly, was also a socialite—at least he was on Ward McAllister's list of the Four Hundred (the only architect to be so honored). He was also a very prominent architect, and a man showered with professional honors in his lifetime, including the presidencies of the Architectural League of New York (1893–1897) and the American Institute of Architects (1896–1899). Teddy Roosevelt even appointed him to a national Bureau of Fine Arts in 1909.

After rising to the rank of colonel during the Civil War, Post returned to New York and studied with Richard Morris Hunt in the latter's famous atelier on West Tenth Street. Everyone who studied with Hunt got a liberal dose of Francophilia and Beaux-Arts theory. Post's subsequent design work never achieved Hunt's level of Europeanized sophistication, however.

George Post is best remembered as a pioneer in the use of steel framing for tall buildings. Many of his New York commissions still stand, among them the Williamsburgh Savings Bank in Brooklyn and the wonderful City College campus overlooking Harlem from Hamilton Heights. During the course of his prolific career, he designed twenty-five hotels, the Wisconsin state capitol, plus hospitals, churches, apartments, and even theaters. He also did over thirty country houses in the Bernardsville colony near Morristown, New Jersey. Post summered there and apparently had a loyal local following. However, he did virtually no country houses elsewhere, and only a handful of city town houses. On the surface of things, he seems an odd choice for an important Fifth Avenue residence.

In 1879, however, there were *no* American architects with a recognized reputation for first-class urban residences. Corneil's father took a gamble when he hired John Snook to design the

Triple Palace. His brother Willie made a similar leap of faith when he commissioned Richard Hunt to do 660 Fifth. Corneil doubtless was impressed by Post's social credentials as well as by his professional expertise. Certainly in 1879, Post was as likely a choice as Snook or Hunt. Hunt's design for 660 Fifth turned out to be the most successful of all the Vanderbilt commissions along Fifth Avenue. No one could have known that in 1879, however.

Corneil and Alice decamped from 742 Fifth on the eve of construction, moving to a house that still stands (albeit massively altered) on the corner of Thirty-second Street and Fifth Avenue. Meanwhile, an early French Renaissance–style château built of bright red brick and very pale limestone rose at 1 West Fifty-seventh Street, as the former sites of 742 and 744 Fifth Avenue would henceforth be known.

The entire city watched, fascinated, as the Vanderbilt family houses rose in concert along what soon came to be called Vanderbilt Row. When completed, they were all the subject of lengthy appraisals from the architectural critics of the day. According to the *American Architect and Building News* of May 1881, Post's Cornelius Vanderbilt II house was "as large and rich" as Hunt's 660 Fifth, but nowhere near as successful. The chief drawback was the "mixture of materials, which results in an effect of color which is not fortunate." Critic Montgomery Schuyler, writing in the *Architectural Record*, didn't think much of the color scheme, either. "The admixture of materials makes the color effect noticeably unfortunate, while the skyline seems out of harmony and very ill proportioned." Schuyler uncharitably summed the place up as a "sad botch, incident to a reaching desire after imposing effect."

According to the *Architectural Record*, 1 West Fifty-seventh Street was "more successful and less interesting" than Hunt's late French Gothic opus down the road. Russell Sturgis, the architect and critic, thought the place suffered from a "lack of decided effect," whatever that might have meant, and further opined that important design opportunities had "gone unimproved."

The *Real Estate Record* in 1881 added its voice to the chorus of boos, condemning the house for its "lack of vigor." This seems rather an odd comment to modern observers of 1 West Fifty-

1 West Fifty-seventh Street; elevations as
originally built.

According to Montgomery Schuyler, "the skyline seems out of harmony. . . ."

George Browne Post, architect of 1 West Fifty-seventh Street, "was on Ward McAllister's list of the Four Hundred."

seventh's multiplicity of pinnacles and bulges. Old pictures show it to have been a truly vigorous and appealing composition, or such is the reaction of modern observers. One West Fifty-seventh Street was, admittedly, trying to do a lot of things at once. The reaction against Victorian exuberance that set in at the beginning of the twentieth century pointed to houses like it as prime aesthetic offenders. In the last twenty years, however, Americans have begun to take a second look at these buildings. Belatedly, many of them again are being seen as beautiful—or, at least, as interesting and historically significant.

If the exterior had its shortcomings, compositional or otherwise, the interior was nothing short of an aesthetic tour de force. Actually, most of the interiors of Post's private houses were brilliant. His experience with commercial palaces seemingly gave him a touch with the grandiose. In his residential commissions, this translated itself far better on the inside than it did on the outside. In the case of 1 West Fifty-seventh, the architect produced a series of carefully executed French revival rooms—a veritable Cook's tour of the various Louis (Quatorze,

Quinze, and Seize)—that were much more beautiful than the structural envelope that contained them.

The stair hall was particularly successful. It had creamy white stone walls and a flying stone stairway that was sinuous, vast, and breathtaking, rather like an upwardly coiling tunnel with open sides and broad, shallow stone treads finished off with thick carpeting. All the doors in this hall were hung with opulent cut-velvet portieres and flanked by elaborate bronze torchères. Every principal room beyond had a massive carved fireplace, equally massive plaster moldings on the ceiling, and as likely as not an old master or two (or three) on the wall.

Mr. Vanderbilt had a cultivated eye for art, and his collection included paintings by artists—Turner, Rousseau, Corot, Ruisdael, Millais, Lely—whose works would in time become priceless. Corneil and his architect further embellished the house with panels by Karl Bitter, sculpture by Augustus Saint-Gaudens, and ceilings and windows by John LaFarge. Everywhere were inlays of ivory, pearl, silver, and gold. The effect was museumlike; one's overwhelming sense was that all conversation should be conducted in a whisper.

The Vanderbilts assumed occupancy in 1882. Three years later, Corneil's father died and left him 75 million tax-free dollars. Only months before his father's death, Corneil had purchased Pierre Lorillard's immense shingled house at Newport, called The Breakers. With his mighty new legacy, he hired the original designers of The Breakers—Peabody & Stearns of Boston—to enlarge and upgrade the house. In 1892, the lavishly renovated Breakers burned to the ground completely. Corneil and Alice decided to rebuild on the most sumptuous scale possible, and they commissioned Richard Morris Hunt to design The Breakers one knows today. What most people do not realize is that during that same year, the Vanderbilts embarked on an equally ambitious house-building scheme: namely, the enlargement of 1 West Fifty-seventh Street.

The additions to Corneil's Manhattan town house were also done by George Post. This time, however, Richard Morris Hunt was invited to advise on the project. By 1892, Post's architectural practice was the largest in the United States, but Hunt's reputation for fine residential design had far and away eclipsed that of the ar-

"The stair hall was particularly successful."

The billiard room at 1 West Fifty-seventh Street.

1 West Fifty-seventh Street as originally built in 1882.

chitect of 1 West Fifty-seventh Street. Unlike Hunt, who had greatly matured as a residential designer from 660 Fifth Avenue onward, Post continued to create dignified but ponderous houses. Corneil and Alice were clearly aware of this, for in 1892, Post had completed a forbidding stone fortress of a house for Collis P. Huntington at 2 East Fifty-seventh Street, right outside the Vanderbilts' windows.

They were not about to hire George Post for the new house at Newport, but they must have felt an obligation toward him in connection with his original work at 1 West Fifty-seventh Street. Hunt's advice on this job was limited to suggestions for the exterior. It was he who designed the tower on the north facade. This tower, in fact, lent not only grandeur and balance to the enlarged house, it was the linchpin of the entire exterior scheme.

Construction began in March of 1892. During the next two years, crews numbering as many as eight hundred laborers swarmed over the site. For speed, much of the work was done at night beneath huge electric lights. Corneil spent $3 million enlarging his New York town house. When completed in 1894, it rated as the largest private house in New York. Overnight, it became a tourist attraction, more famous even than Hunt's masterpiece five blocks to the south at 660 Fifth.

Back in the early eighties, when the original 1 West Fifty-seventh Street was being built, Post was involved in the design of another house on the opposite (Fifty-eighth Street) side of the same block. Four West Fifty-eighth Street was built for William J. Hutchinson in a style that was remarkably similar to the Vanderbilt house around the corner. Hutchinson took occupancy

Left: The new entry courtyard and porte cochere facing the Plaza at Fifty-eighth Street. The Alexander house at 4 West Fifty-eighth Street looks like part of the Vanderbilt château, but predated this section of it by over ten years.

Below: The 1892–3 enlargement of 1 West Fifty-seventh Street consisted principally of a new wing facing the Plaza (looming in the background) at Fifty-eighth Street. The glazed conservatory on the western end of the original house was removed and the west wing increased to three stories. The tops of the dormers on the original central block were also considerably embellished. Most of the orignial house, however, remained unchanged. Note the number of first-class Fifth Avenue brownstones that were demolished for purposes of expanding the Vanderbilt house.

A walk down the new watercolor gallery of 1 West Fifty-seventh Street, towards the ceremonial entry beneath the Fifty-eighth Street porte cochere.

1 West Fifty-seventh Street, bas relief beneath the new porte cochere. This sculpture currently graces the front door of the Sherry Netherland Hotel on Fifth Avenue and Fifty-ninth Street.

in 1882, the same year as the Vanderbilts. He soon sold his house to Charles B. Alexander, whose country house at Tuxedo Park was a showplace for years. For the first ten years of their respective existences, 1 West Fifty-seventh Street and 4 West Fifty-eighth Street remained invisible to one another, separated by half a dozen Italianate brownstones along Fifth Avenue.

In the course of Corneil's expansion of 1 West Fifty-seventh Street, he purchased and then demolished the entire Fifth Avenue blockfront north of the original Post house. The new Post-Hunt addition not only tripled the size of the original house, it visually united 1 West Fifty-seventh Street with the Alexander house around the corner on West Fifty-eighth Street. The architecture of the latter fit so neatly with that of the original Post house and its subsequent additions that most people assumed it was part of the same building. Especially today when one looks at old photos of the Vanderbilt château,

it is hard to recognize that 4 West Fifty-eighth Street isn't really a part of it.

The new additions totally changed the visual focus of the Vanderbilt house from the Fifty-seventh to the Fifty-eighth Street facade. Hunt's tower, surmounting an elaborate porte cochere, rose above a gated garden overlooking the swank new hotels already rising around Grand Army Plaza. The new Fifty-eighth Street entrance was a ceremonial one only, used for weddings and funerals and not much else. The house remained known by its original address and everybody continued to use its original front door on Fifty-seventh Street. Aside from a bit of lacy stonework added to the dormers and a reworking of the conservatory wing, the original Post house of 1882 remained fairly intact as the southern wing of the new house.

The enlarged 1 West Fifty-seventh Street was so wonderfully detailed and so satisfyingly grand that it seems petty to criticize it on mere compositional grounds. However, the truth is, it did have aesthetic shortcomings. Post's original design, whatever one might have thought about it, had made a strong statement on the corner of Fifty-seventh Street. Construction of the new addition robbed the old house of its original coherence, and removed the contrasting brownstones that had heightened its architectural effect. One West Fifty-seventh Street looked ill-proportioned from the south and a little ungainly from Fifth Avenue. However, from the Plaza, thanks largely to Hunt's corner tower, it looked very fine indeed.

The new interiors provided still more opportunities for heedless grandeur. Jules Allard was hired to design and fabricate a Louis XVI music room. It was duly constructed in Paris, dismantled, and reinstalled by a team of imported craftsmen. Alva Vanderbilt's protégé Gilbert Cuel did the new ballroom. Louis C. Tiffany designed a Moorish smoking room with an enormous double-height ceiling and walls inlaid with mother of pearl. And Post himself contributed the obligatory assortment of French-style drawing and sitting rooms.

The fact that Corneil and Alice should choose to enlarge their house on this scale, at this time, and in this neighborhood reveals much about their respective characters. It is one thing to hide oneself away in a palace buried in the middle of a vast estate. One West Fifty-seventh Street, however, sat in one of the most public places in New York City. Grand Army Plaza in the 1890s was witnessing a boom in hotel construction. Both the Savoy and the New Netherlands were already open by 1892, the year that planning for the enlargement of 1 West Fifty-seventh Street was begun. McKim, Mead & White's renovated Plaza Hotel had been open for years. When the new Waldorf Hotel opened next door to Mrs. Astor's house in 1893, she found the resulting noise, traffic, and commotion to be so intolerable that she moved. Corneil and Alice evidently did not mind high visibility or the constant comings and goings of a major hotel district, though. To the contrary, they must have rather enjoyed it.

The Vanderbilts were major subscribers to the "having it and flaunting it" school of thought. By the same token, they were living symbols of American possibility. In the New World, one was not predestined from birth to fill a certain slot in society. The concept of limitlessness—

"The fact that Corneil and Alice should choose to enlarge their house on this scale, at this time, and in this neighborhood reveals much about their respective characters." Looking south across the Plaza from Sixtieth Street. The two towers flanking Fifth Avenue to the south are (right to left) the Gotham and St. Regis hotels.

"Mr. Vanderbilt had a cultivated eye for art." The new watercolor gallery of 1 West Fifty-seventh Street.

from the vast size of the new continent to the huge fortunes that common men were able to amass here—was fundamental to the frontier spirit. The idea of anything being possible, on any scale, was alien to the Old World. This perception of unbounded possibility was what made—and indeed still makes—the United States different.

It might seem bizarre to categorize an urban palace such as 1 West Fifty-seventh Street as a manifestation of U.S. frontier spirit. This is precisely what it was, however. This house and houses like it represented what was then perceived as the apogee of the American experience. They combined the culture of Europe with the unfettered possibility of the New World. They proclaimed the emergence of imperial America, the new leader of Western culture. They resonated with the new political climate and national image of their day. They were vivid, carefully crafted, and enormously meaningful expressions of the most important hallmark of the American psyche—unfettered possibility. Vanderbilt was no nobleman; he was the grandson of a ferryman. Yet he and his family had achieved wealth and prestige that equaled that of any noble house in Europe. This was what the United States was all about; 1 West Fifty-seventh Street was the proof of the pudding.

The profound symbolism of this house and of its owners infused the family scandal that unfolded within it with uncommon meaning and interest for the entire nation. The scandal was sparked by a whirlwind romance between Cornelius (Neily) Vanderbilt III, Corneil and Alice's eldest surviving son, and Miss Grace Graham Wilson. Grace's father, the charming and dignified Richard T. Wilson, was a Southerner who had moved to New York after the Civil War. He was said to have been a war profiteer whose fortune was based on the suffering of the defeated Confederate army. Not even Commodore Vanderbilt was accused of some of the things R. T. Wilson was supposed to have done.

It was an eloquent measure of Mr. Wilson's personal charm that these tales caused negligible social embarrassment. To the contrary, the Wilsons traveled in the very best circles of New York society. They were famous matchmakers, too. Grace's older sister Belle was married to the Honorable Michael Herbert, brother of the Earl of Pembroke. Sister May had wed young Ogden

Right: Cornelius (Neily) Vanderbilt III, at the time of his romance with Grace Wilson.

Above: The Moorish smoking room in the new wing at 1 West Fifty-seventh Street.

Goelet, of Manhattan real estate fame. Brother Orme was the husband of Carrie Astor, daughter of Mrs. Astor. Grace was the youngest of the girls and, with the exception of brother R. T. Wilson, Jr., the last of the siblings to remain unmarried.

Corneil and Alice's eldest son, William Henry Vanderbilt II, met Grace when he was still at Yale. He had liked her enormously, and his parents had not seemed to mind much at the time. In the spring of 1892, Bill Vanderbilt died suddenly of typhoid. And Grace, for the moment, dropped out of the Vanderbilts' lives.

Gertrude Vanderbilt, Neily's sister, "kidded him at first about Grace."

Grace Graham Wilson, a "mirthful and irreverent girl."

Grace was a mirthful and irreverent girl, full of bubbling high spirits and accustomed to the best of everything. The great Mrs. Astor adored her; so did Teddy Roosevelt; Roosevelt's daughter Alice was one of her closest friends. Grace had been presented to royalty on several occasions and had enjoyed particular success with the German imperial family, which had special cachet in American social circles at the time.

In background and temperament, Grace Wilson was not at all Corneil and Alice's favorite

type. She was worldly—at least by the definition of the 1890s. She and her sister Belle had spent too much time with the libidinous Prince of Wales, the future Edward VII. Grace had been to too many parties. She knew her way around wines and foreign cooking to an unseemly degree, at least for a young maiden. She spoke both French and German a bit too fluently, could tell a Millet from a Manet at a glance, and knew how to board a yacht in a long dress and a picture hat. When J. Burden spotted Grace at Cowes in 1894, he noted in his diary that she was there with her sister, Mrs. Goelet, "scanning the Solent for Dukes." Grace's acute social instincts were the subject of fun among the Four Hundred, but it was good-natured fun. She was, after all, invited everywhere. And her brother was Mrs. Astor's son-in-law.

In the summer of 1895, while Alva Vanderbilt was terrorizing her daughter, Consuelo, into marrying the Duke of Marlborough, The Breakers was opened in Newport. Neily's sister Gertrude made her debut there, and Grace Wilson was invited to the party as a matter of course. Neily went, too. They met; they danced; they fell in love.

Grace had been "out" for several seasons already. She had only recently broken an engagement to Cecil Baring, the son of a British lord. Neily had just graduated from Yale that spring. He was an extremely handsome lad, six feet tall, with thick curly hair, determined dark blue eyes, and a full and sensuous mouth. She was the image of the Gibson Girl; wasp-waisted, graceful, with delicate features and pale hair. He was earnest; she was a social butterfly. He dreamed of being a scientist and of applying his inventions to the family railroads. Grace was born to entertain.

Neily's brothers and sisters kidded him at first about Grace. They didn't take the relationship seriously. His parents, however, were alarmed from the outset. They had not objected to Grace in the past, but now they decided she was scheming for a Vanderbilt—any Vanderbilt. Her giddy social life, and especially the recent breakup of her engagement to Cecil Baring, seemed to them to be somehow improper. They soon developed a bizarre image of young Grace Wilson as manipulative, ruthless, and corrupt. On top of everything else, they considered R. T. Wilson to be a cheat and a scoundrel.

1 WEST FIFTY–SEVENTH STREET

Throughout the fall of 1895, Neily paid especial attention to Grace, in spite of his parents' disapproval. Then in November, Alice paid a call on Mrs. Wilson. The call was ostensibly social, but its true purpose was to ascertain Grace's fall travel plans. Mrs. Wilson innocently allowed as how her daughter had none. After which, Corneil and Alice abruptly packed Neily off to Europe.

The Wilsons were understandably insulted when they figured out what had happened. To make matters worse, Corneil then dispatched New York Central president Chauncey Depew as a sort of emissary whose purpose was to enlist R. T. Wilson's aid in quashing the young people's romance. Not surprisingly, this arrogant move outraged Wilson. It is not known whether he and Vanderbilt ever actually spoke on the matter in person or not, but the result of Depew's visit was open warfare. Grace immediately sallied forth to Europe, with parental blessings, in the company of May and Ogden Goelet. When she got there, she went straight to Neily at the Bristol in Paris.

The listening servants and socialite informers of the day made a story like this next to impossible to keep out of the papers. The subsequent behavior of Cornelius Vanderbilt himself gave them a field day. In February of 1896, he sailed to Europe, grimly determined to bring Neily home. He threatened to cut Neily out of his will, a threat that failed to change Neily's mind and, worse, was recounted in society columns on two continents. By the spring of 1896, Neily and Grace were the tabloid press's favorite star-crossed lovers, and Corneil had become an infamous domestic tyrant.

When at last Neily and Grace returned home, a few weeks apart for appearances' sake, Neily went straight to work for the New York Central. Grace's father announced his daughter's intended wedding date: June 18, 1896. On June 10, the New York *World* carried this announcement on the front page, together with news of Neily's sister Gertrude's engagement to Harry Payne Whitney. Corneil heartily approved of his daughter Gertrude's match. As for Neily, Corneil would say only the following for publication: "The engagement of Cornelius Vanderbilt, Jr., to Miss Wilson is against his father's expressed wishes."

As Grace's wedding date approached, society fled New York en masse lest it be forced to take sides. Neily's best man, his roommate from Yale, abruptly left for Europe; the rector at St. Thomas would not commit. Meanwhile, at 1 West Fifty-seventh Street, Neily and his father were having scenes. When the day of the wedding arrived, Neily unexpectedly canceled. He had been felled by an acute attack of rheumatism, which seems an odd affliction for a strapping youth fresh out of college. However, the rheumatism seems to have been genuine. Grace found herself thrust into a very awkward position. Left alone to return the flowers and the gifts, it was to her credit that she bore her situation with aplomb and dignity.

Corneil had won the battle, but the war continued. Angry scenes between father and son continued. In July, after a particularly violent row, Corneil banished his eldest son from the house. Shortly afterward, he had a stroke. The entire nation watched fascinated while death hovered over the head of the House of Vanderbilt. A thick layer of tanbark was actually spread across the width of Fifth Avenue and down a portion of Fifty-seventh Street to muffle the noise of traffic outside the stricken man's windows. Neily's brothers and sisters arrayed themselves immediately on their father's side. Gertrude even claimed quite bluntly that the stroke was Neily's fault.

Neily had learned well the importance of duty. He recognized that his first duty was to Grace. He had spoken for her; it would be caddish to abandon her; and besides, he loved her. The wedding took place at last in August, at the Wilsons' house at 608 Fifth Avenue. It was a hurry-up affair without flowers, music, much gaiety, or any Vanderbilts. Neily's genial Uncle Willie was the only family member who kept in touch with the newlyweds during this period, and the only one to offer them any kindness.

Disinheritance seemed a fait accompli. *Munsey's Magazine* allowed as how Grace had cost her husband $60 million. Neily tried repeatedly to contact his father, whom he truly loved and respected. The latter refused to speak to him until he apologized for his disobedience. By the end of 1896, Neily's torment was further increased by a particularly nasty rumor making the rounds of the New York clubs. It was now alleged that Grace, at this time visiting in Switzerland with her husband, had given birth to a child conceived out of wedlock. This sort of tale barely raises eyebrows today. In 1896, however, it was dirty talk. It was also untrue.

The young Vanderbilts returned to New York in January of 1897. Despite Neily's family travails (or perhaps because of them), public opinion was overwhelmingly in their favor. They were readily welcomed into society and seen everywhere, which must have rankled Neily's parents. The young couple did not languish in self-pity. Grace was as gay as ever. Neily was brimful of the adoration that accompanies the first years of marriage. In 1898, they had a son, Cornelius (Neil) Vanderbilt IV.

The year after that, while working at Central, Neily developed a corrugated furnace device for railroad engines. This promised to be but the first of many creative innovations that the talented young Vanderbilt would devise. *The New York Times* called it a "bold conception" and a "revolution" in boiler construction. Central put Neily's new fireboxes into general use immediately, saving hundreds of thousands of dollars worth of coal in the process.

Neily was briefly celebrated in the scientific press as a "genius." However, according to his son Neil, "Not one single congratulatory word came from the cold marble recesses of The Breakers." That spring, Neily saw his father at cousin W. K. Vanderbilt, Jr.'s wedding in New York. Corneil refused to speak to him. Corneil was fifty-six years old, but he looked closer to seventy. Neily's brothers Alfred and Reggie had to help him to the door as if he were a piece of brittle china. In the early morning hours of Tuesday, September 12, 1899, Corneil sat up in bed at 1 West Fifty-seventh Street, awakened his wife, and said, "I think I am dying." After five minutes of what must have been excruciating pain, it was all over. Cause of death: cerebral hemorrhage.

News of the death spread across the city like wildfire. Crowds began to gather in the street outside 1 West Fifty-seventh Street. By noontime, hundreds of people were obstructing traffic on the avenue. Police were posted both inside the house and out; constables roamed the Plaza moving people on. Corneil's son Neily returned from Newport weeping. Grace, according to Chauncey Depew, was "detained [there] by illness."

The death of Cornelius Vanderbilt II caused

no slump on the stock market, which was down anyway. It did occasion a startling outpouring of public grief. Literal mountains of condolence letters poured into the house and onto the late magnate's desk at Grand Central. His recent reputation as the scourge of youthful love was suddenly obscured by respect for his impressive career as a philanthropist, combined with the sort of breathless awe that accompanies the passing of the great.

On the day of the funeral, a thousand mourners clogged Madison Avenue outside the old St. Bartholomew's. Willie Vanderbilt arrived and his carriage was rushed. In fact, everybody in the clan was rushed and jostled in one of those eerie outpourings of human emotion, the exact nature of which is hard to categorize. Easier to understand was the spontaneous reaction of a vast and silent crowd outside 1 West Fifty-seventh Street. When Alice emerged from the house en route to the funeral, every man on the street, in what must have been quite an affecting scene, silently doffed his hat.

When Cornelius Vanderbilt II died in 1899, he left an estate of something over $70 million. This was approximately what his father had left him fourteen years earlier. Curiously, he had much less of a position in Vanderbilt family railroads than people might have thought. Instead of Nickel Plate, Reading, or Chicago and Northwestern, he had lots of Peoria and Eastern, St. Louis and Kansas City, and something called Quicksilver Mining. Corneil had managed his own investment portfolio, and he was earning less than 4 percent.

His will was dated June 18, 1896, the day Neily and Grace were originally to have gotten married but didn't. About 2 percent of the total estate was earmarked for charity; the rest was divided among Corneil's wife and children. Of his five surviving sons and daughters, three got about 7 million apiece, which was down a bit from what Corneil's father had left his children back in 1885. Alice got the houses in New York and Newport, plus a million in cash and the income from a $7 million trust. Neily got half a million in cash, plus the income from a $1 million trust. Neily's younger brother Alfred was named residuary legatee, to the tune of about $42 million.

Alfred Gwynne Vanderbilt, who would become a leading figure in coaching circles both

Alfred Gwynne Vanderbilt driving his English coach from London to Brighton.

in the United States and in Great Britain, had only just graduated from Yale in 1899. He was away on a world tour when his father died. Upon his return, he voluntarily gave his older brother, Neily, the sum of $6 million. This brought Neily's share to about the same level as that of his other brothers and sisters—not including Alfred. According to Depew, Alfred's was an act of "brotherly affection and for family harmony." Neily told *The New York Times* that the situation had been "met with fairness." The date of the will is worth noting: Corneil had triumphed over his eldest son on June 18, 1896, but he still went out that afternoon and signed a will virtually disinheriting him.

Of course, a half a million in cash and the income from a million-dollar trust (even if the principal can't be touched) is no mean legacy even today. The eldest son of the head of the House of Vanderbilt might still be excused for expecting more—especially if he had anticipated the contents of his father's will. Both Neily and Alfred knew what their father was going to do, and they had made a secret agreement between themselves to ensure fairness. Upon their father's death, Alfred promised to give his elder brother $10 million. When it came time to deliver, Alfred handed over only $6 million.

To get only $6 million, especially back in 1899, when a single million was a sum of stupifying vastness, might not arouse much sympathy. Neily chose not to make an issue of it. However, he felt enormously betrayed by his younger brother. A steady cooling of relations set in between the two. When Alfred arrived at Central to begin his own stint at the boring sequence of jobs the Vanderbilt heirs endured, Neily up and quit. The move was petulant; Neily must have realized that neither Alfred nor their playboy brother Reggie was fit to work at Central. Neily's own interest in the family railroads, however, had been tainted by events. He would go on instead to a career in the army, and display the same bravery on the fields of war that he had in the affairs of the heart.

Six million dollars was enough for Grace, however. Whereas she and Neily had not been starving heretofore, their new riches enabled them to live in Vanderbiltian style. A surface calm was established between Neily and his family. Grace ignored the lot of them, for which she cannot be blamed, and applied herself instead to giving fabulous parties. She and Neily rented an ocean-front villa called Beaulieu in Newport, equipped it with thirty horses, fifteen stable boys, a huge in-house staff, and proceeded to entertain nonstop. Increasingly, Grace Vanderbilt began to assume the position held for so long by the now-faltering Mrs. Astor.

In 1902, Grace catapulted herself to the top of the social pyramid—and became *the* Mrs. Vanderbilt in the process—by means of a clever social coup. A decade or so earlier, she had captivated the German Kaiser during a naval regatta at Kiel. In February of 1902, his son, Crown Prince Henry of Prussia, visited New York. The only private citizen he called upon and dined with in her home was Grace Vanderbilt.

She had arranged this by means of the same calculated strategy that would eventually make her America's greatest society figure. As soon as she heard of the prince's intended visit, she wrote to the German ambassador, recalled her pleasant meeting with the Kaiser years earlier, and asked the ambassador's advice in connection with the prince's upcoming visit. The ambassador forwarded her letter to the Kaiser, who not only remembered Grace very well but proceeded to cable back a command that she entertain his son while the latter was in New York. Neither Alice

nor Mrs. Alfred Vanderbilt were in the same
league with Grace after this. She had outflanked
them both and scored a total rout. She became
the undisputed queen of society, and remained
so until her death a half a century later.

Meanwhile, the case of Grace's mother-in-law
proved that money, name, and great houses do
not necessarily make a social queen. As she grew
older, Alice's youthful prettiness hardened. According to her daughter Gertrude Whitney, she
developed a piercing stare and a fondness for
inflicting heavy moral judgments. It is often asserted that prior to her husband's death, Alice
Vanderbilt had been engaged in a deadly social
competition with her sister-in-law Alva, the wife
of W. K. Vanderbilt of 660 Fifth and Marble
House. This hardly squares with Alice's personality, or her excessively religious attitudes. She
was neither gay nor amusing. She had no finesse
as a hostess and was incapable of attracting—let
alone keeping—a retinue of dancing men, a crucial requisite for serious entertaining.

According to Neil Vanderbilt's *Queen of the
Golden Age*, "the tragic events" of his grandmother's life had "dulled [her social] ambitions
and erased all traces of humor or gaiety in her
somber, plain featured face." Social wit Harry
Lehr could be screamingly funny on the subject
of Alice-of-the-Breakers. However, much of this
humor sprung from the fact that this was not a
very happy woman.

By 1900, Alice Vanderbilt had lost both a
firstborn son and a husband to untimely death.
Her eldest surviving son was married to a woman
who would not even speak to her. In 1915, her
son Alfred died on the *Lusitania* after an attack
by a German U-boat. In 1925, her youngest
boy, Reggie, literally drank himself to death in
Newport.

It should not be supposed that a woman in
Alice Vanderbilt's position, possessed of a large
family, a great deal of money, two palaces, and
a wide circle of acquaintances, would have no
social life at all. However, in an era of great
entertainments, she was not a great entertainer.

"Day after day," wrote Ralph Pulitzer in *New
York Society on Parade*, "the house yawns cav-
ernously, an empty setting for an empty life . . .
and only a few friends are privileged to patter
through its echoing emptiness, to lunch or dine
with its mistress in the comparative comfort of
her breakfast room." Pulitzer was describing an

apocryphal New York palace at the turn of the
century, but he might just as well have been
describing 1 West Fifty-seventh Street. According to Pulitzer, it was only at a ball or a cotillion
that a great house in town "beams and glitters."
Only then will it "be in its element . . . allowed
to perform its proper functions, to fulfill those
purposes for which it was designed five hundred
years ago in the flood-tide of the Renaissance:
to hold the crowded courts of princes; to frame
the gorgeous pageantry of worldly power; to glow
as background to its glory . . . always to be full
of life, rich, vivid, manifold."

Above: After the death of Cornelius Vanderbilt II, most
of the activity at 1 West Fifty-seventh Street took place
outdoors. Here contestants are lined up by the Fifty-
eighth Street gates for the start of the Automobile Club
of America's 1904 race from New York to St. Louis.

Below: "In 1925, her youngest boy, Reggie, literally
drank himself to death in Newport."

There were nights like this at 1 West Fifty-seventh Street. For her daughter Gladys's marriage to Count Lazlo Szechenyi in 1908, the ballroom was converted into an immense grotto of pink and mauve orchids, lit to look like a sunset. On that day, the orchestra alone numbered some seventy souls. Neily, in a measure of normalizing relations, gave away the bride. However, most of the time, things were very quiet, both in New York and at Newport. According to Dixon Wecter's *Saga of American Society*, Alice was the "loneliest figure in American Society." Rare indeed were her New York City entertainments. While at Newport, according to Wecter, she entertained just as infrequently, instead holding court "for a few aging friends at The Breakers."

By 1924, all the Vanderbilts, save Neily and Grace, had despaired of holding out in their Fifth Avenue houses south of Central Park. The avalanche of business and skyscrapers, the mobs of pedestrians, the traffic, and especially the noise had finally gotten to them. Big-time New York real estate interests were perched like so many vultures upon the new Art Deco cornices rising everywhere above the Vanderbilt châteaux. So much underutilized prime real estate, sitting smack in the path of the city's most fashionable business development, could not last for long.

One West Fifty-seventh Street had been put halfheartedly on the market back when Willie Vanderbilt died in 1920. No aggressive sales campaign was launched, but everyone knew it could be had for the right price. Meanwhile, Alice continued her quiet life there—while annual real estate taxes approached $130,000. In 1925, her château was among the very last private houses standing in the Plaza area. And in that year, it was finally sold. The price was $7,100,000, a bargain by today's standards for a blockfront on Fifth Avenue with 125 feet on two side streets. George Post's magnificent creation was to be razed; the new owners wanted only the land.

By the end of 1925, Alice and her butler were installed ten blocks to the north at 1 East Sixty-seventh Street, following a migratory pattern up Fifth Avenue that had characterized New York's footloose plutocratic households for over a century. Her Fifty-seventh Street home of forty years was opened to the public for seven days during January of 1926. The New York *Herald Tribune* raved over the white and gold ballroom with its imported French woodwork, the chandeliers, the marble fireplaces, and the allegorical ceiling paintings. There was even a portrait of Alice's daughter Gertrude Whitney still installed over one mantel in a small salon. Awestruck visitors filed through the rooms between 10:00 A.M. and 10:00 P.M. daily. In a poetic coda to the history of the home of a great philanthropist, the admission fee for the predemolition viewing was donated to the New York Association for the Improvement of the Condition of the Poor, after which, the house was boarded up.

Before the wreckers arrived in 1927, certain architectural fragments were sold at auction. Motion-picture baron Marcus Loew prowled Vanderbilt Row in these years, salvaging fragments from all sorts of people's former Fifth Avenue palazzi. He purchased the Tiffany Moorish Room from 660 Fifth Avenue and transported the whole thing to the Midland Theater in Kansas City. It's there today, outside a ladies' lounge. All manner of chandeliers, benches, hall chairs, sconces, pictures, and so on designed originally for the cream of New York society were scattered across the nation in the new Loew's movie palaces. Later, when Loew's went into the hotel business, a lot of this material was moved into their new hotels. The Moorish Room from 1 West Fifty-seventh Street was too grand for transport, but the fantastical chandelier that once hung from its domed ceiling survives, now enlivens the grand foyer of the Loew's State Theater in Syracuse, New York.

One of the two imposing pairs of wrought-iron gates that had overlooked the Plaza for so many years was salvaged, too. It was reinstalled at the entrance of the Conservatory Gardens—a formal enclave in Central Park—between 104th and 105th streets on Fifth Avenue. Alice's daughter Gertrude Whitney paid for the removal and reinstallation. The Metropolitan Museum of Art possesses a Saint-Gaudens fireplace from the entrance hall and a lunette designed by John LaFarge. With few other exceptions, however, the rest of the house—the magnificent stairway and the tall carved doors, the marble fireplaces and the painted ceilings, the mirrored walls and the white and gold woodwork—was smashed into rubble and hauled out to a New Jersey landfill.

Alice Gwynne Vanderbilt died on April 22, 1934, at the age of eighty-nine, leaving her

"The avalanche of business and skyscrapers . . . and especially the noise, had finally got to them."

sister-in-law Florence Twombly "dowager queen of the old regime." In point of fact, Alice had never been much of a queen, while Florence was already a legend. If, as Ralph Pulitzer maintained, the whole point of American society was entertainment for entertainment's sake, then Alice's reign had been co-opted by others from the outset.

Neily had reconciled with his mother many years before her death. She left him the Gwynne Building in Cincinnati. His sculptress sister, Gertrude Vanderbilt Whitney, received the $7 million her mother had gotten from the sale of 1 West Fifty-seventh Street. The Countess Szechenyi, Alice's last remaining living child, inherited The Breakers, 1 East Sixty-seventh Street, and two-thirds of one of those multimillion-dollar trusts the Vanderbilts were so fond of creating and willing to one another.

One West 57th Street is gone today. In its place is Bergdorf Goodman, department store for the haut monde. Cornelius Vanderbilt II's seemingly invulnerable monument to money, power, beauty, art—and, yes, to vanity—was no match for the juggernaut of "progress." Once again, the city was robbed of an important landmark, one that added romance, mystery, yearning, pride, curiosity—not to mention strongly felt emotions such as contempt, anger, and righteousness—to the texture of everyday life.

We all know that people's lives are crucially affected by physical environment, which includes buildings as well as parks, clean air, and pure water. Inevitably, the architectural environment affects the way we think and the way we perceive the rest of the world. One West Fifty-seventh Street was more than a visual ornament to the nation's greatest metropolis; it was a personal yardstick for anyone who ever laid eyes on it. There wasn't a soul in New York who didn't recognize the place in its day and for whom it didn't have some sort of meaning. Even now, it's the rare person who can look at a picture of it and not be moved.

In February, 1927, 1 West Fifty-seventh Street "was smashed to rubble and hauled out to a New Jersey landfill."

Chapter 4
SHELBURNE FARMS

Shelburne Farms

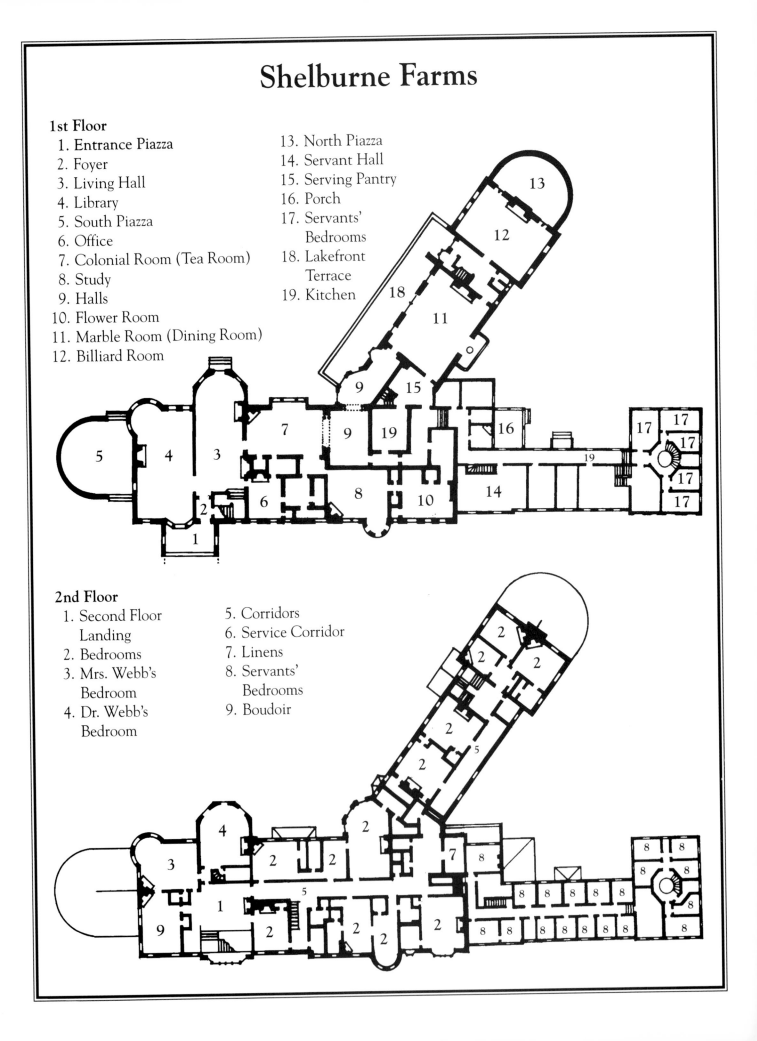

1st Floor
1. Entrance Piazza
2. Foyer
3. Living Hall
4. Library
5. South Piazza
6. Office
7. Colonial Room (Tea Room)
8. Study
9. Halls
10. Flower Room
11. Marble Room (Dining Room)
12. Billiard Room
13. North Piazza
14. Servant Hall
15. Serving Pantry
16. Porch
17. Servants' Bedrooms
18. Lakefront Terrace
19. Kitchen

2nd Floor
1. Second Floor Landing
2. Bedrooms
3. Mrs. Webb's Bedroom
4. Dr. Webb's Bedroom
5. Corridors
6. Service Corridor
7. Linens
8. Servants' Bedrooms
9. Boudoir

The main house at Shelburne Farms "at its peak" in the late 1890s.

Location: Shelburne, Vermont
Architect: Robert Henderson Robertson (1849–1919)
Commissioned by: Dr. William Seward Webb (1851–1926)
and Eliza (Lila) Osgood Vanderbilt Webb (1860–1936)
Main house completed: 1899

*S*HELBURNE Farms is a long way from New York. It lies almost three hundred miles north of Manhattan. The estate today consists of about a thousand acres right on Lake Champlain at a point directly opposite the high peaks of the Adirondacks. The view is more than superb; it is both sublime and beautiful. Likewise, the estate is grand almost beyond imagination. Aesthetically, it is one of those joint undertakings of man and nature where every single element works well.

Shelburne, at its peak in the late 1890s, contained not just a great house but also a farm of satisfyingly stupendous proportions. To illustrate the scale of the place, one must consider the Breeding Barn. This beautifully finished shingled structure, completed in 1891 and devoted to the perfection of the American horse, contained three hundred stalls. They surrounded an indoor ring measuring 375 feet long by 85 feet wide. Not a single pillar supported the immense roof of this ring. For forty years in fact, until the construction of Chicago's Merchandise Mart, the Webbs' Breeding Barn was the largest unsupported interior space in the United States.

At the water's edge, separated from the outside world by miles of carefully designed landscape, sprawled a grand and eclectic manor house. It was, and still is, the largest house in Vermont.

A great hardship ultimately fell upon the Webbs of Shelburne Farms. In the beginning, however, all was romance and light. There is an intimate love story connected with this place, an irony considering its very grand scale. The house and estate always have evoked the warmest kind of memories from everyone who lived or visited here. The Webbs' guest book overflows not just with names but with thanks, oftentimes in verse.

It's hard not to be moved by Shelburne's mixture of spacious natural setting and unfettered architectural grandeur. Everything—mountain vistas, rolling forests, Lake Champlain, the main house, even the barns—is very vast. At the same

"When they met in 1877, he was twenty-six and she was seventeen."

time, it is also extremely homelike and comfortable, not the least bit stiff or formal. The original gracious atmosphere persists to this day, and says much about the people who developed Shelburne in the late 1880s and 1890s. They were Dr. William Seward Webb (1851–1926), Seward to those who knew him well; and his wife, Eliza Osgood Vanderbilt (1860–1936), whom the family called Lila.

When they met in 1877, he was twenty-six and she was seventeen. He was the son of the famous diplomat and newspaper editor James Watson Webb. She was the daughter of the richest man in the world. Travel and education had broadened and cultivated them both. Stern, old-fashioned parenting prevented either from being spoiled. Curiously, however, Lila's father was suspicious of young Seward Webb. At one point in their protracted courtship—according to Lila's diary—her father forbade even the mention of Webb's name in his presence.

Vanderbilt's reaction seems all the more odd, since an alliance with the Webbs then would have seemed a desirable thing. In 1877, the Vanderbilts were acknowledged as rich but still dismissed as socially inconsequential. The Webbs, on the other hand, were a distinguished clan that had all but arrived on the *Mayflower*. Seward's grandfather, General Samuel Blachley Webb, led the Minute Men up Bunker Hill; later, he held the Bible with which George Washington took the first oath of office.

The future Dr. William Seward Webb had a cosmopolitan upbringing. He was the namesake of a distinguished godfather, William Henry Seward, Secretary of State under Abraham Lincoln. This is the man remembered for convincing the United States to buy "Seward's Icebox," as Alaska once was called. As a boy, young Seward Webb enjoyed considerable foreign travel, particularly in South America, where his father was Lincoln's minister plenipotentiary to Brazil. By the time he met his future bride, Webb was a resident at St. Luke's Hospital in New York, just completing ten years of studying medicine both here and abroad.

Being a doctor, interestingly, was considered a risky career choice in the nineteenth century. Professional standards were uneven and most doctors didn't get rich. Early on in Seward's courtship of Lila, William Henry Vanderbilt insisted Seward choose a less precarious job. This is quaint advice from a modern perspective, the more so since the suggestion was that he get a job on Wall Street. In 1878, Webb did precisely that, abandoning a decade of medical training and obtaining a position with W. S. Worden and Company.

Lila was the youngest of William Henry Vanderbilt's daughters, and his youngest child, save for young George, born in 1862. She had been conscientiously educated as a lady and had attended Miss Porter's School in Connecticut. Most of her life had been spent in her father's brownstone mansion at 459 Fifth Avenue. She was a mild, sweet-tempered, and amenable person, with an acute sense of duty and a lively interest in history and biography. She loved to read aloud, and read all of Milton's *Paradise Lost* to her brother George.

Lila was also a lifelong diarist and she poured out her heartfelt thoughts on everything from her brothers and sisters to Charlemagne and the Reformation. Her diaries reveal her as forthright, jolly, and understanding of other people. She had a keen sense of justice and was quite decisive. The many volumes of her diary contain hardly a single word deleted.

She fell very much in love with Seward Webb. In her diary, she described him as "the truest, noblest, loveliest, most affectionate and tender man God ever made." Webb must have cut a dashing figure. He was not only handsome and well-educated, he was idealistic, romantic, and singularly charming.

He was also very much smitten by her. Their romance was what one might call exalted. Webb's charm fell flat with Lila's father, but her siblings were captivated. They were the ones—particularly Emily, Fred, Margaret, and Margaret's husband, Elliott Shepard—who brought the pair together, then kept them in touch behind their father's back. Were it not for Lila's married sister Emily Sloane, who acted as secret postmistress between the lovers, the courtship most certainly would have foundered.

The family watched the progress of Lila's courtship with some apprehension. In fairness to Lila's father, he must have been concerned over his daughter's desire to become engaged at so early an age, and to the first serious suitor to come along. There was also the matter of the age difference. Lila was a mature eighteen in 1878, by which time the romance had become

very serious, but Seward was almost ten years her senior. No doubt, he seemed a very worldly young man to William Henry Vanderbilt, a characteristic not always appreciated by a prospective father-in-law.

Above: Dr. William Seward Webb, dressed for winter sports.

Below: Eliza (Lila) Osgood Vanderbilt Webb, newly married. Note the diamond arrow and crescent on her breast and the diamond bee in her hair.

With other men, Webb's social position might have been persuasive, but the elder Vanderbilts did not pine for the society entertainments from which they were excluded. They were church-goers, operagoers, intelligent tourists, but otherwise homebodies. Then, right in the midst of Lila's romance, her parents suffered another romantically related shock. In December of 1878, their twenty-two-year-old son Fred eloped with a woman who was twelve years his senior, *and* divorced from William Henry's nephew Daniel Torrance.

It was at this point that W. H. Vanderbilt forbade even the mention of Seward Webb's name. Eventually, he relented. He did so, however, in the manner of the classic nineteenth-century authority figure. First, he imposed a six-month separation, during which time letters secretly carried back and forth by Emily Sloane were the couple's only means of communication. When Lila's ardor appeared undampened, her father insisted on a second six-month separation. And when that didn't change her mind either, he took her off on an extended European tour.

During these enforced separations, Seward and Lila maintained secret contact by means of sixty-, eighty-, and sometimes even one-hundred-page letters. Every night at 10:30 P.M., these lovebirds sat down wherever they happened to be and wrote to one another. Whatever wasn't included in their extremely long letters was entered into journals. Emily Sloane also played postmistress with the journals, lending Lila's to Seward and vice versa. The couple submitted, without complaint, to Vanderbilt's demands for three years. They proved their love. After this, Lila's father could only admit defeat.

This he did with ostensible grace in 1881. Seward and Lila became man and wife on December twentieth of that year, at a smart affair officiated at by Bishop Henry C. Potter, the oh-so-social arbiter of who was, and was not, in New York society. The guests included former President U. S. Grant, as well as cotillion leaders and society heavyweights with names such as Fish, Stewart, Mills, and Stevens. Lila ascribed the social glitter of her wedding wholly to the Webbs. Throughout her life, she maintained that had she been born any earlier, she could never have expected to make so prestigious a match.

One is naturally curious as to what in the world took this couple all the way to Vermont. Notwithstanding its classical traditions of education and architecture, Vermont contained nothing remotely resembling the New York world of power and money that had surrounded the newly married Dr. and Mrs. Webb.

Vermont has, however, a special seductiveness for the city dweller, an almost mystical combination of natural beauty and a slower pace of life. Many succumb after the first exposure. In Webb's case, that exposure was the result of a business trip made on his future father-in-law's behalf to Rutland, Vermont, in 1880. Although the New York Central at that time dominated freight transportation throughout the northeast and as far west as Chicago, they had no direct rail link to Montreal. Webb was dispatched to look at a little line called the Rutland Railroad and report whether or not a Central takeover would be in the family's best interests. He decided it would not, and advised Mr. Vanderbilt accordingly.

It was during the course of this trip that he fell totally under the spell of northwestern Vermont. Almost the first thing he did upon his return to New York was arrange a trip for his fiancée and himself back up to Burlington, a vigorous little city on the shores of Lake Champlain, some seventy miles north of Rutland. Lila, too, was captivated by Vermont. The summer after their marriage, they returned to Burlington and rented a house.

Remote as it was, the countryside around Burlington had a spaciousness that appealed to Seward Webb's expansive nature. There were mountains to the east and west, and vast distances every way one looked. The light had a bell-like clarity and the sky seemed immense. The weather patterns, too, were awesome. Entire storm systems could be seen as they rolled dramatically across the peaks of the Adirondacks and advanced across Lake Champlain.

Seward and Lila Webb felt that they had discovered the most beautiful place on earth. They liked Burlington so much, in fact, that they decided to establish year-round residence there. In 1883, after purchasing some fifteen hundred acres on Shelburne Bay, they began building Oakledge. This was a rambling Victorian clapboard affair with multiple angles, towers, and porches; it was situated on the lakefront to the south of town. Oakledge was no mansion, but it was roomy and comfortable. In June of 1884, the family settled into it with two-year-old Frederica. Less than a month later, baby James Watson Webb was born.

Thus began what seemed a wholesome, relatively simple rural existence, removed not just from the dirt and crime of New York but from the frivolities of Saratoga and Newport, as well. All this was shortly to change, however. In De-

petitor. In the early 1880s, W. H. Vanderbilt set Seward Webb the task of rescuing Wagner from a financial slump, which Webb succeeded in doing brilliantly. As president of Wagner, he made a large salary.

It was his wife's inheritance that gave birth to the great dream of Shelburne Farms. However, it was his character that molded the place. Shelburne exemplified a somewhat patronizing ideal-

Aerial view of Shelburne's main house on the shore of Lake Champlain.

cember of 1885, William Henry Vanderbilt died and Lila inherited $10 million. Unlike her siblings, each of whom received $5 million in negotiable securities (as good as cash) and another $5 million in a trust whose principal could not be touched during the lifetime of the heir, Lila's entire $10 million was tied up in trust until she reached the age of thirty—almost five years in the future. Here again was evidence of William Henry's distrust of Seward Webb. As a practical matter, however, the interest on $10 million was so great as to elevate the Webbs into the financial big leagues even without access to their capital.

In addition to this, Seward Webb was making money of his own. Since 1883, he had been president of the Wagner Palace Car Company, a Vanderbilt company that made sleeping cars for railroad trains. It was Pullman's largest com-

ism wedded to a mania for scientific modernism. In this sense, it was truly an American undertaking.

The estate was developed as a country seat in the same manner that country seats existed in class-conscious Europe. Shelburne Farms was to be not just a residence but also a symbol and a source of economic power. As the wealth and privileges of the European gentry derived originally from the land, so the scientific agricultural undertakings of Shelburne Farms would continue to enrich and legitimize Webbs for generations to come. It would do all this, *and* educate the neighbors at the same time.

The Webbs' decision to live full-time in Vermont did not automatically make them Vermonters—at least, not in the eyes of their neighbors. Rural, agricultural Vermont was populated by a rock-ribbed, tight-lipped, slyly hu-

Interior of the "Ellsmere," the Webbs' private railroad car.

"Fortunately, they . . . possessed the Learjet of their time, a private railroad car." It was called the "Ellsmere."

The main house at Shelburne Farms, under construction during the summer of 1886.

morous group who saw the Webbs rather differently than they saw themselves. The world of the Vermonter—then and now—tended to be divided into two camps: themselves and the people from Boston and New York. Vermonters traditionally do not complain about life's hardships; to the contrary, they endure in characteristic silence. They certainly did not welcome rich people coming up from New York and telling them how to run their farms.

The nature of Seward and Lila Webb's Vermont residency was also different from that of their neighbors. They continued, for example, to maintain a Manhattan town house at 680 Fifth Avenue, the gift of Lila's father, to which they could retreat during the very coldest months or whenever mood or necessity struck. Fortunately, they were in the railroad business and possessed the Learjet of their time, a private railroad car. The "Ellsmere," as it was called, could be attached to trains running into Grand Central pretty much at the drop of a hat. This made New York, or alternately Vermont, easily accessible via an overnight train that departed in the evening and delivered them, rested, bathed, and changed, the very next morning. The private car enabled Seward Webb to live in Burlington and work in New York. It allowed his family and guests to travel back and forth virtually at will. Indeed, these people traveled all over the country with an ease and spontaneity that still amazes.

With his wife's full support and encouragement, and with money to do just about anything he wanted, Seward Webb began to plan Shelburne. He was determined from the outset to create an estate that would be more than just a private residence. His personal attitudes embodied the Victorian era's passion for useful instruction. The pursuit of scientific agriculture, then being embarked upon by so many estate-building American millionaires, was a more or less inevitable choice. Webb's personal passion for horseflesh provided him with a specific goal.

Before he started anything, he determined that he would not become a victim of his new neighbors. He wanted to site his new estate on a scenic peninsula called Shelburne Point, located across Shelburne Bay from Oakledge. The land was already in the hands of thirty-two different Vermont farmers. Problem number one became how to acquire it all without paying "Vanderbilt prices."

Webb addressed this problem by hiring a front man named Arthur Taylor. Taylor made tactful visits to the various farmers on Shelburne Point. He told each that an eccentric New York City buyer who wished to remain anonymous was willing to pay two times the value of their land. There was one condition: News of the sale had to be kept secret. If word should leak out prior to March 1, 1886, the deal would be off.

Of course, railroads traditionally acquired land via ploys such as this, and the Vermonters doubtless knew what was going on from the start. The final result was that Webb paid twice the going rate for farmland, and still had to contend with a significant holdout. This was the Shelburne Harbor Shipyard—still extant today—on Shelburne Point. The shipyard was prospering and the owner refused to sell. This scotched a particularly feudal scheme that would have included a main gate on Bay Road, complete with drawbridge over the little La Platte River.

As soon as he got enough land to start (the actual process continued for years), Webb engaged architect Robert Henderson Robertson (1849–1919) to do the design. Robertson was a prolific and successful New York architect, and eventually he became one of Webb's best friends. He was a natural choice, a romantic with high-Victorian, early-English predilections that segued neatly with Dr. Webb's taste. Robertson was an especial fan of H. H. Richardson, whose heavy Romanesque buildings had recently been hunkering down on town squares across the United States. Robertson was also an admirer of the English architect Richard Norman Shaw, famous for his immense and picturesque English country houses.

Robertson was born in Philadelphia and studied architecture in Scotland. His first job was in the Philadelphia office of Henry Sims, a man now dimly remembered for his Gothic-style ecclesiastical work. In 1873, Robertson went to New York and worked briefly for George B. Post, the man who designed 1 West Fifty-seventh Street for Lila's brother Cornelius. After stints in two other firms, he went out on his own in 1881.

At first, Robertson was an architect given to modest designs for churches and country houses. His popularity soon burgeoned and he became rather an expert at complex and weighty-looking railroad stations, and at the newly evolving skyscraper. Among his skyscrapers, the most famous today is probably the old Park Row Building (1899), which still overlooks City Hall Park in New York. Among his railroad clients was the New York Central, which commissioned depot buildings at Mott Haven in the Bronx (1886) and Canandaigua in upstate New York (1888).

It is likely that Robertson met Webb in connection with his work for Central. Just as the commercial nature of most of George Post's work did not dissuade Cornelius Vanderbilt II from hiring him for a personal residence, so Robertson's reputation as an architect of depots and skyscrapers evidently did not dissuade Webb, either.

Both Webb and Robertson were in their thirties when the planning for Shelburne commenced. Both were on a steeply climbing career curve, and each must have recognized the potential of this project to attract nationwide attention. For Robertson, the commission led to many other important residential jobs, notably Hammersmith Farm in Newport for John W.

Auchincloss, and Beechwood at Scarborough-on-Hudson for Seward's brother H. Walter Webb. All this came later, however, and Seward Webb would seem to have been the architect's first estate customer.

By June of 1886, Robertson was in a high state of excitement with regard to the Shelburne project. That month, he wrote to Frederick Law Olmsted, the father of American landscape architecture, describing "a most important country house, stock barns, [and] stables" that he was designing for Dr. Webb. "I hope you can undertake the problem [of the landscape design, since it will be] one of the most important and beautiful country places in America."

As a result of its many famous public parks, the Olmsted office had established itself as the leader of the aesthetic landscape movement. However, the firm's first commission to do a gentleman's estate had been Tanglewood in Lenox, Massachusetts, only three years previously. Ultimately, the Olmsteds would design over nine hundred private estates. In the mid-

Robertson's Farm Barn, "the center for the overall operation of the property."

Dr. Webb's Breeding Barn, designed by Robert H. Robertson, was part of an experiment to perfect the American horse.

eighties, however, they were as new to this type of design as Robertson was.

Frederick Law Olmsted did make sketches and recommendations for the Shelburne Farms estate. Unfortunately, the exact extent of his work for the Webbs, unlike his carefully documented schemes for Lila's brother George at Biltmore, remains unclear. Nor is it known exactly how many of his original proposals were carried out. The overall look of Shelburne Farms—the alternating woods and meadows, the layout and division of the various farm and residential components of the property, and the scenic plan of the roads—is Olmsted-like. However, much of the credit for this is probably due to Arthur Taylor, who stayed on to become the first manager of Shelburne Farms. Webb and Taylor jointly supervised many of the improvements on the property. Olmsted's attention was so scanty that Laura Wood Roper, author of the definitive *FLO: A Biography of Frederick Law Olmsted,* does not even mention Shelburne Farms or Seward Webb.

Webb's grand visions of scientific husbandry sprang from his love of the outdoors. He was typical of the socialite who enjoyed the sporting life, a man who loved riding into the wilderness to hunt, camp, and fish, and had the time and money to do so. He was, of course, a superb

equestrian, and a member of the exclusive New York Coaching Club. Given his lifelong interest in horses, it was only fitting that he concentrated the agricultural emphasis of his new estate on perfecting the breeding of the American horse.

The national economy in the late 1880s still depended on horsepower. According to Dr. Webb, however, the American horse, and particularly its Vermont variety, had descended to a very sorry state. In his 1893 book, *Shelburne Farms Stud: English Hackneys, Harness and Saddle Horses, Ponies and Trotters,* Webb described in detail the degeneration of the formerly famous Vermont horse. He felt that indiscriminate breeding was the culprit, maintaining it had rendered no single horse strong enough to pull a plow *and* good-looking enough to draw a carriage. Ironically, Webb alluded to the proliferation of railroads, a development with which he himself was associated, as having done considerable damage. With the demise of long-distance coach travel, Americans had stopped demanding first-class carriage horses. The result was the unfortunate lot available.

It is likely his Vermont neighbors would have had a few messages for him, had it been in their nature to communicate them. The Vermont Morgan horse, after all, was one of the very few indigenously bred horses in the country. It had been the nation's war-horse, and had virtually carried the Civil War on its back. Webb's suggestion that the local product, even if able to pull a plow, wasn't good enough to pull his elegant carriage only could have insulted his neighbors.

Oblivious to the local reaction to these opinions, Webb set out to teach the nation at large, and Vermont in particular, how to breed a horse. To that end, he had Robertson design what are probably the grandest and most beautiful farm buildings ever erected in the United States: a Farm Barn, which became the center for the overall operation of the property; a Breeding Barn, dedicated exclusively to the hackney stud; and a Coach Barn, which contained numerous horse-drawn vehicles for family use. These buildings are so superb in design and execution that they overshadow the main residence. In fact, the Webbs lived in a temporary house for years precisely because it was the hackney stud and the farm operation that had the higher priorities. Shelburne is unique among Vanderbilt estates in that the barns are—and always have been— more important than the main house.

The Farm Barn was the mecca for all visitors to Shelburne in its heady early days. According to Henry Hazelton writing in the November 1901 issue of *New England Magazine*, it contained "all the appliances which modern ingenuity can devise." These included steam-powered hay-stacking machinery; elevator grain bins; up-to-the-minute shops for carpentry, blacksmithing, and painting; offices for the manager and staff; and accommodations for a herd of cattle and twenty-two mule teams. The Farm Barn was almost as sophisticated in its management of multiple usages as Grand Central Terminal in New York. Both exemplified the wedding of advanced technology to aesthetic design.

The barn was built around a vast courtyard, 400 feet wide and 260 feet deep, with buildings on three sides and an impressive dressed stone gate on the fourth. The main section rises five full stories. It is filled with Victorian-era technology and topped by a tower with a clock. The lower wings contain the workshops and farm offices, all of which are still in use today. The complex sits on a dressed red limestone foundation, but it is primarily a wooden structure. Robertson here demonstrated his skill with shingles, contrasting them with exposed pseudotim-

bers and fields of stucco. The roof, originally shingled, is today covered with copper that has turned a delicate moss green.

The aesthetic composition of the Farm Barn is noble in the extreme. Its towers and complicated roofline, the muted palette of its natural building materials, and, above all, its sumptuous scale give the place a brooding grandeur. Certainly, as a barn it is in a class of its own. Skillfully sited amidst cultivated forests and meadows, it epitomizes everything that was right about American Victorian-era architecture, from sympathetic materials to sensitive siting to vigorous and competent design.

The Coach Barn housed carriages for family use.

At its peak in the nineties, the model farm at Shelburne was arguably the finest in America. For many years, it supplied *all* the butter used on the New York Central's dining cars, every little pat of which was embossed with the initials S.F. Shelburne Farms also produced and exported a large proportion of the milk and cream used by Central, plus eggs, apples, oats, wheat, and rye. Between the main house and the stud and the farm operation, there were five hundred people employed (although not all domiciled) on this property. Shelburne Farms was essentially self-supporting as far as food was concerned. The entire operation hummed with efficiency, and cast a rather feudal glow across the republican landscape of northern Vermont.

At times, the fashion among American millionaires for creating decorative farmsteads resulted in arcane experiments in elegant husbandry, performed amidst laughably elaborate surroundings. Model farms on great estates really did produce better-quality goods, not just for their owners but for households throughout surrounding areas, as well. Very often, they did improve the quality of local produce and livestock, even though they also provoked resentment. Such millionaire farms could operate at a deficit, if their owners so chose. For the locals, deficit farming meant eventual starvation. At Shelburne, the consummate nature of the place at least had a point; and the estate might well have enjoyed the sustained influence for which Webb had hoped had it not been for later and unforeseen complications.

Besides horse breeding and the production of farm goods and crops, Webb also engaged in scientific forestry. Tens (sometimes even hundreds) of thousand of elms, pines, and maples were planted every year. The doctor's goal in forestry, as well as in farming and horse breeding, was to demonstrate advanced technology. The common farmer was thus supposed to be educated by example. It was hoped the nation at large would eventually benefit from increased agricultural production, better sanitation, more efficient use of resources, and all the other advantages that resulted from the informed application of scientific principles.

Shelburne Farms was a quintessentially American undertaking, from the architectural style of its shingled buildings to its preoccupation with scientific advances. Even more important, however, was Shelburne's wedding of aesthetic beauty to technology. The physical beauty of his surroundings was definitely a part of the message Dr. Webb hoped to convey to the farmers of America.

The farming component at Shelburne was extensive, but the primary focus of Webb's energies was horse breeding. His Breeding Barn, which the family called the "BB," was even more cavernous than the Farm Barn. It measured 418 feet long by 107 feet wide, was clad in an undulating skin of gray shingles, and was naturally lighted by enormous glazed lanterns and by dormers positioned picturesquely on the roof. The interior was, in effect, one immense indoor riding ring, big enough for polo. It was seventy-five feet longer than a football field and had not one single column holding up the roof. Instead, the roof was supported by a complicated system of spidery iron rods. These joined together the tops of the side walls and assumed the thrust of the roof. It is an ingenious scheme, visually exciting, and the roofline remains almost as free of sags today as when it was built.

As soon as the "BB" was completed, Webb, at considerable expense, imported thirty-five brood mares and four stallions from England. He then offered stud services to his Vermont neighbors for fifteen dollars. This was a nominal sum compared to Webb's own costs. None of his neighbors came, however. Baffled, Webb eliminated the stud fee altogether. Still nobody came. As a matter of fact, his immense and costly undertaking was shunned by the local population. Try as Dr. Webb would, he could not persuade the locals to improve themselves or their horses. They tended, uncharitably, to view him as a rich New Yorker trying to justify his existence by telling them their own business.

Ignored by the community, Shelburne Stud soon began to produce its own prizewinners. Gradually, the glass cases in the tack room grew crowded with ribbons from society horse shows. However, as far as improving the quality of the local horse, let alone horseflesh on a national basis, Webb's great experiment was a complete failure. Ironically, his efforts were coincident (and at cross-purposes) with those of his nephew W. K. Vanderbilt, Jr. The younger man realized that the era of the horse was over. He subsequently devoted much of his energies to popularizing the automobile. The failure of his Uncle Seward's Shelburne Stud, in a way, boiled down to plain bad timing.

Farm Barns and Breeding Barns were costly (a hundred thousand or so apiece), but nowhere near as dear as marble mansions. In these early years, Lila's capital was still in trust. So on August 1, 1887, at 1:00 P.M., ground was broken for what was intended to be a temporary residence only. The original plan was to live for a few years in the temporary house, get the farm and the stud humming, then crown the whole architectural undertaking with an immense castle atop Lone Tree Hill. This site occupies high ground midway between the Farm Barn and the shore of Lake Champlain. The land there once had belonged to Webb's grandfather, General Samuel B. Webb. Old General Webb never built there, nor did he hold the land for very long, but his prior connection with the property was a pleasing coincidence.

The Shelburne Fox Hounds in front of the Breeding Barn, fall 1918. On horseback from left to right: Harry Hopkins, huntsman; unidentified whip; Mrs. Electra Havemeyer Webb, wife of J. Watson Webb.

Chances are Robertson tossed off the design without a lot of thought. After all, the focus of his efforts was elsewhere. Still, he managed to produce a very charming house. It cost only thirty thousand dollars, and was a deft embodiment of everything attractive in the Shingle Style.

The exterior silhouette was low and sweeping, highlighted by an abundance of sensually curving towers and picturesque redbrick chimneys. The massing was visually interesting, and the surface was full of the contrasting textures possible to achieve with shingles. The muted palette of the house tied together a good many disparate design elements, and it related well to the woodsy surroundings.

The interior plan featured rooms that were grander and better proportioned than those found in most Shingle Style houses. Many of these rooms survive largely unchanged today. Notable, too, were the excellent quality of the Colonial Revival woodwork in the dining room, and the breezy circular piazza on the south with its superb view of the lake.

Even in its original form, the main house at Shelburne Farms might well have been the culmination of most people's dreams. It was no mansion, however, and it proved too small from the start. The family assumed occupancy in 1888, then almost immediately began building additions. First, they enlarged the kitchen and the servants' quarters (there were only four servants' rooms in the original house). Then they built an annex with extra guest and maids' rooms, which angled away from the main body of the house on the lake side. By 1891, even the enlarged kitchen wing was too small, so an addition to the addition was tacked on, tripling the floor space of the service areas.

This supposedly temporary house grew more monumental than anticipated in the course of all this. Robertson continued to work on alternate schemes for the castle on Lone Tree Hill. One version, published in the March 1887 issue of *American Architect and Building News*, was abristle with Arthurian-looking stone battle-

baronial billiard room, eight additional guest rooms, and a huge third-floor playroom was built onto the main house where the annex had been. With the exception of the kitchen wing, all of the original exterior shingles were then covered with a brick facing. The brickwork is actually rather severe, far less competent from a design standpoint than the work on the nearby Coach Barn, finished in 1901.

The wooden roof was raised and slated, the chimneys rebuilt in a more monumental style, the library reworked and fitted out with a marvelous green boiserie that is still in place, and a stair added connecting Dr. Webb's second-floor

Shelburne's main house, still shingle-clad, undergoing a second enlargement of the kitchen wing.

"Once bricked, however, Shelburne ceased being a good Shingle Style house and became something quite different."

ments and medieval keeps. Another was more classically influenced and featured huge columned porticos, acres of creamy-colored pressed brick walls, and hundreds of symmetrically placed windows.

In June of 1893, the Webbs abandoned the idea of building another house and decided instead to make one final enlargement to the existing one. This saved money, but it was still an elaborate undertaking that required years of planning and wasn't completed until 1899. The annex was moved a hundred feet to the north, where it was attached to a new foundation and put into service as extra guest accommodations. A huge new brick wing with marble dining hall, bedroom with a wardrobe room on the floor above.

What emerged in 1899 was a house of some 44,000 square feet. It had the form of one of those aged and added-to English country manses that Americans so admired. Once bricked, however, Shelburne ceased being a good Shingle Style house and became something quite different. Elizabethan Tudor Revival is the tag that has been assigned it in recent years. The name conveys majesty—and maybe a sense of gables —but little else. It is unclear what Robertson himself would have called it.

Shelburne's interiors exemplify some of Robertson's best work. The rooms are spacious, beautifully detailed, and very comfortable. The floor plan, although Queen Anne in its original inspiration, does not share the Queen Anne lack of understanding of the need for privacy. This is a house where parties of thirty or more guests were routinely accommodated. Guests and hosts alike could find uninterrupted solace not just in their bedrooms but in the principal rooms on the main floor, as well. There are places to congregate, such as the tea room, the great main hall with its dual fireplaces, and the wonderful mar-

The library at Shelburne Farms' main house.

The smoking room at the north end of Shelburne Farms' main house.

The oringial main dining room. Note the excellent Colonial Revival woodwork.

Lila Webb's bedroom overlooking Lake Champlain.

ble-floored dining room. There are also places to which one can retreat, such as the library, the Edwardian billiard room at the north end, or Lila's private office, where she spent hours alone at her desk by a window that looked south over Lake Champlain.

The interior finishes at Shelburne are not palace quality. There are no rooms here designed by Allard or Gilbert Cuel, and no custom-made salons imported from Paris. The carving and the plasterwork are first-rate, nonetheless, and some of the marble mantels are quite magnificent. Stylistically, the interior is a successful mixture of Queen Anne domestic sensibilities and Edwardian scale; it manages to be elegant and comfortable at the same time.

The Webbs did not collect art, and nothing precious ever hung on or even near the walls in this house. W. & J. Sloane, the family firm (Lila's sister Emily was married to William D. Sloane), provided rugs, furniture, lighting, bibelots, and so on. In its heyday, the house had a "Pullman" plushness—or perhaps we should call it a "Wagner Palace Car" plushness—that was altogether captivating. Large brocaded and satin striped pillows were flung in abundance on

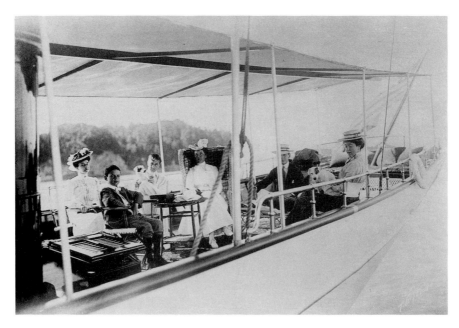

On board the *Elfreda* off Shelburne Point. Lila Webb is in the high-backed wicker chair.

mammoth tucked-velvet sofas. Silk-shaded lamps and silver-framed pictures crowded the tabletops. Every available square foot of floor space was covered with plush carpeting, Oriental rugs, heavily carved and/or upholstered chairs, and quantities of enormous potted palms. It was sumptuous, luxurious, and—joy of joys—endlessly polished and cleaned.

The calculated elegance of Shelburne House was a perfect foil for the relaxed rural atmosphere of its surroundings. It was a working farm, but the first tee of a private eighteen-hole golf course (third oldest course in the country) was right outside the front door. Dr. Webb was a hands-on agriculturalist, but he and his family were served meals by liveried footmen in a marble dining room. There was a nice dichotomy in the experience of staying at Shelburne. Here luxury was an assumption, but one that managed not to be confining.

Vast and elaborate as it was, the Shelburne Farms estate constituted only one-half of the Webbs' northern empire. On the other side of Lake Champlain, deep in the forested Adirondacks, lay a complementary wilderness retreat. Called NE-HA-SA-NE (pronounced nih-HA-snee), meaning "beaver crossing a log," this hunting preserve of forty-seven thousand acres (that's almost seventy-four square miles) was beloved by the family and figured constantly in

their elaborate entertainments. Private trains ferried family and friends from one side of the lake to the other all year long, and a private telegraph line connected each with the other, as well as with the New York house at 680 Fifth Avenue.

The lakeside lodge at NE-HA-SA-NE was designed by Robert H. Robertson in 1893. It was not the most architecturally inventive of the great camps of the Adirondacks, but it was suitably Webbian in scale and comfort. The picturesque main building and the twelve satellite cabins were all filled with fieldstone fireplaces and stuffed animals. Two dozen guests, plus guides, servants, and family members could easily settle in at NE-HA-SA-NE for a week or two of winter sports or summer fishing. One of those guests was the famous forester Gifford Pinchot.

"Considered as a piece of real property," wrote Pinchot in his 1898 volume, *The Adirondack Spruce: A Study of the Forest in NE-HA-SA-NE Park,* "the virgin forest yields no interest. [Present lumber activity] ignores the fact that forest land is productive capital." Pinchot's contribution to American forestry was the introduction of scientific crop management for trees. To him, Webb's private, virginal, almost mystical Adirondack forest was simply an underproducing woodlot.

Pinchot has been incorrectly credited with having helped design Shelburne's historic land-

Family and friends by the toboggan run.

Robert H. Robertson's Adirondack camp for
W. Seward Webb, called NE-HA-SA-NE.

scape plan. True, he was often at the Webbs' Vermont estate, but only as a guest. Pinchot was handsome, socially well connected, and popular among many of the Vanderbilts. Seward's niece Adele Sloane had a crush on him; Seward's brother-in-law George Vanderbilt employed him as the forester at Biltmore. The design of the landscape at Shelburne Farms, however, was the work of Seward Webb and Arthur Taylor, as inspired by Frederick Law Olmsted. All Pinchot did was survey spruce trees at NE-HA-SA-NE.

The Webbs routinely entertained guests by the dozens, and some stayed for weeks at a time. Many were family members, but hundreds of others were just friends who came and wrote their names and impressions in the guest book. The Webbs' style of living was decidedly elaborate. According to those who went to Shelburne, it was fun, too: never stiff like Newport; never too "cultural," as was occasionally the risk at Biltmore; just sheerly pleasurable.

A visit to Shelburne Farms in its heydey often included an excursion by private railroad car to NE-HA-SA-NE. Alternately, guests might attend one of Dr. Webb's big shoots in the fall. He had imported a Scottish gamekeeper and built an enormous pheasantry so that he and his guests could shoot ringnecks, birds that cannot otherwise survive the Vermont winter. As many as five thousand pheasants might have been released on a single day.

In the winter, there was tobogganing on a private run, skating, iceboating, sledding, and sleighing. In the summer, beside the golf links next to the main house, guests could drowse on the lake aboard the Webb's 117-foot steam yacht *Elfreda* (the name was a conjunction of Eliza and Frederica). The *Elfreda* had a crew of fifteen, marble floors in the bathrooms, and mahogany paneling in the staterooms. The bowsprit and aft rail were removable so that the boat could fit through the Chambly Canal locks.

There was also coaching, the ne plus ultra of smart-set diversions at the end of the nineteenth century. Dr. Webb was a member of the New York Coaching Club long before anyone named Vanderbilt had made the grade. Two times the club visited Shelburne, an epic undertaking. During the first visit, Dr. Webb provided a private train to take members, drags, horses, grooms, and so on as far as Rutland, Vermont. Club members tooled their own four-in-hands from there. On the second trip, in June of 1894, members drove their coaches the entire distance from New York City, which would have been a grueling undertaking had Dr. Webb not provided a private train to shadow the party and be available as needed for meals and overnight accommodations.

Ice boating near Burlington, Vermont, one of Shelburne's winter pleasures.

It seemed as if Shelburne House either had or was about to receive prominent guests at all times. Admiral Dewey visited in 1899, at the height of his fame after Manila Bay. Teddy Roosevelt was a guest in 1901; in fact, he was fetched back from the Adirondack wilds by Dr. Webb's yacht after McKinley was shot in Buffalo. Colonel Jack Astor and his beautiful bridge-playing wife, Ava, were guests, as was architect Robertson, Chauncey Depew of the New York Central, and assorted Purdys, Hunnewells, Harrimans, Lymans, and so on. Even the Duke of Marlborough paid a visit in 1890, five years before he married Lila's niece Consuelo. The Webbs also had a house full of children in these years. Fred-

erica (born in 1882), James Watson (born in 1884), Seward Junior (born in 1887), and Vanderbilt (born in 1891) filled the house with parties and friends as only children can.

The Webbs' luxurious Vermont entertainments were interspersed with extravagant excursions by rail. In 1889, Seward Webb took family, friends, two of his brothers, and fifteen servants on an 18,000-mile cross-country tour by private train. The trip was a great success and was followed by many others. In 1896, the family embarked on what was very likely the most deluxe private rail trip ever undertaken in the United States. This time, the private train included both the family cars—the "Ellsmere" (his) and the "Mariquita" (hers)—plus a dining car, a baggage car with accommodations for servants, a wine cellar, a library, and three stock cars for horses and grooms. The entire train numbered ten cars and, besides the Webbs and their guests and servants, carried two chefs, eight porters, a pair of children's nurses, a military guard, and two Pinkerton detectives.

Everything about the Webbs was mythically grand. A journalist named Henry Hazelton, writing in the *New England Magazine* of November 1901, couldn't get over the manicured appearance of Shelburne. Even the railroad station, another Robertson opus, which was located in the adjacent village of Shelburne, had a gemlike look. Nary a twig was out of place on the road between the station and the estate. The carriageways on the property were surfaced with crushed rock and lined with lordly elms. There weren't even any horse droppings; it was one man's job to do nothing but ride around all day and pick these up. Stupendous views were to be had at every turn. "To study these changing pictures," wrote Hazelton, a bit wistfully, "is the delight of a lifetime and the visitor wishes that he might linger."

The main house ran silently and efficiently, the domain of an English majordomo named Walter Woodgate. Woodgate had waited on Seward Webb when the Webbs visited the Duke of Marlborough at Blenheim, and the American visitor hired him away. Mr. Woodgate hired, fired, and purchased, setting a very lofty tone for Shelburne House. He organized its servants into a traditional English hierarchy. Indeed, he and his wife, Nell, were waited on by servants of their own.

Three of the Webbs' four children; left to right, W. Seward Webb, Jr.; J. Watson Webb; Frederica Webb; unidentified friend.

Relaxing in Vermont in the summer of 1885. Adults from left to right: Mrs. James Watson Webb (née Laura Cram), mother of Dr. William Seward Webb; her daughter-in-law, Mrs. H. Walter Webb (holding little H. Walter Webb Jr. on her lap); Lila Webb; Dr. William Seward Webb. The children seated on the little wicker stools are Lila and Seward's eldest, James Watson (left) and Frederica Vanderbilt (right).

Dr. Webb with his two eldest sons, Watson and Seward.

The farming operations, plus such mechanical and repair matters as pertained to the main house, were the province of one E. F. Gebhardt. This man was a sort of executive factotum who supervised literally hundreds of laborers engaged in tasks as diverse as stringing telephone wires, drilling for natural gas, grading roads, harvesting crops, painting, mowing, pruning, mending, hiring and firing outdoor staff, and anything and everything else pertaining to running two large estates.

Despite the prodigious resources he devoted to recreational pursuits, Seward Webb remained an active and energetic businessman. His greatest professional achievement coincided with the establishment of his northern fiefdoms at Shelburne and NE-HA-SA-NE. This was the construction of the famous St. Lawrence and Adirondack Railroad.

During the eighties and nineties, the Adirondacks were just beginning to be opened up as a resort area. The original resorters were rich men who took to the wilds—first at remote hotels and exclusive hunting and fishing clubs, later at elaborate "great camps" whose combination of luxury and log construction was pioneered by the well-known William West Durant. At one point, the Adirondacks were famous as the only spot on earth where one could stand at the edge of a lake in the depths of pristine wilderness and observe a couple in full evening dress paddling a canoe to a formal dinner.

The Adirondacks had few railroads in these early days. And the Vanderbilts still had not acquired a satisfactory rail link to Montreal. In 1890, acting on behalf of the New York Central, Seward Webb began planning a direct route across the Adirondacks that would connect Montreal with Central lines at Utica. He soon began acquiring huge tracts of land, including the future NE-HA-SA-NE Park. Suddenly, however, the Vanderbilts managed to intimidate the owners of the Rome, Watertown, and Ogdensburg Railroad into leasing them their lines to Canada. This rendered Webb's Adirondack efforts superfluous.

The rug had been pulled from beneath him, but Webb was too involved to stop. It's possible that he also felt the Vanderbilts were dead wrong, and that he had the talent and resources to build a railroad without them. Eighteen ninety was the year of Lila's thirtieth birthday, the year

that $5 million of her inheritance was released from trust and available to him in cash for whatever use he chose. Possibly, too, he was damned if he would let his in-laws pressure him into abandoning a pet project. The plan for an Adirondack railroad was also a professional challenge. Several attempts to put a line across the same route had failed.

In the course of this venture, Webb purchased 225 square miles of property, certainly a tract befitting a man with his sense of scale. Together with an entourage, he descended on Saranac Lake in the summer of 1891 to supervise an enormous crew working double shifts. In a mere eighteen months, a 191-mile right-of-way was cleared, graded, and laid with track. The first sleeper pulled into Saranac Lake—midway on the route to Montreal—on July 1, 1892. By October 24, regular scheduled service commenced between New York and Montreal.

Webb's Vanderbilt in-laws were not pleased with the success of his new railroad. The St. Lawrence and Adirondack competed with Central's own connection to Montreal. It also served a high-visibility, high-prestige resort area. Glory as well as profit had been gained for someone else with Vanderbilt money. Such, in any case, was the perception of some family members. When Webb eventually sold his railroad to the New York Central—at a handsome and much-resented profit—it made things that much worse.

The Webbs' Vermont hospitality continued unabated during the construction of the St. Lawrence and Adirondack. Beneath the surface calm, Seward Webb was having trouble, however. The acquisition of rights-of-way over state lands became a bureaucratic nightmare. Lobbyists working for the Delaware and Lackawanna opposed and obstructed the new railroad at every turn. Contractors reneged and went bankrupt; costs spiraled out of control. It was always Webb who dipped into his pocket to make up the difference. There was even an embarrassing scandal, engineered and leaked to the press by an individual at the State Bureau of Labor, wherein Webb was accused of cruel maltreatment of his work force.

The project consumed Seward Webb's attention for most of 1891 and 1892. He endured humiliation in the press, as well as very real financial peril. The double crossing, the back stabbing, and the financial dangers eventually threatened even his own deep pockets. The constant tension brought on a series of excruciating migraine headaches. The pain was blinding, and the threat of failure ever present. Desperate for relief, he turned to a drug that doctors had been prescribing freely since the Civil War. That drug was morphine.

Thus was the seed of disaster planted. Nothing was obvious at first. Probably even his wife didn't realize what was happening. Seward Webb was a principled and hardworking man, but he possessed no immunity to drug addiction. Worse, he and his wife lived in an era when much less was understood about it than is today. Addiction in Seward Webb's day was held to be a curse of the lower classes. Nice people were considered immune by virtue of better moral character.

Few Americans noticed or understood the rise of morphinism in the wake of the Civil War. Morphine had allayed untold suffering on the battlefield, but it also had left the nation with a shockingly large—and unacknowledged—population of addicts. So many were former soldiers that morphine addiction came to be known as "Soldiers' Disease."

By the 1890s, spurred at last by the scenes of degradation and violence that accompany drug problems, public opinion belatedly began to view morphinism as a national problem. Conventional wisdom, however, persisted in the belief that it could easily be remedied by dosage reduction. This thinking ignored the powerful psychological nature of the dependency.

Seward Webb's medical training had taken place at a time when the addictive danger of morphine was unknown. His own addiction coincided with the first stirrings of social disapprobation. Once hooked, he was unable to break the habit himself. His family did not know what to do about it, either.

Other family members soon began to notice Webb's odd behavior. For example, he began to pay undue attention to his attractive young niece, Adele Sloane. His flirtation with Adele Sloane was innocent, ultimately, but it was an early warning signal. A profound barrier of reserve had been breached somewhere within Seward Webb. He was no longer quite himself.

Into the mid-nineties, however, most people did not seem to notice the change. In 1896–1897, Webb served as a member of the Vermont legislature. He maintained an impressive facade as a staunch Republican, a staunch Episcopalian, and a valuable member of the establishment. He was still president of the Wagner Palace Car Company, and he sat on the boards of numerous other railroads, as well as being president general of The National Society of the Sons of the American Revolution. He remained active in developing his Adirondack lands, and as late as 1898 he collaborated with other Adirondack millionaires on the construction of a new railroad called the Racquette Lake Railway.

It was also in 1898 that he considered and abandoned the idea of running for governor of Vermont. Too "aloof and restrained" was the opinion of E. F. Gebhardt. The truth was that by 1898, drug addiction had caught up with Seward Webb.

Things began to unravel. By the first years of the twentieth century, his dream of breeding a perfect American horse was shattered by the rise of the internal-combustion engine. However, no attempt was made either to salvage the horse-breeding operation or to turn it into something else. In 1904, the horses simply were sold and the enormous Breeding Barn relegated to incidental use.

The model farm began to languish, too. Whereas in those same years other farmers were intensifying and streamlining their dairy operations, the farm operations at Shelburne meandered along without real direction. Income from items such as premium-quality butter pats for the New York Central wasn't enough to offset operational expenses. Everything continued to look perfectly groomed, but there was no long-range policy being formulated. Mounting annual deficits were paid out of Lila's capital; nothing was done to avoid them; no solutions were considered.

Seward Webb's other fortunes were fading, too. The Wagner Company had been involved in patent litigation with Pullman for years. By the end of the 1890s, Pullman triumphed and swallowed Wagner whole. Webb resigned as president effective New Year's Eve of 1899.

By 1904, Lila's diaries depict a strangely lonely existence. In the midst of the ceaseless activity occasioned by house parties, growing children, and constant travel, she usually dined alone. Her husband took his meals in his room. The interior stairway connecting the third-floor wardrobe room with Dr. Webb's bedroom on the floor below made it difficult to monitor people going to and from his bedroom ever since its installation. It seemed at times as though no one went in or out at all. Besides his valet, Tom MacIntee, Webb's only regular companion was his physician, Dr. Bingham.

Actually, there were a total of five men discreetly going in and out of Dr. Webb's room all day long. They had no other responsibilities in the household except caring for him. Since Shelburne was typically full of guests, the private stair from the third-floor wardrobe room became a diplomatic necessity. The constant comings and goings of Seward Webb's private retainers otherwise might have looked peculiar. Of course, Lila and the family all knew what was happening, but many who visited did not. Whenever inquiries were made about the doctor himself, the family all colluded in a polite fiction that he was "in poor health."

If Seward Webb was unable to obtain morphine, as occasionally happened, his valet would sleep at the top of the private stairway in order to be close at hand. Even when the supplies of the drug were plentiful, Webb's personal rhythms were totally out of synch with the rest of the household. He took his meals whenever he wanted, sometimes at very odd hours. His food was specially prepared in a private kitchen adjacent to the main one downstairs. Webb's secretary, Graham Kerr, directed what was essentially a shadow staff, operating independently of Walter Woodgate. According to family members, it was Kerr who got the doctor his morphine.

Lila was devastated by her husband's condition, but she didn't stay home and fret. The majestic tides of society swept her from one resort and house party to the next. She would leave New York on a January evening for a day at Shelburne, return the following night, and continue on to a round of receptions and parties. The next month, she might go to NE-HA-SA-NE for a few days to chaperone a party of Frederica's friends. Two weeks later, she would be traveling alone to Palm Beach en route to Havana. At home in New York or Shelburne, she took long walks—sometimes four, sometimes five, sometimes even twelve miles. Her diaries almost never mentioned her husband.

Seward Webb's wife was an intelligent woman, but she was also very much the product of an age where wives deferred totally to their husbands. The commanding man that Lila had married had reneged on his expected role. Trapped in the clutches of morphine, he was no longer able to care about much of anything. She was psychologically unequipped to usurp his traditionally dominant male role. And no one else had the will, or the power, to stand up against the morphine. Humiliated by his condition, and baffled as to what in the world to do about it, Lila resigned herself to the role of coconspirator and did her best to disguise the truth from strangers. The "I told you so" attitude of many of the Vanderbilts made things even more painful.

Every so often, Dr. Webb would pull himself together and make an appearance. He managed to take his private car to Groton to settle his youngest son, Vanderbilt, in school in September 1904. Lila's diary notes the occasional trips he made to New York with his brother Creighton or his son Watson. In the summer of 1905, he chartered the yacht *Sagamore* to cruise along the New England coast. He attended dinners and receptions—his own as well as those of others—occasionally. He tended to show up late, however, impeccably dressed and beautifully mannered, only to disappear again when no one was looking. Lila kept her gracious smile and made excuses.

Increasingly, it was Lila to whom the farm staff turned for instructions. She did her best, but efficient farm management was not her forte. It was the great irony of Shelburne that at its seeming peak, a cancer was eating away at its heart. As if things weren't hard enough for her already, Lila then went completely deaf.

She had been hard of hearing throughout her life, and after the birth of each of her children, the deafness seemed a little worse. By the mid-nineties, she was forced to rely on a little black box with a wire connected to her ear. She would aim this contraption at people, struggle with the volume control, and hope for the best. It never worked very well, and she never entirely mastered the art of reading lips.

However, life went on. "Thirty-two in house party," Lila wrote on one page of her 1905 diary. "Very jolly." On her son Watson's twenty-first birthday, she organized festivities appropriate for the son of an English milord. "Over 100 farmers

came to lunch," she noted in July of 1905. "All
the men wrote their names in our register. . . .
Watson made his first speech." That night there
was a dinner for twenty-four in the marble room
at Shelburne, and a late-night supper in the annex. "Watson says he has had a *great* birthday,"
she noted the following day.

The October 1905 wedding of Frederica Vanderbilt Webb to Ralph Pulitzer, son of publishing
baron Joseph Pulitzer, was one of those glittering
Edwardian social events that still manage to take
our breath away. Shelburne House was brimful
of languid beauties in high-necked dresses and
picture hats, and rich gentlemen up from New
York. The railroad yard at Shelburne village was
full of private Pullmans and the lakeshore was
lined with yachts. Frederica took her vows kneel-
ing on a pillow embroidered with diamonds—
the same one her mother had knelt upon in 1881.
Riotous laughter, dancing, and champagne were
the order of that day. Seward Webb managed an
appearance, but only a brief one. Few of the
guests ever dreamed that Lila Webb later remembered 1905 as the worst period of her life.

Increasingly, her husband remained at Shelburne with his private staff. Every evening at
five, he engaged in the same private ritual: He
drove himself around his property in a carriage.
One can imagine the solitude of the place at that
hour, the workers gone to supper, the guests con-
gregating at the house before dinner. The master
of Shelburne was alone on his manicured thousands of acres, alone to savor the vast mountain
views, the freshness and clarity of the evening
air, the wonders of burgeoning spring or flame-
colored autumn, the beauty of the many fine
buildings he had built. He is a poignant figure
seen from the vantage point of our day, driving
through his deep forests in tweeds and perfect
linen, gazing at the place he loved so very much,
thinking who knows what.

In 1917, at the age of sixty-six, Webb succumbed to rheumatoid arthritis and was confined
to a wheelchair. He still took his evening drives
around Shelburne; he continued to do that by
himself until his death. Other times, he had to
be wheeled around. He sat erect and imposing
in his chair, was gruff to the servants, and especially fond of a pair of Scottie dogs he kept on
his lap. In photographs from this period, he looks
pinched and unhappy. It is to his credit, however, that no one but his valet and Mr. Wood-

Dr. Webb in later years. "Increasingly, [he] remained at
Shelburne with his private staff."

gate ever saw him when he was in less than
perfect control.

By the time of the First World War, Lila was
personally managing all their northern properties, their houses at 136 Dunbar Road in Palm
Beach and 680 Fifth Avenue in New York, their
private cars, and everything else pertaining to
their still-elaborate life-style. Her husband's career was over, and their income was limited to
what was left of her inheritance. The cash portion, of course, had been spent long ago. The
interest from her $5 million trust was substantial,
but in order to keep Shelburne and everything
else going, she had to borrow money. Her
brother Fred, remembering how Lila's intercession with their father long ago had saved his own
inheritance, now came to her aid. For the rest

of her life, he gave her whatever funds she needed.

There was a major change at Shelburne Farms around this time. Back in 1910, Lila's son J. Watson Webb had married Electra Havemeyer, daughter of sugar millionaire and art collector H. O. Havemeyer. In 1913, the young Watson Webbs asked Seward and Lila for permission to fix up one of the unoccupied former farmhouses on the property. The house in question was built of brick and enjoyed a view of the lake and mountains similar to the one from Shelburne House. Delighted, the elder Webbs agreed, tossing in the southern thousand acres of the estate (including the Breeding Barn) as a gift in trust for Watson's, and later Electra's, lifetime. Thus was Southern Acres born. Eventually, the Brick House itself would grow to almost mansion proportions, and the Watson Webbs would divide their time between the polo fields of Old Westbury, Long Island, and the family estate in Vermont.

By 1920, Shelburne Farms was a magnificent anachronism. Seemingly changeless, it had become a monument to the worldview—not to mention the affluence—of a generation that was swiftly passing. Picturesque teams of horses still tilled the fields, an English cook and a large staff still catered to the regular house parties, Walter Woodgate still maintained the luxury for which the Webbs were well known. Although Lila traveled frequently, her home was at Shelburne, and she maintained it as magnificently as ever.

On October 29, 1926, Seward Webb died at Shelburne. The first thing his three sons did was go to his room, empty all the morphine from their father's safe, and make a bonfire of it in the grate. Seward Webb had been little more than a shell for years. However, as long as he lived, the world he had created seemed as though it would never change. Almost the moment he was gone, that world began to show cracks.

Lila had been cutting small corners for twenty years before her husband's death. It would have astonished the world to know it, but the Webbs were in bad financial straits as early as Frederica's 1905 wedding to Ralph Pulitzer. The *Elfreda* had been sold for economy's sake by 1910. After the First World War, the private golf course at Shelburne was reduced from eighteen to nine holes to save on maintenance. At about the same time, their New York house was sold to John D. Rocke-

Ralph and Frederica Pulitzer on their honeymoon in 1905.

feller. Whenever in town thereafter, Lila stayed in a rented apartment on Park Avenue.

In the fall of 1927, a freak frost ruined the specimen box and bay trees in the garden at Shelburne. It was a bad omen. By 1930, the garden was beginning to shrink and the garden staff was reduced. Lila was running ever shorter of cash, in spite of the help from her brother Fred. Mr. Woodgate remained, and Lila still continued her stately progression from house to house, from party to party. Her children now had children of their own and they all gathered regularly at Shelburne.

By 1933, the remote corners of Lila's big house were beginning to look a little shabby. In any case, the mistress of Shelburne House would not be troubled by it for very long. On July 10, 1936, Lila Osgood Vanderbilt Webb died at Shelburne, Vermont. She was seventy-six years old.

Lila left all her property to her four children: Frederica Vanderbilt Webb Jones, married to Ralph Pulitzer in 1905, and to Cyril Jones in 1924; J. Watson Webb, married in 1910 to Electra Havemeyer; W. Seward Webb, Jr., married in 1911 to Gertrude Gaynor; and Vanderbilt Webb, married to Aileen Osborn in 1912. Nineteen thirty-six was not the depth of the Depression, but it was still not a very optimistic period in U.S. history. Shelburne Farms, the great creative achievement of their father's life, to his children must have seemed hopelessly out of step with the times.

Primogeniture, the right of the eldest son to inherit property to the exclusion of other siblings, is alien to American custom. This has avoided much autocratic evil, but many fine and grand old properties are inadvertent victims of our democratic traditions of distribution. In the case of Shelburne, however, the estate was so vast that most of the heirs were already living there, at least for part of each year. There was room for all, and other properties with which to make adjustments, so the estate didn't have to be broken up.

Seward Webb, Jr., and his wife weren't so interested in Shelburne. They took Lila's Palm Beach property and moved down there. Watson and Electra Webb continued to occupy the Brick House on Southern Acres, and took NE-HA-SA-NE, as well. Frederica's share of Shelburne was an undeveloped tract of estate land on Shelburne Point. The youngest sibling, Vanderbilt Webb, took over the main house and the grounds inside the North Gate. The original main gate, or South Gate, now led to Southern Acres. The original farm entrance, or North Gate, had become the new entrance to Shelburne Farms.

Lila's children all loved Shelburne. It was a daughter-in-law, Electra Havemeyer Webb, however, who was the first to appreciate its historic and architectural importance. In 1930, George Vanderbilt's daughter Cornelia and her husband John Cecil had opened Biltmore to tourists. Electra Webb wanted to do the same with

Shelburne, arguing it was unlikely that another estate of its scale or quality would ever be built again in Vermont, or perhaps anywhere. She felt that people would want to see it, that it could and should be the Biltmore of the North. Her husband, Watson, categorically disagreed with her, and nothing came of the idea.

Vanderbilt Webb, the man who now occupied Shelburne House, was forty-five when his mother died. He had a life and a career of his own in New York. He felt a responsibility for the family estate, however, and spent summers in the big house with his own family. There was still a butler at Shelburne in the 1930s, plus assorted maids, a cook and a helper, and a handful of locals hired temporarily each summer. Van's son, Derick, who had attended Cornell Agricultural College, became farm manager in 1938. It was Derick Webb who finally introduced modern methods to Shelburne's diminished farm operation.

At the start of the Second World War, huge old places such as Shelburne Farms seemed to have no future at all. Vanderbilt Webb decided, regretfully, to tear the big house down. In anticipation of this, the heating plant and a delightful cast-iron conservatory adjacent to the marble room were ripped out, and the scrap donated to the war effort. For the first time since its construction, Shelburne House was cold and unoccupied during the long Vermont winter. Plaster cracked, foundations shifted, and dust accumulated.

Dr. Webb at NE-HA-SA-NE, his camp in the Adirondacks.

The Inn at Shelburne Farms today.

However, when good weather returned, so did the Webbs, at least for a month. During the war, gas rationing precluded mowing the fairways of the golf course, and it reverted to meadow. The huge servants' wing was closed off permanently and roof leaks went unattended. The marble swimming pool was filled. The pergola behind it succumbed to rot and had to be pulled down. The retaining wall along the western edge of the gardens collapsed into Lake Champlain. And yet, the place still shambled along rather grandly. It was magnificent in its way, and still much loved by the family. They eventually decided not to tear it down, although that decision may have stemmed more from the cost of demolition than from anything else.

Vanderbilt Webb died in 1956. When summer came, his son, Derick, assumed his father's role as the master of Shelburne House. Derick Webb had farmed Shelburne since the late 1930s and lived with his family in the Orchard House. He had actually made Shelburne self-supporting. Every summer throughout the 1950s and 1960s, he opened the big house, just as his father had. His own children galloped up and down its vast corridors and across its cavernous rooms. They entertained friends from school with cookouts and picnics and rock-and-roll parties.

Webb was able to keep the farm in the black, but costs and taxes were rising at an alarming rate. He was fearful that his own children might not be able to do the same. In 1967, he hired a man named Dan Kiley to devise a plan for the future of Shelburne Farms. The Kiley scheme envisioned preservation of the main house and some of the farm buildings on reduced acreage near the lake. The "outside" land, as it was called, was to be sold off to developers. Webb summoned his children to a family conclave on the south piazza. He described the Kiley plan and invited their reactions.

Whatever one might say about the 1960s, it was a time of idealism and commitment. Derick Webb's children were appalled at the thought of selling off chunks of the family estate to real estate developers. They promised then and there to stay on the land if their father wouldn't sell. Although they did not know how they would save Shelburne Farms, they were determined to find a way.

For a great family estate to survive the passage of time, there must be an emotional attachment to the place. Only the very committed will put up with the hardship, grief, disappointment, financial peril, individual sacrifice, and sheer demands on one's time that the preservation of a great country estate will inevitably require. Shelburne Farms exists today because the Webbs loved it, believed in it, and were willing to devote their lives to it. People such as these are not the norm. The nation is fortunate that this family was in charge here.

In 1972, Derick Webb's children founded Shelburne Farms Resources, Inc. (SFR). The principal goal of this organization was the promotion of sound ecological practices and land preservation; Shelburne's historic architectural fabric was barely a part of the equation. The Webbs tried everything—camps for poor kids, crafts cooperatives, farmers' markets, forestry programs, judicious land sales to a land conservancy, music festivals, you name it. After four years, they convinced their father that Shelburne could indeed survive without dismemberment.

In 1976, Derick Webb donated the big house, the Coach Barn, and the Farm Barn to SFR. Greatly encouraged, his children continued the good fight, rarely making ends meet but always pulling through the year somehow or other. SFR's educational and cultural programs proliferated. However, the big house was a headache. The roof was rotten and the place looked shabbier every year. By the early 1980s, it was approaching a crisis state.

At this point, enter another daughter-in-law, SFR's president Marilyn Webb, married to Derick Webb's son Alec. During functions at the big house, Mrs. Webb had observed that the crowds were always extremely interested to see and know about the house. In 1983, she decided the most logical thing to do with it was to convert it to a country inn. This required the approval of SFR's board. SFR held title to the land now, not the Webbs. Its board of trustees determined future policy, not the Webb family. The board's twenty-five trustees were seriously divided on the issue. Many felt the plan was economically unfeasible. Marilyn and Alec Webb were committed to it, however, and in the end their voices proved the most persuasive.

Plans for the restoration/conversion were drawn up by Burlington architect Martin Tierney. Here, truly, was a man with a feel for old houses. His conversion plan scrupulously respected the original character of the building. As a result of his architectural tact, staying at Shelburne today is quite like staying in a very big private house.

The price tag for the conversion was $1.4 million. SFR had nowhere near this kind of cash. If ever there was a skillful fund-raiser, however, it was Marilyn Webb. The local community, which cares very much about the fate of Shelburne, was mobilized. One individual contributed fifty thousand dollars for a new slate roof. Old Deerfield Fabrics donated all the wallpaper and upholstery fabrics in exchange for rights to market a Shelburne House line of products. The Blodgett Group, after being shown a vintage newspaper article describing the original kitchen they had outfitted for Dr. Webb, donated an entirely new one for the inn. Oneida Silversmiths donated the cutlery; Villeroy and Boch provided china; Sherwin Williams tossed in eighty gallons of paint; and one octogenarian woman sent a twenty-five-dollar check with a note saying, "Shelburne Farms stands for my values and for Vermont." It would seem that at last the Webbs had become real Vermonters.

The people who worked on the restoration put to shame the old saw about the supposed unavailability today of good craftsmanship. Contractor Mark Neagley found plumbers who competently reconditioned the vintage plumbing fixtures, electricians who carefully fished new lines without damaging antique paneling and wall treatments, and a husband and wife plastering team whose repairs to the elaborate molded ceilings and cornices are indistinguishable from the original work.

If there was a fly in the ointment, it was the fate of the kitchen wing. Closed since the Second World War, it was in an advanced state of deterioration. The determination was made that if the inn was to succeed financially, the kitchen wing had to go. Demolition took place in early 1986. What is there now is a discreet parking lot, plus a restoration of the earliest kitchen addition. The work has been done carefully, the restored wing looks precisely as it did before the shingled house was bricked, and 35,000 square feet still do remain at Shelburne House. However, the impressive silhouette of the place has been diminished. And the house today, which in other respects seems miraculously preserved, is deprived of the extensive pantries and service accommodations that were crucial to its existence as a private residence.

The Inn at Shelburne Farms, as the house is now called, opened to the public in 1987. Almost immediately, it became Shelburne Farms' largest source of income, even though it takes guests only from May to October. The heating plant, scrapped in the early forties, has yet to be replaced. As of this writing, Shelburne Farms no longer has deficits, thanks to Seward and Lila's great big house.

One's first impression of the place today is very similar to Henry Hazelton's back in 1901. Certainly the scale is as impressive as ever. Once through the gate, the first building one passes is the aged and noble Farm Barn. Close up, it's not in perfect condition, but a restoration was begun in 1990. The drive winds picturesquely onward through deep forests and sculpted swards of meadow. When one finally glimpses the glittering waters of Lake Champlain, it is across a broad vale, with the peaks of the Adirondacks as a backdrop. In the distance, at water's edge, is the many-chimneyed bulk of Shelburne House. When one finally pulls up beneath the old-fashioned porte cochere and steps inside the big wood paneled hall, there is nary a commercial touch in sight. All the hotel operations are carefully hidden away. One might as well be arriving at one's own great-grandparents' house—assuming one is among the elect.

The interior decor no longer has the density it had in Lila Webb's time. Visually, the house is much brighter and more spare. Shelburne still looks like a period house, however. Three-quarters of the furniture in it today was there in Seward and Lila Webb's time. The experience of staying here certainly has many parallels with—if not quite the same texture as—being a guest of the Webbs.

About 70,000 people visited Shelburne Farms in 1990, not including guests at the inn. Shelburne Farms, Inc., the successor to SFR, employs about fifty people, half of whom work year-round. Another fifty volunteers work as tour guides, bus drivers, program instructors, and so on. There is never a problem getting volunteers; the surrounding community continues to be deeply concerned with Shelburne's welfare. The dairy operation today is modern and profitable. Environmentally oriented educational programs and cultural festivals continue to proliferate. For the moment at least, it would seem that the Webbs' Vermont estate is safe.

At Southern Acres, meanwhile, other Webbs continue to own and live on Webb land as they have for the last century. The Brick House is still private at this writing. It is occupied by J. Watson Webb, Jr., who for many years ran the Shelburne Museum. That museum started when Electra Webb begged her brother-in-law Vanderbilt not to sell his father's amazing collection of carriages, then still in the Coach Barn. It has grown to become a great outdoor museum of early American architecture, and the home of one of the most important collections of American folk art. Its development, it should be noted, has been entirely independent of Shelburne Farms. Other than physical proximity, these institutions have no connection whatsoever.

Nehasane—Lila's grandchildren eventually abandoned the picturesque capitalization—is gone. The Robertson lodge and 7,500 acres of land were sold by Webb heirs to the state of New York in 1979. In keeping with the "forever wild" policies of state conservation land, the abandoned lodge, as well as all other buildings on the property, were burned to the ground.

Such has been the fate of the works of Dr. William Seward Webb, a man crippled in his prime by drugs. However, if a person can be judged at least in part by what he leaves behind, then one should remember Webb kindly. His generous legacy remains. Shelburne Farms is a place of beauty and its purpose is to spread useful knowledge. This was Seward Webb's original intention, and three generations later, his mission is being carried out.

Chapter 5
FLORHAM

Florham

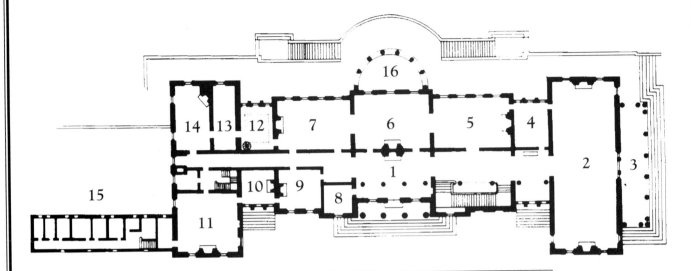

1st Floor
1. Main Hall
2. Drawing Room
3. Piazza
4. Organ Chamber
5. Library
6. Salon
7. Dining Room
8. Dressing Room
9. Reception Room
10. Den
11. Billiard Room
12. Butler's Pantry
13. Serving Pantry
14. Breakfast Room
15. Service Court

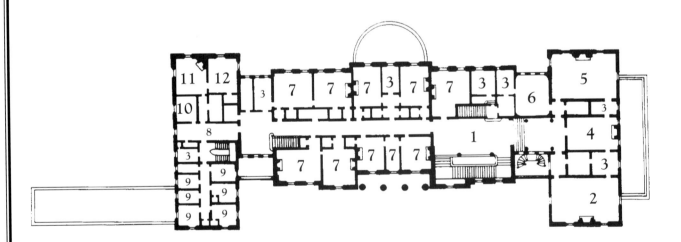

2nd Floor
1. Second Floor Hall
2. Ruth Twombly's Bedroom
3. Baths
4. Boudoir
5. Florence Twombly's Bedroom
6. Mr. Twombly's Bedroom
7. Guestrooms
8. Service Corridor
9. Servant's Bedrooms
10. Sewing Room
11. Housekeeper's Sitting Room
12. Housekeeper's Bedroom

Florham, the New Jersey mansion "whence Florence Vanderbilt Twombly conducted her long reign over old-guard New York society."

Location: Convent Station, Morris County, New Jersey
Architects: McKim, Mead & White
    (William Rutherford Mead [1846–1928], supervising architect)
Commissioned by: Hamilton McKown Twombly (1849–1910)
Main house completed: 1897

FLORHAM is the English-style country manse—located in suburban New Jersey—from which Florence Vanderbilt Twombly conducted her long reign over old-guard New York society. Like Mrs. Astor before her, Florence Twombly possessed a clear personal vision of exactly who was, and was not, acceptable. Her niece Grace (Mrs. Cornelius Vanderbilt III) may have been the queen of society, but Mrs. Twombly was the dean of the New York nobility.

Florence Twombly was a glacial grande dame who bothered little to dispel her intimidating image. She was just a slip of a woman, barely a hundred pounds. Yet the reputation of her enormous fortune, added to that of her cold and imperious manner, produced an image of autocratic terror that few dared to contradict.

Florence Adele Vanderbilt dressed for a masquerade ball in 1883.

Florham is actually a conjunction of its creators' first names, Florence and Hamilton. The estate in both its form and function was imbued with Englishness. It was not a reproduction of any single English house, but, rather, it represented an English way of aristocratic country life, complete with manorial house, working farm, and extensive acreage. Florham was an idealized and technologically up-to-date American version of the English country seat, whose owners unselfconsciously presumed to a certain level of privilege and power.

Hamilton Twombly was a Harvard man (1871) and a New England blue blood whose family had been in this country since 1658. His father was a rich Boston businessman, and he left his son $20 million worth of railroad and paper-manufacturing interests. Young Twombly was more than a fortunate heir; he was also a talented money manager and an inspired venture capitalist. He came to the attention of William Henry Vanderbilt early in his career. Vanderbilt hired him and introduced him to his family. This was how Hamilton met Florence.

The couple married on November 21, 1877, at a time when the case over the Commodore's will was in all the papers. The Twombly wedding, at old St. Bartholomew's on Madison Avenue, was deluged by thousands of uninvited curiosity seekers. Inside the church, a handful of ushers (inaccurately reported by *The New York Times* to have been drunk) struggled to repel mobs of eager street people. Outside, a horse bolted and knocked down the canopy. When the ceremony was over, the newlyweds at first were unable to get out of the church.

Escaping finally from St. Bartholomew's they were pursued by a high-spirited mob of several thousand right to William Henry Vanderbilt's front door at 459 Fifth Avenue. There, 300 invited guests celebrated uneasily within, while an estimated 2,500 potential crashers loitered noisily on the street outside. This experience undoubtedly contributed to the Twomblys' later exaggerated avoidance of publicity.

Hamilton Twombly was William Henry Vanderbilt's favorite son-in-law. After Vanderbilt's death in 1885, it was Twombly who managed the family's extensive investments. He enjoyed close and cordial relations with his brothers-in-law Cornelius and William K. Vanderbilt. When railroad matters or important family business had

Mr. and Mrs. William H. Vanderbilt following the newly married Hamilton Twomblys up the aisle at St. Bartholomew's Church in New York City.

to be settled and no Vanderbilts were available, it was Twombly to whom Chauncey Depew or the elder Morgan or Edward Harriman came.

Eventually, Hamilton Twombly sat on the boards of fifty-nine different corporations, including the New York Central, the Mutual Life Insurance Company, the Depew Improvement Company, Western Union, the New York Mutual Gas Light Company, and multiple railroads. Today, he is remembered primarily as a railroad man. His real genius, however, lay in picking long-shot, nonrailroad-related investments.

Notable among these was the Cerro de Pasco copper mine in Peru, which made him a fortune in and of itself. Another was the sulphur industry in Texas and Louisiana. Shortly after the turn of the century, Twombly met a man named Herman Frasch who had invented a method of extracting sulphur from Louisiana salt domes. Twombly backed Frasch in a fifty-fifty venture, the profits of which exceeded everybody's wildest expectations. Throughout the Depression years, the Texas Gulf Sulphur Company paid Twombly's widow over $3 million a year. (When the sulphur ran out, they struck oil.)

After their marriage, the Twomblys demonstrated the typical Vanderbiltian eagerness to develop a country place. They discovered a sylvan region to the east of Morristown, New Jersey, and proceeded in 1887 to rent a house there. It is uncertain what first attracted them to Morristown. Possibly the fact that Florence's Uncle Jerry (Cornelius Jeremiah Vanderbilt) had rented houses there in summers past played some role. However, Morristown had a reputation for discreet elitism, which appealed to people such as Hamilton and Florence Twombly.

Morristown, according to a 1902 New York Herald, was "the Millionaire City of the Nation. It contains the richest and least known colony of wealthy people in the world." Supposedly, there were once two hundred millionaire residents within a three-mile radius of the center of town. Prominent Morristown estate owners included Marcellus Hartley Dodge, chairman of the Remington Arms Company; Charles W. Harkness of Standard Oil millions; Charles W. Armour of meat-packing fame; and Eugene Higgens, dubbed America's "most luxurious unmarried man" by Ward McAllister.

Madison Avenue, the street on which Florham's imposing gates still stand, was called in the breathless prose of the time, the "Street of Millionaires" and the "Finest Four Miles in the World." Rich men were inundating rural outposts from Georgia to the Adirondacks at the end of the nineteenth century. Those who chose Morristown had a signature expansiveness. The estate of insurance czar Richard McCurdy, for example, struck The New York Times as "a modest place in Morristown. At a quick look one would take it for the Metropolitan Museum of Art, or the Fountainbleau [sic] Palace."

In 1883, the Delaware, Lackawanna and Western Railroad initiated the famous Millionaires' Express. This train boasted a club car that really was a private club. Membership, which cost sixty dollars, was contingent on the approval of the other members. The car was furnished with white wicker armchairs; Bromo-Seltzer was

Hamilton McKown Twombly, "a talented money manager and an inspired venture capitalist."

offered in the morning and high tea (in addition to a full bar) on the way home.

Architect George B. Post commuted to Manhattan on this train, galloping to the station in a four-in-hand. A footman waiting on Market Street would grab the coach and hop aboard as Mr. Post roared by. As they clattered into the station plaza, Post would hand the reins to a groom, pull off his duster, put on his New York jacket, and sprint for the train. A fortune in horseflesh and equipages converged on the Morristown station each morning and evening, in a show perhaps matched only by Bellevue Avenue in Newport during July.

The Twomblys figured prominently among the millionaires who remained generally aloof from Morristown's earlier and more diverse summer colony. These early arrivals included Tom Thumb, the world's most famous dwarf, and

Thomas Nast, the acerbic cartoonist. The publisher Charles Scribner kept a place there, as did the daughter of Hetty Green, the famous miser. For many years Otto Kahn, the cultured and patrician senior partner of Kuhn, Loeb & Company, spent summers at Morristown, until a pervasive local anti-Semitism drove him to Long Island.

Morristown had several attractions for rich newcomers. It had an impressive inventory of picturesque Colonial buildings, quiet streets shaded by gracious elms, a surrounding countryside that was wide and luscious, and historical cachet from its days as one of Washington's Revolutionary War headquarters. The town had an old-line, blue-blooded image. It also enjoyed a longstanding intellectual tradition by virtue of its many "dame schools," which were private boarding academies usually run by educated spinsters.

Despite Morristown's growing grandeur, it managed (as it still does) to preserve a curious anonymity. This suited the Twomblys perfectly. As social historian Dixon Wecter put it, "To the old aristocracy notoriety is a type of social nudism." The passion for privacy dovetailed neatly with other new attitudes then evolving among upper-class Americans. Prime among these was the perception (then quite new to the American experience) that tooting one's own horn was vulgar. Morristown was an ideal kind of a place, at least for a certain sort of person. The Twomblys liked it well enough to rent a house called Cecilhurst, belonging to George H. Danforth. In 1890, they decided to settle there, and they bought the property.

Twombly selected McKim, Mead & White as the architects for his new country seat. William Rutherford Mead was the partner in charge of the project. After working in the office of architect Russell Sturgis and studying in Florence, Mead later became a partner of Charles Follen McKim and Stanford White. Here, he mostly occupied himself with engineering problems and client relations. However, he was in charge of the Twombly job, and his predominating design input made Florham an anomaly among the firm's great houses.

Twombly told Mead he wanted a house "on the order of an English country gentleman." Mead subsequently wrote an amusing letter to Frank Millet, an antiques dealer, in which he

suggested that neither he nor Twombly knew exactly what that might mean. The letter, of course, was tongue-in-cheek. Mead knew perfectly well what Twombly wanted, and he delivered it in full. If Twombly's wife had any say in the design of Florham, there is no record of it.

The project got off to a slow start. For a while—about three years, actually—Twombly couldn't decide whether to "mansionize" Cecilhurst or build something new. He changed his mind repeatedly, driving his architects and landscapers to distraction. The thorn in his side was the railroad bed of the Delaware, Lackawanna and Western, which ran parallel to Madison Avenue a short distance to the north of his house. Cecilhurst was actually sandwiched between the tracks and the avenue; when a train went by, the noise was intrusive. Twombly eventually bought almost a thousand acres to the north of the tracks. However, this did not remedy the problem of the proximity of the tracks to the house.

Well before these land acquisitions were complete, Twombly hired the eminent Frederick Law Olmsted to lay out his new grounds. This was in the early nineties, during which time Olmsted was immersed in his epic labors at Biltmore. Olmsted argued strongly for relocating Twombly's house to a site north of the railroad tracks, out of sight of Madison Avenue. This meant tearing down Cecilhurst, a scheme the client alternately endorsed and refused.

"As you expected," Stanford White wrote to Olmsted in March of 1891, "he has reverted to his idea to change his house . . . changing his entrance and everything." By this time, Olmsted was in failing health, though few people knew it. The great American landscape architect was growing progressively more forgetful, morose, and even violent. Very probably, he was the victim of an undiagnosed case of Alzheimer's disease.

Olmsted lived for another decade, but from a professional standpoint he was disabled by 1893. Fortunately, he had trained his son Frederick from childhood in the art of landscape design. This young man was the repository of all his brilliant father's hopes and dreams, a situation that would have defeated many people. He continued his father's work, and to a great extent disguised the older man's growing incapacity.

Twombly, among many other clients, got a first-class job.

Perhaps due to the Olmsteds' crush of work in those years, combined with the degeneration of the senior partner, the choice of Twombly's new house site fell by default to McKim, Mead & White, and specifically to partner Stanford White. Olmsted approved of White's selection, however, pointing out to Twombly that the new view would be "perfectly within your control; as much so as if you owned the State of New Jersey." The grandeur of this observation finally convinced Hamilton Twombly.

The decision to tear down Cecilhurst, route a new driveway through a tunnel under the tracks, and erect a new house on a high bluff overlooking a thousand private acres to the north profoundly altered the aspect of the property. The Twombly residence would henceforth be invisible from Madison Avenue. Passersby on the street of mansions would marvel at the Twomblys' gates, but only the elect would ever know what lay within. This sense of remoteness from the everyday world is a crucial ingredient in any successful country-estate plan.

Design work on the new house was begun in 1893. Construction started in 1895, and the family was moved in by the spring of 1897. The cost, exclusive of furnishings, was seven hundred thousand dollars.

It is often asserted that Florham is a copy—some go so far as to call it a replica—of Sir Christopher Wren's late-seventeenth-century addition to Hampton Court Palace. Americans love to call their large houses replicas of European palaces, often with little real justification, and frequently out of a residual national sense of cultural inferiority. Florham indeed bears some resemblance to Wren's Hampton Court wing. Wren, working on the eve of the ascension to the English throne of George I, employed symmetry and brickwork in a restrained, classically influenced style whose later examples came to be called Georgian. Florham is an example of fully evolved Georgian Revival architecture. Its design and that of Wren's Hampton Court addition are both drawn from a common architectural vocabulary.

Florham is an enormous three-part composition, built of brick, delicately detailed with limestone, and topped with numerous symmetrically placed chimneys and a classical limestone balustrade. Originally, the house was graced with shutters. The central bay rises three full stories and boasts a recessed, double-height, colonnaded entry. This southern facade looms dramatically at the end of a sweeping, landscaped drive. The garden facade gazes north across an elaborate terraced garden to the blue reaches of a distant horizon.

The interiors of Florham reflected the social prominence of the family for which McKim, Mead & White designed it. The main hall with its marble floors and pilasters ran perpendicular to the front door and extended almost the full length of the house. At its eastern extremity was a vast drawing room, hung with tapestries, lit by a trio of enormous chandeliers, furnished with English antiques and overstuffed velvet sofas, and decorated with silk-shaded lamps and family pictures in silver frames. Outside the door to the drawing room was a built-in organ with a two-story pipe loft.

Elsewhere along the hall, polished mahogany doors led to a library, small salon, dining room, billiard room, and assorted service facilities. The major public rooms were all hung with silk damask and furnished in a decidedly English style. A broad marble stairway led to the second floor, where bathrooms in the larger bedroom suites had working fireplaces. There were more guest suites on the third floor. Kitchens and servants' quarters were found in the basement, as well as in a subsidiary kitchen wing.

By virtue of its magnificence, Florham conveyed a vivid message about the Twomblys. The ultimate impact of this house, however, lies not in its size but in its balanced architectural beauty and the fineness of its detail and craftsmanship.

The distinguished Georgian exteriors of the main house, as well as complementary designs for an adjacent carriage house, are usually attributed to Charles McKim. The design is as competent overall as that of Fred Vanderbilt's very different house at Hyde Park, New York, which was designed by the firm at almost the same time.

For its day, Florham was extremely up-to-date in terms of kitchens, bathrooms, heating plants, refrigeration, and so on. At the same time, it sounded an appropriate stylistic note amidst Morristown's Revolutionary-period Georgian architecture. The classical references of Florham's exterior—and Georgian architecture, after all, drew upon many of the forms and proportions of

Above: Florham from the air. According to Frederick Law Olmsted, Mr. Twombly's view was "perfectly within your control; as much so as if you owned the State of New Jersey."

Below: McKim, Mead & White's Florham; "an example of fully evolved Georgian Revival architecture."

antiquity—also reflected the architectural tastes of the so-called American Renaissance dominating the arts at the time.

As is still the custom with houses of this scale, the interior decoration was contracted out; that for Florham went to the famous New York firm of William Baumgarten & Sons. Baumgarten's founder, interestingly, was the same man who designed the astonishing late-Victorian decor at William Henry Vanderbilt's 640 Fifth Avenue. Florham's Classical Revival interiors illustrate just how quickly and how far fashionable taste had evolved in merely a decade.

Aside from siting the house Stanford White made minimal contributions to the Twombly job. His involvement seems to have been limited to advice concerning the interior decoration and the location of appropriate furnishings. In 1893, for example, he paid $179,000 on Hamilton Twombly's behalf for a set of tapestries from the famous Uffizi Gallery in Florence. This is an indication of the scale on which White was accustomed to operating.

Florham; the main stair.

Florham; the drawing room.

"The main hall with its marble halls and pilasters ran perpendicular to the front door and extended almost the full length of the house."

McKim, Mead & White labored on Florham until 1899. They designed and sited every adjunct necessary for a gentleman's exemplary country seat. The Florham farm complex was completed in 1894. It housed specimen Guernsey cattle and an equestrian stud farm. The carriage house, finished at about the same time as the main house, accommodated forty horses, together with requisite carriages and quarters for grooms. There was a greenhouse complex—reputedly the largest in New Jersey—attached to a handsome orangery. There were scenic drives, distant vistas, and manicured lawns and fields.

In 1899, the firm created an elegant gate lodge on Madison Avenue and attached it to a set of splendid entrance gates—all of which are fortunately extant. The main gate led to a winding drive that proceeded to the mouth of a tunnel handsomely finished in dressed stone. This tunnel, completed at a cost of $23,000, ran beneath the railroad tracks. Due to the architects' skill, one hardly perceived that there were tracks there at all.

The $23,000 railway tunnel on the main
approach to Florham; "one hardly
perceived that there were tracks there
at all."

Florham; the entrance gates on Madison
Avenue, Convent Station, New Jersey."

Plunging into the darkened tunnel, one left
the world of the commonplace. On the other
side, one emerged into a sort of never-never land
of architectural and horticultural perfection.
That level of perfection, in maintenance as well
as design, was a large part of Florham's special
charm.

Hamilton Twombly was a fastidious man and
a perfectionist. Florham was his great passion.
He felt it was not enough simply to raise Guern-
seys; they also had to be prizewinners and champion milkers. He did not engage just any
gardener but, rather, Arthur Harrington, whom
he lured from the royal conservatories at Kew in
England. His orchids and chrysanthemums were
famous prizewinners. The stud farm produced
champion hackneys. Florham's dairy farm was so
productive, it had its own local delivery route.
Under Twombly's meticulous management, the

Florham estate became not only a showplace but
an economically viable agricultural unit. It was,
in fact, one of the few model farms of the era
that actually made a profit. This is not surprising
when one considers its owner's business acumen.

The Twomblys' Morristown estate was a world
unto itself: It had its own water and electrical
system, covered well over a thousand acres, and
employed many local people. Eighty men labored
in the gardens, greenhouses, and on the model
farm. Another thirty-two people worked in the
house itself. The house staff included an imposing butler by the name of Frederick Berles, a
man so formal that he was often taken for a guest.
Assisting Mr. Berles were five footmen dressed
in an elaborate livery of black shoes and stockings, black velvet knee breeches, striped vests in
Vanderbilt maroon and black, and maroon jack-
ets with sterling silver buttons. There was also

The model farm at Florham, designed by McKim, Mead & White. The central tower held a water tank.

The Orangerie, with original fenestration.

a French chef with five full-time helpers, numerous maids, as well as an in-house mason, painter, carpenter, and even a man who did nothing but cut blocks of ice.

The Twomblys gave many elaborate house parties at Florham. On one hand, invited guests could have anything they wanted (one hypochondriacal weekender gave a list of medicines to be stocked in his bathroom cabinet) and were coddled with every conceivable luxury and fashionable diversion. On the other, one had to do things Mrs. Twombly's way—and she was not one to change a habit.

For example, Florence Twombly was among the few in her set to serve cocktails before dinner. But *one* was everybody's limit, and that one drink had to be taken, standing up, in Florham's long marble hall. *Never* could it be taken into the gilt wood and tapestry-filled drawing room. Customs

loosened as the years passed, but Florence flatly refused to change her cocktail routine in any way.

At Florham, nobody was ever late, nothing was ever amiss, and everything invariably happened as planned. Even loud coughing was forbidden, and Florence on more than one occasion exiled her husband from the dinner table to the foot of the stairs until such time as his throat was clear. "I wish someone would just drop a plate!" remarked a guest back in the old days. There wasn't much chance of that, however. Florham was conceived for—and dedicated to—entertaining on a grand scale. It had to work well or it would not have worked at all.

The Twomblys didn't spend all their time at Florham. They had a town house at 684 Fifth Avenue, the gift of Florence's father. In 1896, they purchased a Newport villa on Ochre Point belonging to Catherine Lorillard Wolfe. Vinland, as the Newport house was called, was enlarged greatly by the Twomblys over the winter of 1907 to 1908. It was next door to The Breakers, the house that had been built by Florence's brother Cornelius Vanderbilt II. Florence spent every other summer at Vinland for sixty years.

Florence and Hamilton Twombly had four children, three girls and a boy. These children, incidentally, were forbidden to enter their mother's bedroom under any circumstances, except specific invitation. In 1896, while the main house at Florham was in the final stage of construction, the Twomblys' beautiful daughter Alice died of typhoid fever. The loss of his daughter didn't seem to affect Twombly's ability to press on with the development of his New Jersey estate, or to continue his lavish entertaining, or to husband his growing fortune.

During the July Fourth weekend of 1906, however, he lost his only son, Hamilton Junior. The boy was eighteen at the time, just graduated from Groton and working for the summer as a counselor at the Groton Summer Camp at Squam Lake, New Hampshire. While swimming at night, he developed a cramp and drowned.

Twombly Senior never recovered from the shock. He withdrew from society, began resigning his club memberships, and spent progressively less time at work. Within a few years, he had become almost a recluse, and Florham was dark and quiet. Without a son to inherit, he abandoned his experiments in horse breeding and scientific agriculture. The neglected model farm ceased to be profitable. By 1910, Twombly was dead, ostensibly the victim of tuberculosis. In reality, Hamilton Twombly had died of a broken heart.

His widow did not mourn for years or sequester herself. She was a woman who lived for entertaining and had three magnificent houses that were built expressly for that purpose. Her own $10 million inheritance hardly had been touched during her marriage. When Twombly died, he left her another $75 million. Ironically, the death of Hamilton Twombly signaled a new era of Florence's hospitality and the real beginning of Florham's heydey.

Spring and fall were the seasons for Florham. Every weekend, its mistress was surrounded by guests. This meant between twelve and thirty people staying every single Friday, Saturday, and Sunday. At least that many often went for lunch and dinner during the week. This was simply the routine; sometimes the parties were far larger. The guests arrived, usually with their own chauffeurs, maids, and valets, at teatime on Friday and stayed until after breakfast the following Monday morning. Really *big* dinners might include one hundred and fifty guests. On nights like this, Florence might hire Archer Gibson to come out from New York and play the organ during dinner.

The more Florence Twombly entertained, the more she developed a reputation for a peculiar mixture of intolerance and indulgence. There are many amusing Florence Twombly stories, the best one being the following:

Time: Monday morning, Labor Day, immediately prior to the First World War.

Place: An elegant Florham weekend; perhaps two dozen guests are in the house.

Scene: A gentleman guest spies his packed bags at the foot of the marble steps. "Why are my bags down here?" he inquires of a passing footman. "I was asked for the weekend and today is Labor Day." After communicating the matter to Mrs. Twombly, the footman returns. "Mrs. Twombly says that she has never heard of Labor Day, and that the weekend is over today, sir."

She was also unforgiving, and to decline an invitation to one of her dinners was to risk being dropped from her invitation list with utmost finality. Her nephew J. Watson Webb was once invited to dinner on the night of his wedding anniversary. He and his wife forwarded regrets, which so angered Florence that she didn't invite them again for *ten* years.

She was fussy too. During a visit to her sister Lila Webb at Shelburne, Florence asked the butler for a shawl. Her bags were packed in anticipation of the return trip to New York. Mr. Woodgate brought her one of Lila's shawls. Sweet-tempered Lila Webb looked as if she dressed in thrift shops. Florence glanced once at the proffered shawl and snarled, "I'm not *that* cold."

Florence was famous in society for the quality of her table. Her chef, Monsieur Joseph Donon (pronounced DOE-none—by the Twomblys, anyway) was both culinary artist and superb organizer. When guests asked Florence how she managed to run her houses so well, she always told them, "Go have a talk with my chef."

When he was hired by the Twomblys, Donon

had come directly from the kitchen of Henry Clay Frick. Donon was a protégé of the legendary Auguste Escoffier, who once told him, "Don't get excited in America. Americans don't know how to run a house. You have to *tell* them." Donon was reputed to be the highest-paid private chef in America. Anyone fortunate enough to have spent a weekend at Florham remembered Donon's sumptuous breakfasts, served either on trays or in the breakfast room. Donon maintained that it was he who first introduced the croissant to America—for breakfast at Florham.

Dinner was a more elaborate affair. It would start at eight sharp, perhaps with fresh beluga, on ice with blinis. The menu would list successive courses, such as terrapin (in season), trout in sauce verte, baron d'agneau aux primeurs, or filet de boeuf Richelieu. Then there might be a game course—woodcock, quail, or wild duck, for example—after which pâté de foie gras au vin de porto would be served. Then came a cheese soufflé (Florence's favorite), followed finally by dessert. As likely as not, this might be coeur à la crème, another favorite of Florence's, made of the freshest extra rich Florham cream cheese, cut in the shape of a heart, and covered with fresh strawberries. Madame Donon wrote out each menu by hand.

Donon worked for the Twomblys for thirty-eight years. In all that time, he received but one instruction from his employer, and that was to serve only the best of the best. Fortunately, money was no problem. The Twombly Estate office in New York provided Donon with an annual budget so lavish that he regularly *failed* to spend between thirty and fifty *thousand* dollars of it each year.

Besides what he bought, the production of the Florham farm was entirely at his disposal. Each morning, Donon simply gave the gardener a list of the vegetables needed for the day. Two hours later, they would arrive at the kitchen door, freshly picked. It didn't matter whether it was the depth of winter, since the farm had special greenhouses devoted to produce.

The farm and the greenhouses kept all three of the Twombly houses in produce, dairy products, and fruit and flowers all year long. When the family was at Vinland during July and August, Donon would call New Jersey in the evening with a list of what would be needed for the following day. His order would be loaded onto a railroad car parked at Florham's private siding, then the car would be hauled to Hoboken. During the night, its contents would be shipped by American Express to the Fall River Boat Line, arriving at Vinland by truck in the early morning.

Florence's annual schedule was as predictable as the seasons. Every autumn after Labor Day, she took up residence at Florham. After Thanksgiving, she returned to the Fifth Avenue town house for the winter. She might travel in the early spring, but she always returned to New York until late April. After that, she moved back out to Florham for the months of May and June. And then it was off to Newport, or alternately to Europe, usually for two months, until after Labor Day.

Florham was unoccupied by the Twomblys for the majority of each year. It was never closed, however. There were too many live-in servants who would have needed to be relocated. The house remained heated, polished, and always ready for the occasional out-of-season visit.

As the years passed, Florence delegated more and more of the details of entertaining to her daughter Ruth. Miss Twombly never permitted her mother's Edwardian-era standards to slip, with the result that the great parties increasingly became period pieces.

In her book *The Quiet Millionaires,* historian Marjorie Kaschewski quotes an unidentified lady who dined at Florham long ago. "Mrs. Twombly talked exactly so many minutes to the gentleman on her right, turned and gave exactly the same attention to the one on her left." Everyone at the table took their cue from the hostess and did the same. As a result dinner "looked like a ping pong match in slow motion." Usually some sort of entertainment followed the meal, after which Mrs. Twombly would stand at the door with her fan folded. This meant the party was over. Anyone who missed the point was politely but firmly shown the door.

Florence's second daughter and namesake was born in 1881. She married William A. M. Burden of Troy, New York, who died of leukemia in 1909 after only five years of marriage. He left his widow with two small boys, William Junior and Shirley. Bill Burden, Jr., remembered vividly his early visits to his grandmother in New Jersey. "Everything . . . was imposing," starting with the huge mahogany front door with a "shine you could see your face in."

The cooking stove in Florham's main kitchen.

Florence's third daughter, Ruth, was born in 1885. She never married, and lived—or rather cohosted—with her mother for the duration of the latter's very long life. Ruth was a sportswoman, drove a four-in-hand drag in the days of coaching, and later became an expert tennis player. Before her father's death, she used to drive her own coach to the Morristown station to pick him up, with two coachmen, two footmen, and a postillion in attendance.

Ruth was good-looking and quick-witted but remained in her mother's shadow throughout her life. She was a Red Cross volunteer during the First World War. Upon her return home, she settled into an elegant, if aimless, routine of sports and lavish entertaining. She became her mother's right hand, and as Florence grew older, Ruth gradually assumed responsibility for coordinating their entertainments. At its zenith, then, Florham was the domain of two women who were bound together in an unusual but not always comfortable manner.

Ruth consorted with glamorous people, drank like a man, and drove fast cars. On the eve of Prohibition, she ordered so much liquor for Florham that it lasted until repeal.

At Newport, Ruth Twombly knocked three pavilions together at Bailey's Beach and made it the gaiest spot on the beach. She was in the thick of 1920s high society, always on the go, always partying, always entertaining. At Florham alone, she managed a staff of 126, including a man whose sole job was to give the fifteen cars a daily washing whether they needed it or not.

At Florham, Ruth's administrative talent was reflected in the low gleam of the woodwork, the abundant produce of the greenhouses (filled with luscious nectarines, peaches, and Persian melons so large that they had to be supported with nets), the perfectly mowed lawn, and in the razor-sharp edges where greensward met raked gravel. The ivy was always clipped in front of Florham and the vases inside always filled with perfect blooms. Florence had taught her daughter well; and society hardly noticed as the mantle of responsibility passed from one to the other.

In 1922, Ruth commissioned architect Whitney Warren to design a pool and tennis-court building that she jokingly called her "playhouse." Whitney Warren was involved in many other Vanderbilt projects. The Warren-designed tennis house contained one of the finest indoor courts in the country. Its ultrafast sand surface was watered twice daily for an extraspeedy bounce. A Grecian swimming pool, fifty by twenty-five feet, was decorated with wall and ceiling murals by Robert Chanler. The building contained changing rooms, guest rooms, and a handsome pine-paneled drawing room. Ruth hired an English barman and a Swedish masseur, then she was ready for the Roaring Twenties.

The official opening was on October 12, 1923. It was the largest party in Florham's history. Six hundred guests were invited to a gala tennis tournament. In between the mixed doubles, rollicking dinners were held all around town. The culmination was an awards ceremony and dance at Florham. Donon, who had been feeding 150

for lunch and dinner, laid a buffet in the tennis house that night for the whole 600. He used station wagons to shuttle food back and forth from the kitchens in the main house. When it was over, Ruth gave him a bag of twenty-dollar gold pieces. "I don't see how you did it," she told him. "I could never imagine such perfection."

All through the twenties, the party never stopped. Henry du Pont came, so did Mike Vanderbilt and John Nicholas Brown—"the brainy millionaire" of Providence, Rhode Island. Marshall Field was a guest, as were the Duke and Duchess of Windsor, whose presence was kept a secret to avoid publicity. Florence's sisters and brothers made regular appearances, especially Emily Sloane and Lila Webb.

The thirties came, and so did hard times. That is, hard times for everybody else. At Florham, things remained unchanged. The money from Hamilton Twombly's investments in sulphur continued to pour in, literally. While Florence's siblings were running out of cash in some cases, she was richer than ever.

Monsieur Donon at work in the basement kitchen at Florham.

Above: The swimming pool was decorated with murals by Robert Chanler.

Below: The tennis court building "contained one of the finest indoor courts in the country . . . watered twice daily for an extra-speedy bounce."

Ruth Vanderbilt Twombly's pool and tennis court building which she "jokingly called her 'playhouse,' " designed in 1922 by Whitney Warren.

It was in the 1930s that Bill Burden began to worry about his Aunt Ruth. "I felt more than ever," he wrote in his book *Peggy and I*, "that her administrative ability had been selfishly appropriated by my grandmother and it saddened me that, despite Aunt Ruth's efforts to conceal it, her dependency on alcohol helped her forget what might have been."

Ruth Twombly was homosexual. One wonders if her alcoholism stemmed from having to be her mother's majordomo, or being forced to hide her actual sexuality. As the thirties wore on, she began to binge until dawn and sleep until late afternoon. There were scandals, hushed up by her mother. Florence became an increasingly bitter watchdog. Ruth escaped to her playhouse or decamped for Europe.

Florence was in her nineties by the end of the Second World War. She showed no sign of slowing down; in fact, Cleveland Amory called her part of Newport's "*new* triumvirate" of the late 1940s. The Vanderbilts dominated the Newport social scene by then: Mrs. Cornelius Vanderbilt III (the former Grace Wilson) had the most charm; Daisy Van Alen (Fred Vanderbilt's niece and principal heir) was the most vivacious; and Florence Twombly upheld standards that had fallen elsewhere.

Then, in 1947, Florence's limousine skidded out of control. She was thrown violently against the partition and seriously injured. Resilient as ever, she was up and about for her ninety-fifth birthday in 1949. In 1951, however, she fell and fractured a leg. She never recovered from this second injury and never again saw Florham.

Florence Twombly died in New York on April 11, 1952, at her town house at 1 East Seventy-first Street, which had been designed for her by Whitney Warren. She was ninety-eight years old.

Ruth was sixty-seven years old in 1952, and Florham now was hers. Outside its gates, the "Street of Millionaires" was being demolished. Suburban subdivisions were spreading everywhere. Yet Florham remained as it always had, fully staffed, fully operable, and in mint condition. Ruth visited regularly, but she never again entertained as her mother had; nor did she stay in her mother's house, preferring instead to sleep and entertain in her "playhouse."

Ruth gave her last great fête in Newport, Rhode Island, in August of 1953. It was an original idea, a party at Vinland to commemorate

The grande dame of Florham, at the backgammon table.

the one hundredth anniversary of her mother's birth. The Duke and Duchess of Windsor were there, as well as Ruth's regular coterie. There was only one candle on the cake, a tradition with the Twomblys. "Every year is just *one* more year," Florence used to say. This year would be Ruth's last candle, as well. She died in Paris in the spring of 1954, after disregarding her doctor's warning that one more binge would kill her.

Much of the Twombly money wound up in a family brokerage house, William A. M. Burden and Company. Other portions had been invested in family trusts long ago. In 1917, for example, Florence had given each of her daughters $7.5 million as a hedge against the newly enacted inheritance tax. Still, much of the family money went to taxes. Of the $22 million Ruth left in 1954, the government took $18 million. Legacies of $320,000 to churches and hospitals could not be paid because there wasn't money left to pay them.

After Ruth's death, her sister Florence Burden almost immediately gave Vinland to Salve Regina College. It is largely intact today, used by the college as a combination library/dormitory. Florence's New York City town house was sold, as well; a banal brick apartment house occupies the site today. Florham proved more problematical.

Bill and Peggy Burden did not want to live there, nor did they feel their children would want to be saddled with the responsibilities of running such a house. The question became how best to dispose of a country house and a thousand acres in the middle of suburban New Jersey in a manner that would respect both the community and the Burden family interests.

In retrospect, Florham might have become another Biltmore or Shelburne Farms. Had it remained intact, the estate would have provided needed open space in a rapidly urbanizing area, a cultural resource for the entire metropolitan region, and possibly a business asset of considerable value. Even the canny heirs of William Randolph Hearst viewed his palatial San Simeon as a millstone to be got rid of as soon as possible. Today, San Simeon is the biggest moneymaker in the California State Park System.

The Burdens were alert to the sensitivities of Florham Park, New Jersey, as the borough in which Florham was located had come to be known. Back in 1898, Hamilton Twombly and his neighbor Dr. Leslie Ward seceded from Morristown and formed a borough of their own which included Convent Station. Their two estates occupied 50 percent of the land, employed 80 percent of the population, and provided many of the services that other towns paid for with tax dollars.

Florham Park's peculiar semifeudal organization made it at one time the richest town with the lowest tax rate in the United States. By 1955, however, all that was changing. The Ward estate was a distant memory. The borough's population had grown 40 percent just since 1950. The fate of Florham concerned everybody in town, since it would have a major impact on the local environment.

The fears and gossip were temporarily put aside on June 13, 1955. The headline in the *Newark Evening News* read 7000 GET FIRST—AND LAST—LOOK AT FABULOUS FLORHAM. It was an orderly crowd, permitted entry for the purpose of viewing Twombly furnishings that were about to be auctioned off. Many who attended were just neighbors who wanted a last look.

One East Seventy-first Street was stripped bare by Parke Bernet in January 1955. That auction grossed about $200,000, paltry by today's standards. On June 13 and 14, the contents of Florham—minus some heirlooms kept by the family—went on the block. The catalogue contained 160 pages illustrating tapestries, Chippendale furniture, eighteenth-century English mezzotints, rugs, chandeliers, and so on. It was a record sale at the time, grossing $340,000. After the auction, the staff was cut to a skeleton crew and the house, for the first time in its history, was closed.

The Burdens still owned it, however. They donated a small tract of land for the new Madison Borough High School, but their mansion and all its dependencies remained, as well as nearly a thousand open acres. A master plan for the entire property was prepared in 1955 by Seward H. Mott Associates of Washington, D.C. In the words of this report, "The primary question with regard to the mansion is whether this structure is suitable for conversion to a place of business."

According to the master plan for Florham, the site of the main house was thought most suitable for office and laboratory use; the model farm was to be subdivided into house lots surrounding a golf course; the gate house was to be razed; and the land along Madison Avenue was to be redeveloped with garden apartments.

In June of 1957, the Burdens sold the model farm, consisting of a barn complex designed by McKim, Mead & White and 660 acres of land, to Esso Engineering and Research. During demolition of the existing buildings, Esso invited the neighbors to pry up and take away as many of the Belgian block paving stones as they wished—for a nickel apiece. A research facility stands on the site today. Esso took an option on the main house but declined to exercise it. In September of 1957, local speculators bought Florham. They sold it a year later to Fairleigh Dickinson University.

Fairleigh Dickinson already had two campuses in New Jersey. Enrollment was growing at a rapid pace, reflecting the large-scale development under way in the region. The university's president, Peter Sammartino, had actually looked at Florham prior to its initial sale. He had ruled it out

Ruth Vanderbilt Twombly (left) with her sister, Florence, and her brother, Hamilton, Jr., circa 1900.

as "too rich for our blood." A trustee took a subsequent look and fell in love with the place. The owners lowered the price from $1.5 million to $1 million, took back a mortgage, and the deal was made.

Fairleigh Dickinson recognized that their new campus would put heavy stress on roads, sewers, fixtures, and grounds that had been built for very different purposes. They did not want to do gratuitous harm aesthetically. However, historic preservation was not high on their list of priorities. The first students also were enamored of Florham. Sammartino disapproved of this, complaining in his book *I Dreamed a College* that they "had no understanding of the blood, sweat and tears that had made it possible for their campus to be born. They confused broad acres, magnificent buildings, and idyllic surroundings with academic superiority."

This position, of course, ignores the proven positive impact on education of "broad acres, magnificent buildings, and idyllic surroundings." According to Sammartino, the beauty of Florham was "an artificial and expensive way of building up our importance in the eyes of the

national academic community." Such, he added, "is the hypocrisy of life."

Not surprisingly, Fairleigh Dickinson's attitudes toward Florham were ambivalent from the start. On the positive side, they made no changes to the exterior of the main house, save removal of the shutters. The alterations carried out on the carriage house and tennis house have left each in recognizable form, as well. In addition, the imposing gate-house complex on Madison Avenue has been retained and remains in daily use. A modern library building was constructed out of sight behind the ornate orangery, even though the orangery windows were modernized unaesthetically. In more recent years, paint colors in the main house have been well chosen, and brass chandeliers have replaced fluorescent lighting.

There has been an ongoing sensitivity to Florham's architectural value. Unfortunately, this sensitivity has never been a part of a clearly stated policy on architectural preservation. There was, for example, a scheme put forth in the early days to gut the house completely and add an extra floor. This potential catastrophe was averted only by a shortage of funds. Another scheme proposed major new construction spanning the driveway immediately in front of the entry facade. This time, faculty members banded together into an informal Estate Preservation Committee and were able to convince the administration to build elsewhere. The damage that would have been done to Florham by siting a modern brick and glass box directly in front of it would seem obvious, but it wasn't to the college administration.

Houses such as Florham will never be safe for future generations until their owners assume the duties of stewardship. The failure to perceive oneself as a temporary steward—as opposed to the last in the chain of ownership—too often leads to a slow but steady depredation of historic property. This is especially the case with great houses owned by institutions focused on goals other than preservation and perpetually short of cash.

A chapter from Florham's past aptly illustrates this point and the reactions that occasionally are provoked. The original front door, which shined so brightly that Bill Burden, Jr., could see his face in it, was replaced by Fairleigh Dickinson with modern glass and aluminum doors similar to those found on supermarkets. One morning, the campus arose to find a clutter of supermarket carts and vegetable signs that had been placed there as a student protest. The bronze-colored metal and glass doors there today are only a slight improvement.

Bits and pieces of Florham have been disappearing for years. The organ, larger than the one in Radio City Music Hall, was replaced with modern rest rooms; all the tiled kitchens in the basement were demolished for open office space; a large new stairway to the basement has been inserted, none too gently, into the main stair hall; fireplaces and overscaled bathroom fixtures are routinely removed. No part of the interior is sacred if its continued existence stands in the way of immediate needs. The great majority of Florham's interior remains. This is largely because no one as yet has got around to changing it.

Still, Florham has fared better than most great American houses in institutional hands. The original driveway approach is virtually intact, and the main house is not impinged upon by new construction. In fact, a spacious parkland, complete with original specimen trees, still surrounds the main house. The gardens on the other side of the house may be a bit neglected, but their balustrades, fountains, terraces, stairways, pergolas, and so forth have not been paved over for a parking lot. They remain substantially unaltered, awaiting restoration at some future date.

Fairleigh Dickinson today operates a fifth campus in a stately house in Wroxton, England. Ironically, they have a higher consciousness of the historic value of their English property than they do of Florham. The challenge for American preservationists is to convince our lawmakers that the Florhams of the United States are as valuable as the Wroxtons of England and that they deserve protective legislation. In the absence of that, or of a decisive change of policy on the part of Fairleigh Dickinson, the Twombly house will remain at risk.

Florham: the Fairleigh-Dickinson University campus today.

Chapter 6
ELM COURT

Elm Court

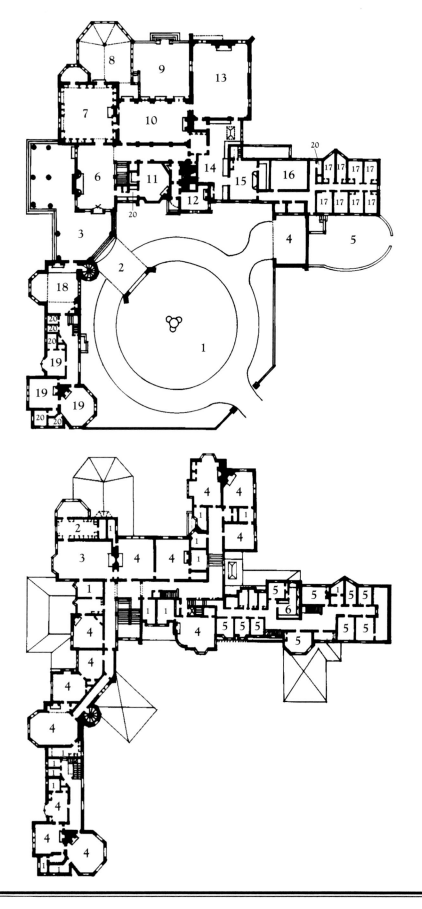

First Floor
1. Entrance Court
2. Porte Cochere
3. Piazza
4. Covered Shed
5. Service Courtyard
6. Entrance Hall
7. Library
8. Conservatory
9. Garden Terrace
10. Drawing Room
11. Reception Room
12. Office
13. Dining Room
14. Serving Pantry
15. Kitchen
16. Servants' Hall
17. Servants' Bedrooms
18. Billiard Room
19. Guest Rooms
20. Bathrooms

Second Floor
1. Bathrooms
2. Master Bathroom
3. Master Bedroom
4. Guest Rooms
5. Servants' Bedrooms
6. Linens

Elm Court from the air.

Location: Lenox, Massachusetts
Architect: Peabody & Stearns
Commissioned by: William Douglas Sloane (1844–1915)
Main house completed: 1887
    Addition: 1889
    Addition: 1892–1894
    Addition: 1895
    Addition: 1899–1900

I DON'T think I have ever spent a more perfect week than this last one; every minute of it has been absolute pleasure to me. So wrote twenty-year-old Adele Sloane during a visit to Elm Court in the summer of 1893. Her diary of that year, published under the title *Maverick in Mauve: Diary of a Romantic Age,* provides evocative glimpses of life at her parents' summer house—and the leisured and patrician world that flourished in the Berkshires—a hundred years ago.

A house party at Elm Court. Joseph Choate, diplomat, lawyer, and Berkshire cottager is at the far right; W. D. Sloane stands third from the right; Sloane's wife, Emily, is second from the left.

Every June through September, the Sloanes, to-gether with four children and a large household staff, moved from Manhattan to Lenox, Mas-sachusetts. At Elm Court, their enormous shin-gled house on Stockbridge Road, they entertained a constant stream of friends and Van-derbilt family relations. Jolly house parties, sometimes with thirty people, often lasted weeks at a stretch.

Adele enjoyed summers at Lenox. Nothing made her parents happier than a houseful of peo-ple, preferably members and close friends of their large family. As the years passed and the Sloane

children took families of their own to Elm Court, the already big house was enlarged to huge pro-portions. Its grandiose size stemmed not from a desire to impress but simply from a need for space.

Emily Thorn Vanderbilt Sloane White (1852–1946) loved family, entertaining, opera, bridge, society, and great houses, in approxi-mately that order. The petite girl the Commo-dore called "my little redhead" was married in 1872, at the age of twenty, to William Douglas Sloane (1844–1915). WD, as the family called him, was a son of the Scotch immigrant who founded the famous rug and furniture emporium called W. & J. Sloane.

When Emily Sloane's father died in December of 1885, she received the same $10 million inheritance as each of her brothers and sisters. However, the Sloanes' prosperity did not depend on Vanderbilt money. WD and his brother Henry were both actively involved in the business of W. & J. Sloane. Both were able to develop elaborate summer estates at Lenox, paid for with their own money, and designed in each case by Peabody & Stearns.

The urban counterpart of the Sloanes' Lenox summer house was a brownstone palace on Fifth Avenue's Vanderbilt Row; 642 Fifth Avenue was part of the famous Triple Palace, built in 1882 by Emily's father, William Henry Vanderbilt. The Sloanes shared the northern pavilion of the block-long complex with Emily's sister Margaret and Margaret's husband, Elliott Shepard. The

The Sloanes of Elm Court, Emily and W. D., circa 1910.

northern pavilion looked like one big house from the outside, but it was actually divided into two completely separate residences, each with its own address. The Shepards' front door was at 2 West Fifty-second Street. The Sloanes shared a lobby on the avenue, which gave access to 640 and 642 Fifth.

"In Lenox you are estimated, in Stockbridge you are esteemed." So said Joseph Choate, fa-

of Athens of New England. It was the home of the famous Lenox Academy, an important seat of classical secondary education in New England, founded in 1803. The equally famous Mrs. Sedgwick's School for Girls was established in 1828.

The local mixture of ancient erudition, New England republicanism, and the immense beauty of the Berkshires was a heady one. Inevitably, summer vacationers began to discover Lenox.

Mrs. Sloane "loved family, entertaining, opera, bridge, society, and great houses, in approximately that order." Here, a family party poses in the flower garden beside the house. Consuelo, Duchess of Marlborough, is second from the left; her uncle, W. D. Sloane, wears a dark coat and skimmer at center.

mous lawyer, ambassador to England, society wit, and summer resident of Stockbridge. There is much truth in this remark, which illumines not only the panache but also one of the reasons behind the ultimate decline of the social colony in Lenox, the village once hailed as the Inland Newport.

For the better part of a century before its discovery by high society, Lenox had been a sort

They were a gentle-mannered, intellectual crowd at first, consisting mainly of Boston Brahmins usually possessed of more culture than money. Mixed among these were literary figures such as Nathaniel Hawthorne and Herman Melville.

Hawthorne, sad to recount, practically starved to death during his financially unremunerative sojourn in Lenox. "I hate Berkshire [County]

with my whole soul and would joyfully see its mountains laid flat," he wrote. Perhaps the winter weather in the mountains prompted a skeptical Ralph Waldo Emerson to ask: "Do the muses speak in these sharp whistling winds?"

However, Henry Ward Beecher, the libidinous Brooklyn churchman, liked the place just fine, noting, "I can see sixty miles simply by rolling an eyeball." Longfellow was transported by the beauty of the countryside. The tragedienne Fanny Kemble made it her summer home from 1836 until 1877.

The first influx of urban riches, it is universally agreed, was the purchase and consolidation of several farms in 1844 by Samuel Gray Ward, the American representative of the British banking house of Baring Brothers. The Ward place was nothing compared to what was to come, but it did mark the first incursion of society into what previously had been an intellectual retreat amidst mountain rusticity.

By the end of the Civil War, the glory days of the Lenox Academy were over, but the reputation of Lenox as a resort continued to grow. Each summer during the 1870s, the village was transformed into a cultural oasis filled with educated wits from New England. The entertainments during this period were modest indeed—charades, twenty questions, taking walks to see the neighbors' cows, and so on. All this would shortly be overwhelmed by an invasion of grand city people building fashionable rural showplaces. Even the cows would soon be replaced by new ones. The oft-repeated joke in later years, vis-à-vis the cows, was that their pedigrees were longer than those of their owners.

Cleveland Amory, in his book *The Last Resorts*, makes an amusing case for the application of Gresham's law of coinage to the development of summer colonies. Just as "bad" coins invariably drive out "good" ones, so the "bad" new millionaires of Lenox drove out the "good" old ones of the Ward and Kemble era. What happened was a radical rise in real estate prices. Soon all the old-line literary and artistic types found themselves priced out of the market.

Lenox had a meteoric rise as an elite watering spot. By 1880, land prices had been bid up to three thousand dollars an acre, big money at the time. Already there were thirty-five major estates in the immediate environs. By 1902, the number of significant estates had risen to seventy-five and

the village had been transformed almost beyond recognition.

According to R. DeWitt Mallary in his 1902 book *Lenox and the Berkshire Highlands,* "More than half of the area of the township has passed into the possession of those who, with large means, have touched the olden picture of scenic charm only to adorn it." The village itself had acquired a "park-like appearance," clipped, and free of dust. Even the population had changed largely. The "cottages and caretakers had arrived." Gone was the "intellectual and social prestige of the ancient Berkshire Capital"; arrived were cut velvet walls on the Berkshire trolley, peacocks on the lawn at the Grenville Winthrops, and footmen in livery everywhere.

The great estates of Lenox were really nothing more than sumptuous private hotels, as great houses everywhere were. Summering here had an interesting flavor in the social heyday, one concocted of wholesomeness, eccentricity, and great wealth. Mrs. George Westinghouse of Erskine Park had a passion for white. The walls and ceilings of her house were quilted with white fabric. Even the driveways at Erskine Park were made of crushed white stone. William C. Whitney maintained a private zoo and a herd of moose on October Mountain. According to Cleveland Amory, Mrs. Charles Lanier rode a pet bull to town for her mail, handed to her on a pitchfork by a frightened postal employee.

Hospitality was dispensed on an Olympian scale in these hills. One of the great tales to this effect pertains to the son of Mr. and Mrs. Anson Phelps Stokes of Shadowbrook, who cabled his mother from Yale that he was arriving with ninety-six men. The hostess is said to have replied, "Many guests here already. Have only room for 50." A truer sounding version of the story has it that young Stokes meant the Class of '96, and that his mother got the joke and responded with wit. Whatever the truth, the story has become a Lenox legend. Indeed, Lenox house parties in the great days were often gargantuan. Shadowbrook was in fact the largest house in the United States, grander even than George Vanderbilt's Biltmore.

Edith Wharton summered at Lenox, in a house called The Mount, whose architectural design incorporated every civilized perfection she and Ogden Codman championed in their 1897 book *The Decoration of Houses.* There was wit in the

Above: The Elm Court cricket team, 1912.

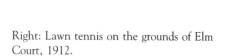

Right: Lawn tennis on the grounds of Elm Court, 1912.

neighborhood, too, most notably that of Joseph Hodges Choate, ambassador to England from 1899 to 1905, and the lawyer who in 1895 successfully argued the unconstitutionality of the income tax. It was Choate who named the Stockbridge graveyard of the august Sedgwick family the "Sedgwick Pie." Concerning a proposal to build a fence around the "Pie," he observed that since no one in it wanted out, and no one outside it wanted in, it made no sense to waste money on a fence. (Choate also remarked of King George that 'he does not reign, he only sprinkles.' And when queried as to who he would most like to be if he could be anyone else, his gallant reply was "Mrs. Choate's second husband.")

Cleveland Amory maintains that during the first decade of the twentieth century, Lenox was the acknowledged "focal point of fall society." Social historian Mary Cable characterized its tone as "aloof exclusivity." The Reverend Nichols was pleased to call it "no place for climbers," being populated predominantly by "old" New York and "old" Boston.

Lenox in those days was scrupulously English. The style of dress, the manner of speech, the mode of living, the taste in servants, the favored sports, and so on all had a heavy British accent.

There were so many English butlers in Lenox that they got together for their own cricket matches. There was also the expected devotion to the horse, which manifested itself in the Berkshire Hunt and in an annual horse show, both great social draws at the time. People came all the way from Newport for the horse shows. Here one saw beautiful women on fine mounts, gay lunches atop elaborate coaches, and, in the evenings, elaborate dinners served on gold plate at the great houses.

Whereas Lenox was certainly elegant, it was also sporty in a peculiarly American way. There was, for example, a women's baseball team in town, one whose players slid into base in long skirts. Another unexpected diversion was the annual tetherball tournament. There was also something called the Tub Parade. A yearly ritual of much hilarity, it revolved around a parade of decorated carriages covered with lavish floral arrangements.

Lenox had a sporting attitude toward chaperonage, too. Whereas propriety—or the appearance thereof—was zealously guarded elsewhere, and no respectable young woman would ever be allowed alone with a young man, in Lenox the practice of chaperonage was dropped entirely. Two of the great Berkshire pastimes were walking and riding, usually deep into the surrounding woods. Young men and women from the very best houses went off by themselves like this every day, sometimes for hours on end. Apparently, no one thought twice about it. It was as if the salubrity of the mountain climate was expected to exercise a wholesome moral check on the appetites of the young. A young society woman in Newport—or in any American city or resort—would not dream of disappearing for the day with a beau and no one else. To do so would guarantee a scandal. In Lenox, however, it was routine.

Natural beauty lured society to the Berkshires. Notwithstanding Nathaniel Hawthorne, it is a truly beautiful place. In choosing Lenox as the site of their summer house, the Sloanes were simply following a current fashion. Evidently, they liked the rustic calm of the woods better than the competitive social clamor of the seaside. Otherwise, they would have gone to Newport. Their choice of Peabody & Stearns as the architects of Elm Court also reflects a sensitivity to the chic of the moment.

The Boston-based partnership of Robert Swain Peabody (1845–1917) and John Goddard Stearns (1843–1917) is much less well known today than that of their New York contemporaries McKim, Mead & White, but at the beginning of the twentieth century, they were nationally famous. Architectural historian Wheaton Holden described Peabody & Stearns as "one of the chief wellsprings of architectural inspiration in their time." Karl Putnam summed the firm up as, "the most important arbiter of building taste after H. H. Richardson." The firm had branches in Boston, New York, Colorado Springs, St. Louis, and Pittsburgh. The total of their opus represents over a thousand commissions.

Peabody was the designer and the business head; Stearns was the construction and field superintendent. Between 1867 and 1870, Peabody had studied in Paris at the École des Beaux-Arts and at the celebrated atelier of Pierre-Gérôme-Honoré Daumet. There he absorbed the architectural doctrines of the École side by side with another young Daumet student, Charles Follen McKim.

Robert Swain Peabody, architect of Elm Court, "the most important arbiter of building taste after H. H. Richardson."

In 1877, Peabody made an enormously influential speech to the annual convention of the American Institute of Architects in Boston. He asserted that America's brightest young architects at long last had found a fitting inspiration for a new national architecture in the Georgian Colonial houses of New England. "In studying this colonial work, we find all the delicacy, grace and picturesqueness that any model can suggest to us; and, combined with it, a familiar aspect, and a fitness to harmonize with heirlooms and old possessions, that might be put to shame by other fashions. In short, we like it all."

Peabody was not talking about copying Georgian architecture. Rather, he wanted to promote the adoption of a new architectural style *based* on American vernacular traditions stemming from the Georgian. He liked the gambrel roofs and the overhanging gables, the bay windows and the delicate interior woodwork of so many of the old New England houses. These elements were not to be employed according to any strict pattern. "What we shall care for in the design," his convention address continued, "is not its historical accuracy, but the artist's clever art in harmonizing whatever his fancy does lead him to." As to where the clever artist would find his elements of fancy, "from no field can suggestions be drawn by an artist more charming, and more fitted to our useages, than from the Georgian mansions of New England."

The houses that emerged from this talk were known, at least in professional circles, as Modernized Colonials. McKim, Mead & White's great shingled houses of the period were designed consciously as Modernized Colonials. So was Peabody & Stearns's shingled mansion for the Sloanes at Lenox.

Peabody & Stearns did buildings in many different styles, notwithstanding their early identification with Colonial architecture. In Newport, they designed Pierre Lorillard's original Breakers (1878), Louis Lorillard's Vinland (1884), and Fred Vanderbilt's Rough Point

Elm Court; entry facade.

"The houses that emerged from this talk were known . . . as Modernized Colonials." Elm Court; the entry facade.

(1891). But they also did Gaum M. Hutton's Shamrock Cliff (1896), a very different-looking sort of place from the above. They also are credited with redefining the look of Boston's financial district, giving it what Adolf Placzek called a "Beaux-Arts panache." They built the Boston Custom House in 1910, filled the better Boston suburbs with brooding stone and shingle mansions, and built eighty town houses in Back Bay alone.

They could be neoclassical or Richardsonian as the occasion demanded. As their shingle period receded, Peabody & Stearns joined ranks with Richard Hunt and McKim, Mead & White as pillars of the American Renaissance. The Machinery Building at the famous World's Columbian Exposition of 1893 at Chicago was a Peabody design. The firm also acted as supervising architect for the Pan-American Exposition of 1901 in Buffalo.

They were very active at Lenox, which was

perhaps a function of the general Boston cast of that Berkshire resort. Besides Elm Court, Mrs. Carlos deHeredia's Wheatleigh was a Peabody & Stearns house, as was John Sloane's Wyndhurst. Peabody seems to have been most at home doing huge private houses. None of these is exactly a palace, however. Peabody houses are typically very large, and often made of stone, but they all have an inherent domesticity that is a Peabody trademark.

The uninitiated might well regard this rambling structure that took asymmetry to undreamt of lengths and wonder how in the world anyone could call it Colonial. However, on closer inspection, the design of Elm Court turns out to incorporate almost the entire vocabulary of America's Colonial architectural heritage, reinterpreted with competence, originality, and considerable panache.

The genius of Elm Court—notwithstanding the many generations of critical abuse heaped upon it and houses like it—is that it has so pure an American accent. As a matter of fact, Elm Court is a tour de force of clever juxtapositions employing early-American architectural elements with the structural and decorative innovations of the industrial age. The exterior of this house is entirely fresh and original. Its silhouette and surface are exceedingly interesting to the eye. And whereas it does indeed ramble, it manages to maintain a decided overall coherence due to its shingled skin and undulating roofline. Its great aesthetic achievement is that it manages simultaneously to be both grand and picturesque. That was characteristic of Peabody.

growing entertainments, and a taste for home improvement. Elm Court soon began to bristle with new wings, all of which were skillfully blended with what had come before. The last alteration was the largest, a complete reworking of the western facade overlooking Lake Mahkeenac (known today as the Stockbridge Bowl). This was the principal axis of the house, and the major rooms here were completely reworked. Originally much smaller and finished modestly in quartered oak, painted pine and varnished cherry, they were replaced by a huge new drawing room, a conservatory, a library, and a noble dining room, each of which was fitted out in

"The last alteration was the largest, a complete reworking of the western facade overlooking Lake Mahkeenac (known today as the Stockbridge Bowl)."

The Sloanes named their house after an elm tree—purported to be the oldest and largest elm in America, thirty feet in circumference—that once stood adjacent to the south facade. When Elm Court was originally built in 1887, the house was about half its eventual size. In 1889, a sort of outrigger room—peculiarly identified on early plans as "own room"—appeared on the west. It was part of a two-story addition, connected to the main body of the house only on the second floor.

More additions followed in rapid succession, a result of the needs of the Sloanes' large family,

high neo-French and Georgian Revival style. The final touch was an enormous set of shallow stone basins and unabashedly naked statues (a replica of the famous Fountain of the Tortoises in Rome's Piazza Mattei) erected in the middle of the entrance courtyard.

Elm Court's interiors represented Peabody & Stearns at their beguiling best. Elegant as these rooms were, the family had them altered early in this century by a skilled, but unfortunately unidentified, interior decorator. Peabody's white and gold drawing room was redecorated with restrained painted paneling, and redesignated as

The original library at Elm Court was changed several times.

". . . whereas it does indeed ramble, it manages to maintain a decided overall coherence."

The library's second incarnation.

139

the library. The conservatory, formerly finished with dark wood paneling under heavy coats of shiny varnish, was reworked in gray and white treillage (decorative latticework) enlivened with gesso ribbons. The original library, with its dark paneled walls and gilded architectural highlights, became the drawing room, again with light-colored paneling.

Emily's grandson Freddy Field told an interesting story about that new library in his book *From Right to Left*. After the redecoration, Emily's husband, WD, asked Freddy's father, W. B. Osgood Field, to fill the new room with books. Neither WD nor Emily were readers, and as Field had contacts with Charles Lauriat, a famous Boston bookbinder, the task was delegated to him. The number of feet of running shelf space, plus a description of the room's pale green and white color scheme were dispatched to Boston. In due time, a beautifully bound collection of great literature arrived at Elm Court, was put on the shelves, and remained there untouched—until stolen by vandals over half a century later.

WD's merchant connections furnished the house copiously with rugs, tapestries, gilt-framed pictures, marble statuary, and antique furniture. According to the Sloanes' grandson Osgood Field, the interiors were "pretty fancy" and could easily have been in New York.

The exterior of Elm Court was originally stained a deep shade of Vanderbilt maroon—a close cousin to the color of Emily's Rolls-Royce—and highlighted with yellowy orange trim. There's a nice symmetry in the idea of Emily Sloane having her shingles stained in Vanderbilt maroon, while her brother Willie liveried his Parisian mistress's servants in the same color.

Elm Court sat on a foundation of rusticated white marble blocks, which seems a peculiar indulgence until one realizes the stone was quarried locally and came quite cheaply. The same marble was used on the first floor of the new western elevation, built in 1899–1900. Vines were allowed to cover the facades with happy abandon, wood and stone alike, giving the entire composition the air of having evolved over generations instead of the decade or so it had actually taken. Elm Court's much-added-to look, with its connotations of family continuity and history, is a part of its distinctive charm.

Fresh flowers and palms—not to mention luscious fruit in all seasons—were supplied by a

Freddy (left) and Osgood (right) Field, two of Mrs. Sloane's grandsons, on the drive at Elm Court in 1912.

major greenhouse complex located just inside the south gate. The glazed area extended over a full two acres. In the height of the season, the Sloanes might use 700 roses and 250 carnations in a single week. On one occasion, the gardener spread mats over night-blooming lillies at 3:00 P.M., heated the greenhouse to ultratropical levels, then rushed the unfurling blossoms to the main house in time for a late-afternoon tea party. This sort of virtuoso undertaking was all in a day's work at Elm Court. For Reggie Vanderbilt's wedding, for example, Emily's gardener dispatched a thousand specially grown orchids to Newport.

The great elm looms over Elm Court during winter alterations to the formal garden, 1924.

The white and gold drawing room, installed at the same time as the library alteration.

The wing with the marble-clad first floor, facing the lake, contained Elm Court's dining room, one of the finest rooms in Lenox.

The grounds at Elm Court were laid out by Frederick Law Olmsted, whose office did work here on and off until 1924. The property covered about a hundred acres and was divided into a mixture of forest, lawn, and formal gardens, calculated for maximum picturesque effect. Elm Court was intended to be used during the Lenox season only, and had no pretensions of being a country seat.

According to her niece Consuelo Vanderbilt, Emily Sloane was a "joyous" person, with a "look of happy expectancy" on her face. The little redhead who sat on the Commodore's knee as he drove his fast trotters up the Harlem Lane grew to become a hostess of legendary charm. Her houses at Lenox and New York were as formal as those of her sister Florence Twombly; but whereas Florence was personally haughty and cold, Emily had a warm and engaging personality.

This charming nature did not allow for lowered standards, however, and Elm Court ran with the same precision as Florham. According to Fred Osborn, when asked how her complex Lenox establishment coped with something unexpected happening, Emily replied, "It never does." For all its outward formality, the atmosphere at Elm Court was anything but Twombly-like. To the contrary, it was relaxed and easygoing, similar to the Webb house at Shelburne Farms. Everybody who went to Elm Court had fun.

The original conservatory, "finished with dark wood paneling under heavy coats of shiny varnish."

Emily loved the opera, and until 1927, she and Florence shared a parterre box at the Met. She also loved society and all the ritual associated therewith. Guests at Elm Court could expect white name cards on the bedroom doors, a daily schedule of activities posted in the downstairs hall, weekend Wagner concerts conducted by the likes of Walter Damrosch, and Archer Gibson organ recitals after dinner on Sunday.

Mrs. Sloane liked punctuality, and indeed lived a very punctual life. Every morning, she took a walk at the same hour. In the afternoon, she took a ritual carriage ride behind a pair of matched horses named Romulus and Remus. When 10:00 P.M. arrived, she always went to bed. Her posture and bearing were immaculately upright. In fact, her grandson Freddy Field said he never once saw her sitting on a soft chair. She enjoyed having guests and expected certain things of them. For example, she thought gentlemen should dance after dinner, whether the ladies were over seventy-five or not.

For all her love of family, Emily Sloane did not much care for intrusions upon her personal privacy. At Elm Court, children dined not with the adults but with the housekeeper, Mrs. Talbot. It also seems that not one of her many grandchildren ever saw the second floor of her New York town house. Nobody ever said to young Field, "Freddy, run upstairs and find Grandma." Instead, the butler would announce, "Madam will be down shortly." Field, who later became a prominent member of the American Communist Party, also asserts that he never once had a real conversation with his grandmother.

Emily's other grandchildren, to all of whom she was known as "Nanan," found her more accessible. John Hammond called her "stunning" and "a swinger for her day." He said her husband, WD, was "one of the most attractive men I ever knew." However, the young Hammonds never got to the second floor of 2 West Fifty-second Street, either.

Emily Sloane's husband was an even-tempered, modest man born to Scotch immigrants who came to America without a dime. He rose to the rank of sergeant in the Civil War, then became treasurer and eventually director of W. & J. Sloane. The Sloane clan was truly a nineteenth-century American success story. It was a long way from steerage to Elm Court, but that voyage took the Sloanes just one generation. Despite his

ascent to the social empyrean—the William Douglas Sloanes were on Ward McAllister's list of the Four Hundred—WD worked regularly at the family business. He did not exactly slave there—as gentlemen in his era and in his position took long and frequent vacations—but he did take an active role in management and policy decisions.

The season at Elm Court was usually from late spring until about October. During this time, any number of the Sloanes' children might be either at Lenox or visiting the estate of some family member or friend. What did young people in the lap of luxury do with one another in Lenox? They read books and discussed them by mail; they talked about religion; they professed love to one another, usually in the most elevated of terms; they visited at the palatial estates or yachts of one another's parents.

At Elm Court, they went on picnics, setting off into the woods on fine horses delivered to the front door groomed and saddled. The picnic itself would be sent ahead on a buckboard, so that when the young people arrived at the sunny orchard or picturesque meadow of their destination, they would find liveried servants awaiting them, ready to serve the lunch on a table set with silver and linen.

Adele adored her room at Elm Court, which, after 1893, she no longer shared with her sister Emily. Over the bed was a picture of "Sleep" sending "Dreams" out into the world. A print of Dante Rossetti's *Beata Beatrix* ornamented another wall, as did a pair of Bouguereaus and a St. John by Carlo Dolci. Outside her window lay the beautiful Berkshires, with Stockbridge Bowl nestled at their feet.

Adele was married at Elm Court to J. Burden of Troy, New York, in June of 1895. The wedding was the most elaborate in Lenox to date. Her cousin Gertrude, the future sculptress and wife-to-be of Harry Whitney, was a bridesmaid. The entire Lenox colony attended, and the wedding gifts were estimated to be worth about $7 million. The route from the church to the reception at Elm Court was completely lined with garlands of flowers. After the party, the new Mr. and Mrs. Burden departed Lenox for ten days at Uncle George's Biltmore. Then they returned to Elm Court for two weeks, proceeded to the Adirondacks with the Twomblys for five days, finally returning home to New York. After this, they went around the world. The parents of the bride then gave the happy couple a mansion on East Ninety-first Street in New York, and a country estate at Syosset, Long Island.

Adele's sister Emily was an earnest woman who could recite whole passages from the Bible from memory. In 1899, she married John Henry Hammond, subsequent to which her parents gave her a mansion adjacent to Adele's on Ninety-first Street, and an estate at Mount Kisco, New York. Emily Hammond progressed from Episcopalianism to Christian Science to an association with Dr. Frank N. D. Buchman's Moral Re-Armament. Son John Hammond, Jr., described Buchman as "successful in obtaining large sums of money from rich widows shortly after the death of their husbands." Emily eventually gave $3 million to Moral Re-Armament, and it was all her children could do to prevent Buchman from becoming their mother's sole heir.

Interestingly, the very earnest Emily Hammond was the mother of the "foremost discoverer of jazz talent in the history of American music," or so reads the jacket on her son's 1977 book *John Hammond on Record*. Hammond is credited with discovering Billie Holiday, Count Basie, Teddy Wilson, Lionel Hampton, Aretha Franklin, George Benson, Bob Dylan, and Bruce Springsteen. In 1933, he met Benny Goodman, helped him form a band, and put together his first recording contract with English Columbia. Goodman eventually married Hammond's sister, Alice.

The youngest of Emily Sloane's daughters, and the closest to her mother, was Lila. Lila married W. B. Osgood Field, who inherited a modest fortune from a bachelor uncle. According to Lila's son, Freddy, his mother was the nicest of the three daughters—Adele being a delirious socialite and Emily a reformer without real vision. Emily and WD gave the newly wedded Fields a fine Lenox mansion called High Lawn, which was technically in neighboring Lee but spiritually in Lenox. In New York, the Fields occupied the Marble Twin at 645 Fifth Avenue, across the street from the Triple Palace.

The Sloanes' youngest surviving child was a boy, Malcolm Douglas. Mike, as his friends called him, labored under the same weight as many of the male Vanderbilt cousins of his generation. The pressure to make something of himself and to live up to the memory of his father

In 1920, Ambassador Henry White asked the widowed Mrs. Sloane to marry him. "Thus, at the age of sixty-eight, the mistress of Elm Court embarked on a new life as a bride."

(not to mention the Commodore himself) proved too much for him. Reggie Vanderbilt suffered from the same syndrome, as did Elliott Shepard, Jr., to a certain extent. As a result, they drank too much. In the case of Reggie and Malcolm Sloane, they literally drank themselves to death. Young Sloane died in 1924 at the age of thirty-nine.

Long before that, in 1915, his father had died. Emily was sixty-three at the time. She was hardly alone, considering the traffic that went in and out of Elm Court during an average week. Having been happily married for forty-three years, she was understandably lonely, however. The following year, a fellow Lenox cottager by the name of Henry White lost his wife. White was a Vanderbilt family friend. Tall, snowy-haired, and urbane, he had at different times been the United States ambassador to both Italy and France. When his wife died in 1916, he had been married for forty-two years. In 1920, at seventy years of age, he asked Emily to marry him, and she accepted.

Thus, at the age of sixty-eight, the mistress of Elm Court embarked on a new life as a bride. Her husband continued unofficially on the diplomatic round. During their honeymoon in Europe, the Whites had lunch in London with the King and Queen, and upon their return home, White hosted Woodrow Wilson, Neville Chamberlain, Winston Churchill, and Generals Pershing and Foch at Elm Court, for a discussion of the League of Nations.

The Whites were not destined to have many summers together after that illustrious beginning. On July 15, 1927, Henry White died, leaving Emily on her own again. She remained healthy and vigorous. In fact, Emily Thorn Vanderbilt Sloane White had never been sick a day in her life. For twenty more years, until her death, she spent her summers at Elm Court. The world changed quickly around her, but Mrs. White maintained the grand standards of the past, just as her sister Florence did at Convent Station, New Jersey.

In New York, however, the changes could not be ignored—especially the enormous intrusion of business and traffic into that formerly tranquil stretch of Fifth Avenue called Vanderbilt Row. In the 1890s, after the death of Elliott Shepard, Emily and WD had combined their city house at 642 Fifth Avenue with that of the Shepards at 2 West Fifty-second Street. In 1925, amidst the Vanderbilts' wholesale abandonment of the area, Emily sold her enlarged house, which by then occupied the entire northern pavilion of the original Triple Mansion, to developers. Subsequently, the DePinna store was erected on the site.

This was an era when everyone, including sisters Lila Webb and Margaret Shepard, seemed to be moving into apartments. Emily Sloane resisted the trend and, instead, purchased a twenty-five-foot-wide town house at 854 Fifth Avenue. Sister Florence Twombly abandoned her house on Vanderbilt Row at about the same time. She, too, resisted the trend toward apartments and moved into a fine Fifth Avenue mansion at 1 East Seventy-first Street. Both Emily and Florence continued to roll up and down the avenue in Rolls-Royces painted Vanderbilt maroon.

All through the 1930s, and even through the war, Elm Court was opened every summer, and grandmother (and great-grandmother) White continued to gather her large and varied clan around her. Then on July 28, 1946, as she turned in for the evening, Emily White sighed and said, "I think I've had it." The next day, she died. She was ninety-four years old.

By this time, Elm Court was almost the last of the estates in Lenox that was still being run in high Edwardian style. The demise of Lenox as an elite resort was already well under way by then. The symptoms had been visible as early as 1908, when Frank Crowninshield's *Manners for the Metropolis* described Lenox as "dull and dowdy, but full of genteel old families in reduced circumstances who are willing to unbend—if properly propitiated."

Lenox remained outwardly magnificent for a long time. As late as 1939, a guidebook compiled by the Works Progress Administration described the houses of Lenox as "enchanted palaces" with "perfection of landscape on every side." The author noted, however, that a very large number of these houses were either boarded up or for sale.

Between the death of Mrs. White and the late 1960s, the old summer colony literally fell apart. Its great mansions were converted to schools, institutions, or simply razed for housing subdivisions. "The astonishing thing," wrote Richard Nunley in the *Berkshire Eagle* in 1984, "is how briefly the era of opulence lasted. . . . The cobbling together of instant ancestral estates and baronies out of Berkshire farm and forest . . . [provided only] the illusion of permanent grandeur, of age-old aristocracy." As for the fashionable throngs who were once "endlessly in transit" between Lenox and the other resorts of that day, Nunley observed that "their circumstances, which condemned them to be consumers exclusively, seem to have consumed them eventually. And now, even before a century since their coming has elapsed, Lenox struggles to draft bylaws regulating the disposition of their remains."

Emily White's granddaughter Marjorie Wilde was determined from the outset to protect Elm Court as best she could. Mrs. Wilde is the daughter of Lila and Osgood Field of neighboring High Lawn. She and her husband, Colonel H. George Wilde, had bought out the interests of her siblings in High Lawn and had been resident there for many years before Emily White's death. The Wildes had transformed High Lawn from a genteel tax loss into a profitable, ultramodern, sci-

Saturday night dinner at the Elm Court Inn, 1949.

Elm Court in the 1940s. "Lenox remained outwardly magnificent for a long time."

SAMPLE MENU
Dinner

Chilled Peach Nectar

Shrimp Cocktail   Chilled Pineapple Juice

Chicken Consomme   Onion Soup, Croutons

Lobster Newburg Casserole

Roast Turkey, Cranberry Sauce

Broiled Half Spring Chicken

Whipped Potatoes or French Fried Potatoes

Green Beans or Buttered Corn Niblets

Chef's Salad

Roquefort, Russian or French Dressing

Hot Rolls   Cheese Tray, Crackers

Green Apple Pie, Cheese   Chocolate Parfait

Iced Honeydew Melon   Sherbet

Tea   Highlawn Farm Milk   Coffee

EUROPEAN PLAN

	Single	Double	Twin
ROOMS	$ 6.00	$12.00	$12.00
		15.00	15.00
ROOMS	12.00	25.00	25.00
With Private Bath	15.00	30.00	30.00

Meals are served in the Tapestry and Empire Rooms and are open to the public.

Breakfast: 8.00-10.00 a.m.   a la carte
Luncheon: 12.00- 2.00 p.m. $2.50
Dinner: 6.00- 8.30 p.m.   3.75

Cocktail Lounge located in the Conservatory overlooking the formal gardens of the estate.

Visit Elm Court Greenhouses

Elm Court is available for small conventions, parties and wedding receptions before and following the Berkshire Festival season.

For Reservations Call Lenox 670

Elm Court
Lenox
Massachusetts

DANCING EVERY SATURDAY NIGHT
NINE TO TWELVE
IN THE

EMPIRE ROOM
AT
ELM COURT, LENOX

TO THE MUSIC OF THE
BEL AIR TRIO

TELEPHONE LENOX 670 $2.50 MINIMUM
FOR RESERVATIONS   PER PERSON

FOR

FROM   *Elm Court*
Lenox, Massachusetts

Elm Court
Elm Court Club, Inc.

Lenox, Massachusetts

MENU

Wednesday, 14 August 1957

LUNCHEON $2.25

Fruit Cup   Marinated Herring   Tomato Juice   Soup   Jellied Madrilene
Shrimp (.50)   Orange-Apricot Juice

POTTED BEEF and NOODLES en casserole
FRIED SCALLOPS with tartar sauce
HAM OR CHEESE OMELET, preserves
CHOPPED SIRLOIN STEAK

Whipped Potatoes   French Fries
Asparagus Spears   Corn Niblets

Tossed Salad Greens   Pineapple-Cheese Salad
Choice of Dressings

Blueberry Pie   Cocoanut Custard Pudding   Sherbet   Cantaloupe
Walnut Russe Sundae   Honeydew Melon   Ice Creams

Teac   High Lawn Milk   Coffee

***   ***

DINNER $3.75

Fruit Cup   Marinated Herring   Tomato Juice   Orange-Apricot Juice
Jellied Madrilene   Soup du jour

PRIME RIBS OF BEEF au jus
BROILED HAM STEAK, pineapp le ring
JUMBO SOFT SHELL CRABS, lemon wedges
TWO PRIME LAMB CHOPS, broiled

Whipped Potatoes   French Fries
Asparagus Spears   Corn Niblets

Salad Greens   Pineapple-Cheese Salad
Hot Rolls

Blueberry Pie   Cocoanut Custard Pudding   Sherbet   Cantaloupe
W alnut Russe Sundae   Honeydew Melon   Ice Creams

Tea   High Lawn Milk   Coffee

STEAK $4.50   LOBSTER $5.00

Massachusetts Old Age Tax 5%

ELM COURT is an inn unique among American hotels.

Formerly the home of Ambassador and Mrs. Henry White, the 110-acre estate is furnished with every luxury imaginable. The mansion, which accommodates about 60 persons, remains almost exactly as it was when it was used as a private home. Fine period furniture still remains on the first floor as well as in many of the guest rooms.

ELM COURT has historical significance, for it was here under the great spreading elm tree which gave the property its name, that Marshall Foch and other great leaders met to confer on preliminary drafts of the peace treaty at the end of World War I.

Nestled in a secluded area of the Berkshire Hills, the main house overlooks nearby Lake Mahkeenac, Tanglewood and the surrounding green rolling hills. It is removed from the highways and hustle and bustle of main roads, offering a quietness and serenity unusual in our age.

Despite its withdrawal from the confusion of everyday life, ELM COURT is close to all the cultural advantages of summer in the Berkshires. Tanglewood is less than three miles distant; the Berkshire Playhouse and Jacobs Pillow Dance Festival within easy driving distance.

Meals are served in the luxurious Tapestry Room. Both this room and the cocktail lounge with its panoramic view of the formal gardens and Berkshire Hills, are open to the public.

Won't you pay us a visit?

Air View of Elm Court

entific dairy farm. They had forty full-time workers in the late 1940s, and 350 head of cattle.

Colonel and Mrs. Wilde had a very sensible plan for Elm Court; they would turn it into an elegant country inn. They purchased the house and grounds from Mrs. White's estate, then spent three months in the spring of 1948 adding bathrooms, a telephone switchboard, modern light sockets (in lieu of the old three-prong models), and a new kitchen. Colonel Wilde hired the Knott Hotels Corporation, operators of the Westbury in New York, as managers. He retained the overwhelming majority of the original luxurious furnishings, reactivated twelve of the original greenhouses, and opened Elm Court to the public in the summer of 1948.

The Wildes' efforts at Elm Court represented an earnest endeavor on the part of private individuals to preserve a heritage they correctly perceived as being in danger. There were eighteen rooms with private baths in the new Elm Court inn, plus a few accommodations for those maids and chauffeurs who still traveled with their employers. The total overnight capacity of the inn was eighty-five guests, who paid between fifteen and sixty dollars nightly for a double room, including meals.

It seemed an altogether fitting solution for the preservation of a very grand house. Many of Elm Court's guests came for the Berkshire Music Festival at Tanglewood. Others came for the polo at nearby Pittsfield. The glorious countryside around Lenox was as alluring as ever.

When *Town & Country* visited in the summer of 1949, things looked as if they were rolling along well. A maître d' named Maurice Colon had been imported from the Taboo Club in Palm Beach. The Tuesday- and Saturday-night black-tie buffets, held in the formal dining room with its framed tapestries and silk curtains, attracted a distinguished crowd, in which musicians visiting Tanglewood often mingled with society figures.

The inn was open only during high summer. America's country-inn craze would not begin until a generation later. Heating a mostly empty house of this size over a Berkshire winter would, in any case, have been prohibitively expensive. The Wildes had started Elm Court as an inn to preserve the house, and also to provide summer employment for the area's many teachers. Their business, however, was farming and they did not possess any great fortune. Their inn had a lovely atmosphere, but unfortunately it never made a profit.

Colonel and Mrs. Wilde made a first-class effort with Elm Court. The conversion to an inn had been done sensitively, without ugly fire escapes or tacky modern additions. They had hired top-quality management, and lavished as much of their own time on the place as they could while running their own full-size dairy farm. Finally, during the late 1950s, there came a point when the Wildes just could not carry it any longer. There seemed to be nothing to do with Elm Court but close it down again.

Actually, there were numerous other things the Wildes could have done. They might have sold it to a religious or educational institution, and watched the property sprout cinder-block megabuildings. Plenty of that was going on in Lenox. They also could have razed the house and subdivided the land. People were doing that

Guests at Elm Court in 1949, pausing on the main stair.

Opposite page: "Colonel and Mrs. Wilde made a first-class effort with Elm Court."

The ruined dining room, Elm Court.

"The tapestries had been cut from their frames on the walls." Elm Court dining room in the late 1980s.

The redecorated conservatory in the late 1980s.

all around town, too. Today, subdivision houses stand right across Stockbridge Road from Elm Court's main gate. Instead, the Wildes chose to hang on.

In the fall of 1957, Elm Court was locked up, the greenhouses were rented to a local florist, and a caretaker was housed nearby to keep an eye on things.

When the inn died, so did the elm tree that had given the house its name. The lawns went unmowed and scrub and brush began to invade the gardens. Trees grew and obscured the view; the mortar began to fall from the chimney joints; and the shingles started to curl. Inexorably, nature began to reclaim her own. Nature, however, played a secondary role in Elm Court's unfolding drama. It was the vandals who played the lead.

Nothing serious happened for a while. Elm Court stood, darkened, boarded, abandoned-looking from the outside, but still completely furnished and intact. Then gradually, kids from nearby schools began to break in. Soon, all sorts of people began to hear tales of treasures sitting around unguarded in Mrs. White's old house. The trickle of kids turned into a steady torrent of marauders. The nonresident caretaker was unable to stop them.

The Wildes tried repeatedly to secure the building, but a house this size is very difficult to

"It is the season of vandals." Elm Court bedroom in the late 1980s.

secure. By the early 1980s, there was not a stick of furniture left. Beautiful old Elm Court had been picked so clean that even the doorknobs and the heat registers were gone. The tapestries had been cut from their frames on the walls and Peabody & Stearns's lovely Colonial Revival stair rail had been kicked to pieces. Impolite suggestions were scrawled in spray paint on the walls; the beautiful damask curtains had been carried off, and such that remained hung in shreds; and there probably wasn't a windowpane intact. People had pried loose the plumbing fixtures, even chipped off chunks of the marble mantelpieces. Meanwhile, the weather had breached the roof in places and whole sections of the masonry chimneys had fallen to the ground. Ruined Elm Court had become, in the words of reporter Rick Hampson, "the Titanic on land." Less sympathetic observers called it "compost."

". . . The house still stands largely because most of the roof miraculously continues to repel water."

"Peabody and Stearns's lovely Colonial Revival stair rail had been kicked to pieces."

As of this writing, the house still stands, largely because most of the roof miraculously continues to repel water. No one has yet stepped forward with a plan to save Elm Court, which is ironic, since this wonderful Shingle Style house probably merits preservation more than any other estate in the region.

Elm Court is a sore point with the Wilde family, who understandably do not care to talk about it with strangers. "Sad, very sad" is Colonel Wilde's only comment. The Wildes have succeeded at least in preserving the land. One is as sorrowful as they, however, over what seems to be the dismal fate of the once-beautiful mansion of Emily Thorn Vanderbilt Sloane White.

Chapter 7
WOODLEA

Woodlea

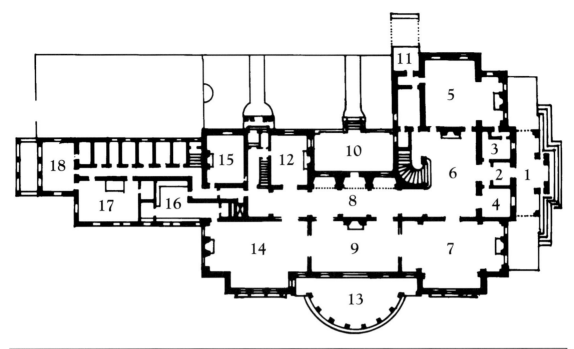

1st Floor

1. Entrance Porch	4. Ladies' Powder Room	9. Music Room	15. Breakfast Room
2. Vestibule	5. Library	10. Terrace	16. Serving Pantry
3. Gentlemen's Room	6. Main Hall	11. Porte Cochere	17. Kitchen
	7. Drawing Room	12. Morning Room	18. Servants' Hall
	8. Gallery	13. Piazza	
		14. Dining Room	

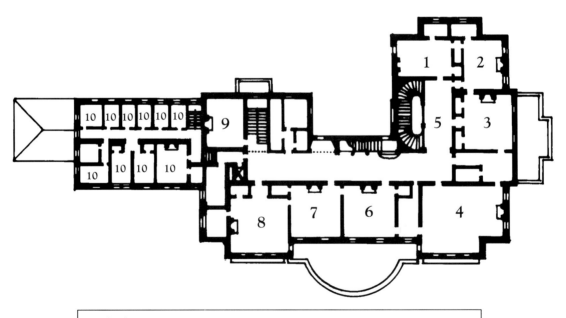

2nd Floor

1–3. Bedrooms	6–9. Bedrooms
4. Mrs. Shepard's Bedroom	10. Servants' Rooms
5. Second Floor Hall	

Woodlea was to be the residence of Colonel and Mrs. Elliott Fitch Shepard. This view is from the north, looking towards the Hudson River facade.

Location: Scarborough, New York
Architect: McKim, Mead & White
    (William Rutherford Mead [1846–1928], supervising architect)
Commissioned by: Colonel Elliott Fitch Shepard (1833–1893)
Main house completed: 1895

*W*OODLEA is probably the best McKim, Mead & White house extant in Westchester County. It is a vast and luxurious place, a marker of the mind-set of its time and of the man who commissioned its construction.

Colonel Elliott Fitch Shepard was able to pay for Woodlea by virtue of his marriage to William Henry Vanderbilt's eldest daughter, Margaret Louisa (1845–1924). He came from a distinguished New England family that included one of the founders of Yale University. Shepard initially rose to prominence during the Civil War. While in charge of a recruiting station at Elmira, New York, he succeeded in mustering 47,000 recruits for the Union cause. Transferred back to New York, he almost single-handedly raised the Fifty-first Regiment of New York Volunteers, widely known at the time as Shepard's Rifles.

153

Colonel Elliott Fitch Shepard, the "perfect type of well-bred clubman."

In the wake of these successes, Shepard became aide-de-camp to New York's governor, E. D. Morgan. President Lincoln himself offered Shepard a commission as brigadier general. Claiming that combat officers deserved the honor more, he settled for the rank of colonel, however.

Shepard was a handsome man, with a thick mane of well-barbered hair, an exquisitely trimmed beard, manicured nails, and an athletic figure. He was, in the words of *The New York Times,* the "perfect type of well-bred clubman," and one who treated his wife with "stately courtesy . . . ever the suitor." Shepard enjoyed close friendships with many prominent persons, most notably Chauncey Depew. However, he was also a controversial figure, continually in the news and caricatured with the celebrities of his day.

Shepard lacked restraint. Once he decided upon a course of action, he would allow no thought of its possible consequences to dissuade him. His judgment was not always good, and his ethics were ambiguous. Like many husbands of heiresses, he spent the majority of his married life trying to decide what to do with himself. His best years were his war years; for twenty years thereafter, he floundered.

Shepard met his future wife, Margaret (Maggie, as the family called her), at a reception for Governor Morgan after the war. They were married in 1868; by 1869, Florence, the first of their six children (only four of whom would survive into adulthood) was born. During his early married years, Shepard practiced law in partnership with a former Supreme Court judge named Heron R. Strong. Shepard and Strong counted the New York Central Railroad among its clients.

The practice of law was not Shepard's forte, and in the early eighties, he turned to banking. He was among the founders of the American Savings Bank, the Bank of the Metropolis, and the Columbia Bank. However, he did not prosper in banking, either. In 1884, he resigned his positions and embarked on a three-year world tour with wife and family.

The Columbia Bank originally bore a catchier name. When it opened its doors at Fifth Avenue and Forty-second Street, Shepard called it the "Bank of Banks." According to *The New York Times,* "People had laughed a little over the Shepardesqueness of this, and they laughed more [upon hearing] the comment of another member of the Vanderbilt contingent—a wee bit of an epic inspired on the spot . . .

> The Bank of Banks
> Started
> By
> The Crank of Cranks."

Woodlea; the river facade.

The *Times* maintained that what was really afoot was a scheme to install a streetcar line down residential Fifth Avenue. This would connect the Vanderbilt-owned Madison Avenue horse-cars with the Desbrosses Street Ferry to New Jersey, with highly profitable results for Colonel Shepard.

According to Shepard's loud protestations to the contrary, all he wanted to do was put a stop to the Sabbath-breaking Sunday stage service. When a rising hue and cry slowed his stock acquisitions, he turned to the courts and tried to get an injunction. Shepard claimed the Sabbath-breaking by the Sunday stages was "imperiling his salvation." The judge threw the case out, telling Shepard to sell his stock if he was concerned about his soul.

Shepard continued to print articles lamenting the decline in Fifth Avenue stock, even though the stock was actually commanding higher prices than ever. By the end of 1888, he had succeeded in capturing the control he sought; there were no more Sunday stages, at least not on Fifth Avenue.

If Shepard bought Vanderbilt stock in hopes of a profitable consolidation of streetcar routes, he was disappointed. No such thing ever came to pass; nor did ownership of the Fifth Avenue Stage Company particularly enrich the Shepard family, especially after it stopped its Sunday stages.

Elliot Shepard had a perverse brand of courage which also led him to speak out on worthy subjects without a care for their unpopularity. He was, for example, an outspoken opponent of anti-Semitism. This was an unpopular stand in the 1890s, when an ugly anti-Jewish sentiment was on the rise in America, and especially in the upper levels of American society. Prominent socialite Poultney Bigelow actually defended the bloody Russian pogroms of the period. Massachusetts patrician Senator Henry Cabot Lodge, together with Bostonians with names like Lowell, Saltonstall, and Aldrich, responded to these same pogroms by founding the Immigration Restriction League.

Shepard, however, together with prominent New Yorkers like Abram Hewitt and Seth Low, attended dinners organized by Jesse Seligman and Jacob Schiff, for the purpose of publicizing and ameliorating the plight of Russian Jews. Shepard regularly addressed the sorts of Jewish religious and social organizations that others of his class shunned.

One of Shepard's greatest unsatisfied hungers was to become a power in the world of politics. According to the New York *World*, "never was man boomed for office as was Depew by Shepard." The colonel actually launched Depew into the race for the 1888 Republican presidential nomination without asking him in advance. When Depew's name was withdrawn at the Chicago convention, Shepard is said to have retreated to his hotel and wept. He supported the ticket, however, and gave $75,000 to the Harrison campaign. Harrison ultimately did nothing for Shepard in return.

Nothing ever came of Shepard's cultivation of ward bosses and Republican business associations. He never achieved important political office, either appointed or elected, but he never stopped trying. The decision to build Woodlea was primarily a result of Shepard's increasing ambition to become a political power. He felt it would be a potent symbol of hoped-for power and influence. The *Mail and Express*, for all its editorial excesses, was a popular money-maker. If its owner and editor in chief wasn't yet taken seriously in the councils of the mighty, he assumed he would be in time.

Elliott Shepard raised his children with uncompromising discipline. He beat his son Elliott Fitch Junior, who was as wild and wayward as his father was rigid and moralizing. He attributed a slight hump on his daughter Alice's back, caused by a mild curvature of the spine, to God's punishment visited upon her for her sins.

His wife was a retiring sort who deferred to her husband's actions and edicts with typical Victorian-era abjectness. Her manner otherwise was that of a thorough Vanderbilt. She was at ease in large households filled with tutors, governesses, and servants. Maggie had been a daring horsewoman when young. In her middle years, however, she settled into a staid and conventional American upper-class routine. She is said to have been fond of giving people surprise gifts, and of entertaining, with butler and footmen in liveries of Vanderbilt maroon. Grand-nephew John Hammond thought her "fascinating." Her nephew J. Watson Webb said that she and Gladys Szechenyi were the only down-to-earth Vanderbilts of the lot. Tall, dark, and good-looking, she is remembered as one of the founders of Miss Spence's School for Girls in New York, and as a patroness of the YWCA.

The Shepards entertained, of course, but they did not go out much in society. His notoriety and moralistic temperament made him unpopular with fashionable hostesses. The Vanderbilts disliked him, too, but they nonetheless included the Shepards in family entertainments, excursions, and house parties.

Proximity to New York was a major factor in Shepard's choice of Scarborough as the location for his dynastic seat. Throughout the nineteenth century, rich New Yorkers had been developing impressive country estates along the east bank of the Hudson. None of these places, in contrast to estate development elsewhere, made any pretense of aping the aristocratic residential forms of the eighteenth century. They were leafy and spacious, and they sported greenhouses, stables, gatehouses, and cottages, often designed in highly romantic architectural styles. However, they did not have the model farms found on the more rural country seats being developed elsewhere at the same time.

Instead of imitating agricultural estates, the large houses along the lower Hudson were suburban from the start. In many cases, their owners actually commuted to offices in Manhattan. Jay Gould at Tarrytown, for instance, went back and forth in his famous yacht, the *Atalanta.* Many others rode the daily trains of the New York Central's Hudson Division.

Even properties of relative size, such as Woodlea's six hundred acres, contained nothing in the way of cultivated fields. Most of the acreage, having been cleared in Revolutionary times and naturally reforested since, was left alone. Rich householders employed large grounds and garden crews, but not to perform any semifeudal agricultural chores. Rather, they kept massive greenswards trimmed, gravel drives raked, stone walls trim, and everything else neat and tidy.

Many prominent people lived along the lower Hudson, including Cyrus Field, the Goulds, Frank Vanderlip (assistant secretary of the U.S. Treasury and president of the First National City Bank), Robert Bonner (the man who bought William H. Vanderbilt's famous trotter, Maud S.), John D. and William Rockefeller, Louis Tiffany, and Amzi Barber. Gen. James Watson Webb, the father-in-law of Margaret's sister Lila, once lived in the area; and Seward Webb's

brother Walter sold his house to Vanderlip.

Scarborough was in Sleepy Hollow country, made famous by Washington Irving. The old Dutch church, from whose graveyard the Headless Horseman issued forth each night, still stands just below Scarborough's southern border. The area originally had been part of a Dutch land grant to the Philipse family, known as the Manor of Philipsborough.

Its pre-Edwardian development had been light: In the early nineties, Scarborough was on the northernmost frontier of estate development along the lower Hudson. Indeed, as a village distinct from Tarrytown and Sleepy Hollow, Scarborough had existed only since 1849. Shepard was looking for a neighborhood that was not only convenient and aesthetic but one in which he could establish a commanding presence. Scarborough seemed made to order.

By the nineties, there were some very fine properties in Scarborough, although they were small by the standards of communities farther downriver. Woodlea, in fact, was one of these, an estate belonging to Butler Wright. Shepard bought the Wright property, built a new house on it, and improved the grounds significantly, but he retained Wright's name for the place. He also kept Wright's house—a painted-brick Victorian structure with porches like bustles and a high tower at one end.

William Rockefeller's Rockwood Hall, an enormous stone castle across Broadway and a little to the south of Woodlea, had been erected in 1886. Shepard's arrival in the early nineties triggered a new burst of building activity in small Scarborough. Soon after the Shepards arrived, Frank Vanderlip purchased Walter Webb's Beechwood, directly across from Woodlea, and proceeded to enlarge the house and transform the grounds in high Westchester style. John D. Rockefeller then began the development of neighboring Pocantico and the Kykuit estate. Thus, Shepard's Woodlea went up at a time when the entire immediate vicinity was feeling the full brunt of an invasion by New York millionaires.

Scarborough already had its own church, and a lovely one at that. It was covered with ivy given to Washington Irving by Sir Walter Scott (the ivy is still there today). St. Mary's parishioners included prominent locals such as Commodore Matthew C. Perry, General Webb, and

Ambrose Kingsland (a former mayor of New York). The trouble was, they weren't Presbyterians. So, having decided to settle in Scarborough, Shepard now decided to build a church of his own. Obviously, he saw it as a fitting complement to the great house on the hill.

Woodlea was designed by McKim, Mead & White, with Rutherford Mead in charge. Mead's sister Joanna was the wife of Colonel Shepard's brother Augustus D. Shepard, president of the American Bank Note Company. Joanna Mead Shepard had a son by the name of August D.

William Rutherford Mead, "Rutherford" to friends and family, was the partner who designed Woodlea.

Shepard, Jr. This young man was an architect, too. In fact, in a bit of nepotism, young Shepard and his partner Abner Heydel got the contract to design Shepard's new church at Scarborough.

In the early months of 1893, when Woodlea was swarming with construction men and ground had not been broken yet for the Scarborough Presbyterian Church, Shepard began to have trouble with his kidneys. The problem was not new, but it *was* a secret. In 1890, the Mutual Life Insurance Company had refused to insure him, based on a diagnosis of Bright's disease, a degenerative kidney ailment, sufferers of which have an inability to tolerate ether.

By March, Shepard was in some pain. He arranged to have his doctors conduct an examination in secret at his home at 2 West Fifty-second Street. Shepard made sure the house was empty. He dispatched his wife and their two youngest daughters to Scarborough to check on construction progress there. Chauncey Depew took Elliott Junior with him on an excursion. Daughter Edith was en route to Europe with the Sloanes. His eldest daughter, married by now to William J. Schieffelin, was at her own home at 35 West Fifty-seventh Street. Elliott Shepard made excuses at the office, ate a light lunch, and waited for his doctors.

Charles McBurney and J. W. McLane arrived at the Shepard house at a little past noon. These men were prominent doctors, McBurney being the attending surgeon at Roosevelt Hospital, and one of the most experienced men in the country. Shepard met them at the door and led them upstairs. He disrobed, lay down on his bed, took one big gulp of ether and promptly vomited. Neither doctor had thought to bring any oxygen. Nearly an hour and a half elapsed before it arrived. When it was finally administered, Shepard regained consciousness and pathetically asked how the examination had gone. Of course, there hadn't been any examination. The doctors had been too frantic trying to keep him alive. They continued their efforts for two more hours. However, Shepard's lungs were full of fluid by that point, and the initial trauma of the ether in combination with his undisclosed Bright's disease finally killed him.

Margaret arrived at Grand Central at five and found her sister Lila Webb waiting for her on the platform. No matter what Shepard's flaws of character may have been, the loss of a husband and father was a wrenching blow. The rest of the city was more surprised than anything else. Various public figures made some attempt to sound grieved. President Smith of the New York Republican Club declared without exaggeration that "This state and county has lost one of its staunchest champions." Boss Platt expressed "sorrow." The *Times*, in a front-page obituary titled "Often Amusing, but Always in Earnest," observed that Elliott should have gained distinction but instead gained only notoriety.

Shepard's widow was probably the only one who truly mourned him. The family made a decent show at the funeral. Most of the mourners, however, consisted of delegations from the various political and social organizations that Shepard had supported in hopes of personal gain. The pallbearers included Depew, John Sloane, and a group of other business friends, but no Vanderbilts.

There was no estate to speak of, at least by Vanderbilt standards. The million or so he left was comprised mostly of real estate bought with his wife's money. In fact, Elliott Shepard already had spent the great majority of Margaret's cash in pursuit of his various projects. It was fortunate for her that half her inheritance had been protected in trust. Shepard did leave a quarter-million dollars to various Presbyterian endeavors, and fifty thousand to his brother Augustus.

This unexpected turn of events left Margaret alone with four unmarried children and a very large house under construction. Instead of shrinking from the responsibility of the latter task, she began to follow its progress more closely than ever. Perhaps overseeing the completion of her husband's great house distracted her from her grief, or perhaps she saw the finished house as a memorial to his memory. She probably enjoyed working with the architects and decorators.

When all the work was done, Woodlea emerged as the very best suburban house possible. It was modern, artistic, grand, comfortable, close to New York, had great views of the Hudson, and sat in handsome grounds designed by the sons of Frederick Law Olmsted. According to an 1897 *Peterson's Magazine,* the fifteen miles between Yonkers and Scarborough constituted "the richest colony in the world." *Peterson's* went on to say that of the great river houses, "none can rival the magnificent Colonial [*sic*] palace of Mrs. E. F. Shepard."

The architectural critic Barr Ferree visited Woodlea in 1906 and recorded his impressions in an article for the December issue of *American Homes and Gardens.* Of the estate in general, he noted that "there is ample room for broad ideas carried out in the broadest way." The Hudson River view, he termed a "marvelous spectacle of nature at her best," one that "is so supremely fine that one may want nothing grander."

Ferree called the grounds "beautifully parked," by which he meant they were attractively planted and well laid out architecturally. He noted in particular the "immense stretches of rolling lawn." The Olmsted brothers created a ravishing plan for Woodlea. Part of what they did, between 1895 and 1901, was to create sinuously elongated lawns—actually view cuts—radiating northward from the mansion. These afforded imposing views of the house from below, and uninterrupted vistas of the river from the house.

". . . [T]he very best suburban house possible."

"The centerpiece, of course, was the main house, a three-story palazzo of cream-colored pressed brick. . . ." Woodlea today is the property of the Sleepy Hollow Country Club.

Taken together, the components of the Shepard estate—the old Wright house (renamed the 'villa'); the handsome stable from the Wright period; the new brick carriage house designed by McKim, Mead & White; the several miles of gravel drives (enjoying calculatedly beautiful views, courtesy of the Olmsteds); and the mansion itself—combined to form an apotheosis of suburban luxury.

The centerpiece, of course, was the main house, a three-story palazzo of creamy-colored pressed brick, ornamented by quoins, window surrounds, pediments, and classical balustrades of pale gray limestone. William Mitchell Kendall, in his authoritative 1920 list of the firm's works, attributes the design of Woodlea to Rutherford Mead. This makes the house unusual in the opus of McKim, Mead & White. Mead was rarely involved in design work, concentrating instead on business and client relations. The fact that he was actively involved in the design of both of the houses the firm executed for this generation of the Vanderbilt family (Woodlea and Florham) is unusual.

William Mitchell Kendall joined the firm of McKim, Mead & White in 1882 and later became McKim's successor. His 1920 list of attributions is considered definitive. Every building produced by the firm was a composite of the work of many different designers. The design of a building such as Woodlea was a complex process. Kendall's attribution to Mead means the latter envisioned the basic look of the house and the overall site plan. Probably he did much more, but in this he was assisted by others in the firm.

In fact, the principals in most large architectural firms, then and now, are often not very involved in design work at all. This was especially the case with Mead. His family connection with the Shepards was no doubt what brought the job to the firm; perhaps it also led to his personal involvement in the design.

Architectural critics say that when in doubt about a certain architectural style, one can avoid potential problems by terming it a "Revival." Woodlea by these lights is in the English Renaissance Revival Style. Its design employs a host of classical devices (urns, pediments, columns, balusters) often seen in seventeenth- and eighteenth-century English architecture. It is certainly a dignified composition.

The house is a full-blown expression of the American Renaissance. Its European and English antecedents are apparent, and the design certainly was inspired by classical cultural traditions. The final product, however, has an unmistakable American gloss.

Such Englishness as Woodlea possesses is entirely superficial and cannot obscure the newness of its overall look. It has a very non-English heaviness about it. Even enormous houses such as Castle Howard and Ickworth possess a certain articulation, despite their bulk and sprawl, that is very much in contrast to great houses on this side of the Atlantic.

American houses of Woodlea's caliber are not as fanciful as their English counterparts. This does not mean they are less imaginative, but, rather, that they exude a recognizable American practicality. This is a result of sustained attention to usability within the context of lavishness. Unlike Chatsworth, Woodlea is clearly not the work of a talented aristocratic amateur. It is too carefully executed, too rife with professional touches in the plan and finish. Unlike Knole or Hampton Court, it is not an agglomeration evolved over centuries. Woodlea was built all of a piece and reflects this. No picturesque wings sprout as a result of afterthoughts. It has a thoroughly contained appearance, which is one of the hallmarks of great American houses. Even the English country houses of the late nineteenth century have a signature sprawl that emanates, perhaps unconsciously, from centuries of the aristocratic tradition of adding on.

Such differences are even more apparent inside. Woodlea demonstrates the typical American preoccupation of the time with up-to-the-minute technology. With regard to the service wing, Barr Ferree noted that "Everything that could possibly be imagined for convenience in serving is here in more than ample abundance."

The carriage house at Woodlea, designed by McKim, Mead & White.

The pantry, for example, was "almost as large as many New York apartments."

The floor plan was also different, and far more sophisticated, than those of English houses. American concepts of efficiency, as opposed to those of social class, dictated the locations of the kitchen, the serving pantries, the service stairs, and quarters for domestic help. American servants did not have to walk half a mile to get from the kitchen to the dining room. These long distances were a common feature of English houses, the idea being to keep cooking smells away from family quarters. Americans would never stand for such inefficiency.

Standards of comfort, as opposed to grandeur alone, determined the arrangement of Woodlea's drawing room, dining room, library, master bedrooms, childrens' quarters, and guest rooms. The house was neither drafty nor were its important rooms inconveniently remote, two of the most frequent criticisms leveled at British stately homes. To the contrary, Woodlea was an easy house in which to live, assuming one had plenty of servants, and quite comfortable if one could afford to heat it.

Woodlea originally had slightly under seventy thousand square feet of living space. It is approached by a landscaped drive that sweeps back and forth up the hill until it arrives at a formal courtyard. The entry facade of Woodlea is a noble one. One perceives immediately that people of substance built this house.

The front door is at the center of the house's short axis. This provides the opportunity of gazing down hallways of impressive length when one enters. The interior proportions are all over-

The library at Woodlea.

Woodlea; a white and gold salon facing the Hudson. "The house was neither drafty nor were its important rooms inconveniently remote. . . ."

scaled, from the height of the ceilings, to the size of the doors, to the length and breadth of the stairway to the second floor. One is impressed immediately by the fabulous woodwork, the massive fireplaces, and the sheer sense of space. There are also myriad sumptuous details throughout: light fixtures, doorknobs, bathroom tiles, and so on, all of which are large and elaborate.

The long axis of the house faces the river and contains an enfilade of three wonderful rooms. To stand in the living room, paneled in green silk and cedar, and look through open doors toward the white and gold drawing room, and then all the way down to the dark mahogany dining room with its tapestry frieze (now painted, alas) is to gaze down a linear distance of over 150 feet.

Woodlea, the main floor hall paralleling the river.

There is a certain satisfaction to be derived from a prospect such as this, a sensation of having arrived.

The design of Woodlea precisely followed the dictates of the Beaux-Arts. The exterior clearly indicated the purposes of the various spaces ceilings, smaller windows, less exterior trim, and a secondary location in relation to the primary approach.

The uses to which Woodlea's various parts were put were quite apparent from the exterior. Both inside and out, the house was coherent,

"The front door is at the center of the house's short axis."

within. For example, the family and their guests occupied the higher and larger southern portion of the house. Here, more exterior ornament, larger windows, and graceful porches indicated the quality of the rooms within. Servants were housed in a northern wing, which had lower comprehensible, and, in the age of abundant servants, efficient, as well.

Vintage photos show the service wing covered with ivy, which did a lot to soften its appearance. An Italian garden—with vine-clad pergolas on each side, precise and symmetrical gravel paths, marble benches, long stone balustrades, and a pool with a fountain in the middle—once occupied a terrace at the foot of the service wing, between the main portion of the house and the view up the Hudson. The delicacy of this garden formed a pleasing counterpart to the functionalism of the service wing. Taken together, the combination of main pavilion, service wing, and Italian garden formed a balanced and beautiful composition.

"The rooms are everywhere large, many of them are immense," commented Ferree. In fact, "immensity is one of the chief characteristics of this great house. Yet it is a beautiful immensity. . . . It is not grandiose nor showy, it is simply grandly large, and large everywhere." Or, as Ferree stated later in the same article, Woodlea is "a large house designed in a large way."

Part of the charm of the Shepard estate stems from the presence of the nearby Presbyterian church. This imposing structure sits on a highly visible crossroads within view of the mansion's hilltop site far to the south. The church walls are of pink granite rubble with limestone trim, topped by a most unusual steeple supported by flying buttresses. Inside are fine fluted pilasters with gilded capitals, a coffered ceiling made of redwood, and lovely stained-glass windows.

Scarborough Presbyterian was a gift of the Shepards to the Scarborough community. By its look and location, it suggested a gracious and accepted relationship between village and house. In England, these relationships developed over centuries; in America, they were fabricated overnight. Although the church was dedicated to her husband's memory (on May 11, 1895), it was Mrs. Shepard who, by virtue of her early active involvement, was most identified with it. According to an old joke in the neighborhood, children in its Sunday school used to recite, "The Lord is Mrs. Shepard, I shall not want."

Maggie Shepard made a noble effort to inhabit her new establishment. Unlike her sister Florence Twombly or her brother Willie K., she was not a great entertainer, however. Woodlea quickly became a house lived in during the spring and fall and visited at Christmas and occasionally at other times of the year. Its mistress, though born an Episcopalian, ran it with strict Presbyterian probity. No meals were prepared on Sunday, Sabbath-breaking being verboten.

However, Mrs. Shepard was not reclusive. She had a large family and a social life that was more active and congenial than it had been when her husband was alive. Once her children were grown and married, though, she found it more enjoyable to visit with them than to maintain elaborate establishments of her own. Without the commanding presence of Colonel Shepard, Woodlea must have seemed a bit much even for a Vanderbilt. Besides, prices were rising and Margaret's income was not.

Shortly after her husband died, Margaret Shepard sold 2 West Fifty-second Street to her sister Emily Sloane. The Sloanes combined it with their own contiguous portion of the original Triple Palace to make a house nearly as large as William Henry's original 640 Fifth. After this, Margaret moved for a while to an apartment in the Belgravia, a building on the site of today's Saks Fifth Avenue, then to another apartment at 998 Fifth Avenue, a building designed in 1910 by the office of McKim, Mead & White. She kept her apartment there until the end of her life.

Margaret Shepard was a typical American grande dame of the early twentieth century. She patronized the best Manhattan shops, was dressed by Worth, summered at Bar Harbor, Maine, and always made an autumn visit to the Homestead in Hot Springs, Virginia. She wintered in Manhattan, with occasional visits to Woodlea, and traveled in the spring, perhaps to a hotel in Cannes or to the villa of her son-in-law Ernesto Fabbri's mother in Florence.

Even prior to 1900, her visits to Woodlea were becoming less frequent. After the turn of the century, she began selling property to her neighbors Frank Vanderlip and William Rockefeller. In 1910, she sold Woodlea itself to these two men. On March 3, 1924, at the age of seventy-nine, Margaret Shepard suffered a heart attack at 998 Fifth Avenue and died within hours. Her $5 million trust was still intact, and she left it in equal shares to her four surviving children. To each of sixteen grandchildren, she bequeathed another twenty thousand dollars apiece.

One might wonder why Vanderlip and Rockefeller would want Woodlea when each already owned a substantial property nearby. According to Vanderlip's 1935 book *From Farm Boy to Financier*, the Shepard house was too big a bargain to pass up. Having spent over $2 million on Woodlea, Mrs. Shepard was prepared to part with it in 1910 for $165,000. Vanderlip says that he did ask his wife whether she wanted to move there. However, that lady declined, on the grounds that Woodlea was simply too large.

In any case, Vanderlip and Rockefeller had another plan in mind: the creation of a first-class country club. This was a pet project in many luxurious American suburbs at that time. The new owners of Woodlea assembled a board of very social directors, including future *Titanic* victim Jack Astor, coal baron E. J. Berwind, cotillion leaders Elisha Dyer and Lispenard Stewart, and dashing young sportsmen such as Averell Harriman, Neily Vanderbilt, and Harrison Williams.

The Sleepy Hollow Country Club was incorporated on May 11, 1911, and the first meeting of its directors took place five days later in Vanderlip's office at 55 Wall Street. To become a member required nine yea votes at a directors'

ficient room for entertaining on any scale; and it positively dripped with Vanderbilt class. For the first few years of its existence, the club rented Woodlea, furnished, for $25,000 a year. In 1912, it purchased the property from Vanderlip and Rockefeller for $350,000.

The club then set about improving the property. In the early years, this was done with a consistently sensitive touch. A golf course was constructed in perfect harmony with the existing landscape, as was an outdoor garden theater, complete with clipped cedars and a sixteenth-century Italian portal. New facilities and structures continued to be built at regular intervals throughout the 1920s. These included a manager's house, a skeet house, a squash house, an indoor riding ring, and eventually a swimming pool. Every bit of this new construction was well sited and skillfully integrated with the existing estate components.

meeting; two blackballs would end one's chances. Initiation was one hundred dollars, yearly dues the same, and, per a 1917 membership guide, "members *must* instruct their chauffeurs to adhere strictly to traffic rules."

Luxurious Woodlea was well suited to become a club. It was just far enough from town to constitute an ideal resort for motorists; it had suf-

The old Butler Wright house became the new golf house, and its appealing porch was soon a favorite spot for lunch. The stables were kept full of horses for members' use. The courts for summertime tennis were flooded for wintertime skating. The house itself was kept carefully polished, reserved for black-tie Saturday dances or such overnight accommodations

Above: The garden at Woodlea; view to the north.

Opposite page: Woodlea; garden adjacent to the river facade.

as club members might require.

Sleepy Hollow Country Club operated at a loss from the beginning. This didn't matter much, as the membership was well able to make up deficits. The twenties were a gay time at Scarborough. The club was busy and famous, and founder Frank Vanderlip's parties—across the road at Beechwood—were legendary. Henry Ford, Sarah Bernhardt, and Isadora Duncan were all guests at Beechwood. The Wright Brothers took off and landed on the lawn.

The collapse of the New York stock market in October of 1929 changed everything. Vanderlip was able to endure the financial storm, but an alarming number of his fellow club members were not. The stock-market crash, in fact, devastated the club. Membership tumbled; the horses had to be sold; Woodlea was closed down except for special occasions, and the club carried on in the golf house. In desperation, five-acre building lots north of the mansion were sold to whatever members could still afford to buy them.

Sleepy Hollow limped through the Depression and the war years, but it did not disband. Instead, it transformed itself from a gentlemen's to a family club. True, it was an upscale family club, but it developed a friendly democracy that contrasted with its original tone and image. In 1950, a member could stay overnight in Woodlea for five dollars (less in the golf house); the first formal dance of that year cost only five dollars a person.

The 1950s saw the start of various renovation programs for Sleepy Hollow's long-neglected physical plant. The aesthetic of the day was not sensitive to vintage architectural fabric. In 1961, Woodlea was redecorated with modern fabrics, warm gold and forest green carpets, dropped lighting, and, in some areas, lowered ceilings. According to the Ossining *Citizen Register*, the redecoration of Woodlea achieved "a new elegance, but retained the splendor of the Victorian era."

Fortunately, there were not very many dropped ceilings. If the new color schemes and furnishings were inappropriate, at least the basic structure of the interior, including most of the old bathrooms, remained intact. However, in the mid-1960s, one very bad thing did happen. The club decided for economic reasons to pull down the golf house and consolidate golfing and meal facilities in a new addition to the Shepard mansion. The Italian garden below the river façade was then demolished and replaced with an enormous modern structure devoted to locker rooms, pro shop, dining facilities, and so on.

The new structure does not rise above the original house, nor is it very noticeable from the grounds below. However, it is dreadfully visible from the house itself. Where once were graceful balustrades, vine-clad pergolas, and reflecting pools, there is now an enormous tar and gravel rooftop covered with hideous—and constantly droning—ventilation machinery. The only good thing that can be said of the new structure is that it probably can be razed at some future date without doing much damage to the original house. The facilities contained within it are modern, spacious, and convenient, but it clashes jarringly with the superb mansion to which it has been appended.

The Sleepy Hollow Country Club is today a part of a National Historic District that encompasses some 376 acres. The existence of the Scarborough Historic District has helped raise awareness of the area's historic and aesthetic worth. It has provided no protection for its historic structures, however, except to mandate environmental reviews in the case of federally funded projects. Anybody in the district, including the club, is quite free to demolish an historic structure or to subdivide historic acres to the maximum extent permitted by local zoning. A great deal of demolition and subdivision occurred in Scarborough during the 1950s and 1960s. The club's several hundred acres of open woodland have become a welcome respite from the spreading ranks of split-levels and condominiums.

The celebrated views from Woodlea's terraces have changed somewhat. In one direction, over the humming machinery atop the golf annex, one now can see Con Edison's nuclear plant at Indian Point. The majority of the house is remarkably intact, however. It even contains more than a little of its original furniture. More important is a new consciousness among the membership of the original building's value. Redecoration schemes afoot as of this writing are far more respectful of the building than those in the past have been.

Woodlea is a good illustration of both the pros and cons of private preservation efforts. One must recognize the Sleepy Hollow Country Club

for its stewardship of the property. They have consistently loved it, which counts for a lot. However, their building policies have suffered from a lack of long-term aesthetic guidelines oriented toward preservation of the original nature of the estate. The Olmsted landscape has been

Woodlea; the garden pergola overlooking the Hudson.

generally respected. It is unfortunate and ironic, though, that the charming and historic Butler Wright house should have survived the worst of economic times only to be demolished in 1967. Even more regrettable is the new addition, an unsympathetic construction that resembles nothing so much as a half-submerged suburban supermarket. If present attitudes are any indication, the same disaster won't happen here again. The adoption of specific and well-articulated preservation guidelines would go a long way toward ensuring Woodlea's future.

169

Chapter 8
IDLE HOUR

Idle Hour

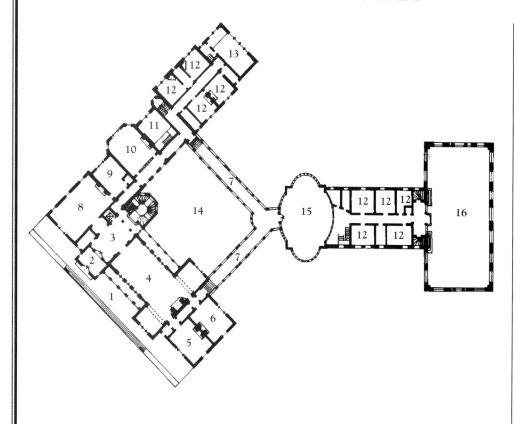

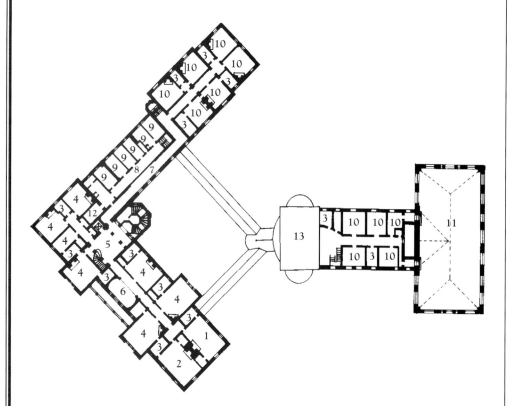

1st Floor
1. River Terrace
2. Foyer
3. Main Hall
4. Living Hall
5. Gold Room
6. Library
7. Cloisters
8. Hunt Room (Dining Room)
9. Serving Pantry
10. Billiard Room
11. Upper Part of Lower Level Kitchen
12. Bachelors' Guestrooms
13. Fives Court
14. Garden Courtyard
15. Palm Room (later Turkish Room)
16. Indoor Tennis Court

2nd Floor
1. Mr. Vanderbilt's Bedroom
2. Mrs. Vanderbilt's Bedroom
3. Bathrooms
4. Married or Ladies' Guestrooms
5. Second Floor Main Hall
6. Alcove
7. Guest Corridor
8. Service Corridor
9. Servants' Bedrooms
10. Bachelors' Guestrooms
11. Upper Part of Tennis Court
12. Linens
13. Upper Part of Original Palm Room

Location: Oakdale, Long Island, New York

Architect: First house: Richard Morris Hunt (1827–1895)

Second house: Richard Howland Hunt (1862–1931)

Commissioned by: William Kissam Vanderbilt (1849–1920)

Main house completed: First house: 1879

Second house: 1901

THIS property was named by the flip of a coin. During an afternoon in the summer of 1877, Willie Vanderbilt and Schuyler Parsons were sitting on the porch of the South Side Sportsmen's Club in Oakdale, Long Island, discussing names for their new country estates. The field had narrowed to two, and both gentlemen preferred "Idle Hour" over "Whileaway." The coin was tossed, and Vanderbilt won.

Such were the concerns of South Side's gentlemen members as the Gilded Age shifted into high gear. The American gentleman, fashioned in the image of the English gentry, seemed a very permanent new fixture on the American scene. His country seat, erected on grand scale and in short order, gave every indication of being as permanent as he. Vanderbilt's new Idle Hour was an apotheosis of the type, a luxurious sanctuary replete with feudal overtones.

The builder of Idle Hour was as authentic a gentleman as America had yet to produce, a man who never shrank from spending a few dollars—or a few million dollars if need be. He had style, education, manners, and came from a family that had been rich for three generations. Frank Crowninshield eulogized him as "the greatest supporter of sport, opera, yachting, racing, art, architecture, coaching, and the theatre in the American social annals," none of the above being a recommended field for undercapitalized supporters.

William Kissam (Willie) Vanderbilt spent a lifetime doing things—particularly things architectural—the right way. His estate at Oakdale on the South Shore of Long Island was his first large architectural venture.

In the 1870s, Oakdale was a famous watering spot for the elite. Fifty miles from Manhattan, it remained intensely rural, intact, hardly changed from the seventeenth century. The South Shore was enchantingly serene in those days.

There were farms, of course, but most were inland. The salt marshes along the shore were a luminous world of waving grasses and glittering bays that together imparted a pale silvery quality to the light. The land was flat and the unspoiled horizons immense. The distant dunes of the Five Islands (later corrupted into Fire Island) kept the ocean surf at a safe remove across the Great South Bay, but the scent of the sea was everywhere. Tranquil rivers and pure streamlets alive with fish meandered through primeval woods. Everywhere was a vast and mysterious silence, broken only by the cry of waterfowl or the distant roll of the Atlantic breakers.

The South Side Club was a hunting and fishing association whose membership, according to social historian Mary Cable, had "more wealth per member than any such club in the United States." Belmonts, Bennetts, Goelets, Tiffanys, Whitneys, Lorillards, Cuttings, and Vanderbilts shot, fished, and socialized there. Guests over the years included everyone from Daniel Webster to Oscar Wilde, from General Sherman to Philip Hone, from Henry Clay to Teddy Roosevelt. The club played an overwhelmingly positive role in the development of the Oakdale-Islip area.

The antecedent of this club was a humble tavern in the wilderness, operated by one Eliphalet (Liff) Snedecor. Snedecor's slowly developed a recherché reputation among gentlemen from New York. What drew them was not just the abundance of hoofed, finned, and feathered game but also the skill and flavor of the local guides (a family of Yankee characters graced with a liberal dose of black and Indian blood), the quality of Liff's table, and the manly conviviality that reigned there.

As early as 1828 the *Smithtown Star* was singing the praises of Snedecor's, where "we find the hunting and fishing . . . something to marvel about." By 1836, Manhattan's man about town Philip Hone noted in his diary that the place was, "so full that, if we had not taken the precaution to write in advance for beds, we might have lain on the floor." *The American Turf Register and Sporting Magazine* urged readers in January 1839 to "get in at Liff's if possible. The way you live there is none of your common doings."

By the 1850s, prosperous locals—some of whose families had lived on Long Island for generations and sometimes even centuries—began to develop exuberant mid-Victorian country estates in the area. These wooden houses were not quite mansions by later standards, but they were undeniably large. Their owners were avid sportsmen, and Snedecor's was their special place.

As long as there was no railroad, the men who made Snedecor's their second home were left pretty much undisturbed. It would be incorrect, however, to assume that they liked it that way, or that they in any way resented the radical changes that were soon to transform little Oakdale (then known as East Islip). Growth and progress were perceived by these men as natural and beneficial. The fragile loveliness that surrounded Islip and Oakdale was not perceived as being in any danger, and it wasn't—at least not yet.

In 1863, great changes began to happen in East Islip. Impending impoverishment forced William Nicoll, the local land baron whose family had been patentees since the seventeenth century, to put huge tracts of southern Suffolk County, including the land beneath Snedecor's, up for sale. This precipitated a sudden influx of outsiders, notably rich sportsmen from New York who were devotees of Snedecor's. One in particular, a man named Robert L. Maitland, bought both a site for a future country house and the land under the old tavern. Never for a moment was the fate of the venerable institution in any peril. Snedecor's son was prevailed upon to stay, and on April 6, 1866, the South Side Sportsmen's Club, numbering one hundred members, was officially incorporated.

Things then began to move quickly. In 1867, the railroad arrived. By the 1870s, South Side's reputation had changed from that of a hinterlands gem known only to the cognoscenti to a favorite retreat of the nation's movers and shakers. Willie Vanderbilt, still virtually clubless at the time of his marriage in 1875, surely appreciated the social value of South Side membership. Its reputation was lofty, but it was not nearly as hard a nut to crack as the elite and snobbish clubs in Manhattan. Out at South Side, what mattered was a man's skill with gun and rod, plus his companionableness at table. Willie's athletic prowess (he was only twenty-seven in 1876), together with his enormous personal charm, made him an ideal candidate. South Side became the first elite social organization in the New York area to invite him to join.

Once he became a member, Willie joined his fellow New Yorkers in the local land rush. By 1877, he had acquired nearly nine hundred acres directly south of the club, bordering Great South Bay and the Connetquot River. He then engaged Richard Morris Hunt to design him a suitable house as a retreat devoted to hunting and fishing. Idle Hour was the commission that began Hunt's long and rewarding relationship with the Vanderbilts.

These were the happy early days of Willie's subsequently unhappy marriage. Although it was his house, its design and construction were very much a project of his wife's. In an unpublished memoir from 1917, Alva called Idle Hour "the first house I ever built . . . without pretension but most spacious and attractive." Naturally, she credited Hunt with the design, but as with 660 Fifth Avenue, she was closely involved. It was probably Alva who made the initial contact with Hunt. Idle Hour was a Stick Style house, very much in Hunt's prepalatial Newport mode, not a great deal larger than the wooden manses of other South Side members. The house was dark in color, bulky, and built entirely of wood, with brick chimneys and foundations. It cost $150,000, which, of course, was nothing to Vanderbilt. Willie just had inherited $3 million from his grandfather's estate in 1877. Construction on Idle Hour began in July of 1878, and the house

The original Idle Hour, designed by Richard Morris Hunt and completed in 1879.

was ready for occupancy by the following summer.

Alva must have been in her glory during this period, deep in daily consultation with Hunt, first on the plans for Idle Hour, then on designs for 660 Fifth. Planning for the latter, a neo-Renaissance château that would set the whole country talking, began in 1878. Two small children joined the household, too: Consuelo in 1877, and W. K. Vanderbilt, Jr., in 1878. Willie's career in the family railroad business was flourishing, even though one wonders how he found time for business between his yachting trips and his hunting parties. In the early eighties, he was promoted to president of the New York, Chicago, and St. Louis Railroad; chairman of the Lake Shore and Michigan Southern Railroad; and director of literally dozens of others.

The Vanderbilts initially used Idle Hour for summers, holidays, and the occasional weekend. They continuously and systematically improved the property, dredging ornamental canals from the marshlands, building scenic drives, and laying out lawns. They added a very large number of ancillary buildings, almost all of which still stand. Isaac Green, a noted local architect whose skillful shingle-clad additions to the South Side Club are still extant, did much of the work. The enormous Vanderbilt coach house is his, as is

The original Idle Hour "underwent more or less continual enlargement, too, always to the designs of Hunt . . ."

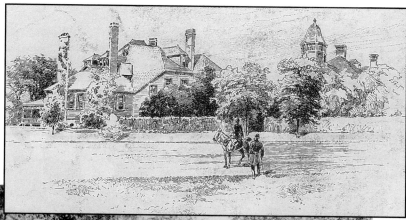

Above: Idle Hour; the main gate and gatehouse.

Opposite page: The model farm at Idle Hour.

the elaborate model farm that at one time provided the estate with livestock, produce, and an air of feudal self-sufficiency.

Besides these, *two* gatehouses, a caretaker's house, a water tower, an icehouse, greenhouses and potting sheds, a bowling alley, a laundry, a house for the superintendent, a house for the palm trees, and even a teahouse on the edge of the Great South Bay went up in rapid succession throughout the 1880s and 1890s.

The main house underwent more or less continual enlargement, too, always to the designs of Hunt. Additions were made in 1883, 1887–1889, and 1892. The bulk of the work went into a new kitchen, plus a bachelor annex reachable via a balcony over a drive-through archway in the rear. The last thing done was an addition to the library on the river side. The resulting structure, by the mid-nineties, had become quite large.

This amount of construction might well have exhausted—not to say bankrupted—the average person, but it was simply a diversion for Willie and Alva Vanderbilt. By the mid-eighties they had already begun to summer in Newport. By 1888, Hunt and Alva were hard at work designing Marble House, an undertaking that would eventually cost Mr. Vanderbilt an amazing $11 million.

Prior to Newport, Alva had loved spending time with her children at Idle Hour. In 1884, her third child, Harold Stirling, was born there. The older children by this time had their own playhouse: a bowling alley imported from Europe and christened "La Récréation." They played in boats and went on picnics; they raised vegetables and sold them to their mother; and explored the network of romantic lagoons and canals their father had created among the salt marshes. They went on the family side-wheeler, the *Mosquito*, down the Connetquot and across the Great South Bay to Fire Island. Life was deliciously free and unstructured, a far cry from the rigid social protocol of New York and Newport.

While the Newport house was being constructed in the early nineties, tension was building in the Vanderbilt household. Willie was a perfect gentleman of his era and always deferred to his wife. However, he also shared the era's double standards of sexual behavior. He had affairs—discreet ones to be sure—but he believed that this was a husband's prerogative. Most society wives tolerated this type of conduct; Alva Vanderbilt did not.

The Vanderbilts' great 1883 ball at 660 Fifth Avenue had helped them to conquer society; so did Idle Hour, since it provided a suitable country house to which Willie could invite the members of the exclusive Coaching Club of New York. They came, too, although it took another eleven months for the governors to invite Willie to join. By 1885, Willie was a member of all the best clubs. The social preeminence he and his wife had struggled so hard to achieve was theirs at last, but it failed to hold together the marriage.

In 1894, upon the family's return from a yachting trip to India, Willie and Alva separated. The penny press was abuzz with nasty rumors. Staid

Cornelius Vanderbilt II voyaged to France in the hopes of convincing his brother and sister-in-law to reconcile. It was hopeless. The couple busied themselves for months denying rumors that anything was wrong, but in January of 1895, Alva filed for divorce.

Since the only ground for divorce in New York State at the time was adultery, Willie graciously provided his wife's lawyers not only with a name but with a time and date, as well. The divorce was granted in a few months. Alva kept Marble House; it had been a birthday present to her and the title was already in her name. Willie offered her 660 Fifth Avenue, but she turned it down as too expensive to run.

Willie kept "his" house, Idle Hour, though in spite of all the steady improvements and alterations, he had not used it for years. By the mid-1890s, trendsetters like Willie Vanderbilt weren't going to Oakdale anymore. The South Side Club still appeared to be at a zenith of popularity and importance, but the initial surge of estate development that it had attracted to the area petered out quickly. If women are excluded from the wellsprings of an area's social cachet, its attraction to society, no matter how potent, will not last long. This was precisely the problem at Oakdale.

Besides Idle Hour, there were only three other grand properties in the area: W. Bayard Cutting's Westbrook, Christopher Rhinelander Roberts's Pepperidge Hall, and Commodore (of the New York Yacht Club) Frederick G. Bourne's Indian Neck Hall. These four houses sat in a splendid row directly across South Country Road (now Montauk Highway) from the South Side Club. Oakdale's truly upscale development was a tiny fraction of what was to be found at Newport or in the other principal resorts of the East.

After his divorce, Willie Vanderbilt seemed to spend most of his time in France (either at the track or at his stud farm) or aboard his yacht *Valiant*. This vessel replaced the *Alva*, sunk off Martha's Vineyard in 1892. The *Valiant* was 331 feet long, brig rigged, and manned by a crew of sixty-two. She served as a kind of floating hotel and restaurant for Vanderbilt and his many guests, and sailed during the summer mostly between Newport and New York.

There's a deep water anchorage in the Connetquot River directly in front of Idle Hour. One naturally imagines Mr. Vanderbilt stepping direct from his yacht into his manorial hall. Interestingly, none of Willie's yachts seems ever to have used it, possibly due to the fact that a 331-foot ocean-going steam yacht will not fit in a river the size of the Connetquot.

Every so often, however, someone did use Idle Hour. Whether Willie Vanderbilt, Sr., occupied it very much or not, it was still a symbolic family seat. His daughter, Consuelo, and her new husband, the ninth Duke of Marlborough, spent the first night of their marriage there in 1895. Four years later, Willie's son W.K.V., Jr., and his bride, Virginia Graham Fair, also spent their wedding night there, but it was not a happy occasion. In the middle of the night, Willie Junior suddenly smelled smoke. A nightmarish comedy ensued. The newlyweds wrapped towels around their heads and beat a hasty retreat to the lawn. A thoughtful servant appeared with a folding chair and a fur-trimmed opera cloak. The new Mrs. Vanderbilt sat down and watched the blaze while her new husband raised the alarm.

The whole countryside was soon in an uproar. The trouble was, nobody did anything about the fire. Worse, no one had the presence of mind to carry out the furniture. There was a pump on the property and men were sent to fetch it. Upon being lowered into the river, it promptly clogged with mud. Another man was dispatched at a gallop to rouse the fire department at Islip, but by the time the department arrived, the main house was already gutted and the annex was aflame.

The timing of the arrival was meaningless, in any case, since none of the fire hoses worked. The department had relied on the hoses kept on the property, all of which had rotted since their installation. Two dozen buckets were eventually produced, but they were inadequate to combat the blaze. Someone managed to drag the billiard table onto the lawn, but little else was saved. By dawn, William K. Vanderbilt's Idle Hour was a pile of smoking ashes.

What would have been a tragedy to an ordinary homeowner was an opportunity to Willie Vanderbilt. He decided to build another house. Considering that he was now single and separated from his children by the terms of a punitive divorce decree, and that he had spent most of the last ten years in Paris or Newport, one might wonder why he bothered to rebuild at all. Part of the answer surely lay in Vanderbilt's percep-

The second Idle Hour, designed by Richard Howland Hunt, son of the architect of the first house.

tion of himself as a gentleman. He had a responsibility to the local people; he was, after all, a major employer—besides which, he still needed a country seat. Paradoxically, this was because business had at last intruded on Willie's life.

During all the years that he had yachted and weekended and shot and attended balls and dinners with the cream of international society, his steadfast brother Cornelius II had tended the family store. Cornelius was badly weakened by a stroke in 1896, which required Willie to pay much more attention to family business affairs than he had in the past. In 1899, Cornelius died, leaving Willie as the head of America's richest and most powerful family. Suddenly, his was the final word in the management of the Vanderbilt railway empire. It was he who now had to attend personally to hundreds of millions of dollars in family trusts. While never in danger of becoming

a workaholic, he did devote himself to business as he never had before. It was at this time that W. K. Vanderbilt came up with the infamous "community of interest" concept, whereby he and his railroad cronies, for a while at least, neatly sidestepped pesky federal antitrust regulations.

In the context of his new position as head of a great family, reconstructing his country estate seemed only appropriate. Richard Morris Hunt had died in 1895, so Vanderbilt turned to Hunt's son to design the new Idle Hour. Richard Howland Hunt had continued his father's practice; he, too, was Beaux-Arts trained, and by 1899 his firm was busy with country- and city-house commissions.

Richard Howland Hunt's new Idle Hour is a brilliant example of everything that was correct about Beaux-Arts houses, although it is the kind of house that is not easily understood today. Idle

Hour was essentially a luxurious private hotel. During large weekend parties, with thirty or more guests invited, plus servants, there might have been seventy or more people eating and sleeping under Mr. Vanderbilt's roof.

The challenge to the architect was to provide everybody, including servants, with appropriate levels of privacy, luxury, and comfort. Servants were distributed discreetly around this enormous structure, and divided according to sex and seniority. Propriety required that a considerable distance be maintained between unmarried serving men and women, and the scale of the house provided for that. Serving men occupied quarters at one end of the basement; maids inhabited the third floor, all the way at the other end of the house.

The kitchens were located in the basement of a special bachelors' wing and connected to a core of service rooms that extended upward to pantries on the first floor and servants' bedrooms on the second floor. The upper tier of this service core was isolated completely from family and guest bedrooms on the same floor. Indeed, there wasn't even a door between them. The result of the plan of the new Idle Hour was the effortless circulation of guests, family, and servants.

In keeping with established Beaux-Arts doctrine, the form or outer shape of the building clearly expressed its various inner functions. Therefore, the exteriors reflected not just the location of major rooms within but also their relative importance to the plan as a whole. The grandest of the main floor's public rooms, as well as the family bedrooms and quarters for married guests on the second floor, were contained in that part of the house running parallel to the Connetquot River. The exterior of this section of the building was consequently the most imposing in terms of scale and decoration. The architect's idea was to prepare the visitor for the grandeur to be experienced upon entering the front door. One couldn't help but be impressed by this facade, separated from the river by a noble courtyard on whose far side was a flight of marble stairs leading down to the water's edge.

Running at a right angle to the main body of the house, and extending a considerable distance to the rear, was a secondary wing containing a marvelously paneled smoking room, a fives court (fives being an arcane indoor racquet sport im-

A view of the second house from the main approach road.

ported from Eton), two floors of bachelor bedrooms, servant halls, pantries, and a main kitchen. The exterior treatment here subtly reinforced the secondary nature of the rooms within. The roofline lacked the pseudo-Flemish gables that distinguish the main part of the house; there were no elaborate arcaded galleries; and doors to the outside were definitely of a secondary scale and nature.

Richard Howland Hunt's Idle Hour; view of the cloister courtyard.

There was drama and anticipation in the approach to Idle Hour: through the great gates on South Country Road, down the long, manicured drives, sweeping past the impressive north facade, and at last pulling into the large courtyard between the front door and the river. Once inside, there was visual excitement in every direction.

The layout of rooms and corridors at Idle Hour was a tour de force of axial arrangement. In Beaux-Arts design, the use of axes is a way of organizing space to provide coherence and aesthetic grandeur. The major rooms—the dining room, main hall, living hall, plus the library and the gold room (as the white and gold reception room was called)—were all arranged along one principal axis that paralleled the river. With all the doors open, one could view its entire length.

The remainder of Idle Hour's interiors were laid out along minor axes that corresponded to this major one. Hunt positioned architectural features in order to compose good views, not just from room to room but from every window and door, as well. The fountain, paths, and covered walkways of the cloistered garden in the rear of the house, for example, were carefully lined up to suggest a continuation of the house's interiors. The concept throughout the design was to create impressive view lines in every direction, both within the building and outside. The result was a sense of expansiveness that was exhilarating.

The interior decoration was an extravaganza of first-class design and workmanship. Karl Bitter, the famed sculptor discovered by Hunt's father, created brilliant things in this house, notably in the dining room, called the Hunt Room. Bitter designed a marble statue of the mythical huntress Diana for a niche above the fireplace, plus an elaborate plaster frieze of hunting scenes, executed in high relief on all four walls above a massive wainscot of Circassian walnut. The bill for the decorative work in this room alone, in 1900, was $75,000.

The vast oak-paneled living hall contained a huge Caen stone fireplace with a mantel supported by life-sized caryatids. Behind the fireplace was an elaborate organ complete with three-story pipe loft. The living hall is best remembered for its fantastic plaster ceiling, covered entirely with richly modeled pendants copied from a ceiling at Gilling Castle in Yorkshire.

Idle Hour; the "living hall."

Idle Hour; the main hall.

The main stairway at Idle Hour rose within a broad tower located at the far end of the entry hall. It looked like the sort of thing an entire medieval English village might have labored on for years, but it was the work of a single craftsman. The richly carved newels were crowned with fanciful creatures, and the stairway was lighted by a stained-glass window with a large V in the middle.

Idle Hour; carved oak screen outside the billiard room.

Idle Hour; organ pipes above the fireplace in the living hall.

The palm garden, before the addition of the Whitney Warren tennis court wing.

The gold room was imported from France and, likely as not, designed by one of the French *décorateurs* to whom Willie gave so many New York and Newport commissions. The boiserie is eighteenth-century French in style, and highlighted with eighteen-carat gold. Equally luxurious, but in an entirely different style, was the medieval smoking or billiard room in the bachelor wing. Along its southern wall was an exquisite ceiling-height carved oak screen whose workmanship was one of Idle Hour's marvels. Even the bathrooms were wonderful, finished off in snow white tile and dark stained mahogany, and equipped with overscaled fixtures.

Idle Hour was furnished with heavy overstuffed furniture, Oriental rugs, potted palms, and a liberal smattering of good French and English antiques. It had damask curtains with fat-tasseled tiebacks, lamps with fringed silk shades, and numerous carved wooden tables covered with silver frames and objets d'art.

When completed, the house had its own domestic telephone system, complete with switchboard and operator, plus phones throughout the main floor and in all the important bedrooms. Steam and electricity lines entered the house via an eight-hundred-foot-tunnel high enough for a man to walk through. The tunnel originated in a powerhouse containing the latest in boiler and generator technology. The reason for this was fire prevention. Although Willie Junior and his bride always maintained that a prowler had torched the original house, the accepted version was that a faulty flue on the boiler had been the culprit. If so, the same thing would not be allowed to happen twice (or three times, if one counts the destruction by fire of brother Cornelius's original Breakers).

Other conveniences abounded. The bedroom closets all had small hidden switches that turned on a light when you opened the door. The butler's pantry contained an immense silver vault

"It was due to [his] close relationship with Vanderbilt that Warren obtained his most famous commission, that for the design of Grand Central Station in Manhattan."

that looked as if it belonged in a bank. There were three elevators: one for baggage, one for guests, and one exclusively for Mr. Vanderbilt.

The design of Idle Hour's exterior, admittedly, was a bit forbidding. It badly needed ivy and important plantings to ameliorate its massiveness, but for much of its history, it had neither. The riverfront gables had a Dutch look, perhaps an unconscious allusion to Vanderbilt family origins. If one takes a photo of the house and covers up the gables, what emerges is something quite transformed and vaguely English in character. Idle Hour remains a building that eludes stylistic categorization.

Altogether, the new Idle Hour had roughly seventy rooms and something fewer than thirty baths. The structure was framed with ten-inch steel beams and sided with twenty inches of solid brick and masonry walls. The oval Palm Garden at the outer edge of the cloistered garden contained ten tons of plate glass. The total cost of construction and decoration approached $3 million.

No sooner was this stupendously big house completed than Vanderbilt set about having it enlarged. He called on Whitney Warren to design a new bachelor annex and an enclosed tennis court. Completed in 1903, this vast addition was constructed on a diagonal from the main axes of the house. It was attached to an existing oval-shaped palm garden, which was reincarnated as a Turkish room dense with Oriental

draperies and hanging brass lamps. The palms, meanwhile, were relocated to a new palm house about a quarter mile from the mansion.

Whitney Warren was a Vanderbilt family favorite who was involved in the construction of several of their houses. He liked to say he was a cousin, though in fact the connection was more remote, and through the Kissams and not the Vanderbilts. He was, however, a close friend of Willie Vanderbilt's and a member of the South Side Club, so he was a logical choice to work on Idle Hour. It was due to this close relationship with Vanderbilt that Warren obtained his most famous commission, that for the design of Grand Central Station in Manhattan. Construction was already well under way in 1906, when Willie Vanderbilt insisted on putting Warren in charge of a project that already had been started by the firm of Reed & Stem. Warren definitely affected the look of Grand Central for the better, but he was not responsible for the majority of the design work. Reed & Stem actually had to sue him for a share of the design fee, in which action they were successful.

In 1903, Willie was married a second time, to Anne Harriman Sands Rutherfurd. The new Mrs. Vanderbilt was twice widowed and had four children of her own. She shared her husband's love of France, and together they spent most of their time in Europe, much of it at Willie's splendid stud farm in Normandy. "If Normandy is the paradise of horses," intoned *The New York Times* in May of 1914, "the studfarm of Mr. Vanderbilt is the inner Eden." Willie was a big winner on the French turf, taking in well over a hundred thousand prize dollars during several prewar seasons. Every fall, the family returned to Idle Hour, where they entertained house parties until Christmas. The rest of the year, the house was closed.

The Great War came, and society as everyone had known it began to disintegrate. No longer were servants willing to labor long hours for low wages; taxes began to rise alarmingly; fashionable life-styles began to change. The new generation of the privileged demanded freedom and mobility, characteristics not associated with semifeudal country estates employing hundreds of people and costing thousands of dollars a day to run— even when no one was there.

As a patriotic gesture during the war, Vanderbilt had the lawns around Idle Hour dug up

The heir of Idle Hour, Howard Stirling (Mike) Vanderbilt, at the wheel of his yacht.

and planted with potatoes. By 1920, the damage was repaired and the estate restored to near-perfection. The landscaping everywhere had matured at last. The house was in an excellent state of repair. The property offered just about any diversion—hunting, fishing, tennis, fives (if you could find an opponent who knew the rules), boating, riding, gardening—that a gentleman might wish. Unfortunately, no one wanted to live there.

Willie Vanderbilt died in 1920 and left Idle Hour to his youngest son, thirty-six-year-old Harold Stirling (Mike) Vanderbilt. Mike Vanderbilt was a handsome and accomplished man. He was a yachtsman who three times successfully defended the America's Cup; he was the first person to apply the rules of the French game Plafond to the popular game of auction bridge, thereby creating today's contract bridge; and he was an active businessman who served for two generations on the board of the New York Central. In fact, he was the last Vanderbilt to sit on that board. In 1920, Mike Vanderbilt had no interest in Idle Hour and he immediately put it up for sale.

Willie Vanderbilt always had been a follower of fashion, and fashion had by now abandoned Oakdale. Places as large as Idle Hour were selling elsewhere, and in some cases even still being built. By 1920, there was no market for palaces in Oakdale, Long Island, however. Pepperidge Hall had been unoccupied for years. In a short time, the Bournes sold Indian Neck Hall to a military academy. That, combined with the demise of Idle Hour, left Mrs. Cutting all alone at Westbrook, the last of Oakdale's great estates.

After the Vanderbilt estate was closed, the furniture was auctioned—by Mr. Parke and Mr. Bernet personally. Plots of land were given to faithful former employees. In 1922, after at least two deals had fallen through, Mike Vanderbilt sold the main house and the bulk of the property to a pair of Brooklyn real estate developers named Edmund G. and Charles F. Burke.

The Burkes at first tried to develop Idle Hour into something called the Oakdale Club. Membership, according to a pompously worded brochure, would be "restricted and attainable only by invitation." The initiation fee in 1922 was two thousand dollars. At the same time they touted the exclusive club, the Burkes began subdividing the property into narrow lots, the av-

erage width of which was barely twenty-five feet. Nobody with any inclination toward owning an exclusive property would have dreamed of buying a lot in so dense a subdivision, which fact no doubt impaired sales. As for the exclusive club, it was a foreseeable flop, and the mansion ended up serving mainly as a sales office.

In 1927, the Burkes changed tactics and hired a new agent named E. A. White. Inspired by the canals and lagoons surviving from the Vanderbilt era, White came up with a marketing strategy that disposed of any lingering notions of exclusivity. The precise inspiration for his concept was unclear, veering between visions of an Idle Hour Riviera and that of a Venice of the north. Conceptual contradictions aside, lot sales improved. A rash of Mediterranean-looking stucco residences went up on spec, and an atmosphere of a Florida land boom invaded the original planned landscape.

Fortunately, the original ancillary buildings on the estate, almost without exception, were converted to residences and thereby preserved. The model farm complex, with its picturesque clock tower, was converted in the late twenties to an artists' colony, noted for wild parties and attendance by a fast set from New York (including the actor William Powell).

Some of these high jinks overlapped to the mansion itself. In 1930, a Gatsby-esque party giver by the name of Mrs. Corinne Groom Cartier announced that she had bought the main house from the Burkes. Mrs. Cartier is still remembered for a pale blue twelve-cylinder Cadillac convertible in which she sported about

1938 promotional flyer for Peace Haven.

briefly. Soon after acquiring this magnificent machine, she urged a local lad named Lavern Wittlock to hide it for her. This he did, savoring his own occasional drives therein, until the dealer in Patchogue found and repossessed it. Mrs. Cartier also hired her neighbors, a couple named Mr. and Mrs. Joseph Seymour, to watch over her new mansion.

Mrs. Cartier never really consummated any deal to buy Idle Hour, and she soon skipped town. However, the Seymours and Wittlock adopted the mansion in her wake. As the Depression deepened and lot sales came to a standstill, this trio became Idle Hour's unofficial guardians.

In 1933, the Burkes held yet another auction at Idle Hour. Incredibly, over five hundred items remained from the Vanderbilt days. Though it was the bottom of the Depression, this second auction raised $134,000. Idle Hour then remained empty for another five years, during which time it grew dusty but remained intact, sitting on a weedy superblock, overlooked by a handful of distant bungalows.

Then an entirely different kind of tenant arrived on the scene. His name was James B. Schafer, a cult leader who preached an ideal state of man based on positive thinking. In 1935, Schafer forsook a career in advertising and founded what he called the Truth Movement. Within three years, he had gathered either four or ten thousand followers—depending on the source one consults—and broadcast weekly lectures from Steinway Hall in New York.

Among other things, Schafer was the creator of the American School of Metaphysics, the Church of the Radiant Life, and the grandiloquently named Royal Fraternity of Master Metaphysicians. In 1938, this latter entity purchased Idle Hour—reportedly for $350,000—and renamed it Peace Haven. According to *Newsweek,* the handsome and charismatic Schafer knew how to "materialize money and dematerialize people." According to Schafer himself, "There is no single problem that money will not solve." Whenever he personally had one, he would simply "reach out to the infinite," as he put it, and the solution would come to hand, typically in the form of "love offerings" from middle-aged female devotees. "Ignorance is death, education is life," intoned the Master Metaphysician, who listed himself in the New York telephone directory with an MM after his name. If the educated

"His name was James B. Schafer, a cult leader who preached an ideal state of man based on positive thinking."

soul be "on constant guard against the forces of evil," then immortality could be achieved easily.

Peace Haven, the "House of the New Commandment," was spruced up—supposedly to the tune of $200,000 (Schafer never quoted reliable figures)—so as to be ready for occupancy by the summer of 1938. On July Fourth, a caravan of buses deposited five hundred followers in the entry court. Thereafter, there was a surge of visitors every weekend, hosted by a semipermanent complement of live-ins headed by Schafer himself.

The following year, Schafer announced he was taking over neighboring Pepperidge Hall, the old Christopher Roberts estate. This relic of Oakdale's salad days recently had been occupied by a Dr. Ludwig Harpootlian, who had been engaged in the indoor cultivation of silkworms.

One of the few alterations Schafer made to Idle Hour was the addition of a swimming pool, visible at upper right, behind the indoor tennis court.

Guests at a weekend program at "Peace Haven," summer, 1938.

Such was the fate of once-exclusive Oakdale. The price of Pepperidge Hall—reportedly only $15,000—bears eloquent testimony to the sorry decline in local real estate prices. It also makes the $350,000 supposedly paid for Idle Hour seem like metaphysical publicity.

In 1939, as war began to engulf Europe, the Master Metaphysician of Peace Haven conceived his greatest plan. In October of that year, he initiated proceedings to adopt a three-month-old girl by the name of Baby Jean. This child was going to be the embodiment of all Schafer's teachings. She would be fed nothing but pure foods and exposed to nothing but pure thoughts. By virtue of this, she would achieve immortality.

Although corny by later standards, Schafer's message of peace, goodness, and immortality actually touched hearts in 1939. In order to affect as many people as possible, he hired a public-relations expert named Lynne Krider to spread the word of Baby Jean across the country. Peace Haven became famous, profiled even in *The New Yorker*.

In early 1940, while Schafer was awaiting finalization of the adoption, Baby Jean's natural mother reappeared without warning and took the baby back. The mother's appearance shattered Schafer's magic aura. Soon afterward a woman named Minna Schmidt demanded the return of her $9,000 love offering. Schafer couldn't pay and Miss Schmidt filed a complaint with the New York District Attorney's office. By November of 1941, Schafer had been indicted for embezzlement, Peace Haven was bankrupt, and Idle Hour had been sold at auction. Six months later, Schafer was in Sing Sing.

Once again, the lawns at Idle Hour grew rank and the old house languished, intact but vacant. Then in 1947, the mansion and its original stable were sold to a subsidiary of the National Dairy Products Corporation of Baltimore, Maryland, for laboratory use. National Dairy took occupancy in 1948 with 127 employees and 250 white rats. The fives court was converted to a chemistry lab; the Hunt Room became a conference facility; boilers were installed in the middle of the former palm room; and executive offices filled the guest rooms. An adjacent tract of undeveloped former estate land was purchased at the same time, rechristened the Connetquot Colony, and earmarked for employee housing.

The most significant change that National Dairy made to Idle Hour was the demolition of the indoor tennis court. The company tore it out and filled the gutted shell with a windowless warren of tiny laboratories devoted to the study of cheese and enzyme biochemistry. Devoid of all architectural merit, these alterations are unfortunately extant today.

Despite this, Idle Hour still remained essentially unchanged. The sumptuous wood paneling remained, as did the carved Caen stone and marble fireplaces, as well as the marvelous Bitter sculptures in the Hunt Room. The enormous kitchen and pantries, as well as a goodly number of the original palatial bathrooms, were still there.

By 1960, National Dairy had outgrown Oakdale and decided to move. Idle Hour, minus the employee subdivision, was put back on the market, with an asking price of $1,750,000. The timing was perfect. Adelphi University's burgeoning new Suffolk County branch, founded in 1958, just then was looking for a new home. Adelphi purchased Idle Hour in 1962 and began conducting classes there in January of the following year. In 1968, Adelphi Suffolk became an independent institution and changed its name to Dowling College in honor of important endowments from a New York financier.

Dowling College seemed to be settling into Idle Hour very happily. It converted the carriage

Baby Jean "was going to be the embodiment of all Schafer's teachings."

house—already disfigured somewhat by National Dairy's attempts to modernize—into a gym, art studios, rathskeller, and a student theater. The old powerhouse became a performing arts center. Whitney Warren's former tennis court, now a maze of laboratories, was converted into a science building. Of course, exit signs, fire walls, institutional furniture, and the occasional steel door all made their inevitable appearance, but the great majority of the Vanderbilt house was unaltered.

While the student body exhibited a pride in Idle Hour, the college's administration did not display the same sensitivity. In the early 1970s, a boxy and ill-proportioned classroom facility was built barely a hundred feet from the Vanderbilt house.

The Learning Center was sadly representative of the new architecture around Oakdale. Idle Hour was now in the middle of the built-up suburbs, surrounded by a sea of Long Island ranch houses. No one seemed to have perceived that the Learning Center would damage the college's priceless original building simply by virtue of its close proximity.

In the early hours of March 18, 1974, a fire broke out in Idle Hour's original smoking room.

It spread rapidly to the main hall, devoured the carved staircase in its entirety, and scorched the Hunt Room and the living hall. Winds of forty miles per hour whipped the flames into a stone-melting inferno, but Idle Hour did not perish. It was a mess the next day, but the roof was still on. Save for smoke and water damage, the second and third floors were hardly touched. The house looked much more damaged than it really was.

A committee was promptly formed to oversee the building's restoration. The design contract went to the New York firm of Wank, Adams, Slavin Associates, one of whose principals had made alterations to Fairleigh Dickinson University's Florham a generation earlier. WASA had a long-standing association with the New York State Dormitory Authority, which actually held the title to Idle Hour as security against bonds it had issued to pay for the Learning Center.

Restoration committee chairman Alan Fortunoff also hired architect Giorgio Cavaglieri to assist on the principal rooms. Cavaglieri had come to Fortunoff's attention because of his alterations to the Jefferson Market Courthouse in Greenwich Village. These alterations had a look typical of the late 1960s, a mixture of old and new highlighted by sheets of smoked glass, dramatic contemporary lighting, and exposed brick walls.

Idle Hour's interiors had been well documented over the years, but no attempt at accurate restoration was even considered. The original Hunt plans never once were consulted. Photos taken immediately after the fire show bubbled veneering on wall paneling, which could have been reglued and repaired. The living hall's soot-stained pendants, shaved off during the alterations, could have been cleaned. Molds could have been made from undamaged pendants in order to replace those that were missing.

The Hunt Room was contiguous to the epicenter of the fire, but here the paneling was restored. This would seem to belie assertions put forth at the time that the original interior was a total loss, save for a few isolated fragments. The staircase was a total loss, and both the entry hall and the smoking room were completely gutted.

The reconstructed main hall, stairway, and living hall are uniformly unsatisfying. These interiors look neither new nor old. They have nothing to do with grand vintage houses, but

neither do they relate much to modern college life. They seem more like meeting rooms in a Ramada Inn. Only the palm room has been restored with sensitivity—and even there, the choice of flooring material strikes a jarring note.

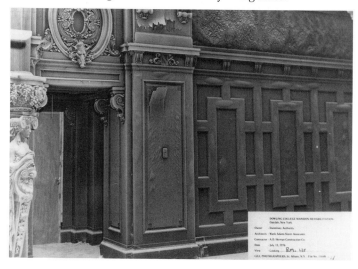

After the fire 1974; ". . . bubbled veneering on the wall paneling . . . could have been reglued and repaired."

Two of the principal rooms on the main floor were largely untouched by the fire. The library remains almost intact, an eloquent reproach to the so-called restored rooms nearby. The gold room, too, is relatively untouched, save for the marble fireplace yanked out by a retreating executive of National Dairy. With the exception of these and the Hunt Room, the rest of the present day interior is bland, functional, and uninteresting.

The architectural details on the upper floors, while filthy from smoke and water, were essentially intact. However, here everything was gutted.

If the $3 million insurance settlement for Idle Hour had been applied to proper restoration of the main rooms and a cleanup of the upper stories, instead of gutting and renovating, this house would again be the showplace it once was.

The renovation of Idle Hour even included some ill-advised alterations to the exterior, the worst of which was the relocation of the main entrance to the cloister in the rear. This has destroyed the entire internal arrangement of the house. The fenestration has been changed, as well; mullioned upper sashes were replaced with single sheets of glass, robbing the facades of an important detail.

Dowling College today; the Learning Center is at upper left.

Idle Hour has now been renamed Max and Clara Fortunoff Hall. As for the village of Oakdale, the former millionaires' country retreat is now densely developed with a mixture of middle-class suburban housing projects and shopping malls. Yet the legacy of the South Side Club and its gentlemen members is still visible. The club existed until 1973, when the Connetquot River State Park Preserve was created in its place. Thus have the lands of a rich man's hunting club been transformed into a sanctuary for precisely what used to be hunted. At this writing, the clubhouse building is undergoing a sensitive restoration, for which New York State is to be commended.

Pepperidge Hall has been demolished, but Indian Neck Hall still stands in fairly extensive grounds, housing the LaSalle Military Academy. The great majority of its important interior is unaltered and in current use. Westbrook, the last of Oakdale's four great estates, has been preserved as the Bayard Cutting Arboretum. Its main house is intact, if unfurnished, and its grounds, designed by Frederick Law Olmsted, still retain the feel of a gentleman's rural estate.

Together with the former South Side lands, this estate provides a welcome wooded greenbelt among the suburban subdivisions.

Mike Vanderbilt lived to be eighty-six, marrying at forty-nine. He died childless in Newport, Rhode Island, in 1970.

As for James B. Schafer, MM, he emerged from prison at the end of the War and went back to doing what he always had. More love offerings enabled him to buy a hundred acres and a big house in West Nyack, New York. On April 26, 1955, he and his second wife were discovered by the latter's daughter, victims of a double suicide. According to an enigmatic note found at the scene, there was "no other way out." Schafer was fifty-nine years old.

As for Baby Jean, the child who was to have been immortal, she was tracked down in 1964 by a Long Island reporter. Then living with a husband and children not ten miles from Idle Hour, she was unwilling to discuss the past. "We are happy the way we are," she said, begging for continued anonymity. "We are just ordinary people and that's what we want to remain."

Chapter 9

HYDE PARK

Hyde Park

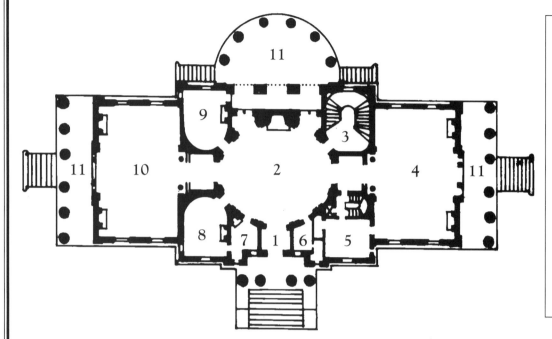

1st Floor
1. Vestibule
2. Main Hall
3. Stairhall
4. Dining Room
5. Serving Pantry
6. Powder Room
7. Office
8. Den
9. Reception Room
10. Drawing Room
11. Piazza

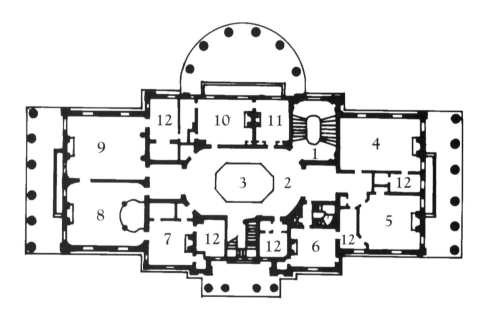

2nd Floor
1. Stairhall
2. Second Floor Hall
3. Upper Part of Main Floor Hall
4–6. Bedrooms
7. Mrs. Vanderbilt's Boudoir
8. Mrs. Vanderbilt's Bedroom
9. Mr. Vanderbilt's Bedroom
10–11. Bedrooms
12. Bathrooms

The original Greek Revival mansion on the property was replaced by this house after a fire in 1847. View shows river facade.

Location: Hyde Park, New York

Architect: McKim, Mead & White

(Charles Follen McKim [1847–1909], supervising architect)

Commissioned by: Frederick William Vanderbilt (1856–1938)

Main house completed: 1899

*O*NE of the most intriguing facts about Hyde Park is that it was named after a famous transvestite. Edward Hyde, Viscount Cornbury, was an early eighteenth-century governor of New York who conducted his administration dressed in women's clothes. This gave rise to perplexity but apparently little more. In 1705, Lord Cornbury rewarded a loyal secretary, one Peter Fauconnier, with a land grant on the east bank of the Hudson, a tract including the site on which Frederick and Louise (Lulu) Vanderbilt's house would eventually stand. In honor of his employer, Fauconnier named the estate Hyde Park.

Entrance facade of the Hyde Park estate house of 1847.

In 1764, Fauconnier's granddaughter and her husband, Dr. John Bard, built a house on the property. Bard was a prominent man in Colonial America, an intimate of Benjamin Franklin, and General Washington's personal physician. His son, Samuel Bard, built a second house on the property, atop a bluff overlooking an awesome panorama of the Hudson and the Catskills. This became the site of the Vanderbilt house.

The Bard estate passed in 1821 to Samuel Bard's son, who sold it a few years later to his father's partner, the famous Dr. David Hosack. Hyde Park was unusual in the United States by this time, because it had been maintained as a gentleman's estate for over sixty years. It was already lovely, but Hosack made it into a show-place. In 1829, he remodeled the Samuel Bard house after the latest Greek fashion, and hired a recently arrived Belgian landscape gardener named André Parmentier to lay out new drives and redesign the landscape.

Parmentier died only six years after coming to this country, and he is little known today. However, he was the first man in the United States to apply architectural—as opposed to merely horticultural—principles to the field of landscape design. Parmentier enunciated pre-

cisely those landscape principles that Freder-ick Law Olmsted would later come to embody. A. J. Downing, in his 1841 *Treatise on the Theory and Practice of Landscape Gardening,* credited Parmentier with being the first important practi-tioner of landscape art in America. Parmentier laid out several estates on the Hudson, the country seat of Dr. Hosack being considered his best.

Hosack was a highly cultured gentleman with a myriad of talents and interests. He was a pro-fessor at the College of Physicians and Surgeons, as well as a professor of botany at Columbia. It was he who laid out the famous Elgin Botanic Gardens in Manhattan, which by 1806 boasted over two thousand horticultural species housed in enormous greenhouses.

Hosack's experience with the Elgin Gardens enabled him to enrich the Parmentier landscape with a sophisticated choice of specimen plant-ings. The estate grew increasingly famous throughout the valley, not just for its sublime mountain and river views and its fine Greek house but for the artistic beauty of the designed landscape. Here Dr. Hosack entertained Philip Hone, Washington Irving, and the poet Fitz-Greene Halleck.

In 1840, John Jacob Astor purchased the Ho-sack estate for his daughter Dorothea and her husband, Walter Langdon. The gentrified, semi-feudalistic atmosphere of the Hudson Valley appealed mightily to the Astor clan, members of which occupied three separate riverfront estates at one point. In 1845, the Langdon house burned to the ground, and two years later, the family replaced it with another fine Greek manse. It was in this house that their son, Walter Langdon, Jr., died childless in 1894. The property was put on the market and Fred Vanderbilt bought it in 1895.

Four years before this, the Vanderbilts had completed a vast stone summer mansion at Newport, designed for them by Peabody & Stearns. It is said that Mr. Vanderbilt was not overly social. If that's the case, Newport hardly could have appealed to him. It's likely, too, that he and his wife encountered unpleasantness at Newport. Affairs were tolerated in American society, as long as they were conducted discreetly, but divorce was considered beyond the pale. Mrs.

Edward Hyde, Lord Cornbury, Governor of the Province of New York between 1702 and 1708.

Vanderbilt was not only a divorced woman, she was divorced from her husband's first cousin. This fact, coupled with the pervasive jealousy toward the Vanderbilt money, probably led to more than one awkward situation. There were plenty of people in Newport who were only too happy to snub a Vanderbilt—as long as they thought they could get away with it.

It has been noted by a number of different researchers that there really isn't much to say or write about Fred Vanderbilt. He was a studious fellow, and an 1878 graduate of the Sheffield Scientific School at Yale University. He was the only one among the four Vanderbilt brothers to graduate from a U.S. college—or, indeed, to graduate from any college at all. He was also the only one of the four to succeed in his own right as a capitalist. He developed his own portfolio of inspired investments, and by the time of his death was an alumnus of every single department of the New York Central. He was a director of Central for sixty-one years, and on the board of the Chicago and Northwestern (the famous "Nickel Plate") for fifty-six years. His neighbor Franklin D. Roosevelt joked that Fred's pockets jingled every time a New York Central train passed below his Hyde Park mansion.

Frederick William Vanderbilt, according to one family member, looked "like a man with a secret."

Aside from his $3 million checking account ('in case I want to buy something') and a passion for yachts, he seems to have kept his head tucked down through most of his life. He never engaged too much with the rest of the world, in spite of his wife's outgoing charm and sociability. His grandnephew Osgood Field remembered him as "painfully shy." John Clermont, construction superintendent of the Vanderbilt house at Hyde Park, called him "humble and shy" and averse to publicity. Fred Osborn, one of the Vanderbilt clan's many relations by marriage, characterized him as looking like a man with a secret.

Grandnephew and namesake Frederick Vanderbilt Field remarked on his great-uncle's curiously unsuitable Christmas gifts. On his fifth birthday, Fred and Lulu sent him a typewriter. When he was seven, they gave him a gold razor. Field, later an ardent communist and author of a memoir titled *From Right to Left*, characterized his great-uncle as "pleasant, gentle and overly shy."

Fred's favorite sister, Lila Webb, described him in her diary as her "pet brother. . . . He is not handsome, has red hair and freckles. But he has the loveliest mouth and teeth and very nice eyes and is a dear good boy." That was in 1878, when the dear boy was twenty-two years old and about to elope with the former Mrs. Daniel Torrance.

Louise Anthony Torrance, or Aunt Lulu as the family came to call her, was twelve years older than Fred. She was also very tall and he was rather short. Theirs was a torrid affair at first, beginning while he was at Yale and she was still married to his cousin Daniel Torrance. They married one another on December 17, 1878, at the Windsor Hotel in New York. It wasn't exactly a secret marriage, but none of his family was present. His father, in fact, didn't hear about it until February of the next year.

Everybody who knew Lulu agreed that she was gracious. Watson Webb remembered with relish that an exaggerated sense of delicacy led her to dress up the high toilet tanks at Hyde Park with tulle. She wore a wig in later years, and Watson claims his Hammond cousins, when small, made a game of trying to snag it off her head with fishing lines. The interesting part of this story is that Aunt Lulu was a willing participant, which says a lot about the sort of woman she was.

According to the Vanderbilts' Hyde Park

Mrs. Louise Anthony Torrance "was twelve years older than Fred."

neighbor Eleanor Roosevelt, Lulu was a perfect example of the old order. She went on a drive precisely at 3:00 P.M. every afternoon, regardless of the weather. During that drive, she did her mental exercises, surely an old-orderish thing to do. These consisted of reciting forward and backward the kings and queens of England, then the

Presidents of the United States. If there was time, she'd do the kings and queens of France, as well. Here, clearly, was a disciplined mind.

Her good humor and discipline couldn't insulate her from the disapproval of her husband's family, however. Apropos of this is the following story from Freddy Field's memoir. Early on, the family's disapproval of Lulu crystalized around the question of an heir. The age difference between her and Fred was paramount in everybody's mind. Could this woman become pregnant? Suddenly, she appeared to be. She and Fred then left for France, innocently on the surface of it all. The next thing anybody knew, there was a cable from Paris: A baby had been born but, alas, had died.

Actually, something very different had been going on. Lulu had been stuffing her dress. Fred colluded with her on the whole plan—including the trip to Paris and the cable home—in an effort to help her win acceptance with his family. When the truth came out, the Vanderbilts took pity on Lulu, never again pressed the issue of children, and forthwith accepted her as one of their own.

Fred and Lulu married for love, and by all accounts the marriage was a good one. However, the elopement angered Fred's father to such a degree that for a while, anyway, he seriously considered disinheriting the young man. According to family tradition, it was only due to Lila's constant intercession on her brother's behalf that this never came to pass. When William Henry Vanderbilt died in December of 1885, his son Fred received the same $10 million inheritance as each of his seven siblings did. Fred never forgot Lila's efforts; in their later years, he helped her liberally with loans, for which he never expected repayment.

Fred and Lulu Vanderbilt first came to know the Hyde Park area while visiting their friends Mr. and Mrs. Ogden Mills. The Mills lived on a riverfront estate in Staatsburg, immediately to the north of Hyde Park. When the Walter Langdon property came on the market, it was Ogden Mills who took Fred Vanderbilt to see it. The property had not been well maintained for some years by 1895. Its landscape and horticultural potential, stemming from the efforts of distinguished past owners, were evident, however. The Vanderbilts were disillusioned with Newport and ready to buy.

There were striking parallels between the Langdon property and that of Ogden Mills. Both were old estates long associated with the local gentry. Both possessed fine vintage houses, neither of which was large enough for the new plutocratic life-style. Mills had hired McKim, Mead & White to enlarge the existing house on his property. Vanderbilt did the same.

The Mills house today, big and wonderful though it may be, is not a design triumph. Flanking wings of an older structure were demolished, and what remained was buried in the middle of gigantic new additions. Much of the lovely interior of the original house was thus preserved,

but the final product looks a bit bland and bulky from the outside, and several of the old rooms seem awkwardly placed in relation to the new interiors. The plan appealed to Fred Vanderbilt, however, and he instructed McKim, Mead & White to do the very same thing to the Langdon house.

The architectural partnership of Charles Follen McKim (1847–1909), William Rutherford Mead (1846–1928), and Stanford White (1853–1906) was among the most prolific artistic associations the United States has ever witnessed. McKim, Mead & White's fine buildings—Pennsylvania Station, the Morgan Library, the University Club, the New York Herald Building, the Washington Arch, the Rhode Island State Capitol, the Boston Public Library, to name only a handful—were consciously intended by their designers to change the world for the better, and specifically to elevate the quality of the American experience. In this respect, the firm didn't differ much from modern architects who similarly see themselves as leading the nation down new and important roads of cultural development.

Professionally, this trio constituted an ideal partnership. McKim was the scholar; Mead, the engineer and manager; and White, the idea man. Their personalities, however, were as different as could be. McKim was an aesthete, sometimes to the point of preciousness. Mead was a Vermonter, so reserved that his office nickname was "Dummy." White was a wild-eyed, hand-pumping, gesticulating, loud-dressing extrovert. McKim once quipped, apropos of his partner's famous excess of activity, that "White, in order to maintain his reputation, is planning to return as soon as he arrives." All three men, however, shared the same belief in the civilizing mission of architecture.

Both McKim and Mead worked briefly in the New York office of architect Russell Sturgis. It was here that both got heavy doses of Sturgis's idol, John Ruskin (1819–1900). Ruskin was a brilliant English critic, utopian socialist, and author of, among many other things, *The Seven Lamps of Architecture.* He was appalled at the depredations—aesthetic as well as social—of the Industrial Revolution. One might summarize Ruskinian doctrine as a vision of a new world order, one suffused with morality, equality, and a picturesque preindustrial Gothic aesthetic. McKim, Mead & White's professional work soon enough left Ruskinian aesthetics in the dust. The exposure was crucial, however, as it instilled in these young men a belief in the ability—and indeed in the duty—of architecture to bring both knowledge and beauty into the everyday life of mankind.

McKim was the only one of the three to attend the famous architectural school at the École des Beaux-Arts in Paris. He arrived in France in 1867, but cut short his Parisian course of study in 1870, the year the Franco-Prussian War broke out and sensible Americans in Paris promptly returned home. Upon his arrival back in the States, the twenty-three-year-old McKim went to work for Henry Hobson Richardson, the great proponent of the Romanesque in American design. Two summers later, in 1872, a nineteen-year-old draftsman named Stanford White began his apprenticeship at Richardson's office. When Richardson moved to Brookline, Massachusetts, in 1874, McKim stayed behind and opened a practice of his own. Among the first things he did was to hire Stanford White.

Meanwhile, in 1872, Mead had returned to New York after a course of study at the Academia delle Belle Arti in Florence. He met McKim, then overburdened with work on new houses, and shortly thereafter they formed a partnership. They called themselves McKim, Mead & Bigelow, the third member being McKim's brother-in-law, William Bigelow. This was a firm well grounded in classical architecture from the start, due to Mead's and McKim's European studies. These young men were typical of America's ambitious and talented young architects of the period: They were consciously searching for unique architectural ways to express the American experience.

Then came a great national event: the Philadelphia Centennial Exposition of 1876. The centennial was quite a show, full of all sorts of cultural and artistic exhibits, plus mechanical contraptions and industrial products that bore eloquent testimony to the nation's cultural and scientific coming-of-age. Its potent patriotic symbolism is hard to overstate. The centennial was an elaborate badge of national accomplishment. The country had completed a century of independent existence, survived the Civil War, and was now in the midst of an enormous pros-

perity. Some citizens had become rich to a degree that surpassed the aristocracies of the Old World. The Centennial was an announcement—to Americans and to the world at large—that the country had shed its former provincial self-image and was now becoming an empire.

For artists and architects, the centennial also focused attention on the question of what, exactly, was the nature of the American culture. This was a subject that had not been taken seriously in the past, most particularly by Europeans. The United States was held by most social observers to be a nation without any real culture—at least not a culture of its own.

In 1877, motivated by a pervasive national quest for identity stimulated by the centennial, McKim, Mead, Bigelow, and White all embarked on a walking tour of New England. Their goal was to discover bona fide examples of indigenous American culture, expressed in the form of Early American architecture. All four came back from this summer with a collection of sketches of everything they had seen, providing them with a well-grounded understanding of the details of Colonial architecture, and a very Ruskinian yearning to improve the lot of Americans everywhere by making architecture a true reflection of American culture.

Colonial architecture was simply a provincial interpretation, usually in wood, of the English Georgian style. English Georgian was really nothing more than the rediscovery—via the Renaissance, Palladio, Inigo Jones, and Christopher Wren—of the forms, proportions, and symmetry of classical Greek and Roman architecture. The Colonial architectural heritage was, therefore, a direct link with Western antiquity. The Greek Revival that swept the country in the wake of the Colonial period was only an extension of established American design traditions.

Then along had come Ruskin, Andrew Jackson Downing, A. J. Davis, Sir Walter Scott, William Morris, and all the others who flooded the mid-nineteenth century with their theories and passions for romantic forms and the revival of the Gothic, the picturesque, and the asymmetrical. McKim, Mead & White matured professionally in the midst of this aesthetic and moralistic ferment, but they were in the forefront of those who moved beyond it. They identified the quality that had informed their country's only indigenous architecture, which, of course, was classicism.

American architects, as much then as today, paid close attention to what one another did and said. In 1877, everybody in the field, including the firm of McKim, Mead & Bigelow, was listening to Robert Swain Peabody, of the eminent Boston firm of Peabody & Stearns. In that year, Peabody delivered an address to the eleventh convention of the American Institute of Architects, an address that would have far-reaching consequences for American architecture.

Peabody, too, had rediscovered Colonial American architecture. He extolled its delicacy and fitness, its picturesqueness, and especially its associations with the American experience. He urged American architects to draw freely from the elements of Colonial design and to take to heart the charm of Georgian models. He believed it was not necessary to reemploy Colonial elements in the same manner as Colonial builders. To the contrary, he said better effects and more originality could be achieved by letting the imagination run wild, and using Colonial details plus modern building materials (notably shingles) to articulate the result.

Peabody's goal was to popularize a new American style of architecture, which he called the Modernized Colonial Style. Of course, buildings designed along these lines look anything but Colonial to modern eyes. To the contrary, Peabody's Modernized Colonials are what people today call Victorian. At the time, in one of those vagaries of terminology, the style was known as Queen Anne.

By late 1879, Bigelow had left the firm and White had taken his place as the new third partner. By the early eighties, McKim, Mead & White had become one of the principal exponents of the Modernized Colonial Style, in particular that version of it which today is called the Shingle Style. Newport, Rhode Island, contains many wonderful McKim, Mead & White houses from this period. They are commodious, visually intriguing, marvelously textured (shingles perfectly achieved that), and showcases of superb domestic carpentry. The Newport Casino on Bellevue Avenue (1879–1881) is a good example of the best of the firm's Shingle Style structures, as is the Robert Goelet house on Narragansett Avenue (1882–1883), and Edna Villa on Bellevue Avenue (1883), to name only a few.

Alas, almost all Modernized Colonials, or Queen Annes as they were popularly called, were afflicted by a very serious shortcoming. The problem was the customary Queen Anne floor plan, which revolved around a very large combination stair hall and living room, located just inside the front door, and called the living hall. Real estate agents in our times often point with pride to so-called "flowing" plans. In Queen Anne houses, the original segregation of living spaces in the Colonial models was replaced by a great openness, wherein vistas in every direction were possible.

The various parts of a well-designed house have their own distinct purposes, however. Once those purposes start to overlap, the possibility of privacy is eliminated. Henry James, in the face of the Queen Anne building boom, declared that privacy was absolutely dead in America.

Each of the partners in McKim, Mead & White was well traveled and well acquainted with how and why the great European houses were laid out as they were. As the United States prospered in the late eighties and nineties, and the firm's commissions for private houses burgeoned, rich clients began to demand more sophisticated architectural packages. The open plan of Shingle Style houses was replaced by arrangements of rooms and hallways that respected individual privacy and protected the sanctity of the household from casual intrusion. The exteriors became more and more symmetrical in massing, and classically influenced in detail. This was simply a natural evolution which reflected the tenets held by the partners a decade earlier.

The more they worked—and this was a firm that rarely turned down a commission—the more historically accurate the designing partners became. The United States was then entering an imperial period. By the nineties, the dynamic financial capital of New York represented the future. McKim, Mead & White took their classical design knowledge and used it to create buildings appropriate to the United States, its background, achievements, and new position in the world. Far from being insipid copyists, the firm became one of the principal exponents of an authentically American architecture.

Americans at the end of the nineteenth century were enthralled by the architectural images of empire. The scale and grandeur of the monuments of antiquity appealed to the nation's collective psyche. Imperialism wasn't yet a dirty word—and imperial architecture, especially that based on models derived from the culture of ancient Greece, seemed altogether appropriate for a nation with democratic traditions and belief in manifest destiny. McKim, Mead & White embodied the national mood.

Both Ogden Mills and Fred Vanderbilt became clients of the firm in the mid-nineties, when it was at the apex of its reputation and influence.

Hyde Park was Charles McKim's project. He had to work with an existing house, but fortunately, it was a serene, classical composition that provided him with inspiration for his own design. The Italian Renaissance, in particular, was McKim's personal standard of beauty. The house he designed for Fred Vanderbilt reflected his fashionable gravitation toward a more literal interpretation of Renaissance form and detail.

Hyde Park is a very grand and formal affair: a rectangular structure rising three floors to a flat roof with a balustrade. On each facade is an imposing two-story porch supported by fluted stone columns with beautifully carved Corinthian capitals. The porch overlooking the river is semicircular in shape, and enjoys what is probably the best view in the entire valley of the Hudson River and the Catskills. The composition is restrained and rigorously classical, but it is also exceedingly sumptuous.

The design and construction process was a frantic blur of activity from the beginning. Measured drawings were done in the summer of 1895. A plan for an adjacent pavilion on the site of an old barn complex was drawn up at the same time. The idea was to erect the pavilion hastily so that the Vanderbilts would have somewhere to stay while the main house was under construction. Later, they would use it as a bachelor annex.

The pavilion is an appealing Georgian structure—far more domestically scaled than the main house. It was constructed of stucco and painted wood rather than stone, and the cornice line beneath the eaves is pierced by second-floor windows in a picturesque domestic manner that subtly reinforces the secondary nature of the structure. The pavilion deftly complements and counterpoints the design of the main house without in any way competing with it. For the sake of speed, a barn on the site of the pavilion was demolished with dynamite in September of 1895. Teams of laborers then worked for sixty-six days,

Architect Charles Follen McKim; Hyde Park was his pet project.

completing the pavilion by November of 1895.

This same fever pitch typified all the construction at Hyde Park. Besides the main house, Vanderbilt commissioned two additional residences on his property: one for his friend and broker Edward Wales and his wife; the other for a New York socialite and cotillion leader, Thomas Howard, who was married to Lulu's niece Rose. The Wales house—a brick Georgian affair on the edge of the estate nearest the village—and the Howard house—a miniature fieldstone manse in the woods across the Post Road—both were designed by McKim; both were built between January and September of 1896. "Mr. and Mrs. Vanderbilt have no children and they seem to have a fondness for making homes for other people," observed the San Francisco *Chronicle* at the time.

Construction of the Wales and Howard houses clipped along briskly. The alterations to the old Langdon house, scheduled to begin at the same time, ran into problems, however. A February 1896 letter from Mead to McKim reached the latter while he was touring the Nile with Mr. and Mrs. Henry White. "Fred Vanderbilt's job has met with a serious delay," wrote Mead. "When we came to tear the old house apart, it was found to be in as bad condition as the annex—no strength to the mortar, walls out of plumb, etc., etc.; in fact, so bad that it seemed foolish to attempt to build anything on it."

One wonders whether a restoration architect today would agree with that verdict. However, in the winter of 1895–1896, the Langdon house wasn't yet fifty years old, and there were plenty of others like it throughout New York and New England. No doubt, it was perceived as expendable, in spite of its history. The architects may have been relieved to get rid of it. The strength of McKim's Vanderbilt house rests as much on its interior as its exterior. If the old house had survived, the present interior would have been very different.

The architect's recommendation to demolish floored Lulu, and put Mead's diplomacy to the test. He continued to McKim:

> As matters stand now, we are rearranging the center on virtually the same lines but with certain changes in plan, and keeping the exterior just as you left it. There has been a good deal of fight to do this, because when it was found the old house had to come down Mrs. Vanderbilt kicked over the traces and was disposed to build an English house as she called it. We have, however, used your name pretty freely as being much interested in this design and likely to be disappointed if anything happened to it.

Fred was less perturbed than Lulu, however, and he agreed with McKim and Mead on the decision to raze. The Langdon house was demolished in the same month the Wales and Howard houses were completed—September 1896. Construction started immediately on the new McKim-designed main house. Norcross Brothers of Worcester, Massachusetts, acted as contractor, John B. Clermont superintendent. Norcross was among the first general contractors in this country and did much work for H. H. Richardson. Before that, architects were expected to deal both with design questions and with a horde of subcontractors. Norcross built 640 Fifth Avenue for Fred's father, as well as the New York Public Library, the New York Central Building, the State Capitol at Albany, the Allegheny County Courthouse, the Cincinnati Chamber of Commerce Building, and Trinity

The Howard house on the Vanderbilt estate at Hyde Park.

Church in Boston, to name but a few. They were the largest construction firm in the United States during the nineties, and maintained a Manhattan office at 160 Fifth Avenue, the same address as that of McKim, Mead & White.

According to Clermont, interviewed in 1954 as part of a local-history project, the Hyde Park house was supervised solely by McKim. He said Mead never even went to the site and that White only popped in once. He apparently annoyed Clermont with his high-pressure, big-city manner. The superintendent recalled him as a "windbag" and "full of hot air."

The men who had labored on the Wales and Howard houses now began construction on the main house. The deep basements were excavated by hand, and the dirt pulled away by horse cart. Millions of bricks—3 million to be precise—were delivered by barge from Kingston, across the river in Ulster County. The house rose steadily, first the steel supporting framework, then the brick infill and partitioning, and finally the limestone skin. Instantly, it became a local sight-seeing attraction. Leon Buller, a German stonemason, did the beautiful carvings on the facade—including the capitals atop the columns—from designs by Charles McKim. Plaster models of those capitals were hoisted aloft and the stone carving done in situ.

The Wales house on the
Vanderbilt estate at Hyde Park.

"The design and construction process was a frantic blur of activity."

Above: Plaster models of the column capitals "were hoisted aloft and the stone carving done *in situ*." Below: Note workmen balancing plaster models.

Charles McKim's completed Hyde Park; entrance facade at left.

By August 1898, the exterior of the house was complete. Inside, the partitions were all in place, but most of the rooms had floors of rough cement and walls of unfinished brick. The final interior work, as was the custom with houses of this caliber, was now entrusted to an entirely different group of decorators and designers. Norcross Brothers did some of the less involved interior work, and they also installed assorted architectural elements designed and/or procured by others. It was at this point, however, that they left center stage. Clermont recalled that the total cost of the building, including interiors, was $2,250,000. Records show that only $660,000 had been expended on it thus far, which gives a good idea of the scope of the work that still remained.

River facade of the new Hyde Park, with semicircular porch overlooking the Hudson and the Catskills.

Ultimately, four of the United States's foremost designers were involved with the interiors at Hyde Park. Though McKim was the principal architect, he did little of the interior design work. Fred wanted French interiors, a natural choice for a rich and cultured individual of that era. French interiors were considered both beautiful and appropriate for great American houses, but good French design work was not McKim's specialty. Stanford White, the firm's best interior designer, played a small role at Hyde Park. He sold Fred assorted rugs, busts, sofas, damask curtains, and so on, and did the original decorating in the large drawing room on the south side of the house. The majority of the interior decorating was done by other designers, however.

Chief among these, strangely enough, was a man wholly unknown now. He was Georges A. Glaenzer, a Manhattan decorator who specialized in the French style. Fred hired Glaenzer directly, and he hired him only for certain specific rooms. Glaenzer did the white and gold

The drawing room at Hyde Park was originally decorated by Stanford White.

The white and gold reception room, decorated by Georges A. Glaenzer.

reception room, a room that was never used or liked very much, for reasons difficult to fathom. He also designed the opulent Circassian walnut and tapestry scheme for Fred's bedroom, although Norcross actually installed the finished paneling. The little den, or library—the room in which Fred spent most of his private time— off the main hall also was done by Glaenzer. As was the original scheme for the great hall on the main floor.

French work was also the forte of the American designer and architect Ogden Codman. In fact, Codman was one of the few Americans whose rooms ever achieved a truly French feeling. Codman, who in 1897 coauthored *The Decoration of Houses* with Edith Wharton, provided Lulu with a delicious French boudoir, plus a bedroom fit for a French queen. The bedroom boiserie is Louis XV in inspiration, and the completed scheme included a ceremonial rail around the bed, itself placed upon a raised platform. W. B. Osgood Field, husband of Fred's niece Lila Sloane, told his children that whenever Uncle Fred wanted to see Aunt Lulu, he dropped a quarter in the gate.

The fourth designer involved with the interior was Whitney Warren, Willie Vanderbilt's good friend and a principal in the famous architectural firm of Warren & Wetmore. Warren was a Beaux-Arts designer with firsthand knowledge of the era's luxurious tastes. His firm's first contract

Glaenzer "also designed the opulent Circassian walnut and tapestry scheme for Fred's bedroom."

was for the aristocratic New York Yacht Club on Forty-fourth Street, built in 1899. The firm's partners traveled in the best circles of New York and Newport society and contributed work to many major houses.

In the case of Hyde Park, Warren became involved years after the house was completed. He substantially redesigned the second-floor balustrade, as well as the ceiling treatment of the large central double-height hall, improving the design greatly. Fred was sensitive to McKim's feelings about other designers altering his original house. In January of 1906, he advised McKim of Warren's projected changes. "We asked Whitney Warren to suggest some plan for improving the appearance of the second floor hall," he wrote, adding solicitously, that "Both my wife and I would indeed be sorry to do anything that would affect our friendly and pleasant relations, especially as we know how interested you are in the place."

". . . [A] bedroom fit for a French queen."

Above and right: Whitney Warren "substantially redesigned the second-floor balustrade, as well as the ceiling treatment of the large central double-height hall."

It was Warren who replaced McKim's vaguely Colonial second-floor railing by using staggered rows of balustrades in heavily carved stone. Warren also reworked White's decoration of the large drawing room, as well as altering Glaenzer's reception room, painting over some murals, among other things. Lulu still was not satisfied with the result, or perhaps she just preferred the large drawing room, where she entertained even small groups.

Fred had a taste for tapestries, which he gratified at the showrooms of Duveen and Glaenzer. The house also had the requisite complement of framed Bouguereaus and Villegas. Most of the furniture was French, but very little of it was antique. Those were the days when you could get reproduction fauteuils and bergères of superlative quality at reasonable prices. Ogden Codman often used reproductions. Most clients found them more durable and comfortable than the originals, and they were just as good-looking.

Hyde Park, notwithstanding the Vanderbilts' hard-to-understand dislike of the reception room, was a gem inside and out. It was wholly inspired by classicism, the pure root of beauty, and showcased America's best architectural and design talent.

While the main house was going up, work continued steadily on the other components of the estate. At the time of his original land purchase, Fred also bought five additional contiguous parcels. The enlarged Hyde Park estate now occupied both sides of the Albany Post Road and totaled over six hundred acres.

In 1897, Norcross built the White Bridge over Crum Elbow Creek, where it intersects the driveway between the house and the main gate. This was among the first steel and concrete bridges in the country, and it is lovely and graceful to this day. Also in that year, Fred hired Robert H. Robertson to design a carriage house. It might seem odd that Vanderbilt would hire another architect after having McKim design all the other structures on the property. However, Robertson at the time was involved with the development of Shelburne Farms, the elaborate Vermont estate of Fred's sister Lila and her husband, Seward Webb. Probably Fred met Robertson socially at Shelburne, admired his work, and gave him the contract. Robertson's Hyde Park carriage house actually looks quite a lot like the Webbs' Vermont mansion, at least in massing and detail. It complements McKim's work and is an ornament to the property.

The main entrance to the estate, a stately gate-house complex located on the Post Road immediately north of the village, was built in early 1898. A model farm east of the Post Road was repaired and upgraded in the summer of 1899. In April of 1899, the furniture was moved into the main house. And on May 12, a special train from New York delivered guests to the Vanderbilts' first house party. Hyde Park was now not just a Vanderbilt house but also a symbol of American taste and power.

What was life like for the Frederick W. Van-

Above: Hyde Park; stair to the third floor. Whitney Warren replaced a similar railing overlooking the main hall.

Below: Hyde Park; the dining room. "Fred had a taste for tapestries, which he gratified at the showrooms of Duveen and Glaenzer."

derbilts of Hyde Park? In a word, it was stately. As soon as the couple arrived in Dutchess County, they assiduously adopted the customs, trappings, and attitudes of the English landed gentry. One would have thought Fred's ancestors had been beautifying Hyde Park and tending to the local populace for centuries.

The Vanderbilts established a grandiose annual routine that was typical of their set and their time. The year started in New York, winter being punctuated with visits to Palm Beach, California, or Europe, or cruises on their yacht. At Eastertime, they opened up the main house at Hyde Park, but by high summer, they were off again. They avoided Newport (even though Rough Point was not sold until 1906), retreating instead to the Adirondacks, to a camp called Pine Tree Point on Upper St. Regis Lake. Fred bought this in 1902 from his brother-in-law Hamilton Twombly. He then had it rebuilt by the same team of Japanese carpenter-mechanics that had built the Japanese Pavilion at the 1901 Pan-American Exposition in Buffalo, New York. The result was so authentic that the Vanderbilts required their maids to wear kimonos.

After 1913, they abandoned the Adirondacks and summered at Bar Harbor, Maine. In the fall, they returned to Hyde Park and New York, dividing their time between the two but staying mostly in the country. Their city addresses reflect the changing patterns of Manhattan's residential districts. They moved out of 459 Fifth Avenue in 1914, when it was torn down and replaced by the Arnold Constable department store. For a few years, they kept an apartment at the Ritz-Carlton, a Whitney Warren design on Madison Avenue and Forty-sixth Street. Then they rented the Oakleigh Thorne house at Seventy-third Street and Park Avenue until 1917. Finally, Fred bought an Ogden Codman–designed limestone town house at 1025 Fifth Avenue, which he kept until his death.

Perhaps because Lulu Vanderbilt was childless, she devoted an inordinate amount of energy to other people's children, particularly those of the underprivileged. For thirty-four years, Mrs. Vanderbilt sponsored an annual Thanksgiving dinner for messengers and newsboys in Newport, complete with music provided by a quartet from the Naval Training Station. Lulu continued to underwrite this dinner every year until her death in 1926, even though her and Fred's last season at Newport was in 1894.

At Hyde Park, the Vanderbilts played the seigneurial role with a vengeance. They gave annual New Year's parties for the entire community, and arranged events such as river cruises and picnics (often with the other river families) for the entire villages of Hyde Park and Staatsburg. In the summer, Lulu always did something special for the local children; for example, chartering a river steamer to take them on an excursion to Kingston, or arranging a strawberry and ice cream festival for them at Hyde Park.

Hyde Park basically was shut down by the beginning of each December, but the Vanderbilts made a point to be in residence there every Christmas. Christmas was Lulu's big holiday. For many years, she loaded a grand sleigh that had belonged to the Romanovs with gifts. Then, swathed in furs and accompanied by Russian wolfhounds, she made the rounds of the village like a society Santa. The Vanderbilts put in huge orders at Macy's every year as a part of this ritual. Lulu continued her Christmas Day calls until she died, although in later years she rode around in a chauffeur-driven Packard.

Throughout these years, her husband paid serious and sustained attention to his estate. Herbert C. Shears managed the estate almost from the beginning until Vanderbilt's death in 1938. There were over sixty full-time employees at Hyde Park—seventeen in the house, two in the pavilion, and about forty-four on the grounds. In 1899, farm workers at Hyde Park received $1.50 in wages for a twelve-hour day. By 1917, the pay had risen to two dollars; the daily hours were down to nine, and Sunday was free. By 1937—the year before Fred's death—the workweek was down to five days, but the daily pay had not hit five dollars yet.

Besides the more than sixty employees at Hyde Park, the Vanderbilts supported twenty-four Jersey cows, fifteen Belgian horses, and two thousand leghorn chickens on their model farm. These latter provided enough milk, eggs, and poultry for everyone connected with the estate. Two times a year, a special railroad car transported Fred's horses back and forth from New York. Two times a week, the greenhouses at Hyde Park sent flowers to the house in town.

The Vanderbilts entertained, of course, and grandly at times, too. The passing years saw a succession of distinguished guests at lunches and dinners. Willie Vanderbilt, Mrs. Potter Palmer of Chicago, Fred's niece Consuelo and her husband, the Duke of Marlborough, niece Gladys Vanderbilt and her husband, Count Szechenyi, Franklin Roosevelt and his mother, the Duke and Duchess of Manchester, William Morse, the

After Aunt Lulu's death, Fred "retreated into a twilight period."

son of the telegraph inventor, plus countless other friends and relatives partook of and enjoyed the Vanderbilt hospitality. Mr. and Mrs. Vanderbilt also spent a lot of time alone, or with just a few friends or family members. When Lulu wasn't entertaining, she kept busy sponsoring events and classes for the villagers, dispatching doctors, coal, and groceries when needed, and even sending local tuberculosis sufferers to Saranac Lake at her own expense. She was, in short, the ideal wife of the model country squire.

Thus the years passed, Fred getting richer and Lulu growing older. In 1926, Lulu died suddenly during a visit to Paris. She had been fibbing about her age for decades, and by the time of her death, she'd given herself the benefit of seventeen years. She was actually eighty-two. However, her death still came as a shock to Fred, who had been—perhaps because they never had children—especially close to his wife. When Lulu died, Fred retreated into a twilight period. He sold the Bar Harbor house to Atwater Kent, the famous inventor and celebrated party giver. He moved out of his Glaenzer-designed bedroom

at Hyde Park into a guest room on the third floor. Increasingly, he spent more of his time alone, and more of it at Hyde Park.

Fred Vanderbilt was in no way incompetent or mentally diminished during his last years. He continued to earn at least a million dollars a year (the last Vanderbilt of his generation to do so), to sit on the boards of twenty-two railroads, and to see to the immaculate maintenance of his estate at Hyde Park. It must have been very quiet, however, alone in that great house.

Ironically, his own end came twelve years after Lulu's, making them the same age at death. In 1886, Fred Vanderbilt had inherited $10 million. After fifty-two years of luxury living, his estate totaled over $70 million. By the time his will was probated—less than a year later—the estate had grown to nearly $77 million.

The federal government and New York State taxes took something in excess of $40 million of this fortune. Herbert Shears, the faithful manager, received a quarter of a million dollars, plus the Wales place, a handsome legacy in any era, and a princely one in 1938. The residue of the estate—over $30 million after taxes—went into a trust with one hundred shares.

Fred's principal heir was Margaret (Daisy) Van Alen. Mrs. Van Alen was Lulu's niece, the sister of Tom Howard's wife, Rose. She had been a favorite of the Vanderbilts and a regular guest at Hyde Park. After Lulu's death, Daisy often had been Fred's hostess and companion. Twenty-five shares of the trust went to her. The rest went to a few institutions, notably Vanderbilt University and Fred's old alma mater at Yale, the Sheffield Scientific School. The only Vanderbilts to benefit from Uncle Fred's will were the four children of his favorite sister, Lila Webb.

Daisy Van Alen was already a rich woman with a Newport mansion of her own, Wakehurst. She didn't need another estate such as Hyde Park, but Fred left it to her, anyway, including all the furniture. He also bequeathed her 1025 Fifth Avenue and all its furniture, as well as the land under the Arnold Constable store, a significant income-producing parcel, which had been the site of 459 Fifth Avenue.

To her credit, Daisy Van Alen did not close down Hyde Park, nor did she attempt to liquidate, subdivide, and/or demolish it. Indeed, it seems she never once considered any course of action that would have compromised the property's aesthetic value. For the several years until its fate was ultimately decided, she continued to maintain it in precisely the grand condition her Uncle Fred had.

This took courage—not just because it cost money but because most people no longer considered Hyde Park to have any aesthetic worth at all. By the late 1930s, the works of McKim, Mead & White were being subjected to relentless criticism. In another ten years, architectural critics such as Vincent Scully and Antoinette Downing would dismiss houses like Hyde Park as sterile and irrelevant, creations of arid mentalities brainwashed by the academic slavishness of the École des Beaux-Arts. The celebrated erudition of a man like Charles McKim was held to be misguided at the least, if not downright subversive to the nation's true architectural needs.

Mrs. Van Alen was undaunted by the supposedly informed aesthetic opinion of her times. She first attempted to sell Hyde Park to someone who would continue to occupy it as a private house. However, in 1938, very few Americans had the money to buy a Vanderbilt mansion, and those who did were reluctant, in the political climate of the day, to set themselves up in such lavish surroundings.

The asking price for the entire six hundred acres, including mansion, pavilion, stable, farm, cottages, boat house, greenhouses, the Howard house—everything but the Wales house—was $350,000. No one even made an offer. The price was then reduced to $250,000, but there were still no offers. A Greek Orthodox church considered the property briefly as a site for a retreat, but Mrs. Van Alen didn't think much of them or of their low offer. Similarly, Father Divine, a cult leader of the day, expressed interest for a while, but Mrs. Van Alen didn't think much of him, either.

A year passed, but still she resisted the temptation to liquidate. Instead, she pursued a wholly new direction, that of giving it to the American people as a memorial to Frederick Vanderbilt. President Franklin D. Roosevelt, himself a neighboring riverfront squire and longtime personal friend of Daisy Van Alen, first proposed the idea to her. "As you know," he wrote to her on September 30, 1939, "I have always thought of the Hyde Park place with the greatest interest and affection, because with the exception of one or two old Van Rensselaer or Livingston places,

The W. B. Osgood Fields of New York and Lenox, Massachusetts, visit Uncle Fred at Hyde Park; Mr. Field takes a picture of his car and driver.

it is the only country place in the north which has been well kept for nearly two centuries. . . . It would be a wonderful thing to have the maintenance of it assured for all time."

Mrs. Van Alen approved immediately. The problem was getting someone to take it. New York State flatly refused. Eventually, due to Roosevelt's persistent intervention, the National Park Service agreed to accept the estate as a gift. In October 1939, Francis S. Ronalds, acting superintendent of Historic Sites, and L. F. Cook, acting chief of the U. S. Forestry Service, visited the property. Their report stated in part: "Although no great event of national moment occurred at Hyde Park, this estate is indicative of a phase of American social history which might well be preserved. The house and grounds represent a way of life, a style, and even a habit of thought which belongs to our past as much as does Colonial Williamsburg. It appears to us that posterity would thank the government for preserving such a site."

There were some legal delays in final transfer of title, but at last, on July 23, 1940, FDR wrote Daisy: "I am made very happy that 'Hyde Park' belongs now to the nation and in memory of your Uncle Fred." The site opened to the public on July 29, 1940. Thirty people went through it that day, paying a quarter apiece for the privilege. The staff came from the Civilian Conservation Corps. There were no interpretive displays or guided tours at that time. People merely wandered around all three floors at will. The pavilion contained a tearoom, and the pavilion bedrooms were rented overnight for reasonable rates.

The Hyde Park estate today is about two hundred acres, the size of the original Langdon parcel. Mrs. Van Alen gladly would have donated the farm on the other side of the Post Road, but even Roosevelt advised against that. The Ogden Mills house in nearby Staatsburg had been accepted at that time by New York's Taconic State Park Commission. This removed it from the tax rolls, and the thought of the same thing happening to the Vanderbilt property caused concern among elected officials in Hyde Park.

Roosevelt also felt that the people of Hyde Park needed land on which to build houses. Therefore, in 1941, Mrs. Van Alen sold the old Howard house and several hundred acres of former model farm for twenty thousand dollars. Small ranch houses occupy most of the land today. The barns survived as the Hyde Park Festival Theater until 1987, when they were destroyed by fire. The Wales house is fortunately extant, in beautiful condition and still in private hands. The Howard house survives, too, on a forested promontory overlooking a sea of split-levels, but it has been considerably altered over the years without much of an eye for historic preservation.

It is fortunate that one can admire the main house intact and in excellent condition. The National Park Service is to be commended not only for overall maintenance but for the skill and sensitivity with which they have interpreted the site and attended to its ongoing restoration.

Perhaps the truest measure of Hyde Park's value today can be seen in the history of its formal gardens. When Fred Vanderbilt bought the property, these gardens were already well

established. They had been ornamented during the Langdon period by a charming brick and frame Victorian gardener's cottage and toolshed complex. Fred saved the Langdon structures, but in 1902, he hired New York City landscape architect James Greenleaf to enlarge the planted area. The Greenleaf scheme was further enlarged on subsequent occasions, and the result was a series of elaborate outdoor rooms descending a hillside across a leafy valley from the Wales house. These large flat terraces were defined by brick retaining walls, connected by stairways, and ornamented by reflecting pools, complicated arbors, a pergola, and ranks of greenhouses.

All of this was in perfect condition in 1938, but in the intervening years, it was the only part of the estate allowed to deteriorate for lack of federal funds and man power. By the 1970s, the cottage and the toolhouse were still in good shape, but the greenhouses had been dismantled in the 1950s and the garden was a ruin. The Park Service then restored the arbors, pergolas, and the retaining walls, but it lacked the money to replant or maintain the garden. In 1984, a Poughkeepsie woman named Martha Stewart visited Hyde Park with a friend and wondered aloud why something couldn't be done about it. Her friend turned to her and asked why she didn't do something about it herself, so she did.

The result of Ms. Stewart's efforts was the Frederick W. Vanderbilt Garden Association, incorporated in 1985. At this writing, it has 125 volunteer members. The Garden Association works in concert with the National Parks Service, which provides an expert site supervisor and a professional horticulturist. All plants and garden maintenance, however, are donated by the Garden Association. Funds come from private individuals, grants, local businesses, and fund-raising events. The 1987 Garden Association budget was fifteen thousand dollars; in that same year, members donated over three thousand hours of volunteer garden work.

Some Garden Association members are senior citizens; others are busy professional people; some are even local teenagers. Most had never gardened before but heard of the Vanderbilt project through word of mouth. Their enthusiasm is reflected in the superb condition of the garden. It is so good, in fact, that in 1988, the Federated Garden Clubs of New York State awarded the Association with a Gold Seal Citation, its high-

Upper terrace, Hyde Park formal gardens, in their original condition.

Mrs. Margaret (Daisy) Van Alen, Fred Vanderbilt's "principal heir."

est award in recognition of work in horticulture and historic preservation.

The garden at Hyde Park once again looks as it did at the turn of the century when Vanderbilt gardeners tended to its every need. Today, however, the workers can stay in the garden when they are done and savor the fruits of their labors. Judging from the Vanderbilt Garden Association experiment, it would seem that volunteerism can and should play a much larger role in historic preservation. Certainly the history of the formal gardens at Hyde Park speaks volumes on the subject of precisely what a millionaire's estate can mean to everyday people, and what those people will be willing to do to preserve it.

Chapter 10
MARBLE HOUSE

Marble House

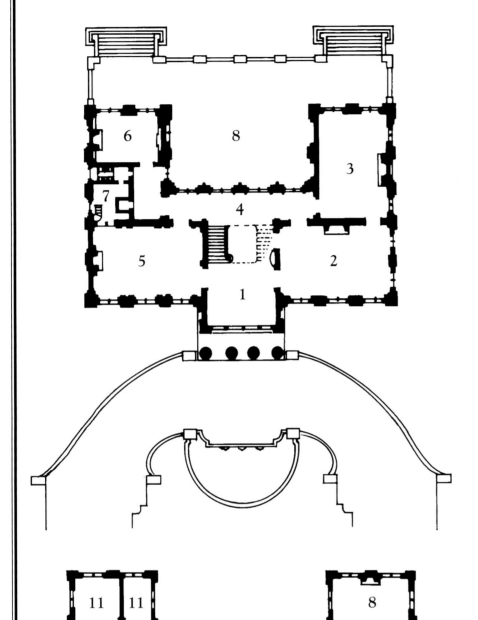

Alva Belmont's Marble House was to her "like a fourth child."

Location: Newport, Rhode Island
Architect: Richard Morris Hunt (1827–1895)
Alva Smith Vanderbilt (1853–1933)
Commissioned by: William Kissam Vanderbilt
(1849–1920)
House completed: 1892

*W*HEN the dowager of Marble House died in February of 1933, *The New York Times* eulogized her as "one of the most colorful female figures in American life." In the course of her eighty years, Alva Erskine Smith Vanderbilt Belmont achieved more than the conquest of American high society. She became one of the great feminists of her time, and deserves considerable personal credit for congressional enactment, in 1920, of the Nineteenth Amendment, granting women the vote.

Mrs. Belmont's funeral, at St. Thomas Episcopal (the "Vanderbilt church") on Fifth Avenue at Fifty-third Street, was no mere society do. It was an emotional farewell to a national figure, attended by thousands. The casket was surrounded by an honor guard of volunteers from the National Women's Party. Across the lid lay a purple, white, and gold banner that read IN TRIBUTE TO OUR COMRADE.

Typically, the individualistic Mrs. Belmont had composed her own funeral hymn, sung at her request by a choir of women. After the service, a flying wedge of motorcycles, sirens ascream, preceded the hearse to Woodlawn Cemetery. In the words of Women's Party Advisory Council member Doris Stevens, speaking from the steps of the Alva Belmont House in Washington, D.C.: "There is not a woman living today who is not nearer the benefits and beauties of freedom because of Mrs. Belmont."

American social historians often ignore the importance of Mrs. Belmont's suffrage activities, or chauvinistically ascribe them to a noxious nature. It makes better reading to dismiss the first wife of William K. Vanderbilt as a social-climbing harridan who bullied her husband's entire clan into high society. The New York *World* enunciated this theme on March 5, 1895, describing Alva as the one who "took Willie K. by the hand and led the way for all the Vanderbilts into the gay world of Society, Fifth Avenue, terrapin, Newport, dry champagne, servants in livery, men who don't work, women with no serious thoughts, and all the other charms of fashionable existence."

It is generally thought that Willie Vanderbilt married Alva Smith because of the help she could supply in his quest for social advancement. The truth is that she needed him more than he needed her. Her father, Murray Forbes Smith, was a man twisting in the breeze, the victim of a long, slow financial decline. His family, for all their southern charm and gentle breeding, had endured a succession of moves to less and less fashionable Manhattan addresses. The last one was at 213 West Forty-fourth Street, alarmingly close to Hell's Kitchen. Smith, bedridden and almost penniless, had reached the point where his daughters would either have to take in boarders or starve.

"When I finally understood the situation, my practical nature at once wanted to help. And help I did, though not in the way I had planned." Alva dictated these words in August of 1917, forty-two years after she dealt with the problem by marrying the second eldest surviving son of William Henry Vanderbilt.

There was a bracing fearlessness about Alva Smith that characterized her entire life. When only a little girl, her mother forbade her to ride bareback. She did anyway, and was regularly whipped for it. "I was probably the worst child that ever lived," she later wrote, adding that neither the bareback riding nor the whipping stopped.

In post–Civil War Newport, the teenaged Alva was a most untypical sort of young society lady. She explored the beach by herself with her own pony, did what she wanted when she wanted, and did not shirk from the consequences. "I loathed girls' occupations and pastimes. . . . There was a static quality to a girl's life, a monotony and restriction in it from which I rebelled from the very first. . . . I wanted activity and I could not find enough of it in the circumscribed life of a girl."

Alva Smith possessed an abundance of sheer animal vitality. At the tender age of twenty-two, newly married to Willie Vanderbilt, she boldly decided to become a reigning monarch of New York society—and she did, achieving equality with Mrs. Astor. Her single-minded determination to succeed was worth as much, if not more, than all the Smith family connections and Vanderbilt millions at her disposal. As she put it, "There was a force in me that seemed to compel me to do what I wanted to do, regardless of what might happen afterwards." Cleveland Amory tartly described this attitude as being "out to prove something." Her daughter, Consuelo, summed her up as a "born dictator."

In truth, any ambitious young woman in Alva's position probably would have aspired to the same goals as she. Society was about the only area in which a motivated woman could advance herself. Politics and business were out of the question. The only other sanctioned alternative for female energies was childbearing. Most men considered these options to be more than sufficient.

Alva's first husband, Willie Vanderbilt, was rich, handsome, athletic, genial, cosmopolitan, and as fluent in French as his well-traveled wife. He was also unfaithful. There was, of course, nothing unusual about this in late-nineteenth-century American society. Infidelity was tolerated as long as it was handled with discretion. Alva's grandnephew Cornelius (Neil) Vanderbilt IV once observed the pervasiveness of the attitude: "Yes, I am his wife," he quotes a Newport society matron in the opening years of the twentieth century, "but I have an assistant down the street."

In France, where much of New York society visited every spring, one's *fille de joie* occupied a recognized position. At table, a man's wife sat on his right, his mistress on his left; that way, no one was confused. European society was glad to condone whatever arrangements best suited its members. The Puritan strain in the American character prohibited such openness.

The double standard probably caught Alva by surprise. Tomboy or no, she had led a morally sheltered life until her marriage. Unlike other society wives, however, Alva rebelled against the typical pattern of upper-class marriages. All around her she saw men marrying women with good social backgrounds merely to gratify the sexual urge. These same men soon tired of their innocent brides, leaving the women on an untouched shelf, with only the duties of respectability and childbearing to occupy them. "Like unpicked sweet peas, they went to seed while it was still blooming time, and their great cry, 'midst all their luxury and material satisfaction was, 'I am so lonely.' "

Willie and Alva Vanderbilt remained married for twenty years and raised three children, but Willie's tact never managed to soothe his wife's growing outrage. Not even the inheritance of $70 million, received in the wake of his father's death in late 1885, could make things right between them. The first fruit of this stupendous inheritance was a steam yacht called *Alva*. The second was a Newport cottage: Marble House.

Price Collier of Tuxedo Park once called Newport, "New York Society's best dish, garnished with a little cold Boston celery and a fringe of Philadelphia and Baltimore parsley." The Willie Vanderbilts began renting there in the middle eighties. Alva and her Marble House eventually became potent symbols of the influx of New York money that Henry James maintained had spoiled the simple pleasures of the earlier Newport.

Alva actually had older ties to Newport than most of the people who lamented her arrival. Her father, harried out of France by an inability to pay his bills, touched down there briefly after the Civil War. It was also there, in the late 1860s, that Alva met the Yznagas, a rich Cuban American family whose children would later have an important impact on her career. The loving patronage of Lady Mandeville, originally Consuelo Yznaga, was a principal reason society went to Alva's great ball of 1883.

There was a modest cottage on the site of Marble House when the Vanderbilts bought the property in 1888. Alva had it torn down posthaste. For architectural help on the new house, she turned to Richard Morris Hunt, the acknowledged dean of American architecture, and a man who had become her dear friend during the design and construction of 660 Fifth Avenue. Before any Newport plans were drawn, Alva insisted that her husband put the property in her name. She felt that she had lavished inordinate time and energy on the design of 660 Fifth Avenue, only to realize that at best she would have nothing more than dower rights to it. She did not intend to make the same mistake twice. Thirteen years of growing marital tension must have figured in this reasoning.

Alva's daughter, Consuelo, called Marble House her mother's second great architectural achievement—after 660 Fifth. In Alva's own words, "It was like a fourth child to me." According to Hunt, Alva was "immersed [in] every aspect of the design." He freely acknowledged her contributions, exclaiming to one and all that she was "a wonder."

Alva involved herself in the process of designing Marble House to a degree possibly greater than Hunt. She studied literally every single plan and elevation, made extensive notes on the working drawings, offered a continuous stream of intelligent suggestions, and even helped research certain of the architectural details. Hunt's files at the American Institute of Architects Foundation in Washington, D.C., testify to the extent of her participation. "This accepted by Mrs. Vanderbilt" reads a note on a seemingly minor drawing of a wall or ceiling cornice; "This absolutely disapproved by Mrs. Vanderbilt" reads another. Every single molding and every last detail received her intense scrutiny. Alva was determined to build for the ages; from the start, Marble House was intended to be a work of art.

The south portico of the White House had a strong influence on the final look of Marble House's Bellevue Avenue facade, but the overall exterior concept was Alva's own. Her most vivid memory from years of foreign travel was that of gazing at the Acropolis in the moonlight from the deck of her yacht. The Parthenon made Alva realize that "the effect of art upon the soul is to make it long for beauty, which is the highest morality." She insisted Hunt use Tuckahoe mar-

"The apogee of the interior is probably the Gold Room . . . designed and fabricated by Jules Allard."

ble for the exterior of Marble House on account of its whiteness. It was too hard to carve—Carrara marble had to be used for the capitals and other carved elements—but it was divinely white in the moonlight.

Construction began in August of 1889. By November, contractor Charles Clarke had leased an entire wharf for the off-loading of building materials. A private ten-ton derrick lifted huge blocks of stone off specially chartered steamboats. Batterson, See and Eisele, who also were marble contractors for Cornelius Vanderbilt's The Breakers and Edward Berwind's The Elms, operated a cutting plant at wharfside. One hundred workmen were imported from Italy, and a studio built for them in the lower part of the town. The marble was cut and polished at dockside; finished blocks then were hauled to the site on Bellevue Avenue for assembly.

Marble House is beautiful from the outside, but its interiors are sumptuous almost beyond belief. It is a glittering, shimmering jewel box, overwhelmingly ornate, brimming with metal, gold, crystal, mirrors, and, above all, marble. As its mistress did, it presented a very hard and shining surface to the world.

The apogee of the interior is probably the Gold Room, most of which was designed and fabricated by Jules Allard, the Paris firm that became a virtual partner with Richard Hunt in many of his mansion commissions. The sculptor Karl Bitter, whom Hunt had discovered, carved the Gold Room's glorious oak wall panels, which were covered with gilt. The Vanderbilts used this dazzling interior space, suggestive of the Hall of Mirrors at Versailles, as a ballroom.

The front door of Marble House was a twenty-five-foot-wide bronze and gold grille. Delicate pale yellow panels of near-translucent Siena marble covered the walls of the main hall. The main stairway, ideal for grand entrances, was composed of solid blocks of the same stone. Alva was particularly proud of the beautiful stair rail, also by Allard, which had been exhibited in Paris before its shipment to Newport. Two fine bas-reliefs by Karl Bitter decorated the landing: one depicted Jules Hardouin-Mansart, architect of Louis XIV; the other was of "Mr. Hunt, his worthy successor."

The dining room was paneled in reddish marble Alva remembered as being shipped from Algiers. Louis XIV makes a symbolic appearance

here, in a portrait above the fireplace. The gorgeous dining chairs are solid bronze, so heavy that each required a footman to push it back and forth from the table.

In contrast to all this neoclassical brilliance is the Gothic Room. Alva had a passion for things Gothic, and she had a Gothic Room in several of her houses. Gilbert Cuel, the *décorateur* who came to the United States at Alva's urging and did such fine work for her at 660 Fifth Avenue, styled the Gothic Room at Newport after an interior in one of Jacques Coeur's houses. (Coeur was the fifteenth-century French financier whose residence had partly inspired the design of 660 Fifth). Like much of the rest of Marble House, the Gothic Room was fabricated entirely in France, disassembled, and then shipped to the United States for installation.

The purpose of the Gothic Room was to house a famous collection of Gothic art that Alva bought from French collector Emile Gabbé. When Marble House was finished, one of M. Gabbé's directors personally accompanied the collection to the States, then supervised its installation in Newport. Such was Alva's commitment to Gothic art. When first completed, the Cuel design included a polychromed ceiling and windows lined with panels of richly stained cathedral glass. This made the room darkly luxurious even in the middle of the day. Alva's daughter, Consuelo, described the decor as "propitious to sacrifice," since it was here

The Gothic Room; originally stained glass windows and a polychromed ceiling made it appear much darker.

"The dining room was paneled in reddish marble Alva remembered as being shipped from Algiers."

that she became engaged to the ninth Duke of Marlborough.

The contrast between the Gold Room and the Gothic Room is startling to say the least. This contrast seems to have been part of the intended effect, however. Taken together, the interiors of Marble House are a tour de force in correct period detailing adapted to the entertaining needs—in terms of floor plan, ease of access, heating requirements, plumbing conveniences, and so on —of the new American nobility. These beautiful rooms are unified less by stylistic similarities than by a common level of magnificence.

Besides the Gothic Room, Gilbert Cuel did Alva's bedroom and boudoir upstairs, plus the dignified morning room at the north end of the seafront. All these luxurious rooms have a special look that historian James T. Maher calls "Alva Vanderbilt French Revival." The detailing is erudite, even though the rooms themselves are not true period rooms. They have an appealing sumptuousness and a look of furnished comfort that is decidedly more nineteenth than eighteenth century.

Gilbert Cuel's bedroom for Alva Vanderbilt; ". . . a special look that historian James T. Maher calls 'Alva Vanderbilt French Revival.' "

The Gothic Room; detail over the fireplace.

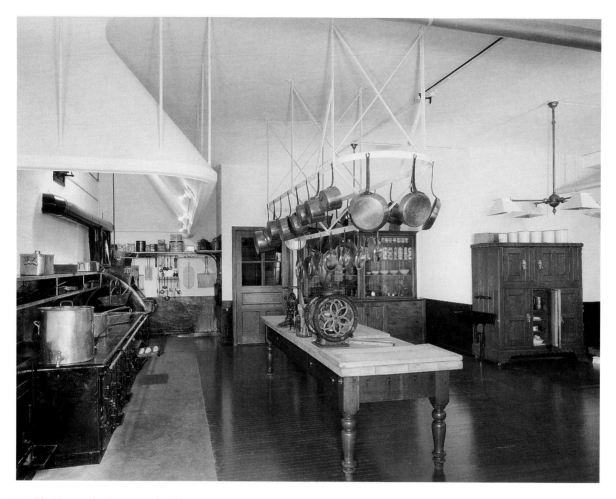

Marble House; the basement kitchen.

Numerous other craftsmen contributed to the interiors of Marble House. The floor plans refer to hardware by Pregaldini and a Hamel ceiling, for example. According to James Maher, there was a pool of first-class artisans in New York in those days, and a steady supply of work. Hunt and Alva jointly supervised the interior decoration of Marble House. However, the finished product was a creative effort that involved the time and talents of many firms and individuals.

The furniture at Marble House was a mixture of antiques, for which Alva had a keen and experienced eye, and the excellent reproductions then available from such French houses as Paul Sourmani and André Dasson. Everything, right down to the pens on the guest-room desks, was personally chosen and precisely positioned by Alva. No rearranging was allowed. No personal

furniture was permitted in any of her children's rooms. When complete, the house required a staff of seventeen, liveried in Vanderbilt maroon, including a butler, three footmen, three housemaids, a French chef, three kitchen assistants, and a trio of laundresses.

The most unusual aspect of the construction of Marble House was Alva's remarkable attempt to keep the process secret. Presumably, she did not want to dissipate the dramatic effect of her great new house, or to lose the element of surprise when it was finally finished. Secrecy was not easily accomplished, considering that the house stands on a smallish lot on the premiere resort street in America. So Alva erected a tall wooden fence around the property, hired watchmen with St. Bernard dogs, and even had her laborers searched at the end of each day lest one might try to sneak home with a written account of the work under way.

Crews engaged in the decoration of the various rooms were not permitted to see each other's work. The imported French craftsmen were intentionally kept apart from both the Newport locals and their countrymen in Allard's Newport office. The papers printed quite a lot about the "Marble Hall," anyway. Frank Leslie's man even managed to sneak onto the site, disguised as an electrician, and escape with a photo.

Marble House was ready for occupancy in time for the season of 1892. On August 18 of that year, Alva and Willie hosted a housewarming dinner and musicale. Prior to the start of the evening, the house was kept in darkness and the guests waited at the gates on Bellevue Avenue. Suddenly, a switch was thrown and the entire facade and grounds were illuminated all at once.

The formal drive between the gates and the main facade was filled entirely with massive beds of white hydrangea. According to *The New York Times*, "The grand portico was a blaze of light and liveried attendants were on hand from carriage to cloakroom." The dinner table was graced with gold plates and centerpieces in the form of miniature lakes filled with night-blooming lilies. The staff wore full-breast cords, gilt garters, and patent-leather shoes.

Willie's friend Winfield Scott Hoyt was there, as were the Sloanes of Elm Court, the Fred Vanderbilts of Rough Point, Colonel and Mrs. Jay of the New York Coaching Club, the architect and Mrs. Hunt, plus assorted Hunnewells, Furmans, and Tookers. It was a fairly young crowd, but then, so were the Vanderbilts. Alva was only thirty-nine in 1892; Marble House was ostensibly her birthday present. Willie Vanderbilt paid a total of $11 million for the construction and decoration of this amazing mansion. The title, of course, had been in his wife's name all along.

Alva's niece, the diarist Adele Sloane, thought Marble House was "far ahead of any palace I have ever seen abroad, [and in fact] far ahead of any I have ever dreamed of." The architectural critic Barr Ferree considered it Hunt's purest expression of French classicism, a beacon of aristocratic orderliness amidst the "disordered picturesque that so strongly marks our domestic architecture."

Marble House was a national sensation in its day, and pictures of it appeared in rotogravures across the nation. Cleveland Amory has called it the "climax of the American dream," doubtless referring to the extreme heights attainable in this striving nation. The house was admittedly a bit grand for the size of the property. Then again, Newport's dramatic effect depends in great part upon its overabundance of grandeur. Vast houses, cheek by jowl, are crucial to its signature charm.

The same year Marble House was opened, the yacht *Alva* was hit by a passing freighter and sunk. If ever there was an omen pertaining to the Vanderbilts' marriage, this was it. Willie set about replacing his yacht with another of even grander proportions. He did not name her *Alva*.

Willie and Alva were the pictures of ease and gentility at a ball or a dinner party, but at home they quarreled constantly. According to their daughter, these bitter scenes wounded her father and "harried" her mother "beyond control." The marriage had become a "horrible mockery"; everyone in the house was miserable. It was in this ominous context that the Vanderbilts embarked, in November of 1893, on a ten-month cruise to India aboard their new yacht, *Valiant*.

Built in England by Laird Brothers, the *Valiant* was quite a ship. Brig-rigged and twin-screwed, she sported two sets of inverted triple-expansion engines that could produce 5,120 horsepower. She was 331 feet long, and carried 651 tons of coal and 10,560 gallons of water. Her extremely wide beam of a bit over thirty-nine feet permitted very luxurious quarters aboard.

The crew included a captain, two officers, twenty-seven deck sailors, twenty-three in the engine department, and twelve stewards to take care of the owner and his guests. On November 23, 1893, the *Valiant* left New York harbor for India. Besides the Vanderbilt family and servants, there were five guests, one of whom was Mr. O. H. P. Belmont.

The party reached Bombay on Christmas Day, then traveled overland by private train to Calcutta. Alva hated India. The poverty, the superstition, the Towers of the Dead in Bombay, the pilgrims on their bloody knees, the oppressed condition of women, all repelled her. In Calcutta, she and Willie left the party and spent a week at Government House with the viceroy. The Vanderbilts were given their own apartment, complete with ten servants.

Landsdowne, as the English viceroy grandly

signed himself a month later on his very own page of the *Valiant's* guestbook, was, among other things, the uncle of the young Duke of Marlborough. Alva and Maud Landsdowne were kindred souls who got on well from the start. Young Marlborough's name must have come up during that week. Nothing official was arranged, but in later years it was Consuelo's opinion that when her mother left Calcutta she had already decided on whom her daughter would marry.

Given the precarious state of their marriage, one might wonder why Willie and Alva cooped themselves up on a yacht for the better part of a year. The private steam yacht, however, was a powerful symbol of privilege and prestige, one to which even a Vanderbilt was not immune. Having ordered the *Valiant* built, Willie was to some extent a victim of the project's momentum. This behemoth demanded a maiden voyage, and it is doubtful Willie could have avoided it even had he wanted to.

He and Alva hardly had to endure close quarters aboard the *Valiant.* To the contrary, except for formal dinners, they hardly saw one another. The rest of the time, Willie played cards with his cronies and left Alva in the sympathetic company of Mr. Belmont. Inevitably, however, the Vanderbilts fought. When the cruise fell apart in the spring of 1894, Alva was not content with a mere separation; she wanted a divorce.

Divorce is so commonplace today that one fails to appreciate what a radical step it was in the 1890s. Among respectable society, it was virtually unknown. Alva had two very fine lawyers: Colonel William Jay and Joseph Hodges Choate. Choate, a summer neighbor of the Sloanes in the Berkshires, had three words of advice for her: "Don't do it." He felt that as a divorced woman, she would be alone and ostracized to a degree she failed to comprehend. Too much power and money, not to mention the weight of common custom, were arrayed against her. Not only the Vanderbilts but every rich man in America would perceive her divorce as personally threatening. Alva was just as insistent that she could, and indeed had to, go through with it, that in so doing she would give courage to others.

The action was commenced on January 3, 1895, and the decree was granted two months later. In the settlement, Alva got to keep the Vanderbilt name, alimony of $100,000 a year, and the offer of 660 Fifth Avenue, which she

declined. She also received custody of her three children: Consuelo, eighteen; Willie Junior, seventeen; and Harold (or Mike, as they called him), eleven. She was rigorous about this custody, absolutely removing the children from any contact with their father.

Successfully divorced, Alva Vanderbilt set forth upon the Newport season. In her words, "society was by turns stunned, horrified, and then savage." When she attended Newport's Trinity Church, all her old friends cut her dead. They actually gathered in cold groups and glared. Fortunately, Alva knew what it was like to be whipped, and knew how to take it.

She probably would have been treated far more harshly were it not for the three social dreadnoughts of Newport: Mamie (Mrs. Stuyvesant) Fish; Tessie (Mrs. Hermann) Oelrichs; and Caroline (*the* Mrs.) Astor. Due to the constancy of these three friends, Alva continued to be invited out. It was often the case that the only woman who would speak to her was her hostess. Men chatted with her as easily as ever, but they did not want their wives to do the same. The women who needed divorce the most, Alva noted later, were the ones who condemned her the most loudly.

Willie Vanderbilt felt badly about the furor. He was not a vindictive man, and he took no pleasure in his former wife's discomfort. He had begged Alva to consider separation for her own sake. She rejected that arrangement as a point of honor. It was manifestly unfair, she maintained, for women to be used by the "J. P. Morgans and Jack Astors" of the world, cheated on, forced to raise children and protect their reputations, while their men went out and did whatever pleased them.

"I always do everything first," was Alva's widely quoted comment in the wake of her divorce. "I was the first girl of my 'set' to marry a Vanderbilt. Then I was the first society woman to ask for a divorce. . . . Within a year [of the divorce] ever so many others had followed my example. . . . They had not dared to do it until I showed them the way."

There is more than a bit of Alva's brand of truculent self-justification in these remarks, and, in fact, she was not the first "society woman" to be divorced. She was, however, the most prominent one to do so, and her divorce did effect a positive change in society at large. Alva's social perseverance, and eventual reacceptance, had the effect of removing the stigma of divorce from the wronged party. In other words, whereas divorce formerly ruined the social prospects of both parties, regardless of who was to blame, henceforth the stigma was reserved for the guilty party alone. At least this was Alva's interpretation of things.

There was another angle to Alva's divorce, however, and it is one that reveals much about her character. The tale begins in 1883, the year of the famous Vanderbilt ball at 660 Fifth Avenue, and also the year of the famous Belmont-Whiting scandal.

Oliver Hazard Perry Belmont was the son of August Belmont, the dashing agent of the Rothschilds in America, and Caroline Perry, niece of naval hero Oliver Hazard Perry. Young Belmont was easy-going, generous, genial, and full of good humor. Bessie Lehr described him as "one of the handsomest men at the Coaching Parade, with his dark eyes, clear cut profile and slender faun-like grace." He was a gentleman of leisure whose great talent was fascinating women.

In 1883, after a protracted courtship disapproved of by his parents, Belmont married the ethereally beautiful Sara Swann (Sallie) Whiting, a socialite. As soon as the honeymooners reached Paris, they were joined by Sallie's manipulative mother and two sisters. Oliver soon found himself part of a ménage à cinq, and discovered to his dismay that the latter three were not leaving.

This situation resulted in domestic turmoil for the young couple, and, in disgust, the bridegroom stormed off with a Spanish dancer. He was subsequently excoriated in the sensation-hungry press for deserting his bride on their honeymoon. Then he received news that Sallie was pregnant. He returned to Paris to attempt a reconciliation, but his scheming mother-in-law now pressed for a divorce. The fruit of this pathetic episode was a daughter named Natica, whom Belmont never acknowledged.

As a result of the double standards of the day, Belmont's divorce never much affected his own social standing. He traveled in the same set as the Vanderbilts, and was their friend and frequent guest. In 1888, he was among those invited on another of their year-long yachting cruises, this one aboard the ill-fated *Alva*. It was a measure of Belmont's popularity that Willie

Vanderbilt sent a private railroad car to Newport to fetch him.

Vanderbilt was a man's man, and a great one for smoking, drinking, and joking with his pals. Belmont was just the opposite; he liked to spend his time with women. As for Alva, she was in her mid-thirties and increasingly angry with life in general and Willie Vanderbilt in particular. The cruise of 1888 was the start of a liaison with Oliver Belmont.

They appeared extremely well suited to one another, and Belmont was on hand at several crucial junctures during the breakup of the Vanderbilts' marriage. He was aboard the *Valiant* when Alva and Willie had their final row. He was waiting in New York when she returned from England with her children and not her husband. Supposedly, Willie found Belmont hiding in Alva's bedroom closet when he paid an unexpected visit to Marble House in January of 1895. Uncowed, Alva had the papers for her divorce, citing Willie's infidelity as cause, filed on the very next day.

Oliver Hazard Perry Belmont, Alva's second husband.

There was gossip about Alva and Oliver even before the *Valiant* left port in 1893. After her divorce, there was open speculation as to when she and Belmont would marry. Alva stoutly denied that there was any such possibility. The reason for this dissimulation was that she had another, more important project afoot, one from which she did not want to be distracted. This was the marriage of her daughter, Consuelo, to the ninth Duke of Marlborough.

One might expect a woman like Alva to be considerate of her daughter's feelings and desires, especially with regard to men. Just the opposite was the case. Alva was a perfect dragon to Consuelo, and Marble House figured boldly in her machinations.

Consuelo Vanderbilt was an enormously "finished" young woman. She spoke three languages by the age of eight and conversed at home with her parents in French. Her mother arranged that she be educated entirely at home by private tutors. During lessons and while reciting for her parents on Saturday nights, Consuelo was required to wear a metal brace to improve her posture. Pictures taken even late in life show her with ramrod posture.

Consuelo met Charles Spencer-Churchill—or "Sonny," as he was informally called—for the first time at a ball in England in 1894. He was interested in her but made no offers. Others were less shy. By the end of that season, the beautiful heiress had received no less than five offers of marriage from all manner of hopeful individuals. Alva wasn't having any of them, nor was she in the mood for any romantic nonsense from her daughter.

Consuelo actually was already engaged, albeit secretly. Her sweetheart was a man named Winthrop Rutherfurd, a pleasant product of New York society of the time. This, in Alva's eyes, was precisely what was wrong with him—plus the fact that he was thirty-one years old and Consuelo was only eighteen.

Alva discovered the clandestine romance and, according to Consuelo's memoir, told her daughter that "I had no right to choose a husband, [and] that I must take the man she had chosen." The daughter had more spirit than the mother expected. She resisted, whereupon Alva raged at her impertinence in a series of astonishingly violent scenes.

Consuelo soon found herself a prisoner in her mother's house, denied visitors and even mail. Alva accused Consuelo of ruining her (Alva's) health, after which she actually shammed a heart attack. She then threatened to rise from her sickbed and shoot Rutherfurd dead should Consuelo attempt to contact him. If such a thing should come to pass, Alva warned, it would be Consuelo who would bear the full responsibility. This heavy-handedness paid off. Consuelo relented, and embarked with a heavy heart on the

dazzling season of 1895, a round of balls, dinners, visits—with Marlborough as her escort. Though Alva was now divorced, Marlborough was happy enough to accept an invitation to Marble House. The climax of his visit came on August 28, 1895, at a great ball ostensibly held to announce nineteen-year-old Consuelo's debut into society. Nine chefs prepared delicacies for the four hundred guests; the society florist Hodgson filled the fountain in the main hall with fairy lamps and floating lotuses, then hung cages full of hummingbirds and butterflies above it. The footmen wore powdered wigs. According to the New York Herald, the grounds "were just as they used to be at Versailles." How could Sonny resist? The fateful proposal was made in the Gothic Room, and the wedding was set for the coming November.

Consuelo Vanderbilt's wedding had everything but Vanderbilts. Alva forced her to return without even so much as a note all the gifts sent her by her father's family. Alva chose the trousseau and the bridesmaids. Consuelo wept uncontrollably on the day itself, so much so that her eyes had to be sponged before she left for the church. Traffic was diverted off Fifth Avenue all the way from Alva's house at 24 East Seventy-second Street to St. Thomas at Fifth and Fifty-third Street. The mournful bride discovered a surging, shouting crowd waiting for her outside the church. Police cordons hundreds strong fought to keep the mob under control. Strangers tore flowers from her bouquet as she struggled for the door. Throughout the ceremony, Marlborough kept his eyes fixed in the air.

To be fair to Sonny, he, too, had been pressured into giving up a love match for an American heiress. The Marlboroughs stayed together for about ten years, and remained married for twenty-five. They had two sons, which didn't bring them any closer to one another. According to Louis Auchincloss, the duke's reply to praise of his wife's beauty was, "I cannot abide tall women." Of her former husband the duke, Consuelo observed, "Of course, I cannot say what a beast my first husband was." As a duchess, Consuelo was an enormous success, especially when one remembers that she undertook this demanding role at the age of nineteen.

Apropos of Alva and the Marlborough wedding, wags of the time suggested that Marble House was the appropriate home for a woman

Consuelo, Duchess of Marlborough.

with a marble heart. However, Alva insisted in her memoir that Consuelo had been glad to escape the vapid uselessness that awaited the wives of the Winthrop Rutherfurds of this world. "I did not see that an American husband could do for her what a foreign husband could." Alva energetically maintained that only in Europe, which was marginally more liberated than the United States—vis-à-vis women, anyway—could Consuelo have a "fitting field for growth and development."

Naturally, many observers believed that Alva had arranged this marriage for her own aggrandizement. Her own explanation seems more credible, however. Alva didn't need a duke in the family to certify her social standing. She was too fearless and too self-confident for any of that. The Marlborough marriage was forced on Consuelo for what Alva believed to be her daughter's own good. If Alva's intentions were misguided, at least they were not selfish.

Alva got through the Marlborough wedding, and within two months she was married again —to Oliver Hazard Perry Belmont. The ceremony was performed on January 11, 1896, at 24 East Seventy-second Street. No priest or minister could be found to marry the pair, since both were divorced. W. L. Strong, mayor of New York, did the honors. The small wedding party included the ubiquitous Colonel and Mrs. Jay, Alva's two sons and her sister, but not a single Belmont. Oliver was thirty-seven; Alva was forty-two.

In describing the Belmont wedding, *The New York Times* characterized the groom as "one of the best known young men in New York society . . . a member of nearly every club of prominence in New York, and . . . an excellent four-in-hand driver." During the season of Consuelo's debut at Marble House, Oliver Belmont had attended so many balls and dinners that he collapsed from exhaustion. According to one story, he passed out inside a suit of armor.

It would be simple to dismiss Oliver Belmont as a useless fop, but for the fact that if he was, a woman like Alva never would have put up with him. He was warm, witty, intuitive, magnificently generous, and an enjoyable companion. He was also a horse fancier. Belmont's Hunt-designed Newport house, Belcourt, was really a luxurious stable-cum-bachelor's lair. After his marriage, Belmont wanted to stay at Belcourt

with his horses. So, beginning in the season of 1896, Alva had Marble House boarded up and closed down, except for the laundry, whose washing and ironing facilities were superior to those at Belcourt.

Alva's urge to build, temporarily stilled by divorce and the English nobility, reasserted itself the moment she became Mrs. Belmont. She and Oliver's journalist friend Arthur Brisbane had introduced them to a bucolic countryside immediately to the east of Hempstead, Long Island, then a pleasant old farming town. Oliver's brother August and Alva's son William K. Junior already had estates nearby. There, in 1897, she commissioned Hunt and Hunt (the successor firm to Richard Morris Hunt's, run by his two sons) to design a Colonial Revival mansion called Brookholt.

Brookholt was one of those heedlessly elaborate-looking wooden mansions, laden with pillared porches and classical balustrades, and designed

Alva at the time of her marriage to Oliver Hazard Perry Belmont.

without the slightest care for the cost of future upkeep. In the course of its construction, Alva studied garden architecture with the French master Achille Duchĕne, much as she had studied town-house architecture twenty years earlier with Richard Morris Hunt.

As squire of Brookholt, Belmont dabbled a bit in journalism and politics (he was his district's two-time congressional representative in 1901 and 1903). What he and his wife did best, however, was entertain. Alva once said she knew of "no profession, art or trade that women are working in today as taxing on mental resources as being a leader in society." To ease the discomfort, Oliver gave her a $300,000 annual entertainment budget.

Alva's and Oliver's entertainments at the beginning of the twentieth century were among the most glittering and elaborate in the annals of American society. In Newport, the great hall on the second floor of Belcourt could accommodate over three hundred guests. This hall was both satisfyingly vast and filled with the sort of picturesque Gothic armorial accoutrements that Alva always loved. At large parties, liveried footmen holding candelabra would stand in powdered ranks along the stairs.

One of the many well-remembered parties at Belcourt was an 1899 auto race. Cars, then called "bubbles" by the Newport cottagers, were a novelty. An obstacle course was laid out on the lawn, incorporating such things as a pony cart with a wooden horse, a stuffed nurse with a stuffed baby, and assorted servants in livery. The judges were a panel of society people.

The "bubbles" were piled with flowers and looked like little floats in a homecoming parade. Alva was teamed up with J. W. Gerard in a car piled with blue hydrangeas; Oliver and Mamie Fish piloted another; Harry Lehr, Mrs. Astor, and Mrs. Astor's dog (complete with flowery collar) were in yet another. After the race, mirth and hilarity reigned as a procession of thirty cars paraded down Bellevue Avenue to a dinner at Grey Crag. This period was a happy one for Alva. In her words, it was an "ideal life, thoroughly refined but full of gaiety and fun." Belmont never interfered with his wife, nor did his attentions stray.

Then without warning, in the wake of a routine appendectomy in June of 1908, Oliver Belmont died. He was only fifty years old and Alva

was devastated. Just the month before, Hunt and Hunt had filed plans for yet *another* enormous mansion, this time a creamy stone town house with a half-block frontage on Madison Avenue between Fifty-first and Fifty-second streets. Conventional belief was that the neighborhood would be entirely commercial within five years, but that didn't stop Alva—nor did the death of her second husband. When completed, 477 Madison Avenue boasted, among other things, an eighty-five-foot-long hall filled with a collection of armor.

Alva, however, was lonely at Brookholt, Belcourt, and at 477 Madison without her gay-spirited husband. She needed an outlet for her energies; after a short European trip in the fall of 1908, she found one.

At about this time, some of the younger women in New York society were becoming involved in the fight for women's suffrage. Mrs. Clarence Mackay, who had been a bridesmaid at Consuelo's wedding, hosted a series of suffrage lectures during the winter of 1908 at her house on Madison Avenue. Ida Husted Harper, the historian and friend of Susan B. Anthony, spoke; so did Mrs. Carrie Chapman Catt, as well as others who were devoting their lives to this cause.

Alva was the only member of society's older generation to join these younger women. She befriended Mrs. Harper and Miss Anthony, and threw herself wholeheartedly into the cause of women's equality. To Alva, the struggle for universal suffrage was a logical attack on one of the root causes of society's ills; it would have been hard to imagine a more perfect outlet for her resources and temperament. The time for polite entreaty had passed; the era of the protest march and the soapbox had arrived. It was Alva's genius to have infused the movement with vigor at a critical moment.

By early 1909, Alva was already a delegate to the International Women's Suffrage Alliance Convention in London. Consuelo, by now separated from Marlborough, attended with her. That summer, Alva reopened Marble House for the first time in a decade. On August 22, 1909, crowds of paying sightseers swarmed all over it to benefit the women's movement.

Alva also established a suffrage headquarters in New York, at 505 Fifth Avenue, at her own expense. Soon she became president of the Political Equality Association, with branches at the Harlem Club, the New York Physicians and Surgeons League, and at Brookholt, which she converted into a training center for women farmers.

By the early teens, Alva was alternately leading tens of thousands of protest marchers down Fifth Avenue (during the famous Suffrage March of 1912); comforting a distraught activist, arrested after pouring carbolic acid into a mailbox, with the famous line "Pray to God, my dear, She will help you"; and traveling constantly back and forth to Europe for the cause, frequently in the company of her daughter.

Consuelo, Duchess of Marlborough, addresses suffragettes at Marble House on July 25, 1914. Her mother sits at the right.

On July 25, 1914, Marble House was again put at the disposal of the women's movement, this time as a convention site. During the conference, Alva introduced Consuelo to the famous Emmeline Pankhurst, and to Pankhurst's daughter Christabel. Consuelo noted that her mother and the elder Pankhurst both "shared a common hatred for the genus man, although they both delighted in men's company." As for the daughter: "To hear Christabel Pankhurst orate against the male sex, as if their presence in this world were altogether superfluous, made one wonder how far prejudice could contaminate a brilliant intellect."

Alva's neighbors were scandalized by the thought of the great unwashed traipsing all over Marble House. After all was said and done, however, not a single precious thing disappeared— except the banner Alva carried down Fifth Avenue during the suffrage parade of 1912. Even

that reappeared. According to Cleveland Amory, Alva was interrupted during the fall of 1914 at a dinner in her New York town house. The butler announced a "Mrs. Catt," instead of whom, Harry Lehr appeared dressed as a woman. Alva gaped at his dress and exclaimed, "*You've got my banner!*"

One might expect that Mrs. Belmont, consumed in the turbulent pursuit of an historic cause, would have had precious little time for building. However, in 1912, a mere two years after the completion of 477 Madison Avenue, she embarked on still another building scheme —the construction of a Chinese teahouse overlooking the sea from the edge of the lawn at Marble House.

A teahouse sounds like a modest undertaking, but Alva was not a person who did things modestly. She wanted something artistic, authentic, and Chinese. To this end, she returned to Hunt and Hunt, whose principals agreed to the extraordinary suggestion that they make a field trip to China, at Alva's expense, in order to properly research the design.

The architects visited Peking, Shanghai, and Hangchow, after which they produced five separate schemes for the teahouse. In the manner of their father before them, they drew freely from different periods of Chinese architecture, and different specific Chinese temples. The teahouse as built followed authentic Chinese models, but it was also a hybrid unlike anything in China. Its finishing touch was a pair of giant blue vases given to Commodore Perry by the emperor of Japan upon the opening of Tokyo Harbor.

The Chinese House, as Alva always called it, was finished in the summer of 1914. Its official opening was at a ball held on July 25. As Europe teetered on the precipice of war, Alva gave her last great party at Marble House. The Chinese Ball started with a dinner at Mamie Fish's. Guests and servants alike wore Oriental costumes; Alva was literally encrusted in jewels; pagoda-shaped ices were served for dessert. After the meal, everyone repaired to Marble House, where the Gold Room was fitted with a throne. Obeisances were made to a costumed emperor, after which guests danced, strolled moonswept lawns ornamented with thousands of white lanterns, and had a supper at 1:00 A.M. It was a magical scene; Alva recalled it as "the most beautiful ball I have ever given."

Three days after Alva's Chinese Ball, the war crashed down upon Europe like one of those stylized waves in an Oriental painting. War or no war, Alva went out and commissioned Hunt and Hunt in 1915 to design another immense house. This time, they gave her an oddly modern-looking Gothic castle called Beacon Towers, which stood at the end of Sands Point near Port Washington, Long Island. Alva was enormously proud of this house, which again contained the requisite portion of medieval art. It was her retreat from New York City at times other than the Newport season.

In early 1917, by now in her mid-sixties, Alva decided to write her memoirs. She asked Doris Stevens, a friend in the women's movement, for the name of a writer. Stevens recommended Sara Bard Field, a woman in her mid-thirties who lived in California. Alva contacted Field, offered to pay her a thousand dollars a month, plus travel and living expenses, and arranged to meet her at Newport in July.

There were things about Sara Field that neither Alva nor Doris Stevens suspected. Mrs. Field's husband had been dispensed with by 1917, and she had taken a radical labor lawyer by the name of Erskine Wood as a lover. Wood was an intimate of Emma Goldman, and a poet who authored a collection called *The Poet in the Desert*. En route to Newport that summer, Sara had stopped in New York in an unsuccessful effort to find him a publisher. She wrote regularly to Wood throughout the summer of 1917, and her letters, now at the Huntington Museum in San Marino, California, provide fascinating and occasionally hilarious glimpses of Newport and Mrs. Belmont.

"She is a terror," Sara wrote to Wood upon arrival in Newport, "and I cringe at the thought of her buying me." Billeted in a guest house on Coggeshall Avenue (as opposed to "Marblehead," where she thought she'd be staying), Sara confided to her lover her first impressions of Newport. Bellevue Avenue to her looked like "a long hall to heaven," quite a contrast to the misery of the tenement families she had observed in New York. "I cannot be glad here. Life is too tragic in its lurid contrasts."

Newport was the site of a major American naval base and the town was filled with servicemen about to embark for war. Field was repeatedly moved by the sight of them. "Here are active

Ocean view from Alva's Chinese teahouse.

preparations to engage in wholesale slaughter and these mindless creatures of inherited wealth or of pirate riches live their lives of selfish indulgence and unvirtuous sloath [sic]. I hate them."

Mrs. Field and Mrs. Belmont soon settled into a routine. "Every morning after breakfast Mrs. Belmont calls for me in her car, takes me shopping or out on business; then home to her palace for lunch, where as a little sister of the rich, I am waited upon by footmen, butler, maids and chauffeurs. I am given a small luxurious car for my own use while here, and, so far as it does not interfere with her ease, treated with a sort of sumptuous consideration, fed delicacies by soft moving servants, given delicious drinks when suffering from heat and generally coddled and made soft. Yet I go to my bed every night with a chill despair in my heart—and I wake every morning, dreading the day."

Despite this, she freely admitted that Marble House was "wonderful, much more breath-taking than (Mrs. Belmont's) New York house." And gradually, she began to soften on Alva as well. "I have sworn to the gods to help this dominant fearless old lady to see the light—more light than she now sees."

Alva and Sara worked each day on the porch of the Chinese House overlooking the sea, the manicured lawn, and the pure white facade of Marble House. For short periods of time, Sara put aside her perception of an onrushing Armageddon, and communed with a fellow woman who was closer to her than she realized.

Sara wrote Wood about "the chapter of (Alva's) terrible marriage to Mr. Vanderbilt, with its sordid selling of her unloving self, but the truly noble desire to save her father who was slowly dying of worry and anxiety . . . a girl barely seventeen (actually Alva was twenty-two) who did not fully know the sex mystery." Unfortunately, Alva wouldn't let her put any of this in the manuscript, claiming her children and the "Vanderbilt family" (about whom she hadn't been overly concerned in the past) might object.

Inevitably, a friendship grew between these two women, and the talk became more personal. We learn from Field's letters that Alva had a crush on a younger man during the summer of 1917. He is identified only as "Ralph," and Sara notes that Alva is forever dropping references to distinguished women in history who took up with younger men. "My heart aches for her," she finally admitted, "selfish to the core and weighted down from babyhood with the heaviness of too much possession . . . (But) what she lacks in gentleness she makes up in justice."

They talked of Erskine Wood as well. Alva's amusing advice was for Sara to drop him and marry a rich man! Sara must have laughed; in any case, she didn't take the advice, and did eventually marry Wood. However, the memoir itself, robbed of interest value by Alva's desire to keep it proper, was never published.

Alva was president of the National Women's Party in 1919 when the constitutional amendment granting women the vote was drafted. After its passage in 1920, she set out to enfranchise all the women in the world. Every time there was an international convention pertaining to law, Alva would set up an office to ensure that, in her own words, "no international code of law would be projected on a basis of inequality for women." As a result, she was in Havana for the Sixth Pan-American Conference, in the Hague for the International Codification of Law Conference, and so on.

Nineteen twenty was not only the year that American women at last got the vote, it was also the year that William K. Vanderbilt died. Consuelo brought her father's body back to New York from France, after which she stayed for a while at her mother's "medieval castle." That year

Consuelo, long estranged from the Duke of Marlborough, obtained a divorce. In July of 1921, she married Jacques Balsan, a French aviator and financier from a devout Catholic family. It was a love match, this time much applauded by her mother.

The Balsans established a handsome summer place called Lou Sueil at Eze on the Riviera. Here, they entertained many of the world's greats, from Charlie Chaplin to Winston Churchill. Alva, too, was a regular visitor. Mother and daughter, despite their conflicts of twenty-five years earlier, by now had become close friends. In 1924, Alva moved to France and two years later she purchased a fine house of her own called Domaine d'Augerville-la-Rivière. This château had been given by Charles VII to none other than Jacques Coeur, the fifteenth-century financier whose architectural career was already much entwined with Alva's own, and who had, in what seems an appropriate spirit, financed Joan of Arc.

Social wit Harry Lehr once observed that Alva was only happy when "knee-deep in mortar." According to her *New York Times* obituary, d'Augerville was her *pièce de résistance*. She was seventy-three when she bought it. She then put to use all her generations of architectural experience in its restoration. She filled the château with museum pieces, restored the park, even widened the river in front. She directed the work force personally, and in the process became something of a force in local provincial life. It was Alva who determined that the local village needed a statue of Joan of Arc. She convinced Bessie Lehr to donate the statue, since Bessie was a Catholic. When Bessie balked at paying the bill, Alva came up with the cash herself.

The same year she bought d'Augerville, 1926, Alva also testified before the rota of a papal court in Rome. She did it for Consuelo, who, as a divorcée, had been spurned by her new husband's family. Alva admitted that in 1895 she had forced her daughter to marry the Duke of Marlborough against her daughter's wishes. She made a clean breast of everything, confessing her threats of suicide and murder. No matter how one judges her prior conduct, Alva's testimony before the rota was unquestionably brave. It succeeded: Consuelo received a papal annulment and was belatedly welcomed into the Balsan family.

By 1981, the teahouse "had fallen into an almost derelict state."

What is not widely known about this annulment is that it was originally the Duke of Marlborough's idea. Sonny had become a Catholic by the mid-twenties and wanted to marry again. Episcopalians across America, however, were livid. Who was this Catholic Pope, they demanded to know, who presumed to annul an Episcopal marriage!

The last decade of Alva Belmont's life was spent pleasantly and comfortably. She was near Consuelo, who was happy at last, and her other children were prospering, too. Then at the age of seventy-nine, in May of 1932, she suffered a paralytic stroke that confined her to a wheelchair. Her physician, Dr. Edmund Gros, and several nurses remained in almost constant attendance.

Undaunted by her failing powers, Alva decided to make another attempt at writing her memoirs. She hired a pair of young American girls named Mary and Matilda Young to help. Unfortunately, the memoirs were as unsatisfying as they had been in 1917, primarily because Alva again insisted on sanitizing them to such a degree

that nothing interesting was left.

Matilda Young's letters to her mother, however, paint an evocative picture of Mrs. Belmont's twilight. While economic chaos slowly enveloped the world, she wheeled Alva around Jacques Coeur's château, and helped her when friends and family visited. "How's this for a funny hand," Alva tells Matilda. "It can take hold of things but it won't let go."

Alva's son Harold came to visit and Alva managed an elegant dinner for him and Dr. Gros. She was too ill to attend herself, so it was just the two men in the vast Gothic hall, attended by a pair of valets with standing orders to keep their quart glasses filled with champagne.

Her sons decided at this point that it was time for her to wrap up her American affairs. On September 10, 1932, Alva signed a contract to sell Marble House, which she had used infrequently since 1918, and not at all since 1924. The buyer was a Chicago financier named Frederick H. Prince. The bottom-of-the-Depression sale price was $100,000, or less than a penny on every 1892 dollar it had taken to build and fur-

The restored Chinese teahouse; the Preservation Society of Newport County "has come to stand for state-of-the-art restoration techniques."

nish Marble House. Alva signed the contract with an *x*, giving rise to speculation that she was more enfeebled than she really was. The real culprit was her paralyzed hand. Within four months of this parting with her "fourth child"—Marble House—she was dead at the age of eighty.

The houses Alva left behind did not fare well. The original Idle Hour, during the design of which she first befriended Richard Morris Hunt, burned in 1899; 660 Fifth Avenue fell to the wreckers in 1926; and 477 Madison Avenue lasted into the late 1950s, when it was replaced by a banal skyscraper. Brookholt was discovered full of illegal liquor stills in the 1920s, and it burned to the ground under mysterious circumstances shortly thereafter. Beacon Towers was demolished in the 1950s by a Long Island developer who replaced it with split-levels.

Marble House, arguably the greatest of her architectural achievements, has had a happier fate, however. Its second owner, Mr. Prince, kept it in splendid condition for thirty seasons. Frederick Prince lived into his nineties, and upon his death in 1963, Marble House became the property of the Preservation Society of Newport County. The funds for its acquisition were donated by Harold Vanderbilt; the original furnishings were the generous gift of the Chicago-based Frederick H. Prince Trust.

One cannot say enough good things about the Preservation Society of Newport County. They have been doing the work of the angels in Newport for over forty years. PSNC today has come to stand for state-of-the-art restoration techniques, as well as innovative and accurate site interpretation. They are not only a source of technical expertise but a beacon of inspiration for preservationists everywhere. Because of them, some of Newport's greatest cultural treasures are not only preserved but accessible to all Americans.

PSNC's meticulous 1981 restoration of the Chinese teahouse, which had fallen into an almost derelict state, was typically accurate and thorough. The teahouse is again the artistic retreat that Alva so enjoyed. Were she alive today, there is no doubt that she would be enormously pleased with the fate of Marble House, and one of the PSNC's most active and committed members.

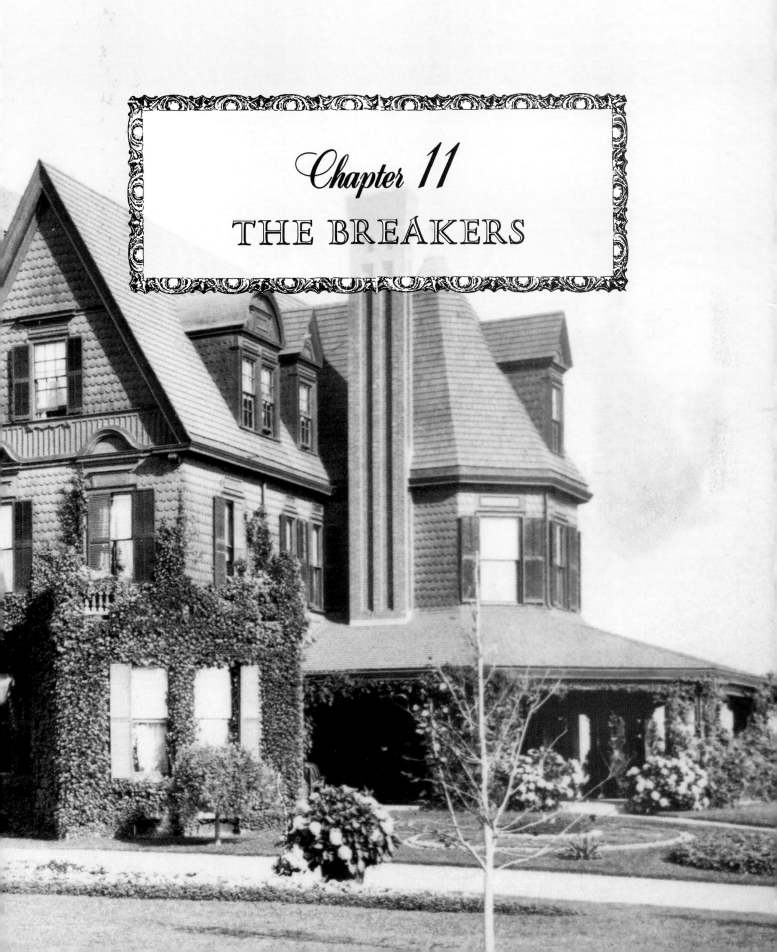

Chapter 11

THE BREAKERS

The Breakers

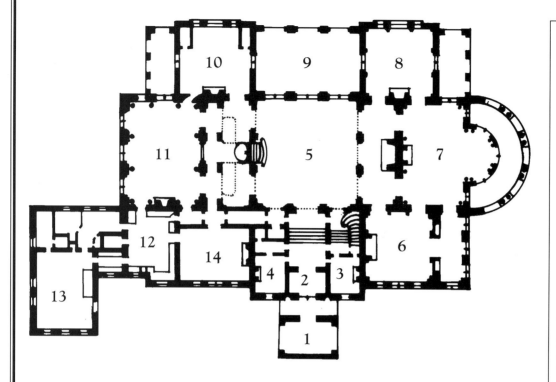

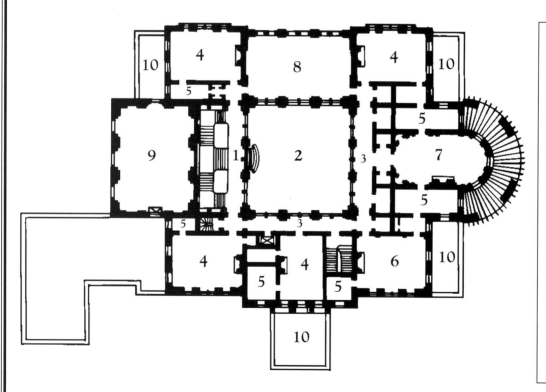

Location: Newport, Rhode Island
Architect: Richard Morris Hunt (1827–1895)
Commissioned by: Cornelius Vanderbilt II (1843–1899)
House completed: 1895

*A*T the end of the nineteenth century, Newport—and above all Ochre Point in
Newport—was the undisputed lotus land of American society. The cottages atop
the little headland, named for the ocher color of its cliffs, were among the most elaborate
in town. It was the consistency of architectural grandeur atop little Ochre Point that gave
it its reputation, however.

"All that has been said in praise of Newport," wrote James Huneker in *The New
Cosmopolis*, "you may safely set down as an understatement." The Russian Grand Duke
Boris, visiting before the First World War, allowed as how he had "never even dreamt of
such luxury." And Czarist Russia, as we all know, was not short on luxury.

Other critics, notably the author Henry James, sneered at Ochre Point's "white elephants," bemoaning the lack of individual thousand-acre estates surrounding each. In truth, however, the luxurious intensity of the neighborhood depended upon the close proximity of its many mansions. Every square foot of property on Ochre Point was manicured to within an inch of its life. Although closely developed, the neighborhood still had spaciousness. Swards of immaculately clipped turf rolled for acres this way and that, specimen trees and/or dazzling formal gardens surrounded every structure, and virtually all the houses were small palaces. Ochre Point was Newport's apotheosis, and at its absolute center, defining it as much for the benefit of the Newport colony as for the United States at large, stood The Breakers.

Cornelius Vanderbilt II had been dead eight years by the time James coined his "white elephant" remark. This was just as well, since it would seem to have been directed squarely at The Breakers. More than any other, this house was a symbol of Newport itself. Richard Hunt's mighty palace by the sea had, by James's day, become a feature of American consciousness, described gushingly and routinely in rotogravure supplements all over the country.

The first of the Vanderbilts to go to Newport was Alva, the wife of Corneil's brother William Kissam Vanderbilt. She'd known Newport before and immediately after the Civil War, when her Southern family had summered there. To a certain extent, she led her husband's family back in the early 1880s, when Newport was first becoming the favorite resort of the Four Hundred. The Vanderbilts probably would have gone there even without Alva. Others in their league were converging on Newport from every corner of the country. Fashion itself was pointing there with all ten fingers.

By the end of the 1880s, Newport had established entirely new parameters for the American definition of magnificence. Two-hundred-thousand-dollar balls became commonplace. According to Cleveland Amory, some Newport hostesses would not invite a guest worth less than $5 million. Mrs. Henry Clews, wife of the famous Wall Street broker, allotted ten thousand dollars in each annual Newport wardrobe budget for "mistakes." Every summer, the very grand (if spuriously hyphenated) Pembroke-Joneses added $300,000 to their Newport entertainment budget simply for "extra expenses."

The most famous street in social Newport was Bellevue Avenue. From its beginning at the Newport Casino all the way to its southern terminus near Bailey's Beach, Bellevue Avenue was lined entirely with sweeping elms and imposing summer houses set in elaborately landscaped grounds. Every afternoon at about three, le tout Newport made its appearance at the famous coaching parade on Bellevue Avenue. This was no organized event but, rather, a ritualized display of money and position—both real and aspirant—described by the participants as "taking a drive." The avenue was clogged with gorgeous carriages, rippling horseflesh, graceful ladies in white gloves and picture hats, grooms and coachmen in immaculate liveries. There were lavish coaching parades elsewhere in America, but Newport set the mark.

According to the French novelist and critic Paul Bourget, writing in 1895, Newport had no adventurers. Presumably, he meant that by that time it had become so inaccessibly high as to be impervious to bounders. Emily Post thought otherwise. According to her, Newport provided fertile fields for the upwardly mobile, or at least more fertile than those of her own Tuxedo Park. "Newport likes to be entertained," Mrs. Post opined. "Tuxedo does not care a bit." The walled community of Tuxedo Park, as a matter of fact, was created precisely in reaction to the ostentation of Newport, and to some of the people who had gotten there from heaven only knew where.

The founder of Tuxedo Park originally summered at Newport himself. His name was Pierre Lorillard, and he was heir to an old and substantial New York fortune based originally on snuff. In 1877, Lorillard hired the prominent Boston architectural firm of Peabody & Stearns to build a summer house on Ochre Point, whose clifftops were as yet not so sumptuously ornamented as they soon would be. The Lorillard house of 1878 was the original Breakers. It was made of wood, and designed in the so-called Modernized Colonial style. Today, most people would call it merely a large, shingled Victorian mansion.

Lorillard's Breakers was famous, and very much on what was then the cutting edge of new architectural design. However, its elitist owner

The original Breakers, designed in 1877 by Robert Swain Peabody for Pierre Lorillard.

soon was dismayed by the booming fashion that had seized little Newport almost as soon as his house was completed. The cultured and literary New England types who had characterized the summer colony in the 1870s were vanishing in a cloud of golden dust. The Four Hundred was on the march. To old-line social conservatives such as Lorillard, the new contingent was too loud, too ostentatious, and contained far too many arrivistes.

By 1885, Lorillard had become sufficiently disenchanted with Newport's gaudy balls and unfettered everyday display that he sold his famous house, together with eleven acres on Ochre Point, to Cornelius Vanderbilt II. The price was $400,000. A year later, Lorillard opened his beautiful planned community of Tuxedo Park in Orange County, New York. Here, it was hoped that an atmosphere of serenity and good breeding would not be disrupted by high-living Vanderbilts or others of their stripe. And it wasn't.

Cornelius Vanderbilt took Lorillard's famous house and did what many a rich new owner does; he remodeled. He did so carefully, however, and with a keen respect for Robert Swain Peabody's original design. In fact, Vanderbilt hired Peabody & Stearns to do the alterations. The kitchen was relocated in a new wing added to the north; the huge central hall was redecorated; a new dining room was created and, when completed, it was said to be the largest in Newport. Meanwhile, on the lawn outside, Peabody designed a freestanding children's playhouse, constructed in three-quarter scale and modeled ironically after an almshouse in Guilford, England.

There was no room on Ochre Point for an adjunct model farm, nor would Newport, being a seasonal resort, seem the sort of place where one would even want one. Cornelius Vanderbilt had no other country residence, however. He needed an upscale agricultural installation of the

The original Breakers; the great hall as remodeled for Cornelius Vanderbilt II.

The "Cigar Box" Edwardian library in the remodeled Breakers.

kind that filled other people's large estates with fresh vegetables and hothouse flowers. So in 1887, he bought a farm from financier August Belmont. Called Oakland Farm, it was situated outside Newport in nearby Portsmouth. Corneil adored the place and poured a great deal of money into its elaborate improvement. Oakland Farm was as much a part of his Rhode Island summers as The Breakers, and he was constantly taking his guests out to see it. He even joined the Farmers Club.

The sober-sided Corneil and Alice Vanderbilt were incongruously at odds with the growing hilarity of their Newport neighbors. He was a committed churchman and stern moralist. She was a rigid stickler for social form. Newport was a hotbed of lapsed morals, dubious standards, out-

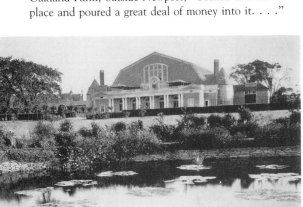

Oakland Farm, outside Newport; "Corneil adored the place and poured a great deal of money into it. . . ."

The new dining room "was said to be the largest in Newport."

right greed, and occasional viciousness. However, the Vanderbilts simply seem to have liked it. They loved the sea, and most of all they liked their house on Ochre Point. They spent a curiously long season there. All the other "cottages" were long closed by the time the Vanderbilts finally moved back to New York. Their young daughters must have felt terribly marooned in Rhode Island by late October, when everybody they knew already had returned to town.

On November 25, 1892, Corneil and Alice were entertaining the author Edith Wharton and her husband, Teddy, at The Breakers. A winter somnolence had settled on the rest of Newport. Alice's daughters Gertrude and Gladys were on the lawn, perhaps lamenting their continued exile, when a great commotion caught their attention. The day was cold and the boilers were stoked to capacity. Suddenly, the flue caught fire. In an appallingly short time, the entire house turned into a pillar of flame. No one was hurt, but The Breakers was incinerated in its entirety.

Much of the blame was laid to Peabody's floor plan, particularly the enormous central hall that efficiently delivered flames to each and every wing and story. Vanderbilt was stoic, at least about the $700,000 loss. There was no question but that he would rebuild. This time, however, he skipped over Peabody & Stearns—and George Post, then working on extensive new additions to Vanderbilt's Fifty-seventh Street town house—and turned instead to Richard Morris Hunt.

Hunt was then at the pinnacle of his career. He was also at work just then "assisting" George Post on the enlargements to 1 West Fifty-seventh Street. Corneil liked Hunt's work. Many in his set did, including his brothers Willie and George, who lived—or in the case of George, would soon live—in Hunt-designed châteaux. Ogden Goelet's Ochre Court, flanking the far side of sister Florence Twombly's Vinland, was a Hunt château. Also, Hunt had only just completed Marble House, opened in 1892 for Corneil's brother Willie and his wife, Alva.

By the end of December 1892, barely a month

Vanderbilt's remodeled Breakers on the morning of November 26, 1892. "In an appallingly short time, the entire house turned into a pillar of flame."

after the old Breakers had burned, Hunt's draftsman Edward Masqueray already had produced beautiful colored studies for a stupendous new château. The proposed house, clad in pale gray stone, was another of Hunt's French Renaissance designs. Perhaps Vanderbilt felt it was too much like Ochre Court, for two weeks later, a quite different plan was proposed—one based on Italian Renaissance models. Both plans required demolition of the existing stables on the site, which were to be relocated a half mile away at the intersection of Coggeshall and Bateman avenues. Forthwith, the new Breakers would stand alone on its manicured eleven-acre lot. Of Peabody & Stearns's extensive original work, only the miniature almshouse would remain.

There is a persistent legend in American social annals to the effect that Alice Vanderbilt urged Hunt to make The Breakers huge in order to upstage her more popular sister-in-law, Alva. These women were poles apart in every way, from their personalities to their self-images. Alva was gay and exuberant; Alice was cold and formal. Alva was a famous party giver; Alice was not.

It is very possible that Alice was consciously jealous of Alva's popularity. After all, it was Alice, the wife of the head of the Vanderbilt family, who should have been the family's social leader. Her sister-in-law Alva was not bothered much over who was, or was not, *the* Mrs. Vanderbilt. Alva gave the better parties and had the better time. She was altogether the more ebullient and attractive of the two. Alice, partly by choice and partly by temperament, never gave Alva much social competition. She was not the sort of hostess who was able to infuse great gatherings with infectious gaiety; she simply didn't have it in her.

In any case, the immensity of Hunt's Breakers had nothing to do with Alice Vanderbilt's frustration, real or imagined. Rather, its size was Hunt's idea. Vanderbilt liked the sixteenth-century Genovese palace scheme—symmetrical layers of classically ornamented stonework surrounding a central court—that Hunt proposed in January of 1893. However, he thought the house should have two principal stories, plus a top floor servants' quarters, instead of three. Hunt's papers reveal that he was absolutely opposed to this idea. Corneil deferred finally to the master, but only when Hunt was able to convince him that the artistic merit of the de-

". . . The immensity of Hunt's Breakers had nothing to do with Alice Vanderbilt's frustration, real or imagined."

sign depended on the larger scale.

Hunt, of course, had read Cornelius Vanderbilt's soul. Although the architect was responsible for the huge scale of the house, the client seized upon the final plans with enthusiasm. Those plans were drawn with remarkable speed considering the complexity of the building and the fact that Hunt was engaged in half a dozen other major projects—including George Vanderbilt's Biltmore—at the same time. Corneil followed the design process closely, traveled to Europe with Hunt to shop for furnishings and artworks, and took a vast pleasure in the entire process. He did not, however, participate in it to the extent his sister-in-law Alva had at Marble House.

The new Breakers was already under construction by the spring of 1893. It was a typical Hunt-Vanderbilt undertaking, conducted at breakneck pace by swarms of laborers. Atop a foundation that measured 250 by 150 feet, rose four stories, framed in steel, filled with brick, and clad in Indiana limestone. There were about seventy rooms and thirty bathrooms, the latter equipped with both fresh and saltwater taps. Facilities for servants occupied fully 50 percent of the floor space. The total cost of construction, including interiors, ran to some $7 million, a sum that didn't faze Cornelius Vanderbilt. The job was completed in just over two years, which was as much a tribute to Hunt's planning and industry as to Vanderbilt's wealth.

Right: "At the heart of the plan is an immense hall."

Below: The Breakers; original gate with main house in the distance.

Bottom: Gate and entry facade of the new Breakers.

The Breakers, from the south lawn.

This time, the heating plant was located well away from the house. Hunt put it under the gate lodge. Steam for heating was transported through enormous mains, housed in a tunnel large enough to drive a carriage through, located beneath the driveway.

Vanderbilt had hired Hunt to create an enduring work of art, one which would almost incidentally be used as a summer house and a place for entertainment. He was well pleased with the result. The finished Breakers was open and airy, possessed of enormously high ceilings, beautiful interiors, an abundance of sunny loggias and terraces, and ocean views in practically every direction. Everything about it was luxurious, even the fence that surrounded the property. Fifty-six wrought-iron panels, each thirty-one feet long and eight feet high, were mounted between dressed limestone piers, all set atop a four-foot limestone wall. The front gate was thirty feet high and topped by elaborate iron scrollwork incorporating the Vanderbilt symbols of acorns and oak leaves.

The Breakers was magnificent from the outside, but the glory of the house was its interiors. According to Antoinette Downing and Vincent

Scully's *Architectural Heritage of Newport, Rhode Island,* the inside of The Breakers had a "constant sense of distance and vista." Although the plan was large, it was also lucid, appealing, and efficient.

This is a house where it was possible both to enjoy solitude (in a billiard room, a library, or a salon) and to entertain hundreds of guests (in a great music room or a state dining room) with equal ease. All such was facilitated by the interior layout.

Service quarters were located skillfully out of the family's way, but the servants still were able to reach any part of the house with ease and to get meals (for hundreds, if necessary) to the dining room with a minimum of wasted steps. Hunt's floor plan is an example of Beaux-Arts design work at its best, a competent unification of plan and function that was adorned by the most opulent ornamentation imaginable.

At the heart of the plan is an immense hall, analogous to the wooden hall in Peabody & Stearns's original house. Had the new Breakers actually stood in Italy, this central hall would have been an open courtyard. In deference to the New England climate, Hunt roofed it with

The Breakers; second floor piazza overlooking the sea.

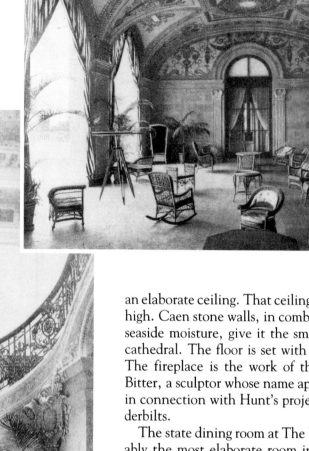

The Breakers; detail of the main hall stairway.

an elaborate ceiling. That ceiling is forty-five feet high. Caen stone walls, in combination with the seaside moisture, give it the smell of a Norman cathedral. The floor is set with colored marble. The fireplace is the work of the talented Karl Bitter, a sculptor whose name appears repeatedly in connection with Hunt's projects for the Vanderbilts.

The state dining room at The Breakers is probably the most elaborate room in Newport. It is fifty-eight feet long, forty-two feet wide, and has walls ornamented with double-height red alabaster columns, each of which is surmounted by a gilded Corinthian capital. The room was designed and fabricated in France by the Paris firm of Richard Bouwens van der Boijen. This designer had a highly developed sense of Second Empire élan. The pumped-up classicism of the Second Empire, with its polychromed stencilings, gilded moldings, elaborate hardware, and crystal chandeliers, looked quite different from the chaste interiors of Louis XVI. The reputations of men like van der Boijen fell badly out of favor in the early twentieth century and have only recently been rehabilitated.

Van der Boijen also designed the grand salon or music room at The Breakers, although fabrication and on-site installation were done by Jules Allard & Fils. Everything in this enormous room, which occupies much of the south side of the main floor, was first assembled in France. The furniture, the gilded hardware, even the chan-

The music room, designed in France by Richard Bouwens van der Boijen.

deliers, were all positioned within completed wall panels, just as they would be in Newport. Then all was disassembled, packed in airtight tin containers, and shipped to the States. A team of Allard's workmen accompanied it and reassembled the entire room within the shell of The Breakers.

Hunt himself is credited with the design of the marble and alabaster billiard room. Cool and richly detailed, its furniture was the work of the famous William Baumgarten. Hunt also did the walnut-paneled library. Perhaps he was the one who chose the peculiar early French motto carved over the fireplace: "Little do I care for riches, and do not miss them, since only cleverness prevails in the end." It seems improbable to ascribe these sentiments to a man such as Cornelius Vanderbilt II, who was neither ambivalent about his riches nor notably clever. Perhaps Hunt meant it as some kind of a joke.

Some of the woodwork at The Breakers is genuinely antique. The reception room to the right of the front door has cream and gold paneling that once graced the Paris house of Mlle. de St. Aulaire, goddaughter of Marie-Antoinette. The family dining room, located behind the state dining room, boasts antique walls from the Louis XV period. In spite of these exceptions, the interior trim of The Breakers was overwhelmingly new at the time of construction.

Everywhere in and around this house are devices of acorns and oak leaves, the same that grace the Vanderbilt family crest. Not only do they crown the front gate, they can be found on the floor of the billiard room, in the cornices, on the walls, and indeed just about everywhere else. This crest is entirely a Vanderbilt invention. Alva claimed she had "discovered" it; actually, she devised it on her own. Acorns and oak leaves are also the symbols of the Desha family, Alva's maternal grandparents. Alva's inlaws had a tolerant attitude toward apocryphal crests. Alva's crest evidently did not offend Alice, who lived most of her adult life within sight of it.

Hunt and Vanderbilt jointly made the decisions concerning the interior decoration. When it came to the second and third floors, however, Vanderbilt entrusted thirteen bedrooms, dressing rooms, and baths to a young man highly recommended by his friend Teddy Wharton. His name was Ogden Codman. Actually, it was Wharton's wife, Edith, who was behind the recommendation. She knew the work of this "clever young Boston architect," as she termed him, quite well. Together, they had transformed her gloomy Victorian Newport cottage into a classically informed villa that exemplified the best of eighteenth-century French decor. She wrote a book with Codman entitled *The Decoration of Houses.* First published in 1897, it has remained in print ever since.

Codman was ecstatic over this contract from "the nicest and richest of them all." It was upstairs work, and the twenty thousand dollars it cost was small change compared to the sums being spent in the public rooms below. This was Codman's big break, however, and his first chance to demonstrate fully the coolly aristocratic French interiors for which he and Edith Wharton later became famous. So many commissions followed this one that young Codman established offices both in Newport and in New York.

Ogden Codman was the son of a Boston Brahmin family that had spent some years at Dinard, France. It was in France that young Ogden was first exposed to French architecture and decoration. He was artistic and evidently possessed a predilection for classic French decor. He readily absorbed the sense of exquisite balance and restraint that characterizes the best of eighteenth-century design. Few Americans before or since have been as totally imbued as Codman with the particular aesthetic essence of the

After a stroke in 1896, Cornelius Vanderbilt II was confined to a wheelchair.

French eighteenth century.

His rooms were revolutionary in 1892. They were uncluttered, very bright, and far more restrained than the usual American "plutocratic palace" look. Codman was famous for painted paneling, controlled color schemes, plaster moldings, discreetely elegant architectural elements—and chintz. Certainly his upstairs bedrooms at The Breakers were a far cry from the heavily ornate work in the main rooms.

Hunt did not like Codman. The elder man's aesthetic, although French, harked back to a far more ebullient and unrestrained period of French decorative history. Possibly there was some professional jealousy at work here, as well. Hunt dismissed Codman as a servile copyist of French architectural models and told Vanderbilt that he would be better off with someone else. This criticism sounds very much like what the rest of the world would soon be saying about Hunt himself.

Despite the opinion of Richard Morris Hunt, Codman's rooms caught on immediately with a certain type of old-guard sophisticate. According to Walter Muir Whitehall, "New England was the warp, and France was the woof" of Codman's

life. His cool and refined interior schemes were at once cosmopolitan and enormously comfortable, fresh and yet refined, and luxurious without being at all overdone. They spoke with a distinct French accent, but it was one modified by comforting English and American influences. Their pervasive impact—the elimination of clutter, the coordination of color, the resurrection of symmetry and restraint—is felt in the world of interior design to this day.

"I hate shabby, dilapidated houses," Ogden Codman once said, "and poor cooks, and all that sort of thing. . . . What I want is comfort. . . . I always decide against poverty when I see very good bric-a-brac." Later, with Edith Wharton, he wrote that "each room should speak with one voice; it should contain one color which at once and unmistakeably [sic] asserts its prominence." The Codman rooms were furnished with elegant beds, chairs, tables, desks, *lits de repos,* and so on, all of it designed by Codman himself in an eighteenth-century fashion. This furniture is elaborated with caning and carved wooden bows, and much of it is as good as any antique made a century earlier.

When The Breakers was finished, *Munsey's Magazine* called it "such a rural palace as an Italian prince or cardinal of the Borgias might have erected." Contemplating the splendor of this summer house, one is reminded of Coco Chanel's remark to a friend who wondered aloud over the extreme luxury of her apartment: "One spends one's life in one's room, no?" Corneil and Alice saw The Breakers the same way.

By July of 1895, the family was in residence. On August 14, the house was opened with a great ball. The occasion was twofold: a housewarming, as well as the debut of twenty-year-old Gertrude. During that same 1895 season, Corneil's sister-in-law Alva was entertaining the Duke of Marlborough at Marble House. Alva had divorced William K. Vanderbilt the previous March. By mutual agreement, she was now persona non grata with the Vanderbilts. A new set of Vanderbilt family troubles was in store, however, and they started at Gertrude's debut.

The party itself was a typical Vanderbilt affair. The guests were rich, the tables elaborate, the favors expensive, the jewels impressive. Lispenard Stewart led the cotillion at midnight. Among the *jeunesse dorée* present that night were many of the Vanderbilt cousins, among them Corneil's eldest son and namesake, Cornelius (Neily) Vanderbilt III. Also present was Neily's future wife, Grace Graham Wilson.

The ill-starred romance between Neily and Grace stood in stark contrast to that between Neily's sister Gertrude and young Harry Payne Whitney. The Whitneys were neighbors of the Vanderbilts across Fifty-seventh Street. Harry was the son of William C. Whitney, a former Secretary of the Navy and a self-made man. Corneil and Alice approved of the Whitneys and welcomed the news of Gertrude's engagement. They were loving and cordial to Harry and Gertrude in exact proportion to their displeasure and intransigence toward Neily and Grace.

In July of 1896, after a violent argument with his son over the latter's continued attentions to Grace Wilson, Cornelius Vanderbilt II suffered a massive stroke. He was subsequently forced to abandon business entirely. Although only fifty-three years of age, Corneil now found himself an invalid confined to a wheelchair.

By its second season, the new Breakers had suddenly become a nursing home. On August 25, 1896, the reverential hush was broken by the joyful wedding of Harry and Gertrude Whitney. He was twenty-four; she was twenty-one; and the two of them truly understood one another. At least there was no suspicion of anyone marrying for money. Gertrude was America's premiere heiress, the eldest daughter of the head of the Vanderbilt family. Harry was handsome and talented, perhaps too much so for his own good. His father wasn't quite a Vanderbilt, but he was still immensely rich.

There were sixty people in the Whitney-Vanderbilt wedding party, a group hardly large enough to be noticed in so vast a house as The Breakers. Corneil, tanned, smiling, and sitting in a plush wheelchair, mustered enough energy to give the bride away, and then was wheeled back to his room. New York's fashionable Episcopal bishop Henry C. Potter performed the ceremony. A squadron of private detectives guarded the gifts.

After the festivities, Gertrude and Harry boarded Uncle Willie's steam yacht *Valiant* for the first leg of their wedding trip. It had been a lovely wedding, marred only by one black cloud. Gertrude had sided with her parents on the subject of Grace Wilson, and she had refused to invite her brother Neily to the wedding.

After Gertrude's wedding, Corneil and Alice embarked on a succession of visits to European spas in the hope of improving Corneil's health. When at Newport, they kept things calm and quiet, at least at The Breakers. By contrast, their younger sons Alfred and Reggie cut increasingly broad swaths through the summer colony and elsewhere. Both these young men were sportsmen, gamblers, and womanizers.

Corneil's health was finally improving by the summer season of 1899. He had begun to make occasional visits to his office again and was moving about without the aid of a wheelchair. The socializing that had never quite got off the ground at the new Breakers was finally showing signs of life. By September, after a season of bracing Newport air and sunshine, Corneil was better than he had been in years. He and Alice planned a dinner in honor of Prince Contacuzene and his fiancée.

The day before the dinner, the entire family made a flying visit to New York in order for Corneil to attend a board meeting. On the night of September 12, at 1 West Fifty-seventh Street, Cornelius Vanderbilt II sat up in bed, said "I think I am dying," and expired on the spot. The cause of death was a massive cerebral hemorrhage. He was fifty-six years old.

His will was read in the paneled library at The Breakers. It was here that Neily learned officially of his disinheritance. He and Grace had been married shortly after Gertrude returned home in 1896. Since that time, Neily had worked diligently at the New York Central, while trying to reconcile himself with his parents. His father's will named Neily's younger brother Alfred as principal heir. Alfred subsequently gave Neily $6 million of his inheritance, but the affair left bitterness on all sides. Its most tangible effect was to drive Neily from the family railroad business.

As a widow, Alice entertained even less than before, but she continued her stately migrations from New York to Newport and back again each year. She also traveled overseas with her children, but the majority of her time was spent quietly and privately in her marble palaces. How different she was from her sister-in-law Florence Twombly. Alice remained in modified mourning, à la Queen Victoria, for the rest of her life; Florence, after the death of her husband, became one of the greatest hostesses in New York and

Alfred Gwynne Vanderbilt, his father's principal heir, was not his eldest son.

Newport. Florence's Newport house, Vinland, was literally across the street from The Breakers, and Alice often visited during the Newport season.

While Alice became more private, her daughter-in-law Grace evolved into Newport's reigning hostess. Grace knew how to throw a party and how to cultivate exciting people. For years, she avoided her mother-in-law—with good cause—while her husband made dutiful visits to the "Rocks," as he called his mother's house.

Neily endured nearly two decades of chilly teas and strained conversation until at last the family worked out a truce of sorts. By 1926, things were sufficiently cordial for Alice to lend the Breakers to Neily and Grace for the summer season. That was the year Neily's brother Reggie drank himself to death, causing Alice yet another heartache. She had already lost her elegant son Alfred, who went down on the *Lusitania* in 1915. Perhaps this latest loss made Alice feel more warmly toward her long-neglected Neily.

She lent them The Breakers, but she was angry when she returned and discovered that Grace had made a number of unauthorized changes to the house. The invitation was never repeated. The following year, Neily and Grace went back to renting Beaulieu. When Alice died in 1934, she left The Breakers to her second daughter, Gladys Szechenyi.

The Countess Szechenyi was then living in Budapest with her husband. She was sweeter and more democratic than her mother but just as private. In 1938, Count Szechenyi died, and Gladys, mindful of gathering war clouds, returned to the United States. She divided her time between New York, Newport, and Washington, D.C., but her official residence, interestingly, was at Newport. Gladys was seldom in the public eye, which suited her. She avoided the tumult and glamour that surrounded Neily and Grace, preferring small parties and quiet afternoons spent reading in her cabana at Bailey's Beach.

Gladys Szechenyi maintained The Breakers, but after the Second World War she stopped going there. In June of 1948, she leased the house to the newly formed Preservation Society of Newport County for a dollar a year. The PSNC had been founded in 1945 by Mrs. George Henry

Warren. Mrs. Warren was appalled by the destruction of Newport's architectural heritage that even then was gathering momentum. Edwardian showplaces were increasingly being abandoned to vandals; others were being torn down to avoid taxes; developers were replacing still others with unsympathetic new construction, sometimes right on Bellevue Avenue.

Mrs. Warren and heiress Doris Duke divided the responsibility for preserving Newport. Mrs. Warren's PSNC concentrated on the mansions in the Bellevue Avenue area; Ms. Duke's Newport Restoration Foundation addressed the problem of preserving the eighteenth-century character of the old town. These two organizations flourish today and are responsible in great part for saving Newport's architectural legacy.

Although tourists roamed the marble halls of The Breakers all summer long, the Countess Szechenyi summered there, in a suite of Codman-designed rooms on the third floor. When she died in 1965, she left the house to her daughter Sylvia, who also had married a Hungarian count, Anthony Szapary. It was a good thing Hunt insisted on that third floor after all. The Countess Szapary has continued to summer there just as her mother did, unseen and unknown to the tourists below.

After 1965, the PSNC continued to rent The Breakers for a dollar a year, but they assumed the costs of maintenance and taxes. In December of 1972, title to the house, the land, and the stables on Coggeshall Avenue all were conveyed to the Society, subject to Countess Szapary's continued summer tenancy in the main house. Since then, the Countess has graciously donated a given amount of the original furnishings every year. Eventually, The Breakers and everything that was originally designed for it will become the property of the PSNC and will be available for public enjoyment and instruction.

The Breakers looks today much as it did in 1895. Because it is the largest and the most sumptuous house in town, it remains the preeminent symbol of social Newport. It is more than a symbol, however; it is also an American work of art. As a nation, Americans are fortunate that this palace has survived so well. It stands today as a beacon of taste and culture and a vivid expression of the American imagination.

Chapter 12
ROUGH POINT

Rough Point

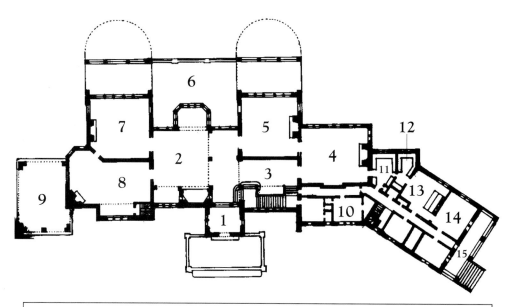

1st Floor

1. Vestibule
2. Great hall
3. Stairhall
4. Dining Room
5. Billiard Room
6. Seafront Terrace
7. Drawing Room
8. Library
9. Piazza
10. Man's Room
11. Serving Pantry
12. Cook's Pantry
13. Kitchen
14. Servants' Hall
15. Service Porch

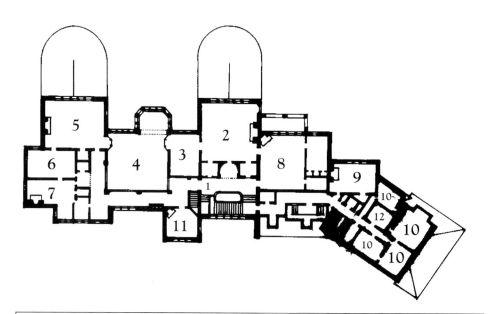

2nd Floor

1. Second Floor Hall
2. Mrs. Vanderbilt's Bedroom
3. Mrs. Vanderbilt's Bathroom
4. Upper Part of Great Hall
5–7. Bedrooms
8. Mr. Vanderbilt's Bedroom
9. Housekeeper's Room
10. Servants' Bedrooms
11. Sewing Room
12. Linens

Rough Point, designed for Frederick W. Vanderbilt by Peabody and Stearns, was completed in 1891.

Location: Newport, Rhode Island

Architect: Original house: Peabody & Stearns

              Additions: Horace Trumbauer (1869–1938)

Commissioned by: Original house: Frederick William Vanderbilt (1856–1938)

                    Additions: James Buchanan Duke (1856–1925)

House completed: Original house: 1891

                Additions: 1924

*T*HE windswept promontory known as Rough Point was the first glimpse of the United States for many an African slave. While unlighted ships lay in the darkness, human beings were rowed ashore and chained in fetid cellars beneath the unvisited desolation of this rocky promontory. The cries of the living went unheeded; the broken bodies of the dead were burned unceremoniously. Some say that on dark and stormy nights eerie cries can still be heard above the sound of the crashing surf.

Frederick Vanderbilt presumably never heard them, for it was upon this point that he and his wife Lulu decided to build a summer house. The year was 1887, at the height of the Vanderbilt family's invasion of Newport. Fred and his brothers Willie and Cornelius, together with their sister Florence Twombly, were simultaneously establishing themselves in Newport, just as they had recently done on New York's Fifth Avenue.

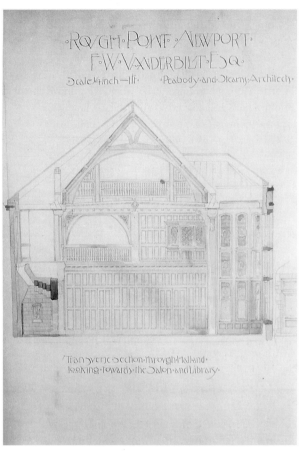

Detail from the original plans for Rough Point.

When Fred bought Rough Point, there were two wooden villas standing on the site. He had them both razed, then turned for the design of his new "cottage" to the Boston architectural firm of Peabody & Stearns. Very probably his choice of architect was a result of family ties. Peabody & Stearns was engaged at the time in the design and construction of Fred's sister's house, Elm Court, at Lenox, Massachusetts.

Besides the respected architectural firm, Fred also hired the fashionable Frederick Law Olmsted to landscape the nine acres of grounds. It was another family member—in this case, brother-in-law Seward Webb—who made the sugges-

tion. Olmsted was then consulting on the landscape at Shelburne Farms, the Webb estate in Vermont. Fred, like many of Olmsted's clients, eventually complained about costs. The result was that the original plans for the grounds at Rough Point were scaled down several times.

The preliminary site plan for the property is dated June 1887. It shows the sites of the two razed villas, as well as a proposed bowling alley, to be built parallel to Bellevue Avenue. Bowling at the time was a diversion of the rich, and private alleys were thought to be attractive inclusions in luxurious residence schemes. Fred followed Peabody's and Olmsted's design work closely and made many suggestions along the way. It was probably he who decided against the bowling alley.

Peabody & Stearns's rambling, asymmetrical, gray granite Rough Point rose during precisely the same time as Richard Morris Hunt's symmetrical and classically formal Marble House. The contrast between them illustrates both the diversity and the vitality of American architecture at the time. Both designs are competent, beautiful, and original. However, whereas Marble House soars, Rough Point sprawls.

From the standpoints of design, engineering, and craftsmanship, both buildings were superb. Rough Point, however, while grand, was not a palace and its construction moved along more quickly. By 1889, the exterior was complete. The principal axis of the house was slightly under 200 feet long, an enormous distance. The house conscientiously complemented the rugged, rocky site. Whereas Marble House was intended as an expression of cultural truth through the medium of pure architectural beauty, Rough Point was an American essay on the fine art of living.

According to *The New York Times* of June 10, 1889, the Frederick Vanderbilt house at Newport "resembles somewhat an English manor house." The resemblance was intentional. English country houses were symbols of refined living on a scale that Americans had only recently achieved. *Munsey's Magazine* in September of 1897 echoed similar sentiments, calling Peabody's design "an attractive mixture of luxury and rustic simplicity," whose impression was that of a "picturesque manor house of the English shires."

The "simplicity" noted by the press was an American notion. The English at that time felt no need to pay lip service to the modest scruples

Rough Point; according to *The New York Times* the house "resembles somewhat an English manor house."

of democracy. American millionaires, however, and indeed much of American society at large, were torn by a peculiar ambivalence. The national distaste for the class stratification of the Old World was tempered by a yearning for the physical trappings of aristocracy. Consciously or not, Englishness was much prized on this side of the Atlantic. Many considered it a badge of cultural maturity.

In fact, Rough Point doesn't look very English at all. There is something altogether American about it. Despite its agglomeration of wings, its picturesque silhouette, and the historical detailing, the house was spanking new, built all of one piece, and looked it. The architectural design, inside and out, was more an expression of the Industrial Age's levels of comfort and technology than a reference to the European roots of American culture.

Even Rough Point's English stylistic allusions were conceived with an American regard for convenience and economy. In the days of plentiful servants, this house was a modern one, vastly easier to maintain and occupy than any English model. Oscar Wilde is said to have remarked, apropos of bathrooms, that if he wanted hot water, he could always ring for it. Even with abundant servants, rich Americans and their architects preferred private bathrooms, a kitchen located sufficiently near to the dining room so that dinner did not get cold en route to the table, comfortable and well-planned accommodations for the in-house work force, and an intelligent floor plan that was convenient both for living and entertaining. These prerequisites would seem universal among owners of large houses, but it was in the American country house, and not those abroad, that they found their most logical expression.

If Rough Point was not truly English, it certainly was picturesque. "In a burly way," the article in *Munsey's* continued, "it asserts its superiority as a claimant to the soil of Newport over the palatial pretensions of a classic pile like Marble House." This writer had a prejudice for the romantic and the asymmetrical over the classic and the symmetrical. However, he made a good point about the house's harmonious relationship to its site. Rough Point is an almost Frank Lloyd Wrightian extension of the spine of rock upon which it sits. Whereas Marble House, beautiful as it may be, is clearly an imported hothouse flower.

By 1891, Rough Point was furnished, landscaped, and officially opened. The original interiors were finished with a great deal of carved dark paneling and ornate marble-faced fireplaces. The glory of the house was a central double-height hall, graced with an elaborate staircase and giant mullioned windows overlooking the sea and the constantly turbulent surf.

Rough Point's oceanfront site, like that of many a grand Newport cottage, faced the Cliff Walk, a public right-of-way along the shore. There were a limited number of access routes to the Cliff Walk, but once on it, the pedestrian was free to wander in either direction. Usually nothing more than a sweeping lawn separated the most humble of folk on the Cliff Walk from the seafronts of the greatest of the mansions. The Newport cottagers would have preferred to close off the Cliff Walk altogether, but as free access to the shore was and is held to be an American birthright, the Vanderbilts and their neighbors were forced to make the best of it.

What they did was to integrate the portion of the walk traversing their property into the overall landscape scheme. Often this was done quite handsomely. At Rough Point, the Olmsted office included a stone bridge that springs picturesquely across a chasm, with the foamy sea below. During the Vanderbilts' 1891 housewarming, the entire property was artfully illuminated, including the stone bridge. Thousands of roses were strewn on the stairs inside. While the summer colony danced to the music of an Hungarian band imported from the Casino, the uninvited stood on the Cliff Walk outside and watched.

The Fred Vanderbilts returned for the seasons of 1892 and 1893; after that, they gave up on Newport and turned their energies to the development of their house and estate at Hyde Park, New York. Rough Point was either kept closed or rented for the next twelve years.

The Newport that Fred and Lulu Vanderbilt abandoned was then entering its grandest phase. During their last season, W. C. Brownell in *Scribner's Magazine* suggested that "Nowhere else

does fashion rest with such feathery lightness on such a solid pedestal." To the Reverend Charles Wilbur de Lyon Nichols, Newport was the "supreme court of social appeals," superior by a social long shot even to the White House.

There was never a shortage of people for whom the Newport season symbolized the ultimate level of personal achievement. This was particularly true of those who lived in New York. Newport, it will be remembered, was what Price Collier of Tuxedo Park called "New York Society's best dish." Especially in the competitive world of New York society, a successful Newport season (or, preferably, a series of the same) was the grail.

Social Newport at the beginning of the twentieth century was ruled by three extraordinary women: Tessie Oelrichs, Mamie Fish, and Alva Belmont (formerly Alva Vanderbilt). During the Newport season of 1905, socialite Harry Lehr introduced Alva to William B. Leeds, the "Tin Plate King," and his attractive and vivacious wife, Nancy. The Leeds, who were renting Rough Point from Fred Vanderbilt, were frankly social climbers. They had style, looks, and

Fred Vanderbilt's yacht, *Vedette.*

money—all on a New York scale. Alva found them altogether charming, but others in her set had adopted a snobbish attitude toward the newcomers.

Interior of Fred Vanderbilt's *Vedette*.

Alva thought this situation was an outrage. In her mind, the Leeds were as good as anybody else in Newport's social set. She decided to "take them up." She and her husband gave a ball at Belcourt, their Newport house on Bellevue Avenue, and the Leeds were the guests of honor. To be recognized thus at a ball at the Belmonts in 1905 was certification of acceptability in Newport. The following year, Billie Leeds bought Rough Point.

Few people have heard of this "Tin Plate King" today, but he was a vivid example of an American type who, by the dawn of this century, was rising in droves from obscurity to prominence through business. Billie Leeds started out as a florist in Richmond, Indiana, and wound up by the age of forty-one as president of the Chicago,

Rock Island and Pacific Railroad. He was additionally a founder of the modern tinplate industry in America. In the process, he amassed a fortune variously estimated at between $30 and $40 million.

In 1896, Leeds divorced his first wife and married Nancy Worthington (née Stewart) of Cleveland, Ohio. The new bride had gotten her own divorce decree a mere three days before her marriage to Leeds. By 1905, the couple was established in a mansion at 987 Fifth Avenue, which was filled with tapestries, Rembrandts, Constables, and a Watteau. The house was served by an enormous stable on East Eighty-ninth Street (only recently demolished). Leeds also kept a 252-foot yacht, *Noma*. Thus equipped, they turned their attention to Newport.

James B. Duke, third owner of Rough Point, with his daughter, Doris.

Then, at his social peak, forty-four-year-old Billie Leeds had a stroke. He lost the use of his voice—temporarily as it turned out. However, instead of becoming the mecca of the 1906 season's most extravagant entertainments, Rough Point was quiet. Leeds made a gradual recovery, but the following year, in the wake of the Wall Street panic of 1907, he was felled again. This time, the stroke paralyzed the entire left side of his body. The following year he suffered a third stroke in Paris and died at the age of forty-six.

The men of the Gilded Age, or at least those who spent their lives in the private clubs and ballrooms of New York and Newport, had a tendency to die young. This was the inevitable outcome of smoking, drinking, playing, working, philandering, worrying, and especially eating to excess. A fitting obituary for Billie Leeds well might be the recipe for "Billi Bi Soup," a dish developed in Paris and named after this American millionaire. It starts off with a rich fish broth. The broth is then thickened with a combination of butter and flour, and finally finished with a mixture of egg yolks and cream. No low-cholesterol mogul he—Billie Leeds was killing himself with his spoon.

The death of William B. Leeds did not put an end to the aspirations of his ambitious wife. She promptly sold 987 Fifth Avenue to Benjamin Duke, brother of the future owner of Rough Point, and moved to Europe. Tales of the immense Leeds fortune opened doors for her everywhere. For the next twelve years, "the widow of the Tin Plate King" entertained in England and on the Continent in the most lavish manner imaginable. She rented yachts at Cowes, threw swank parties in London, hobnobbed with European nobility, and turned down a legion of titled suitors.

In January of 1920, at the age of forty-three, Nancy Leeds finally said yes to one of those suitors and married Prince Christopher, the brother of the king of Greece. Over the next two years, Greece was torn by political havoc. In 1922, the couple fled to the United States.

Before leaving Greece, Princess Christopher had authorized the sale of Rough Point to James B. Duke, brother of the man to whom Nancy Leeds had sold her Fifth Avenue house in 1908. Asked about her Newport real estate, she told reporters that it was "my own private property and not a part of the Leeds estate."

Nancy Leeds, "the widow of the Tin Plate King."

Rough Point then entered a new era. When James B. Duke bought the house in 1922, it had a taxable valuation of $375,000. It had taken Fred Vanderbilt eight years to sell the house. Nancy Leeds hadn't had that kind of time. It was said by the papers that Duke bought the property for under $200,000.

Duke's personal history is an Horatio Alger story that still has the power to inspire. His father had returned from the Confederate navy to find his farm in ruins, his fields destroyed by Union armies, and his boys (Ben, Brodie, and James) on the verge of starvation. The only thing left was a bit of bright leaf tobacco hanging in a blasted barn. Washington Duke and his sons granulated it by hand, loaded it onto a rickety cart drawn by a pair of blind mules, and proceeded to peddle it across the countryside. This was the beginning of the American Tobacco Company, and later the Duke-controlled Tobacco Trust, which by 1910 had devoured 250 rivals and represented a total capital investment of $316 million.

James B. Duke became the manager of the family tobacco business at the age of fourteen.

"I loved business more than anything else," he later said. "I was sorry to leave off at night and glad when morning came." Duke remained a bachelor until 1904, when, at the age of forty-eight, he married a widow by the name of Lillian McCready. The wizard at business was more naïve when it came to matters of the heart. Lillian never really broke off with her boyfriend, one Major Frank T. Huntoon. Duke got wind of things, and by the following year, the couple was divorced. Two years later, he married another widow, this one an Atlanta socialite named Nanaline Holt Inman. Their daughter, Doris, was born in 1912.

By the end of the First World War, the Dukes were established in a grand house on Fifth Avenue (1 East Seventy-eighth Street, designed in 1909 by Philadelphia architect Horace Trumbauer), Duke Farm in New Jersey, and a country estate in North Carolina (called Lynnewood, and also designed by Trumbauer). They soon began to rent in Newport for the summer, liked it, and when Rough Point came on the market in 1922, Duke snapped it up.

Rough Point was large, but not large enough for James B. Duke. He had it significantly enlarged in 1923 to 1924, to the tune of $656,000. The plans were drawn up by Horace Trumbauer. These additions were so skillfully integrated with the existing house that it is difficult to tell where the old exterior ends and the new one begins. The Trumbauer interiors, however, were far more palatial than Peabody & Stearns's originals. Unfortunately, photographs of them have never been published, and as of this date it is only hearsay that accords them a status equal to those at The Elms, Trumbauer's Newport palace for coal magnate Edward J. Berwind.

In December of 1924, Duke announced that he was creating a $40 million trust to aid "educational, religious, and charitable works" in the United States. Six million of these dollars were earmarked for little Trinity College in Durham, North Carolina, on condition that it change its name to Duke University. According to the press, the motivation for this philanthropy was a "love for humanity." In an interview on December 16, 1924, Duke told *The New York Times* that America's rich had a moral obligation to provide for their heirs only to the extent that those heirs might remain "comfortable."

He did not long survive this interview. With his wife and daughter by his side, James B. Duke died in his Fifth Avenue house on October 11, 1925. He was sixty-nine years old. Despite the tens of millions of dollars he had already given to charity and education, there still remained more than $100 million in his estate. His will essentially split the money between his wife and daughter, enabling both to live more than just comfortably.

Two years after his death, Duke's independent-minded daughter, Doris, decided on her own not to allow her father's New Jersey estate to be liquidated. "Girl of 14 to Run 3000-Acre Estate" proclaimed the *Times* on September 24, 1927. Taking over Duke Farm was an early instance of Doris Duke's personal assertiveness, and of her lifelong regard for architectural preservation.

In 1927, the papers described fourteen-year-old Doris as "an unassuming girl . . . keen on outdoor sports." She made her debut in society on August 23, 1930, at Rough Point. It was a large party, with six hundred guests, a giant striped marquee on the lawn, and thousands of colored lights decorating the grounds. It was also one of the last really public events in which she willingly participated.

Doris Duke found herself perpetually described as "the richest girl in the world," an image that would cause inconvenience, exasperation, and occasionally real danger for the rest of her life. Predictably, she became increasingly reclusive.

Doris Duke came of age in November of 1933. The *Times* noted the event in an article entitled DORIS DUKE AT 21 IS WEALTHIEST GIRL. It informed the public that she led a quiet life and was shadowed at all times by private guards. "Ever since her father's death, Miss Duke has been regimented in the art of avoiding attention. . . . She has not gone in for smoked glasses, secret ocean sailings or black veils. She has been seen, if not heard."

Indeed she was seen, and quite often at that. She traveled frequently, chaperoned either by her mother or her half brother, Walker Inman. The papers continued to report that "the menace of the public magnifying glass is always present." Inman stated "Everywhere we go it is the same. She gets to see a few of the sights, goes out to dinner a few times and then her identity becomes known and we have to rush off somewhere else."

In 1935, Doris Duke married James Henry

Above: Rough Point today, behind a high fence of barbed wire.

Right: "Doris Duke found herself perpetually described as 'the richest girl in the world.' "

Roberts Cromwell, son of Mrs. E. T. Stotesbury, in a ceremony described as "unostentatious and somewhat mysterious." She was twenty-two; he was thirty-eight. After visiting India on her honeymoon, the new Mrs. Cromwell announced her intention to remodel her Palm Beach house after the Taj Mahal. The marriage was short-lived, as was a second some years later to Dominican playboy Porfirio Rubirosa.

Over the succeeding decades, the mistress of Rough Point became an even more mysterious figure. Though rarely seen in public, she has continued to champion the cause of historic preservation. Rough Point is the favorite of her many houses, and Newport has been the focus of her preservation efforts. It was a love of that city that led her to found Newport Restoration Foundation, which has focused on the pres-

ervation and restoration of the city's small-scale eighteenth-century districts. Formerly abused, ignored, and/or inappropriately altered, these old parts of the town had fallen to a very low state. The restored charm of much of Newport today is directly due to Doris Duke and Newport Restoration.

Meanwhile, at the far end of Bellevue Avenue, Rough Point remains the only one of the Vanderbilt houses that still serves the original purpose for which it was built. It remains an enormously luxurious summer cottage, still maintained to Vanderbiltian standards. The only difference from the past is the high fence and barbed wire that surrounds it. Unfortunately, Doris Duke has no other way to preserve her privacy.

Chapter 13

BILTMORE

Biltmore

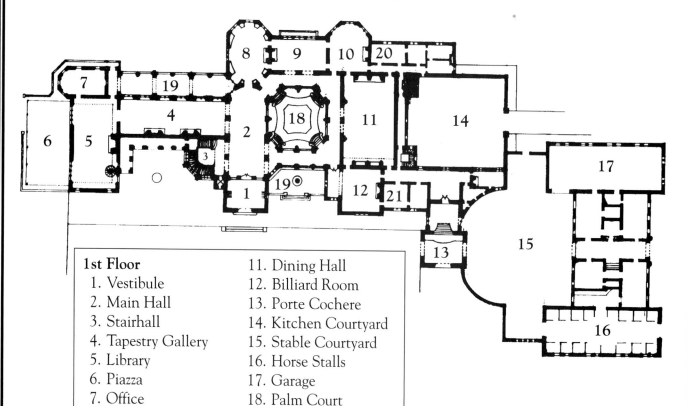

1st Floor

1. Vestibule
2. Main Hall
3. Stairhall
4. Tapestry Gallery
5. Library
6. Piazza
7. Office
8. Sitting Room
9. Morning Room
10. Breakfast Room

11. Dining Hall
12. Billiard Room
13. Porte Cochere
14. Kitchen Courtyard
15. Stable Courtyard
16. Horse Stalls
17. Garage
18. Palm Court
19. Terrace
20. Serving Pantry
21. Smoking Room

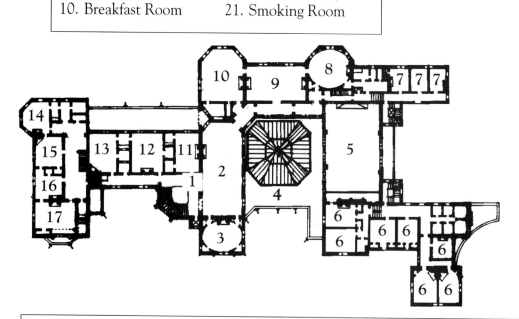

2nd Floor

1. Stairhall
2. Second Floor Hall
3. Bedroom
4. Skylight over Palm Court
5. Upper Part of Dining Hall

6. Bachelor Wing Bedrooms
7. Servants' Rooms
8. Mrs. Vanderbilt's Bedroom
9. Oak Sitting Room
10. Mr. Vanderbilt's Bedroom
11–17. Bedrooms

Biltmore from the air, circa 1930. "No sooner was it completed than George's family began to worry what in the world was going to be done with it. . . ."

Location: Asheville, North Carolina

Architect: Richard Morris Hunt (1827–1895)

Landscape Architect: Frederick Law Olmsted (1822–1903)

Commissioned by: George Washington Vanderbilt (1862–1914)

Main house completed: 1895

*T*HERE are many men in the world like George Vanderbilt—shy, studious, cultured, physically fragile, "unsuited" to business—but rarely do they have any money. In 1885, however, at the age of twenty-three, George Vanderbilt inherited $10 million from his father. The ultimate result of this was an effort to create a great work of art in the form of a major American house.

George Washington Vanderbilt; at first glance he seemed "hardly the type to realize this dream."

Fortunately for George Vanderbilt, he obtained the best artistic advice available. Biltmore actually capped the careers of two titans of nineteenth-century American design. It was Richard Morris Hunt's last completed house—and in the opinion of many, his best. For Frederick Law Olmsted, the pioneer designer of American parks and open spaces, Biltmore was a final opportunity to realize social and ecological creeds he had espoused throughout his career. Biltmore was a monument to personal mission—Vanderbilt's, Hunt's, and Olmsted's. The artists involved were given carte blanche, and Biltmore was paid for almost entirely with capital. Its scale and splendor impressed the entire world.

No sooner was it completed than George's family began to worry what in the world was to be done with it in the long run. It is ironic that many of the sumptuous houses in which such worrying about the future occurred have since been destroyed. However, Biltmore survives, practically intact, and still in Vanderbilt family hands.

It took a certain type of personality to bring a 140,000-acre estate centered around a 255-room house out of the realm of fantasy and into that of reality. At first glance, George Vanderbilt hardly seems the type to have been able to realize this dream. Olmsted called him "delicate"; Henry Clews described him as "not so robust"; Gifford Pinchot thought he was a bit of a dullard.

The great nemesis of George Vanderbilt's life was tuberculosis. He was forever haunted by it. His vulnerability had a positive side, however. In a family whose expectations of its young male heirs could at times be crushing, nothing whatsoever was expected of George. Everyone treated him with special consideration. His ruthless grandfather left him $2 million dollars when he was only fifteen. His doting father, William Henry, gave him another million on his twenty-first birthday. George was living at the time with his parents and neither needed nor appeared to need so extravagant a gift, but his family acted as though the boy might expire at any moment without the extra million to prop him up.

In appearance, George Vanderbilt had the look of a late-Victorian dandy. He had a willowy build, a libidinously thin mustache, thick black hair combed straight back, the aquiline Vanderbilt nose in its most developed form, and a dark complexion—all of which made him look like a Spanish nobleman. However, he dressed with the clothing sense of an English milord. Although he never had a profession, George Vanderbilt received a splendid education in music and art. He developed a passion for opera, sometimes attending the Metropolitan four and five nights in a row. He was a linguist of accomplishment as well, fluent in French, German, Spanish, Italian, and modern and even ancient Greek. He could read Sanskrit, and he stumbled along in Hebrew.

At one point, George considered becoming an Episcopal priest, a vocation that might have suited him well. He did not, however, and instead became a gentleman of leisure. His family was content with this, never having expected him to participate in the rough-and-tumble world of the railway business. After his father's death in 1885, George continued to live quietly with his mother, dabbling in the occasional philanthropy, traveling to Europe, and collecting books on art and architecture.

These living arrangements were anything but constricting. He and his mother inhabited enormous mansions, where each enjoyed abundant personal space and privacy. Their relations were marked by stateliness, good manners, and high mutual regard. Mrs. Vanderbilt's bedroom on the floor plans for Biltmore was not designed for George's wife but, rather, for his mother. Biltmore was to be a permanent country residence for them both, to supplement 640 Fifth in New York, and a summer place called Pointe d'Acadie at Bar Harbor, Maine.

Besides money, George inherited valuable real estate from his father. This included 640 Fifth Avenue, the southern portion of the Triple Palace in which his mother had only a lifetime interest, and a Staten Island country place called the Homestead. The latter property included a modestly pretentious wooden Victorian mansion on New Dorp Road, plus greenhouses and a model farm that together supplied 640 Fifth with all the flowers and produce one could wish.

George's Staten Island neighbors hoped, at the time of his inheritance, that he would become an active member of the community there. By the late 1880s, however, Staten Island was already becoming outré, at least in the eyes of the fashion-conscious. For George Vanderbilt and his mother, select, sedate, and exclusive Bar Harbor was attractive in the summer, and 640

Fifth Avenue was fine for the New York season. Evidently, something else was wanted for the rest of the year, however.

Here George's cultured background came to the fore, for what he eventually developed was a uniquely American version of the traditional European gentleman's country seat. The original vision was more Hunt's and Olmsted's than George's, but he embraced that vision with enthusiasm. Like the estates of the gentry of yore, George's Biltmore would be both a symbol and a source of its owner's economic power.

In 1887, about a year after William Henry Vanderbilt's will was settled, the young millionaire and his mother made a visit to the mountain resort of Asheville, North Carolina. They had gone to stay at Colonel Frank Coxe's Battery Park Hotel. The Battery Park, just completed in 1886, was then enjoying nationwide publicity as the most luxurious hotel in the South. From atop

its little hill in the middle of Asheville, this beporched and betowered wooden behemoth boasted some of the finest mountain vistas in the world.

This, however, was a secondary reason for the Vanderbilts' visit. Since the beginning of the nineteenth century, the little mountain city of Asheville also had enjoyed a reputation as a health resort for consumptives. People went there for the clean air and the mountain climate. By 1871, a modest boom in sanatoria was underway. Tubercular patients flocked to these new establishments, and to little boardinghouses much like the one run, years later, by novelist Thomas Wolfe's mother, which Wolfe recreated in his novel *Look Homeward, Angel.*

Despite the pseudomedical air of the clinic industry, most Asheville cures amounted to little more than taking yourself there and staying for a while. When the railroad arrived in 1880, this

The Homestead, the "modestly pretentious wooden Victorian mansion" on Staten Island which George inherited from his father.

became easy. According to historian Douglas Swaim, "tourists, architects, consumptives, new residents, wealth and business" poured into Asheville. Luxury hotels such as the Battery Park proliferated.

Asheville was and still is the seat of Buncombe County, genesis of the slang term *bunk*. Its reputation as a health resort was ironic, to say the least, since the town sat smack in the middle of a sparse but horribly unhealthy population of mountain people suffering from a combination of poor sanitation, improper diet, and the worst poverty in the United States. Asheville was a little bit of a Dodge City, too. Beyond the manicured grounds of the luxurious hotels were all manner of gambling dens, rowdy saloons, and an established red-light district. Elite visitors could be as insulated from all of this as they chose. Given George's tendency to consumption, his passion for travel, and the national reputation (deserved or not) of Asheville and the Battery Park, a visit here was practically inevitable.

Throughout the 1880s, southern politicos and rich retirees were busy building imposing wooden mansions in and around Asheville. These weren't palaces, but they were often quite elaborate, and they lent a refined and luxurious air to the surroundings. Arriving in 1887, it was very possible for a Vanderbilt to imagine himself established in such an area. Of course, besides the supposedly restorative climate, there were also the sublime mountain views.

Particularly so was the mountain prospect to be had from the piazza of the Battery Park Hotel. George took one look at that view and decided on the spot that he had found the land of his dreams. George Vanderbilt was an impetuous man. He did not weigh carefully the pros and cons of major decisions. Rather, he was quick to decide, and quicker to act.

Leaving his mother at the hotel one day, he rented a horse from the Battery Park stables and rode to a place south of town called Lone Pine Mountain. From the summit, he beheld a vista of mountains and valleys such as he had never seen before, a view that stretched for almost forty miles and included noble Mt. Pisgah. Just as his sister Lila had found a heaven in rural Vermont, George felt that he, too, had discovered paradise.

George bought the land for its view not for the property, which is to say that, notwithstanding the noble vista, the land he set about acquiring was distinctly inferior. It looked picturesque from a distance, but almost every acre in the Asheville region was in terrible condition. That which wasn't devoted to unscientific subsistence farming was comprised of ravaged forests that had been culled so many times for timber that there was scarcely a decent tree left.

Ever since the arrival of the railroad in 1880, local loggers had extended their operations from Asheville in successively wider rings. There was no consciousness of scientific forestry at the time, either in Asheville or anywhere in the United States. The woodcutters would attack a virgin stand of forest like so many locusts, cut down every single good tree, and leave behind them a moonscape of scattered limbs, tangled brush, junk trees, minor fires, and eroding soil. No consideration was given to future harvests. Once the land had been cut, it was considered useless for the future. This was how these forests had been treated since the first settlers arrived; nobody thought much about it one way or another.

Some people in the United States were appalled by the profligate waste of forest land, however. Frederick Law Olmsted was prime among them. When George began to buy his land in North Carolina, Olmsted was already working for him, relandscaping Pointe d'Acadie at Bar Harbor and laying out the grounds for the new Hunt-designed mausoleum on the Vanderbilt family plot in the Moravian Cemetery on Staten Island. Olmsted was quite aware of his client's steady acquisition of huge tracts of ruined forestland, and it fired his imagination.

Olmsted believed that mankind's existence could, and should, be bettered by beautiful parks and a healthy relationship—both aesthetic and ecological—to land and forests. He had been frustrated repeatedly in his efforts to promote these principles. For example, he had tried to induce Leland Stanford to include an arboretum in the landscape scheme for Stanford University, but Stanford wouldn't have any of it, nor was he particularly amenable to Olmsted's naturalistic approach to landscape architecture, preferring more formal designs. Olmsted had encountered similar frustrations in his work on New York's Central Park. He felt the park commissioners were out to ruin completely the carefully contrived bucolic look of the park by their insertion of fast roads and playing fields.

George Vanderbilt was Olmsted's ideal patron. Here was a client with an artistic eye, a sense of moral duty, and the ability to pay for anything. Olmsted saw George's North Carolina estate as a chance to demonstrate all of his most passionately held theories, not just on naturalistic landscaping but on land and resource stewardship, as well. As he worked on the project, he came to believe that posterity would judge everything he stood for on the basis of Biltmore.

Richard Morris Hunt, George's choice of architect, was well known to the nation and to the Vanderbilt family by 1887. The worldwide acclaim for 660 Fifth Avenue, finished in 1882, was fresh in everyone's mind. Hunt was also at that time about to begin work with George's sister-in-law Alva Vanderbilt on the designs for Marble House in Newport. Hunt's and George's desire to build something that would enrich the national culture, plus Olmsted's passion to set influential examples of aesthetic and ecological land stewardship, lent a public character to Biltmore from the very start. This quality was reinforced by an economic scheme that was intended to support George and his estate for generations to come.

Biltmore had a model farm, of course, as every important estate of the period did, but field crops and prize Jersey cattle were not expected to support the estate. Rather, Olmsted's long-range plan was for Biltmore's operating costs to be offset (and then some) with income derived from scientific forestry. This was a bold concept for its time, uniquely different from the models of feudal tenantry that had enriched European nobles of the past. It appealed as much to George's Americanism as it did to his love of the magnificent.

The Biltmore land holdings were acquired piecemeal, but the enormous scale of the property was intended from the start. Even a scientifically managed forest would have to be large in order to generate sufficient income to maintain a place such as Biltmore. The example set to the nation would be just as important as the income. Nobody in the United States, including the government, ever had engaged in scientific forestry before.

Land acquisition commenced in 1888 and site preparation began the following year. By 1890, an army of laborers was at work grading roads, laying out plantations, building bridges, trucking in topsoil, installing waterworks, collecting botanical specimens, upgrading temporary houses, erecting farm buildings, and carving the site for the Hunt-designed château out of a mountainside. A special three-mile railroad spur was constructed up Lone Pine Mountain—at a cost of $77,500—to deliver building materials. This remarkable feature was intended as an economy measure, and it was removed when construction was complete.

George, meanwhile, was seeking a name for his new domain. "Bilton House and Bilton Forest go well together," he wrote to Olmsted in February of 1890. Bildt was the name of the Vanderbilts' ancestral home in Holland. Unfortunately, there turned out to be a Bolton somewhere else in North Carolina and the name was thought so similar as to threaten confusion at the post office. Someone came up with Biltmore, and by the end of the year, that was the official name.

Initially, George wanted a roomy wooden house along the lines of his sister Lila's home at Shelburne (before that house was redesigned), or indeed like many of the other houses then rising in Asheville. Hunt dissuaded him, however, suggesting ever-grander schemes, until at last they agreed on the present Loire-type château. (Cornelius Vanderbilt II would have a similar experience with Hunt in 1892 after the fire that destroyed the original Breakers. Both George and Cornelius would have been satisfied with spacious wooden houses. Instead, Hunt gave each a palace that was grander than Marble House.)

A golden aura of enlightened cooperation characterized everything at Biltmore in the heady early days. Hunt and Olmsted had crossed swords in years past over a rejected Hunt design for a set of gates to Central Park, but at Biltmore, they actually solicited one another's ideas. "There has not been the slightest lack of harmony between us," Olmsted wrote to his wife, adding that Hunt had "accepted every single suggestion that I have made." It was Olmsted's idea to site the stable wing to the north of the château in order to block winter winds, and to construct a sheltered garden to the south for protected walks in blustery weather. Hunt's aesthetic was one of balanced formality, Olmsted's one of naturalism. At Biltmore, their independent visions of beauty actually complemented one another.

Vanderbilt, Hunt, and Olmsted grew to be

George, on the right, clowning with guests during the construction of Biltmore. Gifford Pinchot is seated second from the left.

friends as well as professional associates. All three stayed at the Brick House, a preexisting building on the estate, which is extant today. There was gaiety and laughter, a regular stream of visitors, and a sense of history in the making. George and Hunt made several trips to Europe together to seek appropriate furnishings for the house, returning with rugs, thrones, and even entire ceilings. In the final summer of Biltmore's construction, George commissioned John Singer Sargent to paint Hunt and Olmsted, and brought all three men down in his private railroad car. (The portraits still hang in Biltmore's second-floor hall.) "What a blissful time is ahead for George," Hunt wrote to his wife. "With the fulfillment of his ideals, may he live to a ripe old age to enjoy his work and our work."

George's closeness to his architect and landscape designer had a decided effect on the way Biltmore took shape. The more Hunt talked to George, the grander the architectural scheme became. By 1889, a feudal-style village, fanning out from the entrance lodge, was added to the original plan. Likewise, when Olmsted got his client's ear, the landscape design became more complex, too.

Biltmore's overall landscape plan—which is to say the total of the scenic roads, the model farm, the grounds adjacent to the house, the formal gardens and greenhouses, Olmsted's beloved arboretum, and the great forest itself—evolved in a haphazard fashion. Some elements were intended from the start, such as the enormous esplanade that faces the front door of the château, and the so-called *ramp douce* which rises up the hillside at the esplanade's other end. However, much of the rest of it evolved from impromptu chats between Vanderbilt and Olmsted. The latter would make a suggestion and Vanderbilt would usually agree to give it a try. If George liked what he saw, he would ask for more. Cost was never an issue; the assumption was that the owner's resources were limitless.

Olmsted made two to three trips to Biltmore every year, arriving on the special railroad spur in George's private car and staying for weeks at a stretch. Soon he was bringing along his son Frederick Junior, who was deeply involved in every aspect of his father's work at Biltmore and elsewhere. Richard Hunt also brought his son Richard Howland Hunt to participate on the design and construction of the château. Even-

Sargent's painting of Frederick Law Olmsted; it hangs today on the second floor of Biltmore, beside the picture of Hunt.

tually, it would be the two sons who finished what their illustrious fathers had begun.

It has been suggested by later architectural historians, notably Vincent Scully and Antoinette Downing, that Hunt at the end of his life regretted his period of limestone and marble palaces, preferring instead to be remembered for his earlier work in wood and shingles. However, Biltmore, Hunt's last and grandest commission, was in the French idiom he knew and loved so

blance in parts and detailing.

For Hunt, George Vanderbilt's château was an opportunity to do everything he had ever wanted to do with a large house. Biltmore was a monument to the continuation of Western culture on American shores. It was also an expression of the aesthetics of the French Renaissance, Hunt's favorite period. Hunt's personal visions of architectural beauty were embodied far more in this house than in any of his earlier Stick

Richard Morris Hunt, the architect of Biltmore, painted in 1895 by John Singer Sargent.

well. And it was he who chose that idiom; George did not.

The specific inspiration for the design of the house is very easy to identify. The facade overlooking the esplanade bears a striking resemblance to the house of the fifteenth-century financier Jacques Coeur in Bourges, France. Coeur's house was one of Hunt's favorite buildings. It is often cited as the model for 660 Fifth Avenue, to which it bears some resem-

Style or shingled buildings.

Floor plans were largely completed by 1889. Scaffolds were then erected on the house site to assess the composition of views from what would be the upper floors. The house began to rise in 1890. Thirty-two thousand bricks a day were manufactured on the site. Local stone was used for the foundations, but the superstructure was framed in steel, filled with brick, and clad in Indiana limestone. The house was 375 feet long and 190 feet at its widest. The interior craftsmanship was superb, in particular the library paneling. Much of the wood and stone carving was the work of Karl Bitter. Among other things, Bitter created a bronze statue of a lissome boy struggling with a pair of geese for the center of Vanderbilt's winter garden.

D. C. Weeks and Son was the general contractor at Biltmore. The work continued nonstop, winter and summer. As a measure of the scale of the job, the tiling subcontractor, the firm of Bradley & Currier, took eight months just to tile the twenty bathrooms, the kitchens and pantries, the indoor swimming pool, and such fireplaces as were not faced with marble.

By 1892, the basement was finished; by 1893, they were up to the second floor; and in 1894 work was under way on the roof. Biltmore was habitable and largely furnished by mid-1895, and

by October, George had moved in.

The house itself is far more beautiful in reality than it is in pictures. The pale color of the stone is simply sublime. The interior plan is much more coherent than the vast size of the house would suggest—so much so that Hunt's son later used a markedly similar plan for George Gould's Hempstead House at Sand's Point, Long Island.

The principal rooms at Biltmore radiate from a stone hall that overlooks an enormous winter garden. The plan is impressive but also livable. In a large corner on the south side of the hall, adjacent to the front door, is the circular stone stairway, modeled after that of the Château de Blois, but coiling upward in the opposite direction. Next to the stairway is a carved screen, beyond which lies a long tapestry gallery furnished with overstuffed sofas and carved tables. The French doors along its western wall open

Biltmore under construction; view from the south with walled gardens in the middle distance.

Temporary construction shops on the site of the forecourt lawn; 1894.

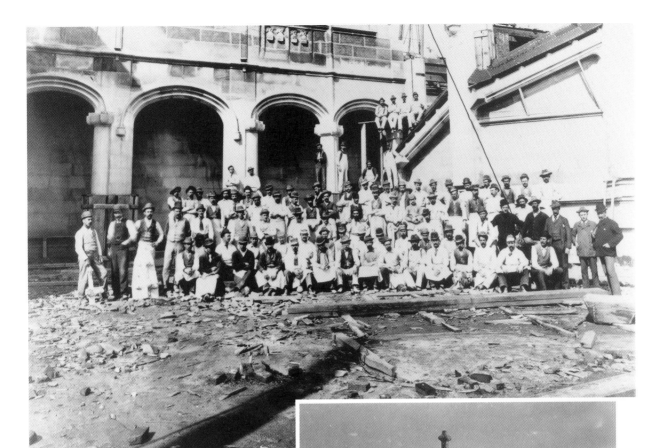

Above: ". . . by 1893, they were up to the second floor. . . ."

Below: Construction site seen from the *ramp douce*; note railroad cars on the temporary spur line.

Above: ". . . and in 1894, work was under way on the roof." Note the Vanderbilt "V" carved in stone above the window.

onto a balcony that overlooks an awesome view.

The tapestry gallery almost functions as a part of the hall itself, and is a dramatic Beaux-Arts approach to the sumptuous paneled library situated at its far end. Although located at the extreme southern edge of the building, this library is the heart of the house. Once inside, one is surrounded by comfort, beauty, and culture in the respective forms of wonderful overscaled furniture, more Karl Bitter carvings, and George Vanderbilt's extraordinary collection of books. It is a welcoming room, and its elaborate dark wood paneling lends an air of coziness despite its enormous size.

At the western end of the main floor hall is the Music Room, unfinished in Vanderbilt's day and decorated and opened to the public only in 1976. How curious to think that during Biltmore's heydey, this prominently placed room had walls of bare brick and a screen across the door. One would never guess that the dark paneling and beamed ceiling were not designed by Hunt himself.

Along the north line of the main hall is the winter garden, a vast palm-filled stone and glass chamber. During daylight hours, the winter garden is lit by a glass ceiling; nighttime illumination comes from eight enormous hanging iron lanterns.

The winter garden doubles as a monumental lobby for the main dining room, or banquet hall. This immense chamber has a triple-bay fireplace,

Biltmore; the main stair.

The winter garden adjacent to the main hall.

a double-height Gothic ceiling, long ranks of velvet chairs, and bearskin rugs. Across a secondary hall to the east is a smoking room, to which gentlemen could retreat after heavy dinners. To the west is a sitting room and a smaller dining room for dinners *en famille.*

There is splendor and an intelligent division of function between the principal rooms on the main floor. A similar coherence typifies the plan for the pantries, kitchens, and service rooms throughout the house, all of which were designed with careful attention to function and convenience, and to the highest standards of nineteenth-century technology.

The two upstairs floors contain roomy and comfortable bedrooms, each furnished with rich and often color-coordinated fabrics and venerable antiques. There is an abundance of private bathrooms, but hardly any of them contains a sink. One rang for hot water at Biltmore, and it was delivered to one's bathroom in one of George's collection of antique pitchers and basins; or, of course, the tap in one's tub could be turned on.

Gazing from these interiors onto the mature woodlands of Biltmore today, it's hard to appreciate the extent to which the surroundings were designed by man. The prospects from almost anywhere on the estate were sculpted and manipulated to provide pleasing vistas and open views. The true measure of Olmsted's brilliance is how utterly natural it all looks.

The library at Biltmore, while located at the southern end of the building, "is the heart of the house."

The double-height banquet hall has a triple-bay fireplace and a seventy-foot-high ceiling.

George's bedroom on the second floor.

Frederick Law Olmsted came late to his life's work. He was well into his thirties when his and Calvert Vaux's "Greensward" plan was accepted as the design for New York's Central Park. Later, together with his son Fred, Olmsted designed parks in Brooklyn, Chicago, Buffalo, Montreal, and Boston, among many other places. The firm's important projects also included the campus of Stanford University in Palo Alto, California, the grounds of the United States Capitol in Washington, D.C., and those of the 1893 World's Columbian Exposition in Chicago.

Olmsted believed that beautiful parks could humanize the ugly industrial cities then arising. He felt that repeated exposure to nature and beauty would alter the daily thoughts of mankind, and eventually help civilize the world. In a sense, his designed landscapes represented a continuation of the naturalistic precepts that informed the work of such English eighteenth-century masters as "Capability" Brown.

Olmstead was widely traveled and had first-hand knowledge of what had been done in Europe with urban parks and forests. Like Hunt, he was a cultural missionary, bringing civilizing ideas from the Old World to the New. Also like Hunt, he adapted what he learned in Europe to American conditions. He was fortunate in that he was able to convert a personal vision of art into a paying business. He was so driven by his visions, however, that he allowed them to ruin his health.

According to Olmsted's biographer, Laura Woods Roper, from the very outset Biltmore was intended to "combine the functions of country retreat and paying enterprise." It was Olmsted who convinced George Vanderbilt that forestry would be "far more interesting to a man of poetic temperament than any of those [other agricultural pursuits] commonly considered appropriate to a country-seat life."

Scientific forestry might be defined as economic management of woodlands designed to maximize timber crops and foster future healthy growth. "Silviculture" was centuries old in Europe but unknown in the United States, where the supply of virgin forest seemed limitless and selective cutting and reforestation were alien concepts.

As early as 1871, Olmsted was writing articles in *The Nation* drawing attention to such things as the interdependence of forests and a pure

289

Left: Vintage canned goods, still in the Biltmore pantries today.

Below: Biltmore's basement laundry room, the height of modernity in 1895.

water supply. Ninety thousand of Biltmore's 140,000 acres of woodlands were in virginal condition in 1890, which fact no doubt contributed to the illusion that the supply of forest land was limitless. The remaining fifty thousand acres, however, were ruinated. The sites of the château

Biltmore as first completed, from the *ramp douce*.

château amidst the dirt farms seemed a "callous anomaly," as Laura Roper termed it, then scientific forestry would constitute its redemption.

At the beginning of 1892, Olmsted hired as Biltmore's chief forester an earnest and intelligent young man named Gifford Pinchot. Pinchot

Biltmore, showing early garden plantings.

and of Biltmore Village were in the devastated area. The soil here was badly eroded, and the remaining woods were so overcut that nothing was left except raggy saplings. Piles of abandoned debris were prone to frequent fires, which had destroyed the precious moisture-holding leaf mold of the original forest floor, further inhibiting healthy new growth.

Thinning, clearing, and replanting of these areas were done on a pharaonic scale. If the great

had graduated from Yale in 1889, after which he had taken a path very different from that of his classmates and had gone to the École Nationale Forestière, in Nancy, France. Here he pursued studies in silviculture for two years. He then returned to the United States qualified for a career that was virtually unheard of in this country, He found a job almost immediately, however.

His background, of course, was an undeniable help. He came from a socially prominent Philadelphia family whose house had been designed by Richard Morris Hunt. Olmsted also knew the Pinchots and doubtless had watched the young man's progress at Nancy. He was willing to entrust Gifford Pinchot with considerable responsibility, and his trust proved well placed. Pinchot went on to become the first chief of the U.S. Bureau of Forestry (1898), founder of the Yale School of Forestry (1903), chairman of the National Conservation Commission (1908), and the state forester and later two-time governor of Pennsylvania.

Pinchot's job at Biltmore was to plan and co-ordinate the surveying, scientific thinning, selective cutting, and large-scale replanting of the devastated areas of Biltmore's forest land. He inherited Olmsted's original forestry plan but greatly expanded it as work progressed.

Everyone at Biltmore felt, quite rightly, that the nation's attention was focused not only on

Biltmore; western elevation overlooking the mountains.

the château but on the experiment in scientific forestry, as well. If all went well, it was believed that the results would have national-policy implications. This was, after all, the first scientific attempt in the New World to rejuvenate a forest that had been overcut, neglected, burned, overgrazed by animals, and allowed to grow infertile. George Vanderbilt set about redressing this situation.

Pinchot stayed at Biltmore for three years. He was succeeded by Carl Alvin Schenck, a forestry graduate of the University of Darmstadt. In 1898, Vanderbilt and Schenck embarked on a

project that would have pleased Frederick Law Olmsted. They founded the Biltmore School of Forestry. This was a well-funded, well-equipped, and intelligently planned scientific undertaking that taught forest land conservation as well as cutting, hauling, milling, stacking, and road building.

The idealistic young men who enrolled in Schenck's school came from all walks of life. At Biltmore, they learned how to estimate the amount of timber in an acre; how to determine what of it was good and how many dollars it was worth; and how to keep the forest healthy so that it could yield repeated timber crops. They were called the Biltmore Boys, or, alternately, the Biltmore Rangers, and they basked in a Teddy Roosevelt–type image of rugged positivism. The Biltmore School of Forestry provided the United States with its first generation of trained foresters, and Schenck's techniques are still taught today.

Olmsted's arboretum plan was less successful. The original idea had been to create a type of tree museum to demonstrate what grew best, in what sorts of soils, under what conditions, and so forth. It was to be a teaching tool with national implications, to which foresters across the country could refer for advice, experience, and planting stock.

Olmsted's ambition was for the Vanderbilt arboretum to contain a greater variety of specimens than the royal gardens at Kew, in England. Interestingly, the idea was not to pack saplings into distant fields but, rather, to line the estate's roads with a dazzling variety of trees, then to wait and see what did and did not do well. Olmsted talked up the arboretum at every possible opportunity. However, perhaps because so many other more visually exciting plans were under way, Vanderbilt had trouble sustaining Olmsted's level of enthusiasm. One crucial segment of the arboretum scheme did come to fruition: the drive from the main gate to the house.

The principal approach road to Biltmore House looks like an enchanted roadway through a magical forest. Actually, it is a calculated composition, planned and executed entirely by Olmsted. Here, he was at his best, creating art through the medium of nature. The distance from the gate lodge at Biltmore Village to the esplanade in front of the main house is about three and a half miles. Richard Morris Hunt re-

An early view of Biltmore Village, showing All Souls Church under construction.

marked that Olmsted's entire career could be measured by this one scenic drive.

Biltmore's main approach road is more than a tour de force of plantsmanship, which, in fact, was never Olmsted's forte. In the words of Laura Roper: "In devising the approach to the house, Olmsted calculated the emotional impact of a deliberately controlled visual experience." One's passage from the main gate to the house is a romantic journey through deep and secluded woodlands. There is a purposeful absence of distracting views. The roadway keeps close to the bottoms of picturesque ravines, crossing back and forth over charming bridges that span mysterious half-hidden pools. Everywhere are beautiful flowering plants and graceful trees.

Olmsted's drive bears no resemblance to the road that led George Vanderbilt to the top of Lone Pine Mountain in 1887. That road followed the ridge lines; Olmsted preferred to save the view until one reached the house. He closed the old road and mapped out a new approach that led through the canopied depths of a flowering forest. This sort of calculated drama was consistent with the Beaux-Arts principles that informed Hunt's design for the château. When one arrived at last at the formal gates to the esplanade, the switch from the winding, bosky drive to the vast and sun-filled formal expanse of the esplanade was extremely effective. However, it was not until one entered the house itself and then actually walked out onto the western piazza that the view was finally visible in its magnificent entirety.

Unfortunately, Olmsted never was able to see his work in completed form. By the summer of 1895, tormented by memory loss, insomnia, and an unrelenting roaring in his ears, he withdrew from his practice and turned the firm over to his son. Sargent's painting of that year shows him appropriately surrounded by leafy plants, but the expression on his face is ominously vacant. The following year, Olmsted became a resident in a private sanitorium in Buckinghamshire, England. By 1897, he had become violent. The following September, his family committed him to a mental hospital in Waverley, Massachusetts, where he died in 1903 at the age of eighty-one, probably another undiagnosed case of Alzheimer's Disease.

Besides forest, château, model farm, scientific dairy, state-of-the-art horticultural installations, enormous landscape and engineering works, cottages, and ancillary buildings, Biltmore also included a manorial village to house the estate employees. George Vanderbilt and Hunt discussed this plan even before the construction of the main house. Hunt collaborated with Olmsted on the design for the village, which spread fanlike just outside the main gate.

Biltmore Village originally had a sort of pseudo–Old English look, characterized by the liberal use of pebbledash stucco and faux halftimbering. This had a significant impact on nearby Asheville; indeed, it set the architectural tone for an entire generation of expensive real estate developments. Although completely new, Biltmore Village, like Tuxedo Park in the North, affected an air of having developed over centuries. Much of it was designed by Richard Sharpe Smith, whom Hunt had sent to North Carolina as a construction supervisor. Smith stayed in Asheville and developed a thriving practice of his own, doing a number of rental villas for George Vanderbilt and houses for other wealthy local clients.

Biltmore Village housed some 2,000 people, 750 of whom were Vanderbilt employees. Like the feudal villages of the Old World that it emulated, it functioned as a service center for the local landowner. Biltmore Village included stores, school, post office, facilities for forestry students, a Hunt-designed church—All Souls—houses, a recreation hall, and even a hospital. The original village laws—lapsed today but not forgotten—prohibited dogs, hen roosts, and live-in servants. For reasons unknown, George Vanderbilt considered these three things to be the primary causes of domestic strife.

Eight and a half years (and $5 million) after George and his mother first checked in at the Battery Park Hotel, Biltmore was opened officially. The housewarming took place over Christmas of 1895, and it received nationwide press coverage. George's artistic niece Gertrude, who later married Harry Whitney, diagramed the

Vanderbilt employees celebrating May Day in front of the main gate to the estate.

Christmas dinner in her journal. Twenty-seven Vanderbilts, Webbs, Sloanes, Shepards, Twomblys, Kissams, and one distantly related Barker made the trip to North Carolina by private railroad car.

A special telegraph line was strung from the house for the occasion. Two hundred and fifty employees and their spouses were invited to join the family by the tree in the banquet hall. Four days after Christmas, another house party descended on Biltmore for a week of hunting, coaching, and shooting. New Year's Eve was particularly festive. Music was provided by the Imperial Trio of the Kenilworth Hotel. There was dancing, speechifying by George, and the passing of a loving cup. Then George and his cousin Mrs. Charles McNamee (married to Biltmore's first estate manager) led a final Virginia reel.

Life was sweet in the largest house in the United States. A typical day for a houseguest might have begun with breakfast in the winter garden, after which the morning's agenda—touring, hunting, riding, or whatever—would have been announced. Then came lunch, followed by afternoons of billiards, swimming in the indoor tank, workouts in the private gym, or leisurely hours in George's superb library. Dinner was usually in the family dining room, unless the party was particularly large, in which case the banquet hall would have been used.

After dinner, guests retired to the tapestry gallery or the library, and then finally headed off to bed. Besides a guest book, George kept a "Nonsense Book" for his visitors' efforts at wit. For example, "Ode to a Bat" was penned by an unknown guest in August of 1900:

> Circle, circle little bat
> How we wonder what you're at
> If you fail to find the door
> You might circle evermore
> When you fly in the library
> We are feeling all quite scary
> Ere you flutter to your lair
> You might grab us by the hair

Sadly, George was not able to share Biltmore with his mother for very long. She died in the autumn of 1896 while visiting her daughter Margaret at Woodlea. Mrs. Vanderbilt was seventy-five; her son was then thirty-four. For a year and a half longer, George remained a bachelor. Then in June of 1898, in Paris, he married Edith Stuy-

vesant Dresser of Oyster Bay, Long Island, and New York. In 1900, a daughter was born. They named her Cornelia, after George's brother Cornelius who had died an untimely death the previous year.

After Cornelia's birth, George and Edith continued to travel and to spend a part of every year at Bar Harbor. However, they always returned to Biltmore, which was their legal residence, and the running of which constituted George's only business.

The guests at Biltmore, despite its hotel-like dimensions, were mostly close friends and family members. Frederick Olmsted, Jr., and his counterpart Richard Howland Hunt were often at Biltmore, as was Richard Morris Hunt's widow, Catherine. Adele Sloane Burden adored her Uncle George and came as often as she could.

There were famous visitors as well. President McKinley arrived unexpectedly in 1897 (George was in France); lawyer and Berkshire wit Joseph Choate came in 1901; and there was a Thanksgiving party in 1902 attended by Edith Wharton, Frederick Olmsted, Jr., and architects Thomas Hastings and Charles McKim. The ubiquitous Chauncey Depew attended a party at Biltmore in April of 1903; and the ill-fated James Hazen Hyde, later giver of too-lavish balls, visited in 1904.

Henry James was a guest during a blizzard in February of 1903. He did not care for Biltmore. "We measure by leagues and we sit in cathedrals," he wrote. Perhaps his low assessment of the house stemmed from the notoriously low temperatures at which tubercular-prone George kept it.

All too soon, however, the Biltmore idyll of beauty, social responsibility, and personal luxury began to develop cracks. In 1893, George was already spending a quarter of a million dollars a year just on grounds care. This was in addition to monies spent on the never-ending proliferation of new horticultural, agricultural, and architectural projects. In the era of the ninety-cent daily wage, the weekly payroll at Biltmore was close to five thousand dollars.

The Olmsted firm preferred budgets, but George would have none of it. Olmsted and his son didn't press the issue because they, like everybody else, assumed George Vanderbilt's riches were inexhaustible. There was also the matter of the client's impulsiveness, particularly in matters of landscape design. George was predisposed to ordering new projects at the drop of a hat. Work was routinely commenced without any consideration of priorities, which led to waste and duplication. When George's financial bubble burst, he found himself suddenly unable to maintain what he had begun.

In truth, George Vanderbilt never had been as rich as people thought. His resources were small compared to his brothers Willie and Cornelius. Even Fred had been busy amassing surplus millions while George had been paying them out. William Henry Vanderbilt must have anticipated something like this when he drew up his will. Half of each child's inheritance was kept in a trust whose principal remained inviolate during the heir's lifetime. The construction of Biltmore absorbed just about all of George's liquid assets. Even though he still had his $5 million trust, the considerable income from that could not cover his expenses.

The first serious tremors came in 1902. Faced for the first time in his life with bills he could not pay, George turned to one of his brothers-in-law, the financial wizard Hamilton Twombly. Twombly was alternately astonished and enraged by George's confessions. "The trouble with you landscape architects," Twombly wrote to Frederick Olmsted, Jr., "is that you don't protect your clients from their own ignorant impulsiveness." Olmsted replied indignantly that if the firm had known George was spending more than his income, they would have arranged things differently.

Overnight, outlays for maintenance of the many landscape projects at Biltmore were cut from $250,000 to $70,000 a year. This was a noble sum, but nowhere near enough to support all that was under way. Almost the entire estate, save the house and a thousand acres, was then leased for a ten-year term to one Edgar H. Moore for use as a private hunting preserve. George's railroad car was sold. Olmsted's beloved arboretum plan was suspended. By the fall of 1903, George and his family were living temporarily in Paris, the traditional retreat of stylish Americans in straitened conditions.

In his absence, Biltmore remained open, but road sweeping was suspended, the greenhouses (except for the palm house) were emptied, and all the farm animals sold. Garden expenditure, which had been running a bit over $10,000 a year, was slashed to just under $1,200. Even the

forestry school suffered a decline in operational appropriations. Fred Olmsted, Jr., observed that "Schenck was much cut up."

George wasn't able to continue funding his forestry school at the levels he had in the past, but he did not abandon it. Instead, he borrowed money. As for the forest itself, he tried to unload it. "Mr. Vanderbilt has no better investment than Pisgah Forest," Schenck wrote Fred Olmsted in September of 1906. "It is difficult, however, to convince him of this because not being a financier, he judges the quality of an investment by actual cash dividends only."

The rich often have a way of living luxuriously even after they have spent their last dime. Such was the case with George Vanderbilt, whose last dime was still in trust. He was back at Biltmore by 1905, entertaining less extensively but still living well. It seemed almost as if things were back to normal. However, a national economic crisis in 1907 hurt George badly and caused yet another round of retrenchment.

It was in 1907 that, except for basic maintenance, everything at Biltmore finally came to a halt. By 1908, George had sold his stable horses, and he was again pressuring Schenck to come up with a buyer for Pisgah Forest. There were signs of domestic tension, too. Schenck on several occasions saw Edith in tears; George was uncharacteristically nervous; guests were few and far between. In July of 1908, the family was off to Paris again and the house was closed for a year. According to *The New York Times* of July 5, 1908, "Mr. Vanderbilt's friends say that in closing Biltmore and selling his horses he is following out the policy of economy he has been practicing elsewhere." By 1909, Schenck, too, was gone, and the Biltmore School of Forestry shortly was closed, as well.

These austerity measures at Biltmore allowed George and his family still to carry on quite comfortably. They continued to summer at Bar Harbor and travel to Europe; they still owned George's father's house at 640 Fifth Avenue in New York, though it was rented out. In 1911, George even bought a substantial Washington, D.C., town house, located at 1612 K Street, N.W., from Pennsylvania senator Matthew Quay. It was there, in late February of 1914, that George suffered an attack of appendicitis. He was hospitalized, operated on, and seemed to be recovering quite well; but within weeks, while con-

Biltmore in the 1920s; Cornelia Stuyvesant Dresser Vanderbilt poses at the wheel of the tractor while her daughter Cornelia looks on.

valescing at home on K Street, George died suddenly of heart failure. He was fifty-two years old.

In retrospect, the death of the master of Biltmore on the eve of the First World War was an omen of impending worldwide change. The newspapers at the time forgot all about George's past financial difficulties. He was reported to have left some $50 million in addition to his real estate. In fact, aside from his trust, George's assets totaled only a little over a million 1914 dollars. Biltmore had cost him all his railroad stock. His securities portfolio was worth eleven thousand dollars on the day he died. Many bequests in the will had to be scaled down because the estate lacked sufficient cash to pay them.

One of them didn't have to be reduced, however, and that was the bequest to his daughter, Cornelia, of the $5 million trust. Nor was the principal any longer inviolate. Fourteen-year-old

Cornelia was now a rich girl with access to capital, should her mother deem it necessary. Edith inherited Biltmore, plus the proceeds of a million-dollar life insurance policy. Not much of that was left after the bills were paid, but at least they had Cornelia's trust.

It will be remembered that back in 1903 George had leased almost his entire estate, minus a large island containing the château and the private village, as a hunting preserve to Edgar Moore. In 1913, that lease expired. George had attempted on several occasions during the intervening years to sell his forest to the government, but he had been repeatedly frustrated by the Moore lease and by the continued existence of unexpired logging contracts.

After George's death, it was Edith who finally succeeded in selling eighty thousand acres to the U.S. Department of Agriculture. The deal took eight years to complete, and the price of

Above: The Hon. John Francis Amherst Cecil and his
bride, the former Cornelia Vanderbilt, April 30, 1924.

Right: Biltmore was first opened to the public in 1930.

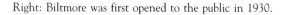

$400,000 was a third less than the appraised value. The government received the nucleus of the future Pisgah Mountain National Forest, however, and Edith got rid of one more headache.

Edith Vanderbilt was equally concerned about what to do with the rest of the land. In 1920, on the eve of perhaps the greatest economic boom in history, she decided to subdivide a portion of it into building lots, to be called Biltmore Forest. That was the name George had used for his woodlands, but it was a name that never really caught on. Mount Pisgah dominated the countryside, and everyone called the wooded tracts that surrounded it Pisgah Forest. So Biltmore Forest was appropriated for the new suburb.

Like other 1920s developments, this one had landscaped drives, an exclusive country club, and a calculated look of Old English charm. It soon became Asheville's most exclusive suburb and the home of many prominent locals. Biltmore Forest even today gives the impression of being an enclave buried deep in untouched woodlands. It was a triumph of site planning, since some of its lots, although well screened, are barely two thousand feet from the greenhouses of the château.

If the death of George Vanderbilt was a metaphor for the close of the Edwardian Age, so his widow's entry into real estate development was a fitting symbol for the Roaring Twenties. As for their daughter, Cornelia became the epitome of the American flapper. Insouciant, determined, projecting immense self-confidence, she even played polo well. Her father's chronic money problems had faded to dim and distant memories. Certainly in the luxurious halls of Biltmore, with paper profits mounting daily and the cream of provincial Asheville scrambling for lots in Biltmore Forest, it must have been hard to remember that life had ever held reverses.

Then, the Honorable John Francis Amherst Cecil (pronounced "Sessle"), third son of Lord Cecil and Baroness Amherst of Hackney, entered Cornelia's life. He was First Secretary at the British Legation in Washington when they met in 1923. They were the ideal couple of the twenties: she, the ultimate American flapper; he, the personification of upper-class English urbanity.

They married on April 30, 1924, in the quasi-feudal setting of All Souls Church in Biltmore Village. The papers promoted Cornelia's $5 million trust to a $50 million fortune, terming her the "world's richest bride." After the marriage, Cornelia's mother hired Addison Mizner to design "The Frith," a soigné pseudo-Spanish residence that still stands in Biltmore Forest. Edith moved there, and by 1925 was remarried to Senator Peter Goelet Gerry of Rhode Island.

Edith Gerry still owned Biltmore, but now it became the domain of Cornelia and John Cecil. They soon produced heirs: George Henry, in 1925; and William Amherst, in 1928. There was plenty of money, if not quite $50 million, and Cecil had found a niche for himself that would last for the rest of his life.

In 1926, a fevered real estate bubble in Asheville suddenly burst. The collapse of the New York stock market three years later proceeded almost to kill the local tourist industry entirely. The Asheville chamber of commerce, desperate for new ways to lure people to town, appealed to Edith Vanderbilt Gerry to open Biltmore to tourists. Visitors had been allowed for years to see the grounds by appointment. By late 1930, with the gracious collaboration of Mr. and Mrs. Cecil, they were admitted to the main house, as well.

With the onset of the Depression, the Cecils moved into a wing, and the staff took a 20 percent pay cut. The butler's record book at Biltmore notes: "Mrs. Cecil had lost quite a lot of her money, and her dividends were not paying much, in fact she was unable to even purchase a new car." As for the pay cut, "this we all accepted in a spirit of loyalty to Mrs. Cecil as no one was to blame for the Depression."

Two years later, everybody took another 20 percent cut in wages. By 1933, the butler at Biltmore was earning a hundred dollars a month and was expected not only to see to the needs of the family but to run a major house museum and maintain it on a shoestring. He and his staff mined the upper floors for upholstery fabrics, untorn curtains, and unbroken furniture. They tenderly wiped off tapestries too frail to brush, redyed damask curtains that had faded in the sun, rubbed oil into thirsty woodwork, and patiently glued back all the little pieces of things that were forever falling off. They shuffled the furniture around when a visible piece became too tatty. All in all, the staff kept up appearances nobly.

The Cecils' marriage, however, did not fare as well. In 1932, Cornelia left her husband and family. By 1934, the couple was divorced. He stayed at Biltmore with the boys, while she relinquished all claims on the property and moved to Europe.

By the late 1930s, Biltmore had become a scene out of an English novel: the faithful butler, the devoted villagers, the magnificent château, the family traditions, and then, the onset of shabby gentility. John Cecil seemed born for the part. The English attitudes he brought with him to the United States—attitudes of noblesse oblige, the duties of the gentry, and the essential rightness of great country seats—inevitably influenced his sons.

Meanwhile, his former wife was cutting a broad swath through European café society, and elsewhere. Cholly Knickerbocker, noting her new pink hair and her new name, Nilcha Baer, termed her "exotic and erratic." The name Nilcha sprang from an obscure numerological source; Baer was the last name of Cornelia's lover, artist Guy Baer, in whose 1938 divorce trial she figured prominently.

With the outbreak of war in 1939, John Cecil closed Biltmore and took his sons to England. For the next half dozen years, he served as a minister of information for the British Foreign Office, and both sons eventually served in the British armed forces. Meanwhile, in North Carolina, Biltmore was shrouded and dark. Stacks of artwork were shipped there from the National Gallery in Washington, D.C., for safekeeping.

After the war, Cecil took his boys back to Biltmore and resumed life as a country squire. The house was reopened, tourism resumed in its mild way, and life went on much as it had in the 1930s. Ironically, it was the model farm and particularly the dairy, neither of which had been taken very seriously by Biltmore's original planners, that provided the income to support the place. Under Cecil's direction, the Biltmore Dairy became an Asheville institution, famous throughout the South, and a serious money-maker.

In 1949, Cornelia Cecil executed another volte-face and married an English banker named Vivian Francis Bulkeley-Johnson. She was living in Sussex, England, in 1954 when John Cecil

William Amherst Vanderbilt Cecil, the current owner of Biltmore. "This is a piece of history and it shall be preserved."

died at Asheville Hospital. He was sixty-four years old. The management of Biltmore, now divested of its manorial village and reduced to something under twelve thousand acres, devolved for a while on a board of trustees that included the Cecil sons. Slowly and quietly, the old ways at Biltmore wound down. George and Bill Cecil shared the house for a while in the mid and late fifties, spending at least part of their time there. George and his wife, Nancy, finally moved out in March of 1956. The last guests—or at least the last to sign the guest book—came for a week in May of 1959. Charles and Joan Withington of Washington, D.C., wrote their names with a ballpoint pen.

By the early 1960s, Biltmore was becoming shabby and sliding into debt. The dairy business, run by George Cecil, was prosperous enough, but it was no longer able to support the entire estate. In 1964, George's younger brother abandoned a career in New York banking and returned to save the family estate. Most people thought he was crazy. Great estates such as Biltmore were held to be unpreservable at the time. Cecil rebelled against this perception and set about finding a solution to the seemingly intractable dilemma of making Biltmore pay for itself.

"This is a piece of history and it shall be preserved," says William Amherst Vanderbilt Cecil, present owner of Biltmore. He is an imposing and assertive man who has concocted his own blend of preservation and entrepreneurism. Cecil's policies and practices do not always sit well with strict-minded preservationists. A case in point was a recent decision to relocate a second-floor bedroom door. The old location interrupted the smooth flow of visiting tourists. Even though the installation was done in such a manner that no one actually can tell it's not original, this would never happen at Mt. Vernon, for example.

On the other hand, Cecil's policies at Biltmore attract in the vicinity of 700,000 annual visitors. The corporate offices of the Biltmore Company are now housed in a sleek black glass office tower, designed by I. M. Pei, and situated in the heart of downtown Asheville. The profits of this family-held corporation exceed a million dollars a year, although much of this goes right back into Biltmore for repairs.

Being privately owned, Biltmore is run the way Cecil sees fit, without interference from boards or historic commissions. However, unlike pub-

Biltmore today, "far more beautiful in reality than it is in pictures."

licly owned properties of equivalent scale—notably, W. R. Hearst's San Simeon in California—Biltmore enjoys no state or federal subsidies, nor is it exempt from taxes. Biltmore, in fact, is Buncombe County's largest taxpayer, facing a six-figure annual bill. It is a major regional employer as well, with a yearly payroll that approaches $6 million.

"Most of my time," Cecil recently told *Historic Preservation Magazine*, "is spent getting this whole operation into the hands of the next generation." Punitive inheritance taxes are the cause of that. Attracting a high volume of visitors to the estate (at $18.95 a head in 1990) is Cecil's primary strategy. "People come here to experience the house; they don't want history rammed down their throats." As a result, there are no guides at Biltmore. Visitors simply roam around at their own speed. There are restaurants, however, and gift shops, and the new Biltmore

Biltmore; south elevation.

Biltmore; exterior of the main stair hall.

Winery, bringing with them the unmistakable whiff of commercialism. One hesitates to criticize any of this, however. Bill Cecil freely acknowledges his commercial efforts, rightly pointing out that economic survival depends on them.

The important difference between Biltmore and many other historic properties is that profit here is seen as the servant of preservation, and not vice versa. Commercialism notwithstanding, Biltmore has become a showplace for American restoration technology. The music room on the main floor is a case in point. Designed in 1976 by Alan Burnham, an authority on Richard Morris Hunt, it is indistinguishable from the Hunt work in adjoining rooms. The British firm of Campbell Smith originally came to Biltmore to restore a ceiling. Today, the American branch of the firm is called Biltmore Campbell Smith and is owned by William Cecil. It is based at

Biltmore, where it designs and coordinates on-site restoration, as well as other projects across the nation.

Two hundred head of beef cattle today roam the Olmsted-planned fields of Biltmore, and something over a hundred acres of potatoes and carrots are grown there, as well—the latter destined for inclusion in Campbell's soups. An elaborate new winery—situated in revamped quarters originally designed for a dairy herd—opened in 1985. Approximately one out of every two visitors to Biltmore leaves with a ten-dollar bottle of Biltmore Estate wine. There are also movie-location fees and revenues from souvenirs and dining facilities, which range from snack bars to the elegant Deer Park Restaurant. All of these reflect Cecil's determination that his grandfather's estate will endure. Fortunately for the rest of us, Cecil's children seem as committed to Biltmore as he is.

Biltmore Village, unfortunately, has been engulfed by suburban sprawl from nearby Asheville. It has become a mishmash of muffler shops, fast-food outlets, gas stations, drive-in banks, and discount stores. Much of Hunt's and Olmsted's original planned hamlet endures, including many delightful old buildings and Hunt's All Souls Church. The original charm of the place is no longer readily apparent, however, certainly not to those who are just driving through on the way to Biltmore.

Still, Richard Morris Hunt's main gate to the estate itself survives intact, and to drive through it is to enter a fairy realm untouched by mufflers or Big Macs. The plantings along Olmsted's drive have grown to grand maturity and the forest is beautifully maintained. After winding slowly upward through enchanted glens, one emerges at last before the imposing gates to the esplanade. Everything is just as Hunt and Olmsted wished it. The calculated approach still delivers the intended surprise.

The exterior of the house is as majestic as ever. Inside, the rooms are filled with books and flowers, framed family pictures, beautiful furniture, and fine rugs. Despite heavy tourist traffic, everything appears to be in immaculate condition. George Vanderbilt would find it all quite recognizable.

Today, the owner of Biltmore lives in Biltmore Forest, in the house his grandmother built in the twenties. (Edith died in 1958 in Providence, Rhode Island; her daughter, Cornelia, died in

Biltmore's gardens and greenhouses remain in perfect condition today.

England in 1976). In 1979, the Cecil brothers amicably divided their interests in the estate. Bill took the château and some 7,500 acres; George took the Biltmore Dairy and about 3,500 acres. In 1985, George Cecil sold the dairy to Pet Milk, and that is what Biltmore Dairy bottles contain today.

How is it that Biltmore has survived, when so many other great houses have perished? The great houses of the Vanderbilt era were built in a nation that lacked the traditions and attitudes necessary to foster preservation. In the United States, one rarely finds families who possess centuries of association with a single property or who are willing to devote their entire lives if necessary to preserving great houses. It takes a special connection with houses and land to produce people such as the Cecils. John Cecil's gift to American culture was the English attitudes he passed along to his sons. The result of these is the preservation of Biltmore.

The view up Vanderbilt Row from Fifty-first Street, circa 1900.

640 Fifth Avenue, completed in 1882, "was both a symbol of the family's presence on Fifth Avenue and a metaphor for their eventual fate."

Location: New York City

Architect: Original house: John Butler Snook (1815–1901)

Charles B. Atwood (1849–1895)

Reconstruction: Horace Trumbauer (1869–1938)

Commissioned by: Original house: William Henry Vanderbilt (1821–1885)

Reconstruction: General Cornelius Vanderbilt III (1873–1942)

House completed: Original house: 1882

Reconstruction: 1916

THE construction of this house, begun in 1879, marked the beginning of the Vanderbilt presence on Fifth Avenue in the Fifties. As it marked the beginning, so, too, did it mark the end. This Triple Palace, built for the families of William Henry Vanderbilt and two of his married daughters, turned out to be the last of the family houses on Vanderbilt Row to fall to the wreckers. Although not strictly within the bounds of our stated subject matter, 640 Fifth was both a symbol of the family's presence on Fifth Avenue and a metaphor for their eventual fate.

The palace at 640 Fifth was the work of William Henry Vanderbilt, eldest son of Commodore Vanderbilt, and the man whose estate financed the Vanderbilt houses. It was W. H. Vanderbilt who led the family migration uptown from the Forties. Collectively, he and his children built ten important residences between Fifty-first and Fifty-eighth streets. In so doing, they set the standard for the cityscape around them.

Until their arrival, Upper Fifth, as it then was called, was a frontier. By the 1850s, the massive grading and earthworks occasioned by the northward extension of the street grid had ruined its previous rural-suburban charm. The majority of new construction on the eve of the Civil War consisted of unfashionable institutional buildings. Among these were St. Luke's Hospital, the New York Institution for the Deaf and Dumb, and St. Patrick's Cathedral, the latter of which drew regular crowds of despised Irish Catholic immigrants. On broad vacant lots between the institutional buildings were ugly shacks, the occasional rotting country mansion, herds of roaming pigs, blowsy-looking vegetable farms, and ragged hillsides sheared violently away in order to maintain grade at the new street level.

After the Civil War, the situation improved. In the late 1860s, Mary Mason Jones (Edith Wharton's aunt and her model for Mrs. Manson Mingott in *The Age of Innocence,*) built her famous Marble Row between Fifty-seventh and Fifty-eighth streets. Her sister, Rebecca Jones, built another row of French-style town houses between Fifty-fifth and Fifty-sixth streets.

By the early 1870s, despite the financial boom that the nation then was enjoying, caution still prevailed on Upper Fifth. Fashion remained comfortably housed on Washington, Stuyvesant and Madison squares, and in the Forties and elsewhere south on Fifth Avenue. Its leaders saw no reason to move as yet. A few churches and the odd brownstone went up here and there in the Fifties, but the area retained an unformed look.

One of the new brownstones in the Fifties was a pretentious Italianate structure on the northeast corner of Fifth Avenue and Fifty-first Street. Its handsome exterior did nothing at all for the reputation of Upper Fifth. To the contrary, this house was the definition of disreputability in nineteenth-century New York.

It belonged to a Mrs. Anne Lohman—wife of a certain "Doctor" Lohman—who was known professionally as Madame Restall. She regularly advertised something called "infallible French female pills," which was a code for illegal abortions. For many years, Mme. Restall operated what amounted to an abortion clinic in a fancy mansion on Fifth Avenue, literally in the shadow of St. Patrick's Cathedral. She had a powerful society clientele, and supposedly the "goods" on everybody in town—at least this is the oft-repeated explanation for her long-standing immunity to the law.

640 Fifth Avenue was "the ultimate expression" of Mr. Vanderbilt's own taste.

Mme. Restall remained an unassailable institution until 1876, when "Doctor" Lohman died. Then a rising tide of vilification commenced, culminating in 1878. In that year, as a result of the efforts of Anthony Comstock and the Society for the Suppression of Vice, a warrant was issued for Mme. Restall's arrest. According to one story, she attempted to bribe Comstock with forty thousand dollars in cash. He refused, and she was booked and released on bail. Days later, rather than face disgrace and prison, Mme. Restall climbed into a hot bath and, depending on the source one consults, slit either her throat or her wrists.

This sensational business seemed not to have bothered William Henry Vanderbilt at all, however. In that same year, he purchased the entire blockfront across the street from Mme. Restall's house, then newly infamous due to the lurid illustrations in the penny-dreadful press. Vanderbilt paid half a million 1878 dollars for a dozen

150-foot-deep building lots that occupied the west side of Fifth Avenue from Fifty-first to Fifty-second streets. The land was a bargain; just prior to the Panic of 1873, the former owner turned down $800,000 for the same parcel.

Vanderbilt's son Willie K. got an even better deal for five lots located on the same side of the street, one block north. According to the *Real Estate Record and Guide* of January 18, 1879, Willie paid $200,000 to sellers who had turned down $700,000 seven years earlier. The Vanderbilts realized, of course, that they were moving into a neighborhood that was not as yet fashionable. However, they were doing so in sufficient numbers that they would have an opportunity to set its tone, both socially and architecturally, without paying too dearly for the privilege. They accomplished this to such an extent that the Fifties on Fifth eventually became known colloquially as Vanderbilt Alley or Vanderbilt Row.

William Henry Vanderbilt, the builder of 640 Fifth Avenue; the sensational Restall affair "seemed not to have bothered [him] at all."

William Henry Vanderbilt's new house on Fifty-first Street was the ultimate expression of his personal taste. It was a monument not only to the man but to the era, as well. The house was intended from the outset to be a national showcase of art and culture. W. H. Vanderbilt was a cautious man, as cautious with art as he was with business. For his architect, he shied away from the untested fashionability of Richard Morris Hunt, whom his son chose at almost the same time to design 660 Fifth Avenue. Instead, he turned to a firm both he and his father had known quite well.

Snook and Trench did not have a prestigious-sounding name but they did have a solid reputation in New York. They had done hotels (the Metropolitan and the Hoffman House); pleasure grounds (the famous Niblo's Garden); and numerous commercial buildings (including the still extant A. T. Stewart Dry Goods Store overlooking City Hall Park). John Butler Snook also designed the St. John's Freight Depot for Commodore Vanderbilt. This vast and brutal structure occupied all of the former St. John's Park in downtown Manhattan. It together with Commodore Vanderbilt changed that charming residential square into a grim warehouse district almost overnight. Snook also designed the Commodore's house at 10 Washington Place, and the original Grand Central Terminal at Forty-second Street and Park Avenue.

William Henry Vanderbilt was a longtime patron of the United States Hotel in Saratoga Springs, New York; he is seen here on the famous porch, surrounded by fellow resorters.

Above: 640 Fifth Avenue; detail of the Fifth Avenue facade as originally built.

Above: The double-height central hall at 640 Fifth, as originally decorated by Herter Brothers.

Right: Plot plan of 640 Fifth; what looked like a single house with two pavilions was actually a residence for three separate families.

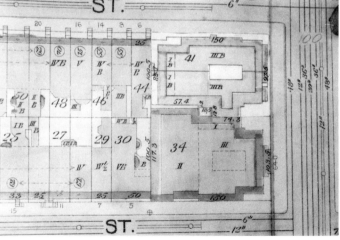

Snook was competent if uninspired, an assessment that also might have been made of William Henry Vanderbilt. Perhaps sensing his architect's shortcomings, Vanderbilt hired another man, Charles B. Atwood, to do the interiors of the new house. Atwood worked for Christian Herter, the famous decorator of New York in the 1880s. Herter Brothers was the New York analogue of French *décorateurs* such as Allard and Alavoine. They are remembered today more for the fine craftsmanship of their furniture than for the decor of the rooms they created.

Snook filed plans for the new Vanderbilt house in August of 1879, four months after the Commodore's will was settled. Actually, the plans were not for a single house but for a complex of three separate residences housed in a pair of symmetrical cube-shaped pavilions. The southern of the two, known as 640 Fifth, would be W. H. Vanderbilt's home. The northern pavilion, divided into two separate residences, would house two of the Vanderbilts' married daughters—Mrs. William Douglas Sloane at 642 Fifth Avenue; and Mrs. Elliott Fitch Shepard at 2 West Fifty-second Street.

Snook also designed, at the same time, another pair of houses for Vanderbilt's other two married daughters—Mrs. William Seward Webb at 680 Fifth; and Mrs. Hamilton Twombly at 684 Fifth. These elaborate brownstones stood at the southwest corner of Fifth and Fifty-fourth Street.

Plans not just for 640 Fifth but for Willie K's 660 Fifth and Cornelius II's 1 West Fifty-seventh Street were all filed in 1879. All three houses were completed in 1882, the year of the famous "public be damned" remark. Although 660 was the most talked about of the three, 640 was by far the largest and most elaborate. Between 600 and 700 men labored on the Triple Palace for a year and a half; 250 were hired simply to execute interior wood carving.

According to designer William Baumgarten, who was then manager of Herter Brothers, Vanderbilt was closely involved with every aspect of the design of 640 Fifth. He was either at the site or in the Herter Brothers' shops on a daily basis, examining progress and encouraging workmen with compliments and generous tips. Two-thirds of the $2 million he spent on the project went into his own fifty-eight-room house in the southern pavilion. According to Baumgarten, Van-

derbilt reviewed every single thing, from the "first stone to the last piece of decoration."

The exterior of the house was clad in brownstone. Snook and Atwood argued for a skin of light-colored Ohio limestone, detailed in red and black marble. The conservative William Henry Vanderbilt insisted on brownstone as the material most appropriate for a New York gentleman's house. In so doing, he left the field open for his son Willie K. and his son's architect, Richard Morris Hunt, to shock and revolutionize New York's architectural sensibilities with a palace one block to the north made of pale Indiana limestone.

The interiors of 640 Fifth were designed, with only a few exceptions, by C. B. Atwood of Herter Brothers. They all bore the client's personal stamp, however. Vanderbilt bought much of the furniture himself, including an eight-foot green malachite vase, one of a pair that originally came from Russia. The Czar owned the matching vase. Mrs. Vanderbilt's boudoir was the first American commission executed by the Parisian firm of Jules Allard et Fils. The ceiling mural was Mr. Vanderbilt's choice, commissioned by him in Paris after a personal visit to the studio of artist Jules LeFebvre.

The pride of 640 Fifth Avenue was its collection of pictures. William Henry Vanderbilt was an avid collector, and a major client of New York art dealer Samuel Putnam Avery. Vanderbilt had his own ideas about art, however, and tramped all over Paris making his own choices. After his death, his taste in painting was mocked, but the artists he liked have returned to favor in the present day. He ignored the Impressionists, preferring the work of artists such as Bouguereau, Tissot, Alma-Tadema, Delacroix, Constable, and most particularly Jean Louis Ernest Meissonier. In fact, the railroad king bought seven canvasses from Meissonier for an unheard-of (in those days) total of $182,000. He had a particular taste for rural scenes, and a parallel horror of nudity. Supposedly, he refused even to look at depictions of undraped mythological figures.

There might not have been much undraped flesh depicted in the decor of 640 Fifth Avenue, but there surely was a lot of glitter. According to the *Magazine of Art*, Mr. Vanderbilt's drawing room was a "harmony in crimson and gold." The double-height hall was lit by gorgeous polychromed stained-glass windows executed by John

The art gallery on Fifty-first Street; "the growing collection was opened to the public on Thursdays. . . ."

The green malachite Demidoff vase, from a Russian auction, originally stood in the foyer connecting 640 and 642 Fifth.

La Farge. In the words of M. S. Euen, author of a vanity publication entitled *Mr. Vanderbilt's House and Collection*, everything inside 640 Fifth "sparkles and flashes with gold and color—with mother-of-pearl, with marble, with jewel effects in glass—and every surface is covered, one might say weighted, with ornament."

Some sixty years later, Frank Crowninshield put it another way:

> The house, at the time of its debut, was a terrifying conglomeration of . . . marble and bronze, and mosaic and stained glass. There were incredible combinations too, of mother-of-pearl tables, Japanese bric-a-brac, silk butterflies, Pompeian frescoes, stamped leather seats, bamboo curtains, and pillars of grained onyx. There were also a figure of a female falconer, a brace of sentimental Venuses, a Moorish den, and, here and there, statues upholding heavily gilded gasoliers.

While 2 West Fifty-second Street had its own front door around the corner, 640 Fifth Avenue shared a mid-block entrance lobby with 642 Fifth. Whereas the interiors of 640 glittered with a jeweled complexity, those at 642 and 2 West Fifty-second were far more subdued. Old photos

of 2 West Fifty-second show expanses of darkly shining woodwork, heavily curtained windows, lots of potted palms and gilt-framed pictures, tapestry chairs, Oriental rugs, and damask-covered walls. Each house in the northern pavilion had its obligatory French drawing room in white and gold, but otherwise they were unrelentingly dark and gloomy. In fact, the old flash pictures illuminated surprising accumulations of dust along the baseboards and under the chairs, and this in an era of plentiful and low-cost help. In the

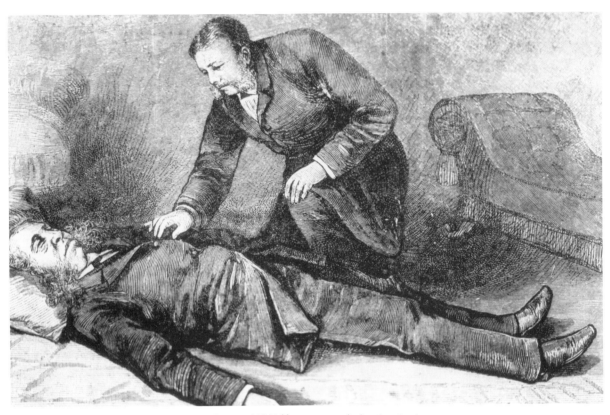

William Henry Vanderbilt on the library floor at 640 Fifth, moments before his death.

absence of exploding flash powder, it seems to have been too dark inside these houses to see what was clean and what was not.

A block north, 660 Fifth Avenue basked in fame and praise from the start. The brownstone cubes of William Henry's Triple Palace had a different reception, however. "It is a marvel," stated the *Real Estate Record* of June 4, 1881, "that so well constructed buildings [*sic*] should appear so ineffective. . . . Strictly speaking, there is a conspicuous absence of architectural design." The *Record* took particular issue with Snook's treatment of the exterior surfaces, terming the applied ornament "promiscuous and inartistic."

"If these Vanderbilt houses are the result of entrusting architectural design to decorators," sniffed the *American Architect and Building News* of May 21, 1881, "it is to be hoped the experiment may not be repeated." The *American Architect*, while noting the superior nature of the craftsmanship, dismissed the design as a case of "boxes of brownstone with architecture appliqué." In later years, historian Stewart Holbrook would call 640's exterior a "glorious hash of styles and periods from much of the known world,"

and its interior a bizarre exercise "lined with bamboo and fairly acrawl with jewelled crickets and dragonflies."

Although it was no beauty in its original form, it was certainly grand, and very comfortable. Here Mr. and Mrs. W. H. Vanderbilt lived quietly with their delicate son George. The art gallery at 640 Fifth was enlarged barely a year after the house was completed. The growing collection was opened to the public on Thursdays, access being via a door on Fifty-first Street. Occasionally, a red carpet would roll across the Fifth Avenue sidewalk to signal a reception or dinner. In general, however, the Vanderbilts' social life was quiet and uneventful, the most frequent visitors being family members.

It was in December of 1885, at the age of sixty-four, that William H. Vanderbilt died. The provisions of his will—detailed in the Introduction of this book—were largely responsible for the building of the Vanderbilt houses. With the exception of young George, all of William Henry's sons and daughters already had houses of their own by 1885. So it was to this young man of twenty-three that William Henry left his beloved 640 Fifth Avenue and his Staten Island farm.

The great changes that were to come, both in the fortunes of the Vanderbilts and upon the face of Fifth Avenue, were undreamed of in 1885. George and his mother continued to live quietly together at 640 Fifth. Aside from a renovation of the art gallery—done to the designs of Richard Morris Hunt—George did very little to the house. From 1887 onward, his principal energies were devoted to the creation of Biltmore. After his mother's death in 1896, 640 Fifth was rarely used at all. In 1905, pressed for funds, George leased the house to steel baron Henry Clay Frick.

Frick first had gazed upon 640 Fifth Avenue some twenty years earlier, when it was brand new and ranked as the most luxurious private house in New York. He and Andrew Mellon, just back from a grand tour of Europe, had stared at it in rapt admiration. Frick calculated it would take a thousand dollars a day to live there. "That would be six percent on five million dollars," he told Mellon, adding "that is all I shall ever want."

By 1905, abetted by the onset of George Vanderbilt's financial woes, Frick was able to realize his residential fantasy by signing a ten-year lease. During his tenancy, Frick spent over $100,000 improving 640 Fifth Avenue. He abandoned the original mid-block entrance and constructed an elaborate new porte cochere in the center of the Fifth Avenue facade. Overall, however, the house retained its original—and increasingly dated—Snook/Atwood/Vanderbilt look.

Fifth Avenue, by contrast, was entering a period of dramatic change. It had always been a unique feature of this fashionable thoroughfare that as soon as the beau monde deserted one stretch of it, they would reestablish themselves immediately to the north. The former houses of the privileged were then either torn down or converted to business usage. It had taken only fifty years for commerce to chase residences all the way from Washington Square to St. Patrick's Cathedral. It was a leitmotiv of nineteenth-century New York to lament the rapid and profligate abandonment of fine Fifth Avenue residences.

By the dawn of the twentieth century, the march of progress, which is to say the advent of office buildings, busy shops, traffic-clogged streets, and crowded sidewalks, had all but destroyed the tranquil residential atmosphere of the Forties. Immediately to the north, in the still sacrosanct Fifties, hotels such as the Gotham,

St. Regis, and the Netherlands, and exclusive clubs such as the Metropolitan and University were springing up everywhere. Each of these new buildings, luxurious as they undoubtedly were, represented nonresidential uses in what had been formerly the premiere residential district of New York.

The Vanderbilts fought this invasion to the best of their collective abilities—a struggle described in Chapter 1—but it was a losing battle. In 1907, the first office building opened in the Fifties at 712 Fifth. It may have looked like a private mansion, but the ramifications of its arrival between Fifty-fifth and Fifty-sixth streets were not lost on anyone. In 1910, the Vanderbilt family sold the northeast corner of Fifth and Fifty-second Street to the developers of an eight-story loft building. Within a few years, the jeweler Cartier was established in the former Morton Plant mansion across the street. This latter transaction marked the triumphant invasion of smart shops, traditionally the stalking horses of worse change, into the very heart of Vanderbilt Row.

In 1911, the city itself perpetrated a major indignity by widening Fifth Avenue to accommodate increased traffic. UPPER FIFTH AVENUE IN WRECKERS' HANDS—BUSINESS ROUTS SOCIETY—VANDERBILT RAILINGS MUST GO, *The New York Times* proclaimed. Previously, the city had been casual about letting house owners erect stoops and ornamental railings beyond the building line. When Fifth Avenue was widened, the sidewalk boundaries were enforced, and the result was considerable architectural mutilation of numerous avenue-fronting town houses. This was the last straw for many an already-exasperated householder.

Soon, fine residences in the Fifties were being demolished or converted to shops in great numbers, usually at advantageous terms to their former owners. It is hard to imagine the degree of change in this neighborhood between 1900 and 1916. The avenue was transformed from the nineteenth century's most exclusive and palatial residential boulevard into what the *Brickbuilder* in 1916 described as "the most interesting and most gorgeous shopping district in the world." Some home owners on the avenue clung to their properties for a while longer, but they did so amidst a new context of crowded sidewalks, lunch-hour crushes, and the growing clamor of skyscraper construction.

In 1915, Henry Clay Frick was among those preparing to abandon the Fifties. Soon, he would move to a new palazzo designed by Carrère & Hastings at Fifth Avenue and Seventieth Street. The fate of 640 Fifth looked dim indeed. However, it was to remain a residence for many more years; in fact, it was about to become an even more glamorous one.

In 1914, George Vanderbilt died suddenly in Washington, D.C. His father had left him 640 Fifth Avenue on condition that he, in turn, leave it to his eldest son. In the event that George should have no male issue, 640 Fifth was to go to the eldest son of George's eldest brother, Cornelius Vanderbilt II, of 1 West Fifty-seventh Street and The Breakers.

George Vanderbilt's only child was a daughter. As it happened, Cornelius II's eldest living son, Neily, had been disinherited by his father in 1899 as a result of his marriage to Grace Wilson. Even in 1914, Neily was laboring under some residual family resentment springing from his parents' disapproval of his wife. Then suddenly, the family outcast found himself in possession of his grandfather's famous New York house. It evidently did not matter to Neily and Grace that the neighborhood was changing. They needed a larger house for their elaborate entertainments, and here was one obtained at no cost.

After Neily's disinheritance, his younger brother Alfred had given him the sum of $6 million. This was much less than Neily would have inherited had he not quarreled with his dictatorial father, but it was still a handsome fortune. It was certainly sufficient to enable Grace to achieve the social position for which she yearned. In fact, during the first decade of this century, Mr. and Mrs. Cornelius Vanderbilt III set the mark in splendid living. They summered in Newport at Beaulieu, and whereas they didn't actually own the house, they inhabited it with great panache. Their Newport stable alone provided an interesting glimpse of grandeur. Neily kept a calèche, two broughams, two victorias, an Irish jaunting cart, an Irish dogcart, a black phaeton, Grace's wicker phaeton, two Brewster station wagons, a carryall for the servants, an express wagon for the luggage of family and guests, and a pair of sulkies. Thirty horses and fifteen stable boys were required to keep all this equipment on the road. To this were added assorted Packards and Stanley Steamers, pur-

chased in an era when motorized vehicles cost between ten and fifteen thousand dollars apiece.

It was Grace's parties, however, that really made people sit up and take notice. Her Fête des Roses, given in Newport during August of 1902, is still remembered for its extravagance. This party was supposedly an "at home," to which only two hundred invitations were issued. Grace received her guests in a gown of pale green mousseline de soie, with a huge black plumed hat. She wore a fortune in cabochon emeralds and her signature diamond stomacher. Behind her on the lawns of Beaulieu stretched a midway, 275 feet long, blazing with lights and lined with carnival diversions. There was a wheel of fortune, a Punch-and-Judy show, dancing girls, strength machines, fortune-tellers, and all manner of similar attractions, each of which somehow incorporated the motif of roses.

At midnight, the guests sat down in a huge temporary theater—constructed on the lawn especially for the evening—to see Irene Bentley perform in the hit play *Wild Rose*. Grace had imported the whole show—sets, costumes, actors, orchestra, everything—from Broadway just for this party. She even paid the producers for lost income occasioned by closing the New York theater for two nights. There was thunderous applause after the final curtain, and Neily himself handed bouquets of roses over the footlights. After the performance came a supper, and then a cotillion, where guests received favors of sterling atomizers and cigarette cases. Dancing continued until dawn. One of the guests, the Russian Grand Duke Boris, remarked to Harry Lehr, "I have never even dreamt of such luxury. . . . It is like walking on gold."

Grace was a great one for lists. She had a private roster of potential guests, which she updated and rearranged continually. According to her son Neil, she also kept a special list of 138 single men, arranged according to what they could do (dance, play the piano, be available for lunch, and so on). For a broader social reference, she kept 114 *Social Registers* in the house.

Grace Vanderbilt personally supervised the organization of all her parties. Her abilities as a hostess, together with the Vanderbilt name, quickly brought her to the forefront of American society. She was unashamedly in love with luxury and was surrounded by it daily. Causes held no allure for her. When Alva Belmont invited

Grace to march down Fifth Avenue in support of the Red Cross, Grace scrawled the following pithy note to her secretary: "Regret. What does she think I am—a suffragette?"

Grace was, however, more than just a party giver; she viewed herself as a "fixer," a catalyst who introduced interesting and important people to one another, one who arranged and smoothed things from behind the scenes. It was Grace Vanderbilt who reconciled Taft and Teddy Roosevelt. The latter held her in highest esteem throughout his life. She was never shy about inviting prestigious foreign visitors to her home, whether she had met them or not. As the years passed, dinner with Mrs. Vanderbilt became almost a semiofficial stop on the itineraries of visiting foreign dignitaries.

For Grace, inheriting a huge mansion on Fifth Avenue was providential. However, if she was ecstatic about the house, she was appalled by the decor. "The Black Hole of Calcutta," she called it, with some justification. In response to his

"For Grace, inheriting a huge mansion on Fifth Avenue was providential." The double-height central hall at 640 Fifth, redecorated in 1915 by Horace Trumbauer. The vase was the only thing they kept.

wife's complaints, Neily drew up preliminary plans for a lavish alteration of 640 Fifth, then turned those plans over to society architect Horace Trumbauer for perfection and execution.

Trumbauer was a fascinating man who could turn out an elegant building in almost any style imaginable. Although prominent in his day, he suffered from a curious inferiority complex said to stem from his lack of formal education above the tenth grade. Trumbauer never allowed interviews or photographs. Despite his personal shyness, he managed to acquire many prominent society clients. Notable Trumbauer commissions included Whitemarsh Hall on the Philadelphia Main Line for Morgan partner E. T. Stotesbury; numerous mansions for members of Philadelphia's powerful Widener and Elkins families; The Elms at Newport for Edwin J. Berwind; Deepdale at Lake Success, Long Island, for Willie Vanderbilt's son W. K. Vanderbilt, Jr.; and the entire Gothic campus of Duke University in North Carolina for James B. Duke.

Trumbauer's chief designer, who ran the office for thirty years, was a man named Julian Abele. In 1906, Abele was the first black graduate of the École des Beaux-Arts in Paris. It was Trumbauer who recognized his talent, sent him to Paris, and paid for his studies. Abele was a modest, self-effacing man whose own predilection for the French *Dix-huitième* dovetailed neatly with that of his employer. The best of Trumbauer's buildings were based on French eighteenth-century models, and he had a particularly deft touch with French interiors, unmatched perhaps except by Ogden Codman.

The alteration of 640 Fifth Avenue took almost two years and cost half a million dollars. The brownstone exterior was stripped of most of its applied ornament, and the interior was completely redecorated. All of the Atwood work was ripped out and replaced by pale new color schemes and Classical Revival architectural treatments. The only thing saved from the original decor was William Henry's enormous green malachite vase. According to Neily's son, Neil, once the house was fitted out with its new "Louis XVI boiseries, Gobelin tapestries, Savonnerie carpets, petit-point chairs, and suites of furniture, some from Versailles, it was generally considered the most impressive and elegant house in New York City."

There were Caen stone walls, formal balus-

Right: The new music room at 640 Fifth Avenue.

Above: The ballroom at 640 Fifth; Trumbauer's chief designer, Julian Abele, was the first black graduate of the École des Beaux-Arts in Paris.

trades, marble floors, and a feeling of lightness and grandeur everywhere. The dining room contained a single table large enough for fifty guests; the Music Room had a floor of parquet de Versailles so beautiful that no one even considered covering it. When completed in early 1917, the new 640 Fifth Avenue contained seventy rooms and thirty-three bathrooms. The live-in staff totaled thirty-six. Male servants slept in the sub-basement; female servants were quartered on the fifth and sixth floors. The English butler and the French chef each had a private apartment off premises.

Grace's footmen wore a livery consisting of knee pants and tailcoats in Vanderbilt maroon, with white stockings and black pumps. Her maids wore black dresses with frilly organdy aprons and caps. There were more miles of phone wire in Grace and Neily's Fifth Avenue house than there were in the new Biltmore Hotel. Heat was provided by enormous coal furnaces that were stoked by hand. The main floor dressing rooms could accommodate up to six hundred topcoats.

Visiting the Vanderbilts in New York was an experience in comfort. There was a card file kept for every guest. Grace's housekeeper, Miss Henderson, saw to it that visitors invariably would find their favorite novel and personal brand of cigarettes at bedside, their favorite flowers in vases in their rooms, and their favorite snacks

319

on silver trays. As a matter of fact, hotelier J. Leslie Kincaid had a running joke with Grace that he would pay her $100,000 a year should she ever decide to go professional and be his head housekeeper.

In 1915, Neily's brother, Alfred, died aboard the *Lusitania.* Thus Neily at last became the official head of the Vanderbilt family. He had never completely patched things up with his family, however. Pictures taken of him on the eve of the U.S. entry into the First World War show a tortured-looking man.

His marriage to Grace had undergone a sad and familiar transformation since its dramatic beginning in 1896. The truth was that his parents had been correct. He and Grace really were not well suited to one another. He was sensitive and private, with a tendency to brood; she was extroverted and vivacious, with a passion for society. They stayed together and raised children. As the years passed, Neily became progressively estranged from his wife and despondent about his life, however. This had been his frame of mind when he inherited 640 Fifth Avenue. Ironically, he had not spoken to his Uncle George in decades, as the latter had sided firmly with the family against Grace in 1896.

". . . [A]s the years passed, Neily became progressively estranged from his wife. . . ."

Therefore, in 1916, Neily did what many men in similar mental states do: He joined the army. Specifically, he joined the National Guard, and then was dispatched as part of an expedition against Pancho Villa in Mexico. After this, he returned to New York a colonel. When the United States declared war on Germany, Neily embarked for the front.

World War I was his finest hour. For a while, he was able to set aside all his disappointments and frustrations for the sake of a patriotic cause. Whatever his failings, Neily Vanderbilt most certainly was brave, talented, and intelligent. He rose meteorically through the ranks, not due to high-level contacts but, rather, to genuine merit. On June 26, 1918, he was promoted to brigadier general in the course of combat.

Grace was only too delighted to refer to him as "the General," and she did so for the rest of their lives. As soon as the war was over, however, Neily sank back into his old malaise. He spent increasing amounts of his time aboard a succession of luxurious yachts—usually without his wife—and he began to develop a drinking problem.

Vanderbilt Row, meanwhile, was disintegrating. By the middle of the twenties, Fifth Avenue in the Fifties was halfway to becoming a skyscraper district. In 1925, Neily's Aunt Emily sold 2 West Fifty-second Street, which she had combined in the 1890s with 642 Fifth to form a single house. Shortly after the sale, the northern pavilion of the Triple Palace was razed and replaced with the skyscraper DePinna building. In 1927, 1 West Fifty-seventh Street, Neily's father's château on Grand Army Plaza was demolished for the Bergdorf Goodman store. What once had been known as Upper Fifth had now become midtown. By the end of the decade, except for Neily's cousins the Fields across the street in one of the Marble Twins, he and Grace were the last residential holdouts on a decimated Vanderbilt Row.

Nonetheless, they lived on as grand a scale as ever. Grace's New York staff was superbly trained and constantly busy. Her in-house laundry at 640 washed and ironed between 180 and 200 sheets every week. She entertained an average of ten thousand people annually. During one particularly sumptuous year, between Newport and New York, Grace personally hosted over 37,000 guests. Their New York home became a symbol of old-guard New York society's last stand.

Florence Twombly might have represented the old guard more properly, but Grace became its public personification, and 640 its architectural one. The guests who danced in its gilded ballroom included King Albert of Belgium, the queen of Spain, Lord Balfour, the Duke of Kent, Winston Churchill, the crown prince of Norway,

Below: Grace and her sister-in-law, Countess Szechenyi, in Grace's car in New York.

Above: "Vanderbilt Row, meanwhile, was disintegrating." The northern pavilion of the Triple Mansion in 1925, about to be razed for a thirty-story skyscraper. Note the commercial building at the right, which had replaced 660 Fifth Avenue a few years earlier.

Calvin Coolidge, Herbert Hoover, General Pershing, Toscanini, and Paderewski.

A typical dinner party at 640 Fifth Avenue invariably was preceded by sherry (no other predinner drinks were served), then it commenced with clear turtle soup, fish (presented on a silver platter, complete with head and tail), turkey with chestnut stuffing (at which point the footmen would stop pouring sherry and begin with champagne), asparagus, and finally a mix of raspberry and vanilla ice cream in a chocolate sauce (Grace's favorite dessert). After this, there would be fruit, coffee, and liqueurs, and an opportunity to admire what Grace's son, Neil, called the "dazzling array of diamond bosoms" without the distraction of food.

When the New York season was over, 640 Fifth would be mothballed—the shades drawn, the furniture encased in white muslin, and the chandeliers bagged. While Grace retreated to Europe or the Homestead to recuperate, the Steinway grand piano, the Gobelin tapestry, the gold plates, and the silver flatware all would be transported to Newport. That way, when she

arrived there for the summer season, everything at Beaulieu would be in place.

During the stock-market crash of 1929, Neily lost $8 million in twenty minutes. However, that didn't stop the gilded couple. They had established themselves irrevocably as big spenders by then; if they had to spend capital to maintain their life-style, they did. Neily declined to cancel the order he had placed for a yacht. Called the *Winchester*, she measured 225 feet overall and was capable of achieving a speed of thirty knots. Grace decorated her with paneled walls, thick carpets, Chinese chests, and taffeta curtains. It cost seven thousand dollars a month in the early 1930s just to keep this vessel docked. Neily really could not afford it. His mother, with whom he had reconciled, began discreetly helping him out. By the middle of the decade, he was broke, but for her money. His health was beginning to fail, as well. He suffered a series of heart attacks and retired more or less permanently to the *Winchester*.

Nothing seemed to stop Grace, however. In 1939, she was still rolling a red carpet across

One of the last great parties at 640 Fifth Avenue, held on June 5, 1941.

the sidewalk outside 640 whenever a big party was planned. She still was summering in Newport, and her servants were still in livery. However, the end was drawing near. When the Second World War broke out, Neily donated the *Winchester* to the Canadian government for use as a mine chaser. Instead of returning home, however, he rented a smaller yacht called the *Ambassadress* and stayed on in Miami. His marriage by now had become a hollow sham, and he was convinced that he had been a failure in life. He was a Vanderbilt, after all, and he had not increased his fortune. In fact, he had spent it all, and more.

By 1940, General Vanderbilt had become a shadow of his former self. His mind was wandering and he had become a virtual invalid, confined to his rented yacht. Badly in need of cash, he stunned New York in that year by announcing that a contract had been signed to sell 640 Fifth Avenue. The buyer was Lord Astor of Cliveden, the son of William Waldorf Astor. The price was $1.5 million. Twelve years earlier, Neily had refused $9 million.

The terms of the sale permitted Neily and Grace to remain in the house as tenants for a period of one year after the closing. The spread of hostilities in Europe and the United States's entry into the war delayed their departure, however. Grace carried on at 640 Fifth as best she could, even though her brand of extravagant socializing was curtailed by the war. At one point, she took in child refugees from the London Blitz. True to form, however, Grace's refugees were the children of Lord Mountbatten.

In February of 1942, Neily's health took a turn for the worse. Grace and her two children, and Neily's sisters Gladys Szechenyi and Gertrude Whitney, all flew to Miami to be at his side. A pair of doctors was in constant attendance aboard the *Ambassadress*. Neily lay semiconscious in an oxygen tent. On March 1, 1942, he opened his eyes, looked around him, uttered a short, amazed laugh, and died. Cause of death: a cerebral hemorrhage, the same thing that had killed his father. Neily was sixty-eight years old. Aware of his financial problems, his sister Gertrude paid to have his body shipped back to New York.

At the time of his death, Neily Vanderbilt belonged to more social clubs than any other man in New York. Despite their money problems, he and Grace had been spending a quarter of a million dollars annually just to run their Newport and New York houses. Still, Grace refused to cut expenses.

Neily's estate totaled about $4 million, not very much for a Vanderbilt. It would have been less, except for the sale of 640 and the remains of a $3.5 million legacy received in 1935 from the estate of his mother, Alice.

Grace received half of Neily's estate, and the balance was theoretically to be divided between their two children, Cornelius Vanderbilt IV and his sister, Grace Davis Stevens. However, Neil had borrowed $900,000 from his father some years earlier, when he was attempting to establish a chain of newspapers. Neily's will stipulated that the amount of this loan be deducted from his son's inheritance. Since the loan equaled approximately the amount of the legacy, the result was that Neily had disinherited his son, as Neily's father had disinherited him.

In the year before General Vanderbilt's death, Grace hosted three large public benefits at 640. A fourth and final ball, to benefit the Red Cross, was held in 1942. After that, there were no more great parties at 640 Fifth. Grace continued to live there during the New York season, however, and to summer at Newport, just as she had in the past.

When the war ended, the Astors took possession of 640 Fifth Avenue, and Grace finally had to move. In the fall of 1945, she purchased a brick and limestone château at 1048 Fifth Avenue, on the southeast corner of Eighty-sixth Street. For a few more years, she continued to entertain almost as grandly as she had in the past.

By 1949, Grace was growing feeble and blind. The woman who had been involved with so many social activities and who had entertained people at lunch, tea, and dinner during almost every day of her adult life was now almost an invalid. After 1949, she no longer was able to attend the opera. No one society figure before her had been on intimate terms with so many crowned heads, poets, statesmen, writers, and musicians, not to mention the amusing members of the world of high society. The luxurious guest rooms at Newport and New York were suddenly empty. The Christmas Day receptions for a thousand, the never-ending procession of powerful and famous guests, the jewels, the music, the laughter, the champagne, all of it disappeared, leaving Grace alone.

By 1951, she was confined to bed in her Fifth Avenue château, worrying whether the money would last. During the Christmas holiday of 1952, Grace Vanderbilt contracted pneumonia. She died in bed at 1048 Fifth Avenue on January 8, 1953, at the age of eighty-two. Frank Crowninshield, the society wit and litterateur, summed up Grace's life with characteristic generosity as well as fairness. "All in all," he wrote, "her influence has been restorative, her loyalties unswerving, and her hospitality at all times unbounded." Grace struggled hard for her status as a Vanderbilt, and she rests today in the family plot on Staten Island.

When she finally moved from 640 Fifth Avenue, the last of the great Mrs. Vanderbilts left behind a soot-stained anachronism, a building that crouched in a canyon of midtown skyscrapers vibrating at all hours with the roar of traffic. Architectural historian Christopher Gray has described Fifth Avenue in the Fifties as the "grandest street ever built." Indeed it was. Vanderbilt Row consisted of an almost unbroken succession of real palaces, interspersed with the finest brownstones in New York. Taken together, the streetscape was visually sumptuous and satisfyingly elaborate.

At the end of 1946, 640 Fifth Avenue finally fell to the wrecker's ball. The Crowell-Collier Building was constructed on the site. This utilitarian structure survives today, and is presently occupied by a bank.

640 Fifth at the end, ". . . a soot-stained anachronism . . . crouched in a canyon of midtown skyscrapers. . . ."

Bibliography

Books

Adler, Cyrus. *Jacob H. Schiff: His Life and Letters.* Garden City, New York: Doubleday Doran & Co., 1929.

Alpern, Andrew. *Apartments for the Affluent.* New York: McGraw-Hill, 1975.

Amory, Cleveland. *The Last Resorts.* New York: Harper & Bros., 1948.

————. *Who Killed Society?* New York: Harper & Bros., 1960.

Andrews, Wayne. *The Vanderbilt Legend.* New York: Harcourt Brace, 1941.

Auchincloss, Louis. *The Vanderbilt Era.* New York: Macmillan Scribner, 1989.

Baker, Paul R. *Richard Morris Hunt.* Cambridge, Massachusetts: MIT Press, 1980.

Balsan, Consuelo Vanderbilt. *The Glitter and the Gold.* New York: Harper & Bros., 1952.

Black, David. *The King of Fifth Avenue: The Fortunes of August Belmont.* New York: Dial Press, 1981.

Brown, Henry Collins. *Fifth Avenue Old and New.* New York: Fifth Avenue Association (in commemoration of the 100th anniversary of the founding of Fifth Avenue), 1924.

Burden, Shirley. *The Vanderbilts in My Life.* New Haven and New York: Ticknor and Fields, 1981.

Burden, William A. M. *Peggy and I.* New York: William A. M. Burden, 1982.

Burnett, Charles H. *Conquering the Wilderness: The Building of the Adirondack and St. Lawrence Railroad.* Privately printed, 1932.

Cable, Mary. *Top Drawer: American High Society from the Gilded Age to the Roaring Twenties.* New York: Atheneum, 1984.

Churchill, Allen. *The Upper Crust: An Informal History of New York's Highest Society.* Englewood Cliffs, New Jersey: Prentice-Hall, 1970.

Clews, Henry. *Fifty Years in Wall Street.* New York: Irving Publishing Co., 1915.

Cooke, Rollin Hillyer, ed. *Historic Homes and Institutions and Geneological and Personal Memoirs of Berkshire County, Mass.* Lewis Publishing Co., 1906.

Croffut, William A. *The Vanderbilts.* Chicago and New York: Belford Clarke & Co., 1886.

Crowninshield, Francis W. *Manners for the Metropolis.* New York: D. Appleton & Co., 1908.

DeSha, Wallace Eugene. *Sprays of Oak Leaves and Acorns: A Geneology of the Various DeSha Families.* Privately printed, 1969.

Dow, Joy Wheeler. *American Renaissance: A Review of Domestic Architecture.* New York: William T. Comstock, 1904.

Downing, Antoinette F., and Scully, Vincent, Jr. *The Architectural Heritage of Newport, Rhode Island 1640–1915.* Cambridge, Massachusetts: Harvard University Press, 1952.

Federal Writers' Project, Works Progress Administration for Massachusetts. *The Berkshire Hills.* New York: Duell, Sloane & Pearce, 1939.

Field, Frederick Vanderbilt. *From Right to Left.* Westport, Connecticut: Lawrence Hill & Co., 1983.

Folsom, Merrill. *Great American Mansions and Their Stories.* New York: Hastings House, 1963.

————. *More Great American Mansions and Their Stories.* New York: Hastings House, 1967.

Friedman, B. H. *Gertrude Vanderbilt Whitney.* Garden City, New York: Doubleday & Co., 1978.

Gannon, Thomas. *Newport Mansions: The Gilded Age.* Dublin, New Hampshire: Foremost Publications, 1982.

Griffin, Ernest, ed. *Westchester County and Its People: A Record.* New York: Lewis Historical Publishing Co., 1946.

Grover, Kathryn, ed. *Dining in America.* Amherst, Massachusetts: University of Massachusetts Press and Margaret Woodbury Strong Museum, 1987.

Hammond, John. *John Hammond on Record.* New York: Summit Books, 1977.

Harrison, Mrs. Burton. *Recollections Grave and Gay.* New York: Charles Scribner's Sons, 1911.

Hill, Napoleon. *Think and Grow Rich.* North Hollywood, California: Wilshire Book Co., 1937.

Holbrook, Stewart H. *The Age of the Moguls.* Garden City, New York: Doubleday, 1953.

Hosmer, Charles B., Jr. *Preservation Comes of Age.* Charlottesville: University Press of Virginia, 1981.

Hoyt, Edwin P. *The Vanderbilts and Their Fortune.* New York: Doubleday & Co., 1962.

Hunekar, James. *New Cosmopolis.* New York: Charles Scribner's Sons, 1925.

Jaher, Frederic Cople, ed. *The Rich, The Well Born,*

and the Powerful. Urbana: University of Illinois Press, 1973.

Jenkins, John Wilbur. *James B. Duke: Master Builder.* New York: George H. Doran Co., 1927.

Johnson, Allen, and Malone, Dumas, eds. *Dictionary of American Biography.* New York: Charles Scribner's Sons, 1939.

Jordy, William H., and Monkhouse, Chris P. *Buildings on Paper: Rhode Island Drawings 1825–1945.* Providence, Rhode Island: Brown University, Rhode Island Historical Society, Rhode Island School of Design, 1982.

Kaiser, Harvey H. *Great Camps of the Adirondacks.* Boston: David R. Godine, 1982.

Kaschewski, Marjorie. *The Quiet Millionaires.* Morristown, New Jersey: *Morris County's Daily Record,* 1970.

Kerr, Albert Boardman. *Jacques Coeur Merchant Prince of the Middle Ages.* New York: Charles Scribner's Sons, 1927.

Kimball, Fiske. *The Creation of the Rococo Decorative Style.* New York: Dover Press, 1980.

King, Robert B. *Raising a Fallen Treasure.* Mattituck, New York: Mad Printers of Mattituck, 1985.

Lehr, Elizabeth Drexel. *"King Lehr" and the Gilded Age.* Philadelphia: J. B. Lippincott Co., 1935.

LeMoyne, Louis Valcoulon. *Country Residences in Europe and America.* New York: Doubleday Page & Co., 1908.

Lewis, Arnold. *American Country Houses of the Gilded Age,* (a reprint with commentary of *Sheldon's Artistic Country Seats* of 1887). New York: Dover Publications, 1982.

Lipke, William C., ed. *Shelburne Farms: The History of an Agricultural Estate.* Burlington: University of Vermont, 1979.

Maher, James T. *The Twilight of Splendor.* Boston: Little, Brown & Co., 1975.

Mallary, R. DeWitt. *Lenox and the Berkshire Highlands.* New York: G. P. Putnam's Sons, 1902.

Mann, William D'Alton. *Fads and Fancies of Representative Americans.* New York: Town Topics Publishing Co., 1905.

Maurice, Arthur Bartlett. *Fifth Avenue.* New York: Dodd Mead & Co., 1918.

Middleton, William D. *Grand Central: The World's Greatest Railroad Terminal.* San Marino, California: Golden West Book, 1977.

Moore, Charles. *The Life and Times of Charles Follen McKim.* Boston: Houghton-Mifflin, 1929.

Naylor, David. *American Picture Palaces: The Architecture of Fantasy.* New York: Van Nostrand Reinhold Co., 1981.

National Americana Society. *Morris, Hennen, Shepard, Vanderbilt and Allied Families Geneology and Biography.* New York: 1954.

Nichols, Charles Wilbur de Lyon. *The Ultra-Fashionable Peerage of America.* New York: George Harjes, 1904.

Oakes, Donald T., ed. *A Pride of Palaces: Lenox Summer Cottages 1883–1933.* Lenox, Massachusetts: Lenox Library Association, 1981.

Obolensky, Serge. *One Man in His Time: The Memoirs of Serge Obolensky.* New York: McDowell, Obolensky, 1958.

Owens, Carole. *The Berkshire Cottages.* Englewood Cliffs, New Jersey: Cottage Press, 1980.

Placzek, Adolf K., ed. *The Macmillan Encyclopedia of Architects.* London: The Free Press, 1982.

Porzelt, Paul. *The Metropolitan Club of New York.* New York: Rizzoli, 1982.

Pulitzer, Ralph. *New York Society on Parade.* New York: Harper & Bros., 1910.

Rae, John W., and Rae, John W., Jr. *Morristown's Forgotten Past: "The Gilded Age."* Morristown, New Jersey: John W. Rae, 1979.

Roper, Laura Wood. *FLO: The Biography of Frederick Law Olmsted.* Baltimore: Johns Hopkins University Press, 1973.

Roth, Leland. *A Monograph of the Work of McKim, Mead & White 1879–1915.* New York: Benjamin Blom, 1973.

———. *McKim, Mead & White, Architects.* New York: Harper & Row, 1983.

Sammartino, Peter. *I Dreamed a College.* Cranbury, New Jersey: A. S. Barnes & Co., 1977.

Sanchis, Frank E. *Westchester County, New York, Colonial to Contemporary.* North River Press, New York, 1977.

Schriftgiessen, Karl. *Families.* New York: Howell, Soskin, 1940.

Sclare, Lisa, and Sclare, Donald. *Beaux-Arts Estates: A Guide to the Architecture of Long Island.* New York: Viking, 1980.

Sherman, Joe. *The House at Shelburne Farms.* Middlebury, Vermont: Paul S. Eriksson, 1986.

Sirkis, Nancy. *Newport Pleasures and Palaces.* New York: Viking Press, 1963.

Sloane, Florence Adele, with commentary by Louis Auchincloss. *Maverick in Mauve: The Diary of a Romantic Age.* Garden City, New York: Doubleday & Co., 1983.

Smith, Matthew Hale. *Sunshine and Shadow in New York*. Hartford: J. B. Burr, 1880.

Snell, Charles W. *Vanderbilt Museum National Historic Site*. Washington, D.C.: National Park Service, 1960.

Stein, Susan R., ed. *The Architecture of Richard Morris Hunt*. Chicago: University of Chicago Press, 1986.

Sterling, Albert Mack. *The Sterling Geneology*. New York: Grafton Press: 1909.

Stern, Robert A. M.; Gilmartin, Greg; and Massengale, John Montague. *New York 1900: Metropolitan Architecture and Urbanism 1890–1915*. New York: Rizzoli, 1983.

Swaim, Douglas, ed. *Cabins and Castles: The History and Architecture of Buncombe County, North Carolina*. North Carolina Department of Cultural Resources, Asheville, 1981.

Tague, William H.; Kimball, Robert B.; and Happel, Richard V. *Berkshire: The First 300 Years 1676–1976*. Pittsfield, Massachusetts: Eagle Publishing, Co., 1976.

Valentine, Tony, and Hahn, Patrick. *Daddy's Duchess*. Secaucus, New Jersey: Lyle Stuart, 1987.

Van Pelt, John Vredenburgh. *A Monograph of the William K. Vanderbilt House*. New York: John V. Van Pelt, 1925.

Vanderbilt, Cornelius, Jr. *Queen of the Golden Age*. New York: McGraw-Hill, 1956.

Vanderbilt, William K. Historical Society. *The Story of Idle Hour*. Miller Place, New York: Laurel Publications, 1984.

———. *The Old Oakdale History*. Oakdale, New York: 1983.

Webb, Colonel G. Creighton. *Webb and Allied Family Histories*. New York: National Americana Society, 1938.

Wechter, Dixon. *The Saga of American Society: A Record of Social Aspirations 1607–1937*. New York: Charles Scribner's Sons, 1937.

Weitzenhoffer, Frances. *The Havemeyers: Impressionism Comes to America*. New York: Harry N. Abrams, 1986.

Williams, Henry Lionel, and Williams, Ottalie K. *A Treasury of Great American Houses*. New York: G. P. Putnam's Sons, 1970.

Wilson, Richard Guy. *McKim, Mead & White Architects*. New York: Rizzoli, 1983.

Withey, Henry F., and Withey, Elsie Rathburn. *Biographical Dictionary of American Architects (deceased)*. Los Angeles: Hennessey & Ingalls, Inc., 1970.

Zukowsky, John, and Stimson, Robbe Pierce. *Hudson River Villas*. New York: Rizzoli, 1985.

Newspapers and Periodicals

American Architect
April 20, 1926. "Scrapping an Architectural Masterpiece."

American Architect and Building News
May 21, 1881. "Recent Building in New York—The Vanderbilt Houses."
August 29, 1891. A. A. Cox. "The Residence of Mr. William K. Vanderbilt, New York."

American Houses and Gardens
December 1906. Barr Ferree. "Notable American Homes: 'Woodlea,' the Estate of Mrs. E. F. Shepard, Scarborough, N.Y."

The Magazine Antiques
April 1980. Susanne Brindel-Pandich. "Biltmore in Asheville, North Carolina."
September 1980. Pauline C. Metcalf. "The Interiors of Ogden Codman, Jr., in Newport, Rhode Island."

Architecture & Building
December 7, 1895. Barr Ferree. "Richard Morris Hunt: His Art and Work."

Architectural Digest
November 1985. "Historic Architecture: Richard Morris Hunt."

Architectural Forum
October 1916. Aymar Embury II. "From Twenty-Third Street Up."

Architectural Record
Vol 6, 1896. Montgomery Schuyler. "The Works of R. H. Robertson."
July 1896. Russell Sturgis. "A Critique of the Works of Shepley, Rutan & Coolidge, and Peabody & Stearns."
June 1898. Russell Sturgis. "A Review of the Work of George B. Post."
June 1903. " 'Idlehour' [sic] The Estate of William K. Vanderbilt."
July 1914. Montgomery Schuyler. "Notes and Comments, Obituary of George Browne Post."
September 1925. Arthur W. Colton. "The Architect's Library," being a review of *A Monograph of the William K. Vanderbilt House* by John Vredenburgh Van Pelt.

July 1926. Herbert Croly. "Notes and Comments, The Work of Richard Morris Hunt."

Atlantic Monthly
August 1908. Jonathan Thayer Lincoln. "Newport: The City of Luxury."

Avenue Magazine
November and December 1984. Christopher Gray. "The Most Gilded Street."
November 1985. Christopher Gray. "The Rise and Fall of Midtown's Most Civilized Avenue."

Century Magazine
November 1893. M. G. van Rensselaer. "Fifth Avenue."

Citizen Register (Ossining, NY)
September 23, 1961. "Anniversary Party Will Reopen Main Clubhouse of Sleepy Hollow Country Club."

Cosmopolitan Magazine
Vol. 36, 1903. Robert N. Burnett. "Captains of Industry, Part XXIII, William Kissam Vanderbilt."

Country Journal
June 1986. Patricia G. McWilliams. "Be It Ever So Humble . . ."

Democrat Register (Ossining, NY)
April 1, 1893. "Elliott F. Shepard's Death."

Forum
March, 1924. Arthur Train. "The Billionaire Era."

Garden and Forest
December 4, 1895. "Mr. Vanderbilt's Forest."

Harper's Magazine
August 1906. Henry James. "The Sense of Newport." (Note: the piece in which James coined the term *white elephant*).
February 1948. Cleveland Amory. "Newport: There She Sits."

Herald Tribune
July 3, 1938. "Peace Haven."

Herald Statesman (Yonkers, NY)
April 22, 1960. "Sleepy Hollow Family Atmosphere Unchanged."

Historic Preservation
July/August 1987. Jonathan Walters. "When a Grand Estate Goes Public."
May 1988. Jonathan Walters. "The Baron of Biltmore."

House and Garden
September 1984. Pauline Metcalf. "Restoring Rooms in Newport by Ogden Codman, Jr."
February 1988. Steve M. L. Aronson. "High Bohemia: The Spirited Side of Flora Whitney Miller."

Journal of the Society of Architectural Historians
Vol. 32, no. 2 (1973). Wheaton A. Holden. "The Peabody Touch: Peabody & Stearns of Boston, 1870–1917."

Life
October 16, 1944. "Life Visits a Fading Newport."
August 14, 1964. George Plimpton. "The Voices of Two Venerable Vanderbilts."

Lippincott's Magazine
Vol. 46, 1890. Review of *Society as I Have Found It*, by Ward McAllister.

Locust Valley Leader
May 24, 1979. "Idle Hour."

Long Island Forum
October/November 1980. Lavern A. Wittlock. "When Idle Hour was Peace Haven."

Magazine of Art
N.d. S. G. W. Benjamin. "An American Palace"

Munsey's Magazine
Vol. 1892–6. Richard H. Titherington. "The Vanderbilts."
Vol. 1896–00. John W. Harrington. "Summer Homes on the Hudson River."
Vol. 1900–4. Frank Lewis Ford. "The Vanderbilts and the Vanderbilt Millions."
Vol. 1904–6. William S. Bridgeman. "Mrs. Cornelius Vanderbilt."

New England Magazine
November 1901. Henry I. Hazelton. "Shelburne Farms."

New York Herald
January 25, 1903. "The Baronial Parks of Long Island, Mr. W. K. Vanderbilt, Jr., and his Success Lake Purchases and Plans."

New York Post
July 28, 1939. "Schafer and His Long Island Cult Seem to Grub Along Nicely on W. K. Vanderbilt Estate."

The New York Times
December 26, 1888. "Col. Shepard's Victory."
December 26, 1888. Editorial: "Reforming Journalism."

March 26, 1893. "Elliott F. Shepard Dead."

February 1, 1895. "Ward McAllister Dead."

February 2, 1895. "Funeral of Ward McAllister."

August 1, 1895. "Death of Richard Morris Hunt."

July 6, 1906. "H. M. K. Twombly, Jr., Drowned in Squam Lake."

July 10, 1906. "Young Twombly's Funeral."

March 2, 1914. "George W. Vanderbilt Improves."

March 7, 1914. "George W. Vanderbilt Dies Suddenly."

March 8, 1914. "Vanderbilt Funeral Plans."

March 20, 1915. "William Douglas Sloane" (obituary).

March 4, 1924. "Mrs. Shepard Dies of a Heart Attack."

April 11, 1927. "Elliott F. Shepard Dead in Florida."

July 13, 1931. "Richard Howland Hunt, Architect, Dies."

January 26, 1933. "Mrs. O. H. P. Belmont Dies at Paris Home."

January 27, 1933. "Mrs. O. H. P. Belmont to be Buried Here."

January 29, 1933. "Mrs. Belmont's Funeral."

February 4, 1933. "Marble House of Mrs. Belmont Was Sold for About $100,000."

July 11, 1936. "Mrs. Seward Webb Dead in Vermont."

September 6, 1937. "General Vanderbilt, 64, Honored at Party."

June 1, 1938. "Peace Haven Will Open with 100 Students."

July 11, 1938. "Vanderbilt Reply Ordered in Legacy."

July 22, 1938. "Vanderbilt Bequest Is Argued in Court."

April 21, 1940. "Mrs. Vanderbilt Dies in Hospital."

May 17, 1940. "Vanderbilt Home in Fifth Avenue is Sold."

March 2, 1942. "General Cornelius Vanderbilt Dies on His Yacht."

March 6, 1942. "Notables at Rites for Cornelius Vanderbilt."

May 8, 1942. "Vanderbilt's Will Gives Family All."

January 8, 1944. "William K. Vanderbilt Dies in Home Here."

February 4, 1955. "Twombly Estate Slashed by Taxes."

April 27, 1955. "A Double Suicide Recalls Old Cult."

December 7, 1964. "Mrs. Balsan Dies; Former Vanderbilt."

December 10, 1964. "Members of Leading Families Attend Service for Mrs. Balsan."

December 12, 1964. "Burial in Britain for Mrs. Balsan."

July 6, 1970. "Harold Vanderbilt, Yachtsman, Is Dead."

July 9, 1970. "Vanderbilt's Will Gives $41 Million to the University."

New York *Tribune*

January 21, 1893. "Judgement in Favor of E. F. Shepard."

March 25, 1893. "Col. E. F. Shepard Dead."

New York *World*

March 25, 1893. "Colonel Shepard Dead."

June 4, 1889. "How He Stopped the Stages."

The New Yorker

March 16, 1940. E. J. Kahn. "A Reporter At Large, A Place to Think." (Peace Haven)

March 10, 1962. G. T. Hellman. "The Best of the Best." (A profile of Joseph Donon.)

Newsweek

May 9, 1955. "New York: At the End." (Concerns James B. Schafer.)

Outing Magazine

March 28, 1888. "Men and Women of the Outdoor World."

Real Estate Record and Guide

January 18, 1879. "The Vanderbilt Purchases."

June 4, 1881. "The Vanderbilt Houses Criticized."

April 20, 1901. "Middle Fifth Avenue, The Evolution of the New Piccadilly."

October 9, 1915. "Passing of the Last Vacant Corner."

St. Nicholas Magazine

June 1909. Day Allen Willey. "The Boy Lumber Cruisers of Carolina."

Scribner's Magazine

August 1894. W. C. Brownell. "Newport."

Southern Living

December 1985. James T. Black. "The Season's Special at Biltmore House."

Suffolk County News

January 27, 1922. "Oakdale Club."

September 8, 1960. " 'Peace Haven' is National Dairy."

Trenton *Evening Times*

April 11, 1927. "New York Burial for E. F. Shepard."

Town & Country

August 5, 1905. "Does Newport Pay?"

September 1, 1906. "Town and Country Life."

August 20, 1915. "This week in Society."

June 1959. "Newport: Past Perfect."

Vogue
November 15, 1941. Frank Crowninshield. "The House of Vanderbilt, Sixty Years of New York Society."
September 15, 1958. Candace A. Van Alen. "Newport DeClichéed."
February 1, 1963. Valentine Lawford. "Consuelo Vanderbilt Balsan: Portrait of a Unique American."

Westchester Illustrated
September 1982. Carole Harrmann. "Greek Revival Revived: Vanderlip Estate will be 34 Luxury Houses."

Miscellany

Address of Mr. Walter T. Savage, delivered March 26, 1988, to the Federated Art Associations of New Jersey at Florham.

Address of Mrs. John J. Slocum, delivered March 9, 1987, to the Newport Historical Society.

Biltmore Estate, guidebook to the house, gardens, and winery. Biltmore Co., 1985.

Brochure of The "Idle Hour" Development, exclusive sales agents, E. A. White Organization, 225 West 34th St., NYC, for Edmund G. and Charles F. Burke, Inc., owners, 146 Pierrepont St., Brooklyn, New York.

The Chinese Teahouse, guidebook. Preservation Society of Newport County, 1988.

"Documentation of the Construction of Biltmore House, Through Drawings, Correspondence and Photos," masters thesis. Susanne Brendel, Graduate School of Architecture and Planning, Columbia University, 1978.

Dowling Caliber, former student newspaper of Dowling College. March 26, 1974. "Mansion to Be Restored." "A Strange Semester."

Last Will and Testament of Frederick William Vanderbilt, dated October 28, 1936, admitted to probate in New York City, September 1, 1938.

"The Legend" of the Sleepy Hollow Country Club, members' publication. June–November 1986. Joan Goldsborough. "Sleepy Hollow Memoirs."

Log of the Steam Yacht *Valiant*, in the collection of the New York Historical Society.

Literature Search for a Cultural Resource Survey of the Beechwood Project (former Vanderlip Estate). Louis A. Brennan, prepared for MTS Associates, property developers, 1981.

Marble House, guidebook to the house. Preservation Society of Newport County, 1965.

Museum of the City of New York Bulletin, March 1942, vol. V, no. 5. John Walden Myer. "The New York Work of Stanford White."

Newport Gazette, printed for the Preservation Society of Newport County. February 1968. "About Marble House, 1892."

Office ledgers from the architectural office of Horace Trumbauer, in the collection of the Philadelphia Athenaeum.

Scarborough Historic District, National Register of Historic Places Inventory-Nominating Form. U.S. Department of the Interior, National Park Service.

Scrapbooks at Eagle's Nest, Vanderbilt Museum, Centerport, Long Island, N.Y.

Shelburne House Interior. Typed ms. study of conditions in the Shelburne archives at the time of the conversion of the main house to an inn, by Emilie Mead.

"Six Generations 1800–1960," an unpublished family history by Frederick H. Osborn, 1962.

Sleepy Hollow Country Club: A Brief Description of its Grounds and Buildings, brochure, illustrated with photos, privately printed for the membership, 1919.

Sleepy Hollow Country Club, prospectus, 1917.

Slide show of the history of the Sleepy Hollow Country Club, researched and written by Karolyn Wrightson, exec. dir., Westchester County Historical Society, for presentation at Senior's Golf Tour Dinner, July 29, 1987.

Society of Architectural Historians Journal, vol II, May 1952. Alan Burnham. "The New York Architecture of Richard Morris Hunt."

Unpublished autobiography of Alva Belmont (1917), in the Wood Collection of the Huntington Library, San Marino, California.

Unpublished autobiography of Alva Belmont (1933), in the collection of Duke University Library, Durham, North Carolina.

The Westchester Historian, Quarterly of the Westchester County Historical Society, vol. 52, no. 4. Mildred E. Struble. "Sleepy Hollow Country Club."

List of Photo Illustrations and Photo Credits

Introduction
p. 3: Culver Pictures, Inc.
p. 5, left: New York Public Library Archives.
p. 5, right: Courtesy J. Watson Webb, Jr.
p. 6: Biltmore Co.
p. 8: After a photo by Matthew Brady, in *Munsey's Magazine*, March 5, 1859.
p. 9, both: *Frank Leslie's*, January 22, 1877.
p. 11: Courtesy J. Watson Webb, Jr.
p. 12: *Cosmopolitan*, September, 1908.
p. 13, upper left: The Bettmann Archive
p. 13, others: New York Public Library Archives.
p. 14: *Harper's Weekly*, June 7, 1889.
p. 16: *Harper's Weekly*, August 28, 1880.
p. 17: New York Public Library Archives.
p. 18: Courtesy J. Watson Webb, Jr.
p. 19, left: *Harper's Magazine*, September, 1883.
p. 19, right: *Architectural Record*, June, 1898.

660 Fifth Avenue
p. 23: New York State Library Archives.
p. 24: Culver Pictures, Inc.
p. 25: *American Architect*, January-March, 1929.
p. 26: New York Public Library Archives.
p. 27: New York Public Library Archives.
p. 28: *McClure's Magazine*, November, 1908.
p. 29: William K. Vanderbilt Historical Society, Islip, NY.
p. 30: *Harper's Weekly*, January 30, 1892.
p. 33, above: *The Magazine of Art*, 1883.
p. 33, below: *Architectural Record*, January, 1926.
p. 38: Culver Pictures, Inc.
p. 39: Culver Pictures, Inc.
p. 40: *American Architect*, April-June, 1926.
p. 41, top: *Harper's Weekly*, September 10, 1902.
p. 41, below: *Munsey's Magazine*, October, 1894.
p. 42: *American Architect and Building News*, November 2, 1907.
p. 44: *Country Life in America*, March, 1934.

1 West 57th Street
p. 49: Culver Pictures, Inc.
p. 51, top: *Munsey's Magazine*, June, 1898.
p. 51, bottom: Courtesy J. Watson Webb, Jr.
p. 53, top and right: *American Architect and Building News*, May 21, 1881.
p. 53, middle and bottom: *Munsey's Magazine*, October, 1894.
p. 54, top: *Harper's Magazine*, September, 1883.
p. 54, inset: Culver Pictures, Inc.
p. 55: *Architectural Record*, June 1898.
p. 56: Culver Pictures, Inc.
p. 57, top: Courtesy J. Watson Webb, Jr.
p. 57, bottom: Culver Pictures, Inc.
p. 58: *Architectural Record*, June, 1898.
p. 59: *Architectural Record*, June, 1898.
p. 60, top: *King's Views of New York*, 1909.
p. 60, bottom: *Architectural Record*, June, 1898.
p. 61, top: *Munsey's Magazine*, February, 1902.
p. 61, below: *Architectural Record*, June, 1898.
p. 62, top: *Series of the Home Journal*, June 4, 1910.
p. 62, below: *Munsey's Magazine*, November, 1905.
p. 65: *McClure's Magazine*, November, 1908.

p. 66, above: *Harper's Weekly*, August 6, 1904.
p. 66, below: Courtesy J. Watson Webb, Jr.
p. 68, top: *Old New York Yesterday and Today*, Meiry Collins Brown, 1922.
pp. 68–69: The Bettmann Archive.

Shelburne Farms
p. 73: Courtesy J. Watson Webb, Jr.
p. 74: Courtesy J. Watson Webb, Jr.
p. 75: Courtesy J. Watson Webb, Jr.
p. 77: Courtesy J. Watson Webb, Jr.
p. 78: Courtesy J. Watson Webb, Jr.
p. 80: Courtesy J. Watson Webb, Jr.
p. 81: Courtesy J. Watson Webb, Jr.
p. 82: Courtesy J. Watson Webb, Jr.
p. 84: Courtesy J. Watson Webb, Jr.
p. 84, above: Courtesy J. Watson Webb, Jr.
p. 84, below: Shelburne Farms, Inc.
p. 86: Courtesy J. Watson Webb, Jr.
p. 87: Shelburne Farms, Inc.
p. 88: Courtesy J. Watson Webb, Jr.
p. 89, above: Courtesy J. Watson Webb, Jr.
p. 89, below: Shelburne Farms, Inc.
p. 90: Courtesy J. Watson Webb, Jr.
p. 91, top: Shelburne Farms, Inc.
p. 91, below: Courtesy J. Watson Webb, Jr.
p. 95: Courtesy J. Watson Webb, Jr.
p. 96: Courtesy J. Watson Webb, Jr.
p. 97: Courtesy J. Watson Webb, Jr.
pp. 98–99: Shelburne Farms, Inc.

Florham
p. 105: Fairleigh-Dickinson University Archives.
p. 106: Courtesy Condé Nast Publications.
p. 107: *Frank Leslie's*, December 6, 1877.
p. 108: Fairleigh-Dickinson University Archives.
p. 111: Fairleigh-Dickinson University Archives.
p. 112: Fairleigh-Dickinson University Archives.
p. 113: Fairleigh-Dickinson University Archives.
p. 114: Fairleigh-Dickinson University Archives.
p. 115: Fairleigh-Dickinson University Archives.
p. 118: Fairleigh-Dickinson University Archives.
p. 119: Fairleigh-Dickinson University Archives.
pp. 120–121: Fairleigh-Dickinson University Archives.
p. 122: Fairleigh-Dickinson University Archives.
p. 124: Courtesy J. Watson Webb, Jr.
p. 125: John Foreman.

Elm Court
p. 129: Private collection.
p. 130: Courtesy Osgood Field.
p. 131: Courtesy Osgood Field.
p. 132: Courtesy Osgood Field.
p. 134: Courtesy Osgood Field.
p. 135: Culver Pictures, Inc.
p. 136: *The American Architect*, April 5, 1902.
p. 137: *The American Architect*, April 5, 1902.
p. 138: *The American Architect*, April 5, 1902.
p. 139, top and bottom: Lenox Library.
p. 139, middle: Courtesy Osgood Field.
p. 140: Courtesy Osgood Field.
p. 141, left column: Lenox Library.
p. 141, right: National Park Service, Frederick Law Olmsted National Historic Site.

p. 143: Lenox Library.
p. 145: Ewing Krainin.
p. 146: Private collection.
p. 147: Ewing Krainin.
p. 148: Private collection.
p. 149: Private collection.

Woodlea

p. 153: A Monograph of the Works of McKim, Mead & White, 1909.
p. 154, top: The National Cyclopedia of American Biography, Vol. 1, James T. White, 1898.
p. 154, bottom: A Monograph of the Works of McKim, Mead & White, 1909.
p. 156: Courtesy *Vogue Magazine*, Condé Nast Publications.
p. 159: *King's Notable New Yorkers, 1896-99.*
p. 160: *American Home and Garden*, December, 1906.
p. 161: Robbe Pierce Stimson.
p. 162: *Architectural Record*, October, 1902.
p. 163, top and middle: *American Home and Garden*, December, 1906.
p. 163, bottom: *American Home and Garden*, December, 1906.
p. 164: Joseph Meehan.
p. 166: *American Home and Garden*, December, 1906.
p. 167: *Architectural Record*, October, 1902.
pp. 168–169: *American Home and Garden*, December, 1906.

Idle Hour

p. 173: William K. Vanderbilt Historical Society.
p. 175: William K. Vanderbilt Historical Society.
p. 176, top: Culver Pictures, Inc.
p. 176, below: William K. Vanderbilt Historical Society.
p. 177: *Architectural Record*, June, 1903.
p. 179: William K. Vanderbilt Historical Society.
p. 180: *Architectural Record*, May, 1903.
p. 181: *Architectural Record*, May, 1903.
p. 182: *Architectural Record*, May, 1903.
p. 183: *Architectural Record*, May, 1903.
p. 184: New York State Library Archives.
p. 185: The Bettmann Archive.
p. 186: William K. Vanderbilt Historical Society.
p. 187: Courtesy Laverne Wittlock.
p. 188, top: William K. Vanderbilt Historical Society.
p. 188, below: Courtesy Laverne Wittlock.
p. 189: Courtesy Laverne Wittlock.
p. 190: New York State Dormitory Authority Archives.
p. 191: Courtesy Dowling College.

Hyde Park

p. 195: National Park Service.
p. 196: National Park Service.
p. 197, top: Private collection.
p. 197, bottom: *King's Notable New Yorker*, 1899.
pp. 198–199: National Park Service.
p. 203: Culver Pictures, Inc.
p. 204: National Park Service.
p. 205: National Park Service.
p. 206: National Park Service.
p. 207, top: National Park Service.
p. 207, bottom: *Architectural Record*, October, 1900.
p. 208: National Park Service.
p. 209: National Park Service.
p. 210, top: Peter Klose.
p. 210, bottom: National Park Service.
p. 212: National Park Service.

p. 213: Courtesy Osgood Field.
p. 215: National Park Service.

Marble House

p. 219: Preservation Society of Newport County.
p. 222: Preservation Society of Newport County.
p. 223: Preservation Society of Newport County.
p. 224: Preservation Society of Newport County.
p. 225: Preservation Society of Newport County.
p. 226: Preservation Society of Newport County.
p. 229: *King's Notable New Yorkers, 1899.*
p. 231: The Bettmann Archive.
p. 232: Culver Pictures, Inc.
p. 234: *Town and Country*, July 25, 1914.
p. 235: Private collection.
p. 237: Robbe Pierce Stimson.
pp. 238–239: Preservation Society of Newport County.

The Breakers

p. 243: *Architectural Record*, October-December, 1895.
p. 245: Redwood Library.
p. 246: Redwood Library.
p. 247: Redwood Library.
p. 248: *Harper's Weekly*, December 10, 1892.
p. 249: Redwood Library.
p. 250: Redwood Library.
p. 251: Robbe Pierce Stimson.
p. 252, above: *Architectural Record*, October-December, 1895.
p. 252, below: *Munsey's Magazine*, July, 1900.
p. 253: Redwood Library.
p. 254: *Harper's Weekly*, September 23, 1899.
p. 256: Culver Pictures, Inc.

Rough Point

p. 261: *Architectural Record*, July, 1896.
p. 262: Boston Public Library.
p. 263: *Architectural Record*, July, 1896.
p. 264: *Arts and Decoration*, November, 1927.
p. 265: *Arts and Decoration*, November, 1927.
p. 266: Duke University Archives.
p. 267: *Series of the Home Journal*, September 10, 1919.
p. 269, top: Duke University Archives.
p. 269, below: Robbe Pierce Stimson.

Biltmore

p. 273: Biltmore Company.
p. 274: Biltmore Company.
p. 276: *Frank Leslie's*, February, 1886.
p. 279: Biltmore Company.
p. 280: Biltmore Company.
p. 281: Biltmore Company.
p. 282: Biltmore Company.
p. 283: Biltmore Company.
p. 284: Biltmore Company.
p. 285: Biltmore Company.
p. 286: Biltmore Company.
p. 287: Biltmore Company.
pp. 288–289: Biltmore Company.
p. 290: Biltmore Company.
p. 291, above: Courtesy Richard Marchand.
p. 291, below: *Architectural Record*, July–September, 1895.
p. 292: Biltmore Company.
p. 294: Biltmore Company.
p. 297: Biltmore Company.
p. 298, top: The Bettmann Archive.
p. 298, bottom: Biltmore Company.
p. 300: Biltmore Company.

Acknowledgments

MANY individuals provided generous amounts of help and advice during the course of this research. The authors wish to express particular thanks to J. Watson Webb, Jr., of Shelburne, Vermont, and Los Angeles, California; Alfred Branam, Jr., of Philadelphia, Pennsylvania; James T. Maher of New York City; and Peter Thyrre of Ardsley, New York. The text of this book owes much of its depth and authority to all of them.

We are also indebted for their kind efforts to the following: W. B. Osgood Field, Jr., of Great Barrington, Massachusetts; Richard Champlin of the Redwood Library in Newport, Rhode Island; Diane Cleaver and the Sanford J. Greenburger Associates; Elizabeth Kuss and Richard Baldwin of the William K. Vanderbilt Historical Society in Islip, Long Island; Christopher Gray of the Office for Metropolitan History in New York City; Richard Jenrette of N.Y.C.; Alix St. Claire at the Sleepy Hollow Country Club in Scarborough, New York; W. Knight Sturgis of Ardsley-on-Hudson, New York; Larry Gobrecht at the N.Y.S Department of Parks, Recreation & Historic Preservation; Duane Pierson, Don McTernan, and Craig Jessup at the National Park Service Archives in Hyde Park, New York; Sally Hall of Fairleigh Dickinson University in Madison, New Jersey; John Fritz of the United States Equestrian Team; Dini Pickering and Dan Ingram at Biltmore House in Asheville, North Carolina; Lavern A. Wittlock of Bayport, Long Island; Megan Camp of Shelburne Farms Inc. in Shelburne, Vermont; Carole Owens and Lila Berle of Stockbridge, Massachusetts; the Preservation Society of Newport County; and our editors, Peter Ginna and Robert Weil, editorial assistant Richard Romano, production editor, David Stanford Burr, and our book designer, Glen Edelstein, all of St. Martin's Press.

Index